# MASTERS OF AMERICAN COOKERY

# MASTERS OF AMERICAN COOKERY

M. F. K. FISHER

JAMES ANDREWS BEARD

RAYMOND CRAIG CLAIBORNE

JULIA McWILLIAMS CHILD

## BETTY FUSSELL

Times
BOOKS

Grateful acknowledgment is made for permission to quote from the following:

*Serve It Forth, How to Cook a Wolf,* and *The Gastronomical Me,* reprinted by permission of Macmillan Publishing Company from *The Art of Eating* by M. F. K. Fisher. Copyright © 1937, 1942, 1943, 1954, and renewed 1970, 1971, by M. F. K. Fisher.

"The Anatomy of a Recipe," "Teasers and Titbits," and "Once a Tramp, Always . . ." reprinted by permission of G. P. Putnam's Sons from *With Bold Knife & Fork* by M. F. K. Fisher. Copyright © 1969 by M. F. K. Fisher.

*Theory & Practice of Good Cooking* and *The New James Beard* by James Beard, reprinted by permission of Alfred A. Knopf, Inc. Copyright © 1977, 1981 by James Beard.

The works of Julia Child, reprinted by permission of Alfred A. Knopf, Inc. Copyright © 1961, 1970, 1975, 1978, and 1980 by Julia Child.

The works of Craig Claiborne, reprinted by permission of TIMES BOOKS/The New York Times Book Company, Inc. Copyright © 1975, 1976, 1977, 1978 by The New York Times Company. *Craig Claiborne's Gourmet Diet* by Craig Claiborne and Pierre Franey, copyright © 1980 by Craig Claiborne and Pierre Franey.

Published by TIMES BOOKS, a division of
The New York Times Book Co., Inc.
Three Park Avenue, New York, N.Y. 10016

Published simultaneously in Canada by
Fitzhenry & Whiteside, Ltd., Toronto

**Library of Congress Cataloging in Publication Data**
Fussell, Betty Harper.
Masters of American cookery.

Bibliography: p. 401
Includes index.
1. Cookery, American. 2. Cooks—United States—
Biography. I. Title,
TX715.F98 1982    641.5     82-40467
ISBN 0-8129-1062-1

Manufactured in the United States of America
83 84 85 86 87 5 4 3 2 1

*For Tucky and Sam*

# ACKNOWLEDGMENTS

I would like to thank many who over the years have shared food talk and recipe lore, but most particularly these: Alfred Bush, Edward Cone, Marion Cunningham, Narsai David, Michael Dorn, Lynn Fagles, Peggy Fergusson, Joseph Frank, Cynthia Gooding, Annette Grant, Georgine Hall, Moira Hodgson, Elizabeth Jane Howard, Maureen Howard, Lili Kahler, Mary Keeley, Marion Kelleher, Mina Kempton, Nancy Lewis, Florence and Norman Lind, Gloria Loomis, Milton Lyon, Fleury Mackie, Judy McConnell, John McCormick, Philip Miller, Elizabeth Moynahan, Honora Neumann, George Pitcher, Virginia Priester, Glenna Putt, Caroline Roth, Leonard Schwartz, Patricia Sides, Albert Sonnenfeld, Elizabeth Sturz, Harriet Vicente, Alexandra Wahl, Nancy Wood, Beverly Williams.

Thanks also to James Beard, John Clancy, and Karen Lee for their cooking and teaching skills and to Julia Child, Craig Claiborne, and M. F. K. Fisher for their generosity of time and spirit.

# CONTENTS

# PART ONE

*A man accustomed to American food and American domestic cookery would not starve to death suddenly in Europe; but I think he would gradually waste away, and eventually die.*

—*Mark Twain*
**A Tramp Abroad** *(1880)*

# EVERYMAN
# A COOK

*. . . the American character has not been much more deeply studied than that
of the Anthropophagi. . . .*

> —*Frances Trollope*
> Domestic Manners of the
> Americans *(1832)*

Something happened to the American character during the Second
World War that would revolutionize the eating habits of us Yankee
Anthropophagi. Boys who had never been farther from home than
Tuscaloosa, Iowa, landed on the banks of the Rhine and the sands of Iwo
Jima. Boys whose lips had never touched anything but milk and peanut
butter guzzled beer and ate coconuts. Boys who had never loved anyone
but mother lined up for whores on the Via Roma of Naples or Grant
Street in Bombay. In the forties, Americans discovered, along with a
world at war, a whole new world of travel, food, and sex.

Before the war, while travel had had the glamour of the rich and while
sex had had the allure of the forbidden, food was thought to be pretty
dull stuff. Food was fodder or fuel or whatever liquid or solid it was that
came in cans. But during the war our boys in the trenches found themselves dreaming of thick ribs and T-bones as well as of slender waists and
ankles of fair creatures left behind. It took us by surprise that the memory
of a last hot dog could be as powerful as the memory of a first kiss. On
the Home Front, civilians dreamed of butter on their bread and sugar in
their coffee. Food became symbolic of home, happiness, and the American way of life. As we began to speak of a national destiny and to become
conscious of a national style, a Norman Rockwell roasted turkey became
as symbolic of what we held dear as Betty Grable's dimpled knees. We
began, in other words, to take food as seriously as we took other pleasures. And, since we were Puritan Anthropophagi, we took our pleasures
seriously indeed.

The war that had mixed up classes, colors, regions, and menus had also mixed up the rules. The end of the war liberated America from its traditional small-town tribal taboos with a burst of energy and cash that transformed the old Eleventh Commandment "Thou Shalt Not" into the new imperative, "Enjoy!" With the earnestness of born-again converts, we pursued first the *Joy of Cooking* and then *The Joy of Sex*. We chorused "Joy to the World," less for the coming of the Lord than for the coming of tourism and a new age of travel. The world was our new-found oyster, on the half shell, with cayenne.

The end of the war was the beginning of our palate revolution. Craig Claiborne dates that beginning precisely: June 17, 1947. On that day Pan American airlines launched its first round-the-world flight at a cost of $1,700 a passenger. Soon everyone from impoverished students to fat-cat corn brokers could become adventurers and conquerors of the strange eating and drinking habits of exotic tribes elsewhere. We hungered and thirsted for romance, and we found it in the *bratwurst* and Liebfraumilch of Frankfurt, in *sushi* bars and *saki* in Tokyo, in stuffed vine leaves and *ouzo* in Greece. The threats of the cold war and of extermination by the atom bomb did not diminish but increased our appetites. For the next three decades, we enjoyed the money and mobility that produced all kinds of revolutions of which food was but one. In the 1950s, those of us who had been born into Prohibition and weaned on Depression threw lavish cocktail and dinner parties like refugees from the Jazz Age. In the 1960s, those of us who worried about the fate of a whole earth and the diet of a small planet channeled our food pleasures into vegetables and the delights of tofu. In the 1970s, those of us who had earlier scorned cooking as woman's work now rushed to fashionable cooking classes and converted our dining rooms and living rooms into one-room live-in kitchens.

By the 1980s, food that had once been thought as vulgar a subject for discourse as religion or money had become our common language, our coin of the realm. Stockbrokers and truck drivers would dispute the right way to broil a steak. Children and parents would argue the nutritive values of yogurt. Husbands and wives would come to blows over the primal and secondary causes of a failed soufflé. Food had become our main performing art, our chief entertainment, and even, perhaps, with the burgeoning of both fancy and fast-food restaurants, our last communal center. Today America is in the grips of what French journalists have called "une frénésie culinaire," or a national food orgy.

Before the war, America still looked to England for standards of taste and decorum in eating and other social actions regimented by Mrs. Frances Trollope and similar matrons of the middle-class manor. After the war, America looked to France, where so many birds had been eaten and bottles uncorked in the villages that had become battlegrounds. But once again Americans were overcome by feelings of inferiority. When, in

1958, Waverley Root compared American to English and French food in his fine ode to *The Food of France,* most of us believed him when he said that the English cook in their awful way "because that is the way they like it," whereas Americans cook in their awful way because they do not really like to eat. Awed by a grand and grandiose culinary tradition of some four centuries in France, we Frenchified our cooking habits as eagerly and as pretentiously as the Russians had in the century of Peter the Great.

We were ignorant, most of us, of our own rich traditions, which were rooted less in the courts of Versailles than in the grills of the Bastille. Descendants of regicides, misfits, rebels, and buccaneers, what had we to do with the high and mighty cuisine of the Sun King and the order of monarchies? A French term such as *cuisine bourgeoise* is as inappropriate to the barbecued ribs of Arthur Bryant in Kansas City as an American term such as "uppity" would be to a *gigot en croûte* in Paris. The categories of France are not ours. The French categorical habit was expressed by Julia Child and her French collaborators in *Mastering the Art of French Cooking,* when they dedicated their first volume to La Belle France and her peoples—"peasants, fishermen, housewives, and princes—not to mention chefs."

The American way, by contrast, is to deny categories. The American anticategorical habit was expressed by the author of the first American cookbook, the self-proclaimed orphan (defying categories of birth) Amelia Simmons, in her *American Cookery* of 1796, which was "adapted to This Country & All Grades of Life." Instead of classes, grades—not immutable by birth but changeable by education—grades, as in school. In France even schools for cooking were rigidly categorized in a pecking order from the lowest scullery boy to the master chef, where the chef ruled as a despotic prince or priest. After the French Revolution got rid of both, chefs became substitute princes and priests, hoarding their knowledge like alchemists who could make or break the new merchant princes by their wizardry.

Antonin Carême, father of classic French cuisine at the end of the eighteenth century, so elevated the art of cooking that he made architecture a mere branch of his empyreal confectionery. Auguste Escoffier, at the end of the nineteenth century, so classified the art of cooking that he measured every dish by a scale of *gloire,* from *haute* to *bas.*

It was Escoffier, "the great codifier," as Child calls him, who drew up rules of cooking for the correct, the predictable, and the invariable. In the early 1900s, such rules were useful and even necessary in expanding the art of cooking from the privacy of noble or rich houses and restaurants to the public industry of the hotel business, even hotels as deluxe as the Ritz. In the 1960s, however, when a group of French chefs rebelled against Escoffier's codifications in the name of *nouvelle cuisine,* they were doing what Americans had always done with categories and codes. Americans had always heeded Ezra Pound's imperative to the artist, "MAKE IT NEW."

America by definition has always been defiant of rules and codifications. By Old World standards, America is a permanent *Saturday-Night-Live* joke, with its wild and crazy clash of cultures. For simple survival, Americans have always had to improvise, experiment, translate, assimilate, and combine what other nations kept separate. When Waverley Root and others praise French food, they speak of measure, balance, proportion, and of rules of culinary decorum as fixed as the classical unities of drama. My 1938 *Larousse Gastronomique* scolds Americans for combining the opposing tastes of salt and sweet in their cooking, as if those were opposites fixed by nature. Because the French assumed their tastes were founded on universals, such amalgams seemed unnatural and immoral until their own *nouvelle* chefs discovered the salt and sweet of Oriental cooking and began to sprinkle French ducks with analogues of soy sauce and plum jam. Even today, however, French logic is offended by the American amalgam of salt, sweet, *and* crisp. American ads proclaim the pleasures of a crisp glass of beer. What rational Frenchman would call beer crisp?

Clearly, American cooking is as expressive of its own culture as French cooking is. "The idea," Child said in introducing *Mastering the Art of French Cooking* to the American public, "was to take French cooking out of cuckoo land and bring it down to where everybody is." To a European, the idea stinks of a demotic swampland. Nobody wants to be "where everybody is." To an American, the idea is invigorating. Everybody wants to be in on the action. James Beard, recalling forgotten traditions in his *American Cookery,* finds that American cooking "occasionally reaches greatness in its own melting-pot way." To illustrate, Beard cites the cooking of a currently renowned Chinese-American chef who learned his arts from his mother. She had cooked in the wilds of Oregon, where she wandered with her preacher husband in the early part of this century to feed Chinese immigrant workers with whatever ingredients she found. The result was not Cantonese, but Oregonese, a new amalgam of East and West. Our melting-pot way has created French-Italian-German-Jewish-Dutch-Irish-Mexican-Japanese-Indian-Cuban-Chinese-Americanese cooking of a kind that defies definition, appalls the tidy minded, and delights the muddlers and mixers. Eclectic is a pale Greek word for the chaos of where everybody is.

If French cooking is balanced, orderly, and classic, American cooking is its opposite. American cooking is based not only on amalgam, in the melting-pot way, but on motion and speed. American cooking is romantic, absurd, full of excess, extravagance, given to self-parody and bizarre contradictions. We are a nation, Claiborne has said recently, of culinary schizophrenics, who binge and purge with equal frenzy, addicted to sugar and vitamins alike, caught between anorexia and bulimia and saved by Overeaters Anonymous. So strong is our simultaneous sugar lust and diet fantasy, say the French journalists Gault and Millau, that if Dracula were to eat six months at a Howard Johnson's, his teeth would fall out until he could only suck yogurt through a straw. American dentists, they add, are the best in the world and American gastroenterologists the busiest.

By French standards, our extremes are incomprehensible except by class divisions—the masses so victimized by industry and advertising that they salivate over tomato-less ketchup and orange-less orangeade, the elite so snobbish that they collect "French" restaurants as they would framed reproductions of Van Gogh and Lautrec. Our extremes, however, belong to the contradictions of the American character and to our impossible amalgamations of technology and art, consumerism and cultism, the salt, the sweet, *and* the crisp. If our sugar fixation has produced the world's best dentists, so, too, our health fixation has produced the world's best-equipped kitchens. If we have bred a race of amateur engineers, we have also bred a race of professional home cooks on an unprecedented scale and of unparalleled quality. If we are technological Anthropophagi who gobble up blenders, electric mixers, and food processors, we also regurgitate the airiest of *quenelles,* mousses, and soufflés. If we are the nation that has produced the world's worst factory-made bread, we have also produced the world's largest number of excellent homemade bread bakers.

Such contradictions belong to a country without servants, where cooking is everybody's business because everybody inhabits some kind of frontier. Our kitchens may be a chuck wagon in the Wild West or a space capsule on the moon, but what defines our cooking is the idea that every man is his own cook. What and how he eats depends on the frontier of the moment. A homesteader at the turn of the century, an ex-washlady named Elinore Pruitt Stewart, described one such moment in Burnt Fork, Wyoming, when she wrote to a friend describing a "Stocking-Leg" dinner wrassled up by the men, women, and children of Burnt Fork. They aimed to recreate the foods mentioned by an earlier pioneer, the Pathfinder of James Fenimore Cooper in his *Leather-Stocking Tales.*

> We had venison served in half a dozen different ways. We had antelope; we had porcupine, or hedgehog, as Pathfinder called it; and also we had beaver-tail, which we found toothsome, but which I did *not.* We had grouse and sage hen. They broke the ice and snared a lot of trout. In their cellar they had a barrel of trout prepared exactly like mackerel, and they were more delicious than mackerel because they were finer-grained.

If hunting was everybody's business, so were the preserving arts. And it's not hard to see that the taste for salt and sweet was strongly rooted in the need to salt, pickle, and preserve everything from beaver tail and trout to melons and cackleberries.

Such contradictions belong also to a country always on the move. We don't just eat and run. We eat while running. The tube a spaceman squeezes for his supper is not all that different from the cube of portable soup Miss Eliza Leslie devised for the traveler in 1828. Movable food is as necessary to a nation of joggers as fast food is to a nation of cars. A can of Campbell's tomato soup is as expressive of our mobile homes and mobile·food as the electronic Pac-Man is expressive of our mobile eaters. And if motion and speed characterize American cooking and eating, so does the humor by which we laugh at our own excesses. Describing the pop-architecture of our highways, one comic has called us a nation of "strutting cereal boxes and wise-cracking vegetables, utterly silly, with a skewed sense of scale." Our scale is skewed by the hyperbole of our self-burlesque. Our strutting cereal boxes, giant ice-cream cones, and big Big Macs mock the greed of our combustion engines as they eat up the miles. Our jolly Green Giants mock the pretensions of our would-be giant killers who climb the bean stalk to cloud cuckoo land.

The place of the action is ground zero, where everybody can start over and make it new. One of the most obvious contradictions of our cooking, as of our culture, is the American professionalism of amateurs, which is yet another expression of mobility. Most of us who learned to cook in the first decades after the war learned not at our grandmother's knee— grandmother was maybe miles and maybe continents away. Nor did we learn in cooking schools, geared to technical and vocational training. We learned from books and, later, from television, the most mobile media of all. And the books we learned most from were the work not of professional chefs or restaurateurs, but of amateurs, not one of whom had set out to be a cook.

The leaders of our cooking revolution were four, one a journalist, one an actor, one a publicist, and one a copywriter. But when they all eventually focused on food, they responded like pioneers and revolutionaries colonizing a new land. Many of the old ways of nineteenth-century America, with its fresh beaver tail and salted fine-grained trout, had been processed out of existence in the heady days of new technology at the turn of the century. As our native wilderness became a wasteland of Campbell's soup, Wonderbread, and Spam, our food revolutionists were grass-root radicals who changed our palates by compelling us to taste for ourselves and to have the courage of our own sensations. More than cooks, they were teachers and persuaders. In good American fashion, their sexual division was equal. They were two women and two men and their names were M. F. K. Fisher, James Beard, Craig Claiborne, and Julia Child.

All born in the first two decades of this century, they all looked to

France for standards of good cooking. Yet each was a quintessential Yank, characterized by honesty, stubbornness, openness, generosity, originality, and, above all, a strong sense of humor. Their quirky individualism revealed shared roots and aims. While they shared epiphanies in the kitchens of Europe, they also analyzed what they found there with the obsession of pragmatic Americans determined to learn and eager to share their knowledge. They were mentors and mediators, translating and domesticating foreign arts into a common American idiom and a whole new battery of melting pots.

All of them had tasted good food at home and in that they were fortunate. They brought the regionalism of the four corners of the country in which they lived to bear on the cooking they learned in other countries. Fisher mined the materials of California, Beard of the Pacific Northwest, Claiborne of the deep South, and Child of New England. As they talked about food in print or other media, each developed an idiosyncratic style. Fisher was a sexy siren, Beard a Bunyanesque gourmand, Claiborne an urbane dandy, Child a stand-up comedian. Performing in print, at demonstrations, on television, they showed us that cooking and eating were performing arts, that we were all performers as well as consumers, that with a little daring and imagination, taste was not the prerogative of an elite but available to all. They de-mythicized and de snobbed the mystique of French cuisine by Americanizing it. They translated high cooking into home cooking. They said, "If I can do it, you can, too."

In the postwar decades, these were our masters: Fisher in the forties, Beard in the fifties, Claiborne and Child in the sixties and seventies. There were others of course, predecessors, contemporaries, and followers whom I'll mention later, people like Irma Rombauer, Michael Field, Richard Olney, John Clancy, Jacques Pépin, and a host of current successors. Together, they have spawned a new breed of young American chefs and a new breed of sophisticated eaters. As in other revolutions, the fervor of the originators has also brought changes they deplore, such as the mass-marketing of "gourmet," pronounced "gore-may," into a term of affectation and pretense.

These four became our masters because they came at the right time. Until they began to forge a national style, American cookery was thought to be either a form of industrial waste or an historical anachronism. American cookery meant the quaintly regional. Writers would cite the Cornish pasties of Keweenaw County, Michigan, the hot slaws of Cincinnati, Ohio, the funnel cakes of Marietta, Pennsylvania, in a kind of lyric litany. Cookbooks were either manuals of instruction on nutrition and health or gourmet nostalgia about How Aunt Hettie Made Hush Puppies. Officially, we were back on the farm in small-town rural America. Unofficially, we were food technologists bulldozing underground anything live that couldn't be canned, frozen, dehydrated, biogenetically altered, or otherwise faked. More culinary schizophrenia. Our masters came at the right time to mediate between technology and tradition by insisting on the primacy of taste. We were ready for them. And when they transformed our cooking into a native American art, we were ready to transform them into celebrities. If cooking was to become our chief entertainment, our cooks would have to become stars.

In the middle of the twentieth century, out of the war that destroyed so much of Europe and the East, America came of age in her typical helter-skelter motorized melting-pot way. "This has been America's Elizabethan era, her Bourbon Louis romp, her season of the rising sap," Tom Wolfe writes in *From Bauhaus to Our House,* in lamenting our failure to invent a native architecture that would express our newfound "exuberance, power, empire, grandeur, or even high spirits and playfulness." In architecture, it would seem, we cowered before the authority of the Germans, as in cooking we once cowered before the authority of the French. But maybe architecture is too public, too institutional an art to express our anarchic spirit. Maybe the domestic arts are more truly expressive of the contradictory dimensions of that place where everybody is.

Maybe we should look to the pop-art food stands of our highways and city streets, to the skyscraper canyons of our supermarkets, to the electrifying hardware of our kitchens, and to the dazzling abundance of our tables for the fullest native expression of the American character. The phrase "plain home cooking" doesn't begin to cover the inventive, titillating, extravagant, playful, and far-out foods we serve up as a nation of amateur cooks. As Josh Billings said of the American sense of humor, "We must have it on the half-shell, with cayenne." Everyman his own cook—and don't hold the pepper—excites us by the challenge of new frontiers. To show how this is true and how everybody can have the pleasure of it is the purpose of this book. I begin with How I Learned to Cook as Exhibit A. I learned by following in the footsteps of our four pathfinders, trekking across a continent of salt seas and sugar loafs to a promised land of cooking joy. If I could do it, coming from an anthropophagous outback in the West, believe me, you can, too.

# HOW I LEARNED
# TO COOK

❦

*. . . if, in its diverse manifestations, the American table is distinctly different from ours, that in no way means that it is fundamentally bad.*

—*"Cuisine Americaine"*
Larousse Gastronomique *(1938 edition)*

In 1938, I had never heard of *cuisine américaine* or *gastronomique* or even gourmet. The American table I sat down to was covered with oilcloth as the floor was covered with linoleum. We ate with Wm. Rogers silver plate on diverse manifestations of china and drank from ex-jelly glasses and Bakelite cups. Our napkins were paper and we kept them in a box next to the Zenith radio. When company came, we put a machine-made lace tablecloth over the oilcloth. Lace was gracious living.

Nobody at my American table asked whether the food was fundamentally bad or good. Was there food? That was the question. Good taste meant the thing was edible. Bad taste meant spoiled meat or rotten fish. Food was good or bad only in so far as it was good or bad *for* you. At my table most food was bad for you. Our food talk centered not on the palate but on the colon and food was judged more by its ease of egress than its speed of entrance. Because our scale was colonic, food was better the closer it aspired to the condition of water. Water was the main ingredient of our boiled fish, flesh, and fowl, not to mention vegetable, beverage, and dessert. Dessert was Jell-O. Beverage was Koolaid or Postum, but even Postum was too dangerous a stimulant for my grandmother without additional watering. To ¼ teaspoon powder, she would add a cup of boiling hot water. Water, despite clear evidence to the contrary, was thought to be pure. Purity was the function of our food, because the body needed less to be fueled than cleansed.

By 1938, the American table should have improved, by the standards of *Larousse Gastronomique,* since the bad years of the "régime sec" were over and tastebuds should have recovered from the " 'ersatz' de vin" furnished by "les bootleggers." Good cuisine could not be savored, said *Larousse,* unless accompanied by good wine. There was little hope, in that case, for our savoring.

But our table, as I say, was distinctly different from that of the French. Food that was good for you was soft, bland, and branded: Wheatena, Quaker Oats, Mott's Apple Sauce, Franco-American Spaghetti, Kraft's Macaroni and Cheese, Campbell's Cream of Tomato, Del Monte's Peaches, Dinty Moore's Beef Stew. Food that was bad for you was chewy, binding, and anonymous. Foods that could not be Fletcherized—that is, ground to a paste with thirty-two chews, one for each tooth—were out. Unprocessed cheese might bind. Fresh anonymous fruits and vegetables were indigestible. Most of the foods listed by *Larousse* as characteristically American—le clam chowder, le razor back ham, le canvas back duck, le clambake, le burgou—I had never heard of.

My American table in a small Southern California town was not, obviously, everyman's table, but it was typical of Middle Bible-belted America for whom there were saintly foods and forbidden foods. By some trick of communion, food was meant to turn flesh into spirit and if bran didn't work colonic irrigation did. Ranged against the evangelists like Alma White and Jethro Tull who preached water cures were the libertines who swilled champagne. By some trick of moral economy, libertines were invariably rich and they proved their swinishness by enjoying . . . their FOOD!

My table followed the dictates of Harriet Beecher Stowe, who told us in *The American Woman's Home* that "The customs of society, rather than the order of nature designed by Providence, lead us to eat merely to gratify the palate." We were not about to violate the order of God and nature even if we could have afforded to join in the customs of society. Because we couldn't, we were spared agonizing over the questions posed by Ida Bailey Allen, in 1940, in her *Money-Saving Cookbook:* "Should we entertain when we are in debt?" Or "Are salads an extravagance?" Or "My family doesn't like fish, but as it is one of the cheapest foods I'd like to use more. How can I cook fish so they will like it?"

We were also spared the worry and expense of the servant problem. "This want of servants is the one thing that must modify everything in American Life," Harriet Beecher Stowe wrote in a chapter entitled "The Lady Who Does Her Own Work." Nothing drove Mrs. Frances Trollope up the wall faster than the "coarse familiarity, untempered by any shadow of respect, which is assumed by the grossest and lowest in their intercourse with the highest and most refined." When Mrs. Trollope, struggling with the servant problem in Cincinnati, was forced to dismiss one Nancy Fletcher for gross intercourse of another kind, she wrote her son Anthony that she was faced with "the dread of cooking my own dinner before my eyes."

It was a dread my family faced with fortitude and self-reliance. My schoolteacher father did most of the cooking and all of the canning because he had been raised on a farm. My stepmother, on the other hand, was a career woman before and during her marriage and, as an osteopath, knew how to treat human bones but not beef bones. Her mother had learned to cook perforce when the banks failed and she turned her home into a boardinghouse. My father's mother, however, had learned to cook from her mother and sisters and from the 1910 *Our Women's Exchange,* put out by the Women's General Missionary Society in Xenia, Ohio, and dedicated "To our Modern Marys and Marthas whose lives are channels of blessing in the church and home." She learned from recipes salted between scripture of an appropriate sort, like "While I was musing the fire burned . . ." She learned from recipes such as Cheap Steak Made Palatable, and how to make Mock Fish. That one was a puzzler because it called for ground nuts, bread crumbs, and hominy, shaped into a fishy form and decorated by using almonds for fins and, for an eye, "using a bit of truffle or anything at hand, to make it look natural." One wonders about the nets cast by the Marys and Marthas of the Xenia Women's Exchange.

Real Fish did not figure large in the contents of *Our Women's Exchange.* A recipe for Parsley Fish begins, "Take any kind of best fish and boil in water with a little salt." Nor did Real Meat. Everything the women had to say about fish and meat could be said in fifteen pages under the rubric "Fish, Meats, Etc." They had to leave space for Bread, Cereals, Corn Recipes, Pies and Pastry, Cake, Puddings and Desserts, Beverages, Confections, and Hints for the Sick. Those who did not heed the appropriate scripture for the latter—"Men die, and many because they know not how to live"—could take comfort from the Cure for Pneumonia. It was a poultice of chopped onions, rye, and vinegar, stirred to a paste in a large spider (frying pan) over a hot fire and put in a cotton bag to cover the lungs as hot as the patient can bear. "This simple remedy has never failed in this too-often fatal malady."

The kitchen appropriate to the contents of *Our Women's Exchange* was half sickroom and half candy shop, but the two halves never came together, for the cook was occupied with matters of faith rather than logic. The whole duty of a cook was not only medical—men die, and many—but spiritual. A cook of the true faith believed with Sarah Tyson Rorer, the Julia Child of 1902, that Christianity and indigestion were incompatible. Because everybody complained of dyspepsia, common sense might have suggested that the cause was less a spiritual falling away than a greedy falling to on all those cakes, puddings, desserts, pies, and confections. Curiously, the only food that seemed exempt from the general charge of poison was candy. One of my grandmother's favorite recipes was a fudge called Divinity.

Candy could always be rationalized as high-octane fuel. Our kitchen was sickroom, candy shop, *and* pit stop for the racing motors of our depreciating machines. In her lesson on Animal Combustion, Mrs. A. D. Lincoln of the Boston School Kitchen explains that the service of food is three-fold to "that most wonderful machine, the human body." Food furnishes heat, keeps it in repair, and gives it the energy to do its work. Science and industry met in the kitchen and redubbed the cook a domestic scientist, a home economist, and auto mechanic. The ladies who did their own work might "become better and more *useful* women," Mrs. Lincoln advised, by understanding the chemical principles of their laboratories and the physical principles of their machine shops.

Our kitchen was a lab-shop not by design but lack of space. Except for the yellow enamel coating on the cast-iron stove and matching water heater, everything was functional, if seldom modern. Our idea of modern was a hand-turned Dazy can opener screwed into the wall. Our idea of efficient was a human dish washer and dish dryer standing side by side.

The real laboratory kitchen was a classroom in my junior high school, equipped with burners and sinks, where girls were required to take a year of Domestic Science. Boys, on the other hand, were required to take Auto Shop, which neatly divided the sexes into fuelers and fixers. Our domestic science teacher wore a white laboratory coat and followed Mrs. Lincoln's precepts to the letter: "Cooking cannot be well done by guesswork. There is a right way and a wrong way." Exact measurement, we learned, was the key to all cooking. We performed our experiments with the precision of technicians working on the cure for pneumonia. We wrote up lab reports on the experiments we were forced to conduct in the septic conditions of the lab at home. I cannot remember a single dish that we cooked. I cannot remember even cooking a dish. Perhaps in the first year we only learned to measure and there was an advanced course in which we were allowed to apply a Bunsen burner to our tubes.

By the time I was ready for an advanced course, the war had removed needed ingredients. Now scarcity provoked appetites the way sin had before. While the coffee shortage did not affect my family table, the sugar shortage did. The sugar shortage brought in Ration Book Number One that lasted four years. Morale sank. But our Depression stretchers for making cheap meat palatable or making mock fish were readily applicable to wartime stretchers, and we made do with honey, corn and maple syrup, sorghum, and molasses.

The most severe problem was not sugar but cans. We who had lived on canned Bartlett pear halves and canned tomatoes were forced, by the metal shortage, to actually grow things in the backyard as if we'd never left the farm. We called it a Victory Garden and went to war with the Japanese beetles that descended in little yellow hordes on anything green. We couldn't wait for the war to be over to get back to the security of our cans.

We did try to do our best for our boys over there. We saved bacon fat and Crisco to recycle for explosives. We colored our margarine yellow and sent butter to our boys. Girls my age at high school became Victory Girls, who harvested tomatoes and onions and grapes on outlying commercial farms and determined never again to eat or even smell a tomato, onion, or grape. We resisted buying bubble gum on the black market to fill K-rations abroad. But the war didn't make a dent in my clichés about food. If before, food was fuel, now it was ammunition. If before, eating for fun was wicked, now it was unpatriotic.

The dents didn't come until after the war. During the war everyone was geared to quick meals, said Rosie the Riveter, but afterward the magazines were full of stuff that'd take you a whole day to make. The stuff that'd take you a whole day to make was appearing regularly in the pages of a new Magazine of Good Living that had begun in 1941 but didn't take off until the war's end. During the war the stubborn Scot Earle MacAusland, who founded *Gourmet,* had had to defend his depiction of lush food in posh surroundings from outraged patriots and purists by claiming that he showed the things that were "worth fighting for." In the postwar climate, however, he could confess openly that his "dream-like cookery" appealed to fantasy and snobbery with food never meant to be eaten from recipes never meant to be cooked. It was the beginning of gourmet chic and the cuisine of the *moi* generation.

The word "gourmet" had still not penetrated my brain, however, because my graduate-student husband and I were trying to survive on fried foods and beer in quarts paid for by the GI bill. For a wedding present, the wife of a tough ex-Marine sergeant, turned Harvard English grad student, had given me a looseleaf notebook with three basic survival recipes: 1. Spaghetti Sauce; 2. Brownies; and 3. Fudge. Somebody else had given us a Waring blender, which we thought a magic machine for turning out whiskey sours and gin slings. It never occurred to me to use it for *food.* If you wanted a magic machine for *food,* you threw something into the pressure cooker and hoped it would not end up on the ceiling.

My cooking horizons did not expand significantly beyond spaghetti, brownies, and fudge until the summer of 1952, when we hopped aboard the reconverted *Bremen,* now called the *Liberté,* and sailed to France. My husband had fallen in love with France as an infantryman, despite, or because of, mortar-shell wounds that kept him for a year in a hospital in Nancy. I fell in love with France at first bite—into one of the crusty rolls baked on the *Liberté* and served fresh at every meal. I was so dazzled by the experience that I put out my cigarette on the empty butter plate and was soundly rapped by the very French waiter. It was my initiation into just how different the French table was from the one back home.

Since it was far cheaper to eat and sleep abroad than at home, we used our combined teaching salaries of $3,800 a year to explore the differences at first hand as often as possible. We had lots of company—about three and a half million fellow travelers a year, to make a tourist boom second only to a baby boom. But eating out was not at all the same as cooking in. Not, in fact, until we joined the baby boom did I look seriously at a cookbook and then only because the apartment was too noisy for Eliot or Joyce.

In 1959, I discovered *The James Beard Cookbook.* Somebody must have given it to me, because I certainly wouldn't have spent good money on a book about food. It was simple, practical, and good for finding out how to roast a turkey or cook up a chili con carne from scratch. I still hadn't got the message. I didn't get it until I skimmed the Women's Page of *The New York Times* one day in 1961 and discovered a man talking about restaurants the way Brooks Atkinson talked about theater or Bosley Crowther about movies. A *man* on the Women's Page taking food *seriously?* It was a double whammy.

At first, intellectual snobs that we were, we read Craig Claiborne's Dining Guide for entertainment, for the novelty of anyone criticizing restaurants the way we criticized novels and poems. Not until the author published *The New York Times Cook Book* in 1961 did I make the cooking connection between the dream-like food we ate in France and the dreck we ate at home. Here were ten detailed recipes for *pâtés,* of all things, specifying mysterious ingredients like fresh pork fat, of all things. And just as were learning what fresh pork fat was and how come our supermarket didn't have it, Claiborne reviewed a book that called for quantities of it, along with other French-type ingredients. This book, astonishingly, was *only* about French-type ingredients because it was about *Mastering the Art of French Cooking.*

The authors had unlikely names from a Brecht play—Bertholle, Beck, and Child—but they addressed likely readers, "the servantless American cook," as they said, "who has the occasional leisure to cook for fun." *To cook for fun!* Was it possible? It was certainly a new idea to me, as was their assurance, "Anyone can cook in the French manner anywhere with the right instruction." A whole fifties generation of us who were kitchen-bound by babies, and by the postwar mystique that a wife in the kitchen was what our boys had been fighting for, took them at their word.

If it was wrong to compete with vets in the marketplace, we would instead compete with each other, fiercely, in the kitchen. Our kitchen tournaments belonged to the good clean teeth-baring fun of suburban tennis tournaments. We devoted our workdays as well as our leisure to perfecting our culinary strokes with balloon whisk and crêpe pan. Cooking in the French manner became a full-time profession for the ladies who do their own work. Cooking in the French manner became a plausible unsalaried profession because it was a creative art. A few radicals snarled that creative cooking kept a woman from being creative as a stockbroker or astronomer, but they underestimated the power of creative cooking to draw men, as well as women, into the workshop of conspicuous leisure. "Julia," as we came to know her in the intimacy of our living rooms once her television series began, appealed to men. Behind the warm and comic mask was the mind, men thought, of an engineer.

Men as well as women worked their way through *Julia I* as they might a night-school course in Welding or Public Speaking. Graduates of *Julia II* knew far more about French tables than the French generally knew. It was a highly specialized course and, for all that it seemed to be an art, it was in fact a high-tech science that demanded high-tech equipment. That was part of its appeal. My old Waring blender looked like a Victorian relic beside my heavy-duty Kitchen-Aid electric mixer with attachments: a complete set of rotary graters, slicers, and shredders, plus dough hook and pastry paddle and jack attachment for holding hot water or ice water. All this *before* the Cuisinart.

Julia had made the kitchen both fun and intellectually respectable by making it hard and serious work. Instead of the chemical lab of my high school days, my kitchen was now a splendidly equipped electrical shop humming with the eight-part harmony of dishwasher, disposal, food processor, coffee grinder, juicer, can opener, oven timer, and the old Waring blender. The evolution was logical and even inevitable. I had learned that eating was fun. I had learned that cooking was fun. What was wrong? Fun was wrong. What was the text I dimly recalled from the pages of *Our Women's Exchange?* "Be not anxious for your life . . . What ye shall eat, or what ye shall drink."

I remembered that text after I had spent five days on a *cassoulet.* Was it really okay to spend five days on a *cassoulet?* Or ten on a *confit d'oie?* The Puritan work ethic that drove me through two volumes of mastering French cooking stopped short with a backlash of guilt. Was I going to spend the rest of my life on what ye shall eat and what ye shall drink?

The answer was "yes" and I couldn't have been more surprised. The answer came from another book, or rather, five books in one, titled *The Art of Eating* by M. F. K. Fisher. She had written the books between 1937 and 1949 and a publisher had had the good sense to combine them in 1954, but I didn't discover her until nearly a decade later. I wasn't ready for her earlier. Something labeled "Gastronomical Works" would have seemed to me earlier a waste of time. Gastronomical Works were what libertines like Lucius Beebe wrote.

To my surprise, this gastronomer was as witty as Jane Austen and as sensual as Colette. Could it be that reading about cooking and eating was as much fun, maybe more, than doing it? It was Fisher, finally, who took the sting out of fun by addressing food in a language I knew. She spoke in the language of the Fisher of Men, because she spoke of human need and the hunger for sex, love, warmth, and cherishing that bound creatures of the earth each to each. Her voice of velvet seduction concealed an American moralist, and a tough one at that, who knew that men die, and many because they know not how to live.

It was Fisher who brought me back full circle to that austere American table of my childhood in which food was good or bad according to how you thought about it. It was Fisher, too, who revived the long dead words of my childhood, words like "purity" that I thought to have escaped forever. Purity, she taught me, had meaning after all. Purity need not mean the Puritan vision of flesh polluting spirit with the poisons of food. Purity might mean seeing life clearly and seeing it whole, with food at the center of the civilities that distinguish human creatures from other kinds. It was Fisher, finally, who taught me most about the differences between the American and French tables in order to show how much they shared in easing the common hunger not just to live but to live well.

# PART TWO

# THE MAKING OF FOUR AMERICAN MASTERS

M. F. K. FISHER

JAMES ANDREWS BEARD

RAYMOND CRAIG CLAIBORNE

JULIA McWILLIAMS CHILD

M. F. K. FISHER

*Philosopher-Poet of the Stove*

*Mary Frances Fisher* (signature)

*I was alone, which seems to be indicated for many such sensual rites. The potatoes were light, whipped to a firm cloud with rich hot milk, faintly yellow from ample butter. I put them in a big warmed bowl, made a dent about the size of a respectable coffee cup, and filled it to the brim with catsup from a large, full* vulgar *bottle that stood beside my table mat where a wineglass would be at an ordinary, commonplace, everyday banquet. Mine was, as I have said, delicious.*

—*from "Once a Tramp, Always . . ."*
With Bold Knife and Fork *(1968)*

Who could make mashed potatoes and ketchup sound like *that,* invoking Mark Twain on the one hand and the secret life of Frank Harris on the other? Whose words were both so bold and so curiously devious that the poet W. H. Auden had called the wielder of them one of the best prose writers in the United States today?

Who in fact *was* the mysterious M. F. K., whom the gastronome Lucius Beebe assumed was "a wispy young Oxford don" and with whom he promptly fell in love until the truth was exposed? I am wary as I search for a nearly invisible house on the Bouverie Ranch near a dinky cross-roads called Glen Ellen, California, in the Valley of the Moon.

The person who comes to the wrought-iron gate at the sound of my bell is surprisingly tall, surprisingly young. Mary Frances Kennedy Fisher, born July 3, 1908, is full of surprises—like her prose. She wears a loose cotton smock over trousers and walks slowly. A snub nose, a red cupid's mouth, and a girlish whisper contradict the gray hair pulled back from an imperious brow and the cool of gray-green eyes. I am right to be wary. I remember her writing about a great-grandmother who was "part witch, part empress." Fisher's disguise as a simple girl of the West doesn't fool me a bit.

We enter a room of such simplicity that I instantly sense a trap. Along one wall is the "kitchen"—a stove, sink, refrigerator lined up a step away from the round oak table set with a centerpiece of Santa Rosa plums. A floor of black tiles, a ceiling of weathered redwood, a sofa covered with mirrored Indian cushions: It is all too comfortable, too real, too inviting. A Siamese of infinite breeding, whose name is Charles II, pretends to sleep beneath a Spanish arch that looks west to the hills where Jack London built Wolf House in 1906. From Bouverie Ranch he had hauled red lava rock by ox sled. Fisher, I note, enjoys telling how London's macho bohemianism had shocked the citizens of Sonoma Valley in the days when the California wine country was inhabited by a handful of Italians and Russians and the odd Scottish Presbyter. This is her room for food and people, she says, simply, to throw me off the track.

She shows me the room for work and sleep. A typewriter, a clutter of manuscripts, a purple spread on the bed, and some 5,000 books—Colette, Virginia Woolf, Thackeray and Dickens, Simenon and Maigret, Shakespeare, Blake and Donne, books on gypsies, persecution, and old age. And cookbooks, of course. "I consult Irma Rombauer and Julia and Escoffier or *Larousse* and then I go ahead and do it *my* way." It is all too plausible.

Then, she shows me the room between. At last, a clue. A bathroom of Roman splendor—a six-foot tub, Oriental rugs, an easy chair beside the books and magazines, Pompeian red walls covered by the brilliant canvases of her second husband, the painter Dillwyn Parrish. I remember how she has written about the strategies of food in confronting grief, after his slow and painful death. "I ate with a rapt, voluptuous concentration which had little to do with bodily hunger, but seemed to nourish some other part of me," she wrote in *The Gastronomical Me.* "Sometimes I would go to the best restaurant I knew about, and order dishes and good wines as if I were a guest of myself, to be treated with infinite courtesy." Anyone who could eat like that could bathe like this, with voluptuous concentration. She is a voluptuary. She said so herself.

When she pours me a glass of Johannisberg Riesling 1981 from Napa, in the room for food and people, she recalls the toast of her newspaper father, Rex. "Here's to myself. A good man is scarce." I remember her envying his "great beak of a nose," but I also remember how she's written of the women in her family, a strong matriarchal line: "women like Mother and Grandmother and Baunie and even Aunt Gwen and Isobel and my little sister Anne and—yes, and me."

On the ranch in Whittier, where she'd been raised and where her father published and wrote 1,000 words a day for sixty years of the *Whittier Daily News,* the battle lines were drawn between women. On one side were her Anglomanic mother, Edith, joined by Aunt Gwen of the delicious Fried-Egg Sandwiches and French-Fried Onion Rings. On the other was Grandmother Holbrook of the Nervous Stomach and Ritual Enemas and Puritan Hunger for White Sauce. Grandmother Holbrook, when she was not refurbishing her bowels in Battle Creek, Michigan, oversaw the series of kitchen hirelings who were all women, "trying to survive among savages." The story of Fisher's life, I realize, is the story of a woman's struggle, setback, and eventual triumph over Grandmother Holbrook's Boiled Dressing and White Sauce. That is the person who could make the eating of mashed potatoes and ketchup a pornographic rite.

I realize that all of Fisher's thirteen volumes, from 1937 to 1982, comprise a unique autobiography. They are kitchen allegories about A Cook's Progress from cradle to grave with Pilgrim stops along the way in Aix-en-Provence, Marseilles, Switzerland, beginning and ending in California, a wholly allegorical place. Her initials are part of her disguise, like the invented name of Samuel Clemens. Yes, she is as tricky as Mark Twain, who pretended to write simple stories about the Mississippi in order to lure us into experiencing something else. Fisher and Twain were both writing about the American journey from innocence to knowledge and about all the hungers, yearnings, and cravings of that perilous trip.

If Twain disguised himself as a tramp, Fisher disguises herself as a kitchen tramp. Once a tramp, always . . . And if Twain measured his powers by plumbing the depths of the Mississippi River bottom, Fisher measures hers by plumbing the depths of her family kitchens. She discovered at twelve, she wrote, the pleasures of kitchen power when she began to cook dinner on the cook's night off. "I felt powerful," she said, "and I loved that feeling."

She was the natural leader of her savage tribe of two younger sisters, Anne and Nora, and a brother David. Their 100-acre ranch, halfway between country and town, mountains and sea, seemed an ideal place for savages. They grew everything—oranges, blackberries, mirabelles, guavas and dates, asparagus and artichokes. They raised everything— pigeons, chickens, turkeys, a pig, a cow, even a horse named "Hi-Ho Silver." They cooked everything—they canned fruits in Aunt Maggie's Cookhouse in the desert beyond Mount Baldy. They collected mussels in ten-gallon cans on the beach at Laguna. When they slept out after their barbecues, they circled their bedrolls with a lariat of horsehair to keep out the rattlesnakes. It was the savage West, where *la vie mondaine* meant a trip to the Victor Hugo restaurant in Los Angeles to order grandly a chicken à la king.

But there were other snakes in this Eden. The Whittier that produced Richard Milhous Nixon was entirely Quaker. As Episcopalians and midwestern Campbellites, the Kennedy family was heathen. She titled her family memoir *Among Friends*, but she had wanted a stronger less ambiguous title. "I wanted to call it *Child of an Inner Ghetto*," she tells me, "because it was the Quakers who first taught me the lessons of apartheid." It was a lesson, she says, that she never forgot. That lesson took her to Mississippi in the long hot summer of 1962 to teach black students, age seventeen to twenty-two, at Piney Woods Junior High School. It took her six months to win their trust and when the whites discovered the barriers were beginning to melt a little, she was asked not to come back. Her voice is still whispery, but I feel the cutting edge of her rage.

To escape the Friends and Grandmother Holbrook's Boiled Dressing, Fisher, at nineteen, married a son of a Presbyterian minister, Alfred Fisher, and fled to France. They lived in Dijon on $25 a month each. They were tramps and innocents abroad, and she writes of their wonderment on first biting into a hot croissant on the Quai Voltaire. Or on first ordering a *diner deluxe au prix fixe* at a fancy Dijon restaurant because they were unable to read a French menu. They learned French at the University of Dijon and they learned food in the marketplace and kitchen. She learned how to buy hard cheese by the kilo and grated cheese in grams. She learned how to cook a simple meatless casserole of cauliflower, with bread and fruit afterward. And she learned, when she returned to America to get a divorce, that everything in America was different—the cauliflower, the bread, the marriage. "It was never so *innocent,* so simple," she wrote of those days, "and then where was the crisp bread, where the honest wine? And where were our young uncomplicated hungers, too?"

She had fallen in love with "Timmy," son of the painter Maxfield Parrish. And when they went to live in Switzerland, in the small town of Vevey, she learned anew the power of the kitchen. They built their own onto the living room "so that we, the owners of the place, could be its cooks and servants." Their conventional Swiss neighbors were shocked and disbelieving. After one dinner party, the Parrishes were accused of concealing the cook so that no one else could hire her.

She also learned from this idyllic place, where fresh green peas seemed to pop from the garden into the pot, the power of food to evoke our senses. Later she would write of the way contemporary American women seemed to have lost that power and that pleasure by shunning contact with food as such, by pretending to live like aristocrats above the kitchen matters of servants. Long before est or other voguish sensory therapies, Fisher was writing about the therapy of food, how one might recover the immediacy of lost senses "by touching an egg yolk, smelling a fresh lettuce leaf or berry, tasting either the product of their own hands, such as a fresh loaf of bread, or a fresh body."

In the early forties, the idyl ended. The death of her husband, the suicide of her brother, the outbreak of war required new strategies of survival and once again she found them in food. When the wolf is at the door, ask him in, seduce him, and cook him up for supper. *How to Cook a Wolf* (1942) is a book like no other, with excursions on How to Boil Water, How to Keep Alive, How Not to Boil an Egg, How to Make a Pigeon Cry. It is a parody of American how-to books with a bucketful of anti-recipes. Here the artful strategist contrives recipes for Prune Roast and Mock Duck, for Aunt Gwen's Cold Shape (which turns out to be headcheese) and Addie's Quick Bucket Bread, for Rice Fats Waller, and Eggs in Hell (garlic and tomato sauce, ketchup will do). And, of course, her famous anti-recipe for Sludge.

"Borrow 50 cents," her anti-recipe begins, along with a food grinder and a kettle. Spend 10 cents on whole-grain cereal and the rest on vegetables—the withered, battered, or big ugly kind are cheaper. Grind everything together, cover with water, and cook slowly until the sludge is a "stiff cold mush, and a rather unpleasant murky brown-gray in color." You can make it *look* better, she assures us, by adding a blob of Kitchen Bouquet, but why bother? Gastronomically speaking, sludge is the means to an end "like ethyl gasoline."

A wolf-seducer, she was caught by a wolf in gastronome's clothing in the form of her third husband, Donald Friede. "He was expert in caviar and smoked salmon and had never eaten a muffin in his life," Fisher said. "I was his fifth wife and we lasted seven years." Fisher had one daughter, Anne, by Parrish and now she had a new daughter, Kennedy. Their marriage broke over children. "He was appalled by babies," she says, so she took them to Aix and wrote, in *A Map of Another Town* (1970), about the strategies of food in combating loneliness. ("Place three tangerines on the sill above the radiator until they have distilled their juice.")

Her strategies with food were never simple. The rites of cooking and eating were her way of coping with the "atavistic realities" of man's essential cannibalism. Since eat we must, what and how we eat is everything. She turns the eating of snails, for instance, into an erotic and disturbing act of necrophilia:

> Then there were snails, the best in the world, green and spitting in their little delicate coffins, each in its own hollow on the metal plates. After you pulled out the snail, and blew upon it cautiously and ate it, you tipped up the shell for every drop inside, and then with bread you polished the hollow it had lain in, not to miss any of the herby butter.

"Their little delicate coffins"? Another ambush of the seductress. I recall that her one adult novel, with the intriguing Samuel Beckett title *Not Now But Now*, is about a modern Lilith, "a wandering wanton."

And I remember the entrapments that lay in the depths of even the most ordinary of her institutional kitchens. She wrote about the kitchen of Miss Huntingdon's School for Girls, which the young Mary Frances attended until she was sixteen. Mrs. Cheever ran Miss Huntingdon's kitchens. "She ran her kitchens with such skill," Fisher wrote, "that in spite of ordinary domestic troubles like flooded basements and soured cream, and even an occasional extraordinary thing like the double murder and harakiri committed by the head-boy one Good Friday, our meals were never late and never bad." I begin to understand fully why I was uneasy when I found out that Fisher's present kitchen lay in the Valley of the Moon.

I remember, too, that even in the security of her own childhood kitchen, there were insights of what was to come. Fisher recalled the elderly spinster cook named Ora whom her Grandmother Holbrook disliked. She disliked the affectation of Ora's long "French" knife and the way she was always polishing and sharpening it. Grandmother Holbrook thought Ora way above herself when she failed to return after her Sunday off. Grandmother Holbrook was not surprised to learn that Ora *could* not return: She had cut first her mother into neat pieces and then her own wrists and throat without inflicting a single scratch or nick in the knife.

Even so, I did not make the full Fisher connection between strategies of survival and "the dark necessity of eating" until the reissue, in 1981, of a very small book of recipes called *A Cordiall Water*, first published twenty years earlier. I knew that writing was as natural as sneezing to a woman born into a fifth generation of journalists and broadside pamphleteers, including a great-grandfather who fled Ireland to escape being shot for printing tirades against the queen. "With my own discovery of the printed word I came into focus," she once said, and proceeded to write a novel at age nine and short stories all her life. But her real writing is halfway between essay and meditation, meditations like those of Brillat-Savarin in *The Physiology of Taste* she has so finely translated. Her meditations, she tells me, are little ways of saying "what I think about omelettes or nosebleeds or warts." And the meditations she likes best, "the pick of the litter," are those collected in the "Garland of Odd and Old Receipts to Assuage the Ills of Man & Beast" that she has titled *A Cordiall Water*.

"While writing about horny cats and aching bones . . . and all that clutter of life," she writes in her preface, "I was stripped of banality, and I wrote simply in my native tongue . . ." She wrote simply and purely of recipes for healing our wounded condition as human beasts. She wrote of recipes For a Consumption, or To make ye Green Ointment that cured Lady Probyn's Coachman's Back, or a Sure Cure for a Scorpion Bite—all of them incantations compounded of age-old science, magic, poetry, faith—the true ingredients of our recipes for death and life. She wrote of an Elizabethan receipt that called for thirty garden snails and thirty earthworms, and of a contemporary French workman's receipt that called for the Laying on of Hands. "Both spoke," she said, "of incantation, and mystery, and ageless faith: the essentials of healing." She wrote of cures using urine and dung, "the liquid and the solid, which all animal bodies must make and then excrete in order to exist."

Finally, I had reached the truth of her siren song. Her strategies were addressed to a single overwhelming question: "What must we do in order to exist?" She was a philosopher in an existential kitchen, a poet who saw Plato in a bean pot, love in a baked potato, death in a bowl of chicken soup. With cunning and daring, she wrested food from the exploitive hands of pseudo-science, commerce, and industry, from the wasteland of mass mediocrity, from the corruptions of greed and self-loathing, to restore it to its rightful place at the center of those "ageless celebrations of life" expressed in feasts and fairs. She was a philosopher who believed in "Nothingness probably, like an oyster or a seed." But she was a poet for whom an oyster or a seed is everything.

As a poet, she observed precisely her fellow creatures, a toad's throat pulsing like a baby's fontanel, the three stiff hairs by the single nostril of a bifurcated *tête de veau*. As a philosopher, she wrote about hunger instead of about wars and love because "There is a communion of more than our bodies when bread is broken and wine drunk." Food was, in truth, a sacrament, and she has seduced me like Circe into confronting that hard fact as I sit at her round oak table with the plums she will pickle that night.

By this time I would willingly eat mashed potatoes and ketchup but she is too canny for that. She serves forth a Moroccan *chermoula*, a dish of green and red peppers bonded by oil, garlic, and coriander. There are thin slices of smoked salmon prepared by an Eskimo friend in nearby Petaluma, exiled for a year from his tribe because of a death in his family. "Not a bad custom," she says. There is a loaf of sourdough wheat bread from a family of Basque bakers in the village of Sonoma. "Like the bread in Marseilles," she says. There are blueberries from Alaska macerated in brown sugar and a very crisp shortbread. "Just put a little too much sugar on before you bake it," she says. Her receipts are exact.

"I went to the woods because I wished to live deliberately," Thoreau wrote in *Walden Pond,* "to front only the essential facts of life, and see if I could not learn what it has to teach." What Thoreau learned in the woods, Fisher learned in the kitchen. The essential facts that Thoreau fronted in the wildness of nature, Fisher fronts in that "art which may be one of our last firm grasps on reality, that of eating and drinking with intelligence and grace on evil days." Her cook's progress begins and ends in that real and symbolic kitchen in which she took the measure of her powers, tasted the fruits of her passion, and learned her place in the world. She has caught me by the throat. I am spooked by her powers and food will never again be entirely innocent of them. As she says, "Once a tramp, always . . ."

## JAMES ANDREWS BEARD

*King of the Pots*

*It has always been my contention that the people of the Western European countries ate pretty dull food until the discovery of America.*

—*from* Delights and Prejudices *(1964)*

To discover America through its food is to discover James Beard, a continent in himself. "How much garlic?" a student asks in one of the cooking classes Beard has taught for nearly thirty years to amateurs and professionals, stockbrokers and plumbers, secretaries and housewives and chefs. "Half an acre," the master of masters replies. "He's the giant of the food world—physically, mentally, spiritually—in every way," M. F. K. Fisher says. Beard is bigger than life, like some Paul Bunyan folk hero, who thinks in acres of garlic, hectares of butter, and rivers of cream. As the father of American cookery in this century, he has probably done more than anyone else to reshape the American palate to the freedom and largesse incarnate in his own girth. Now, at eighty, he can say along with Whitman, "I am large; I contain multitudes."

His students are his extended family, many returning year after year in a new-found liberation from parsimony and prissiness. "Get your hands into it," he tells a student folding egg whites with a spatula. "Get your hips into it," he tells a student rolling out pasta. At six feet, four inches and reduced to a mere 260 pounds from his peak of 310 before a no-salt, low-fat diet, Beard reeks authority, and we hustle to obey. With his bald dome and pointy ears, he is a cross between Bacchus and Sydney Greenstreet. "I have disliked several students with a passion," he confesses in his autobiographical *Delights and Prejudices,* the title of which speaks for itself. "There have been a few students for whom I would not have wept had they mistaken a flagon of hemlock for the *apéritif!*"

But we are not apprentices, cowering before the *batterie de cuisine* aimed by some despotic French chef. We are extras in a Marx Brothers' movie, fighting for space like gnomes in the giant's workshop, where cleavers whack, ovens smoke, mixers whir, engulfed by walls of copper vats, by blocks bristling with knives, by a ceiling consumed with a Rand-McNally map of the globe. Beneath a strip of theater lights, seated in an outsized director's chair in the middle of the U-shaped counter he calls his "grand piano," the giant in a red Chinese smock and blue trousers directs our garlic epics like a veteran of Hollywood. The scene is a Twelfth Street brownstone in Greenwich Village, but the style is *A Night at the Opera.*

How else explain "the pot boy," as he calls himself? Clay Triplet, an Irish-Polish black with a gap-toothed grin, who hollers, "Leave your diamonds and emeralds in the hall and go put on your aprons." Clay, I notice, is wearing a discreet necklace, given him by chef Julie Dannenbaum, that spells out in diamonds his favorite phrase, "Oh Shit." And where else would you find a *sous-chef,* Richard Nimmo, Beard's assistant of many years, explaining as he kneads a loaf of saffron bread with expert hands that he got into cooking by way of the clarinet? He came to Juilliard, met Beard, and that was the end of the clarinet.

"Never skimp," the giant says to a student who asks, "How much cream?" "I've never had a cooking class," another student confesses, and the giant roars, "Me, too." Born a thirteen and a half pounder on May 5, 1903, Beard learned to cook as he learned to breathe, because what he breathed were the incredible aromas of the kitchen of the Gladstone Hotel in Portland, Oregon. His father, Jonathan, was a charmer with a good palate and lots of debts. His mother, Mary Elizabeth Jones, was an English adventuress turned hotel manager, who produced, at forty-two, her first and only child. "I have always said that Mother brought me up in the same way she ran her hotel," Beard says, "more manager than Mother." Of his father, Beard says, "He was a Mississippi gambler type who wore a red carnation, smelled of fine soaps and colognes and was loved by all the ladies." Of his mother, he says, "That incredible woman who was my father."

That incredible woman had come to America at sixteen to serve as a governess. She traveled through America and most of Europe and Central America before she settled in Portland and, in 1896, bought a hotel as dignified as its Gladstone name. The Portland that Beard remembers, however, was a port of waterfront hearties, of sporting ladies and pimps, of imported French and Italian chefs who would catch gold fever and head for the Yukon to leave Mother Beard fuming among her pots. She solved the cook problem by hiring Chinese, men like Let, Gin, Poy, and Billy, immortalized now in Beard's recipes.

It was an idyllic world that Beard evokes, where the ancient arts of China, England, and France were applied to the provender of the western shores. The waters teemed with Olympia oysters, Dungeness crab, razor clams, and Columbia River salmon. The woods were blue with huckleberries and blackberries. They ate terrapin stew and chicken sautéed with wild mushrooms. The Yamhill Street public market offered seasonal rarities such as white raspberries, husk tomatoes, morels, lemon cucumbers, and a dozen varieties of apples—Gravenstein and Newtown Pippins. Italian truck gardeners brought in cardoons, fava beans, leeks, and Savoy cabbage. La Grande Creamery offered Brie and Camembert from French cheese makers in California. And Mother Beard and Chef Let battled over the proper way to make aspic, capon, and curries.

Beard remembers Let brandishing a knife in the heat of battle, and Mother parrying with a stick of firewood. But such quarrels ended in laughter and renewed argument over the proper way to preserve a fig. With the arrival of James, the pair battled harder "to instill in me a love for food . . . the most varied gastronomic experiences any child ever had." There was Let's Wonderful Sweet Cream Biscuit and My Mother's Black Fruitcake and even My Father's Pear Preserves. It was the great American amalgam, where Mother imported the muffin and crumpet rings of her youth so that Chinese Let could make perfect English crumpets, "dripping with butter and daubed with our strawberry jam." It was a social amalgam, too, of backyard, carside, and oceanside picnics. There were champagne parties, whist parties, bridge parties, fashionable luncheons, and after-theater suppers. For a large fat boy, it was bliss.

He was so pampered by the entire hotel staff, Beard recalls, that he became "as precocious and nasty a child as ever inhabited Portland." His lifelong friend Mary Hamblet agrees that he was a holy terror on occasion but so generous always that to admire a toy was to be given it to keep. She also remembers what may have been his first culinary act, playing on the beach at Gearhart, where they made a sand pie and frosted it with a pink marshmallow whipped with salt water. "Eat it," said James. "And I did," said Mary, "because I adored him—and he was big."

Gifted with a taste memory as acute as perfect pitch, Beard remembers his first gastronomic act, when he crawled into the vegetable bin and ate a giant onion, skin and all. At three, sick with malaria, he remembers feeding on a superb chicken jelly. At four, he began to discriminate among restaurants when his father took him to dine out in Portland once a week. At five, his mother in a lapse of discretion took him to the Louvre, "a palace of high living," where he sampled French cuisine in the most notorious place in town. And at all ages his Chinese godfather took him to eat in Chinatown.

Still, even as a child prodigy of the knife and fork, his first love was not eating but acting. He advanced from charades in his mother's hotel to playing Tweedledum in the Red Lantern Players' production of *Alice* and Mr. Fuzzywig in their annual performance of *A Christmas Carol*. At nineteen, he was to be an opera singer, and he set out for London and Paris by way of a freighter, the *Highland Heather,* and the Panama Canal. When a vocal ailment ended that ambition, he returned to play in *Cyrano* and *Othello* at Walter Hampden's Theater in New York. Then on to radio, where he did food commercials for a station in San Francisco.

But since acting often meant not eating, he determined to make a living from food and became a "gastronomic gigolo" in New York. Jobs were scarce in 1937, so he cooked for his supper at the houses of friends and still he went hungry. He went hungry until, with a pair of friends, he opened a catering shop on Sixty-sixth Street and Park Avenue and went after the carriage trade. With Hors d'Oeuvre, he revolutionized the current canapé style, with its soggy dabs he called "doots," by offering he-man stuff: artichokes stuffed with caviar, smoked salmon rolls, brioche-onion rings, and similar "highball sandwiches." He was on the road to both cooking and writing. He published the first major cookbook devoted exclusively to drink food in *Hors d'Oeuvres & Canapés,* in 1940, and followed it with the first serious work on outdoor cooking, *Cook It Outdoors,* in 1942.

The war interrupted this promising beginning with the draft and a stint at cryptography school. Released from the army at thirty-eight, he joined the United Seamen's Service to direct USS clubs from Marseilles to Rio. "Get him to take his teeth out and sing 'Sylvie,' " said one of his oldest Portland friends, who remembered dying with laughter at his tales of service trips. As he became a pro at entertainment, he also picked up tips on food, such as the Avocado Purée dessert made with lime and sugar by a cook in Brazil.

At the end of the war, he found a new theater for food when NBC asked him to do the first commercial food program for television. "At last," he thought, "a chance to cook and act at the same time." He shared billing with a bovine star fashioned by Bill Baird and produced by the Borden Company, Elsie the Cow: *ELSIE PRESENTS—James Beard in I Love to Eat."* A new medium inaugurated a new theater of cooking and new "cuisines of advertisement," as they have been called. From now on food images would confer status and Beard's image was the biggest around. By 1959, with the publication of the first *James Beard Cookbook,* James Beard became the majordomo of the food establishment, a Gargantua beaming over platters of fat sausages and hams and chops that fit the mood of the decades of affluence.

Some have criticized Beard for working too closely with the food industry, for endorsing products like Omaha Steaks and Camp Maple Syrup. But that's the kind of purism that Beard laughs off as loudly as he does prissiness. People take food too damn seriously, he says. "It's something you enjoy and have fun with, and if you don't, to hell with it. It's no ritual; it's . . . good and amusing and a pleasant part of life."

Having fun in the Beard way is the story of his twenty-five years of cooking classes. He began in 1955 by borrowing the kitchen of chef

André Surmain and of other food-industry professionals until he could set up a kitchen in a Village brownstone of his own. It's more fun to cook at home, he says, where you can open another bottle of Beaujolais when the class gets merry and dry.

He expressed his credo in *Theory & Practice of Good Cooking* (1977), when he wrote, "In my twenty-five years of teaching I have tried to make people realize that cooking is primarily fun and that the more they know about what they are doing, the more fun it is." To learn from Beard is to discard diet books altogether as dreary and depressing. Forced onto a no-salt low-cal diet a few years ago, Beard discovered new ways of flavoring that he hadn't imagined, as he discovered new intensities of ignored friends like strong rooty vegetables, a plain saltless baked potato, the creamy sour of yogurt.

To learn from Beard is to learn *good cooking*, whether its roots are French, Italian, English, Oriental, or down-home American. In his recipes, in his classes, he teaches the virtues of simplicity. "Don't gussy up spareribs with all that gunk," he instructs. "Just sprinkle with plain salt and pepper and half an acre of garlic." His books are all basic teaching books and are the most practical of our four masters. The first *James Beard Cookbook* begins with a chapter on how to boil water—to assure his readers that much of cooking is no more difficult than that. "Be bold," he tells us. "Taste for yourself," he commands. "Taste things half-done, done— and overdone, if that happens; mistakes are to learn from, not to pine over."

Beard's voice is as American as Whitman's as he sings the body electric, knocks over old categories in the name of "freshness and freedom," insists that we improvise, experiment, and shake up our ideas about menus to feature "whatever you want to star." "I like this class, you're all rebels," he told us one night, after we'd learned to talk back. As a rebel himself, he has always celebrated America first. "I can assure you," he writes, "that the smell of good smoked country ham sizzling in a black iron skillet in the early morning is as intoxicating and as mouth-watering as the bouquet of a fine Château Lafite-Rothschild or an Haut-Brion of a great year."

While we cut hominy grits into squares, spread it with Jack cheese, roasted peppers, and lots of Parmesan, he laments the attrition of regional cooking and eating in this century. But he has done more than anybody to stalk the wild traditions of our past and to honor earlier giants. In his *American Cookery* (1972), he acknowledges his debts to a trio of strong women: Mary Randolph of *The Virginia Housewife*, Eliza Leslie of *Directions for Cookery,* and Mrs. Thomas Crowen of *Every Lady's Book.* "I would like to have known all three," he says, taking down volumes at random from his immense library of cooking Americana. He, more than anybody, has traced the great American tradition from the trio before the

Civil War to the postwar stars, Mrs. Sarah Tyson Rorer in Philadelphia, Mrs. A. D. Lincoln in Boston, and her former pupil and subsequent rival, Fannie Farmer. And on into this century, through Irma Rombauer, Louis DeGouy, Mrs. Simon Kander, his friend Helen Evans Brown, Helen McCully, Michael Field ("a theorist who didn't like food but wrote well about it"), and then, finally, "Claiborne, Child and me."

Of Claiborne he believes that it was his writing that mattered. "He excited people about cooking." Of Child he believes that it was "her brilliant sense of humor" that mattered because "she kept people from being too earnest about it all." Of Fisher he believes that it was her context that mattered. "She is not a great cook but a great writer *about* cooking." Of himself he believes that he dramatized cooking, made it theatrically fun.

A sense of theater, the grand gesture, explains such typical Beard productions as his Forty-Garlic Chicken or his Game-Stuffed Turkey, in which a turkey is stuffed with a goose which is stuffed with a capon which is stuffed with a partridge which is stuffed with a quail. Typical also is the Beard method behind the latter madness, in which he arranges fat birds to baste drier ones and in which he bones all the birds to make slicing and serving dramatically a snap.

A sense of theater explains the wild eclecticism of his melting-pot menus. "What you cook is a reflection of *you,*" he tells us. "Don't be afraid to try new combinations." It's the cook that unifies a meal, not a country or a culture. That's why our student meal may begin with a mustard-broiled quail for a finger-food appetizer while we chop, knead, sieve, and pound a Noodle and Eggplant Dumpling, a Carrot-Beet Soufflé, Chantarelles in Madeira, a Roast Lamb with Italian Orzo, bagels with three different flavorings, and why our meal may end with an arpeggio of Chestnut-Raisin Ice Cream, a Pound Cake with Grand Marnier, a dozen pecan-studded Schnecken. With the king of pots, anything good goes good together in one combination or another.

The setting of our final consummation, where we gather in the bamboo-papered dining room to eat the lesson, is grand opera in little. We consume flagons of Beaujolais beneath the boar's head in porcelain, beside the pitchers and tureens of Wedgwood corn, while the wall dances with turquoise oysters and pink sardines in Minton china from France. Or we wander into the walled garden of pink and red geraniums and potted herbs beside the pig in copper. A glass greenhouse hangs above us on the second floor, with a desk at one end and a shower at the other, extending the throne room of Chinese porcelains and paintings guarded by life-sized terra-cotta nudes representing Terpsichoria Nectambrosia, the spirit of gastronomy. Half an acre of collectibles. Everything in excess. We have starred with James Beard in "I Love to Eat."

If cooking is not fun, to hell with it. "Put on a fine show!" Beard exhorts the readers of *Delights and Prejudices*. "Like the theater, offering food and hospitality to people is matter of showmanship, and no matter how simple the performance, unless you do it well, with love and originality, you have a flop on your hands." Beard speaks the language of P. T. Barnum as well as of Whitman and knows that imagination, rather than money, is the secret ingredient of a hit. Like a good showman, Beard boosts the future of American cooking and believes that we are about to recover the gastronomic excellence into which he was born, but which declined rapidly in the industrialization of food before the war. For the sake of health, he has at last forsaken cream for yogurt, meat for vegetables and grains. But why not? Limitations are a challenge, and there are acres of garlic to chop before he sleeps.

DAN WYNN

# RAYMOND CRAIG CLAIBORNE

*Hayseed Connoisseur*

*Craig Claiborne* [signature]

---

*Under umbrellas on a driftwood bench*
*Beside a sea that wore Parisian ruffles*
*We drank champagne, ate food divinely French*
*Viz: hamburgers—with truffles.*

*With love for Craig*
Phyllis McGinley
—*from* The New New York Times Cookbook *(1980)*

Hamburgers with truffles describes a marriage unique in the world of cooking and eating and of writing about both, a marriage both divinely French and just-folks American. It's a marriage that was consummated by the most famous—and some said infamous—dinner of our times, the $4,000 banquet for two paid for by American Express at Chez Denis in Paris and washed down by plenty of champagne. It's a marriage of nearly twenty-five years that began in the spring of 1959, when Craig Claiborne fell in love with a striped bass in champagne sauce at Le Pavillon and met the man who cooked it, Pierre Franey. "The greatest event in my life," Claiborne says, and confesses that he owes it all to *The New York Times.*

Becoming food editor of *The Times* but two years earlier, in August of 1957, was the first "miracle" in the life of this Walter Mitty of gastronomy, who describes himself then as "a ninety-six-pound weakling" —shy, reticent, awkward, and backward and, worst of all, a man. Until Claiborne, the media assumed that food was strictly women's work, at least the nitty-gritty cooking of it in recipes sandwiched between marriage announcements in newspapers and between ads in ladies' magazines. The eating of it might be work for men if they were famous restaurateurs like George Rector, famous gastronomes like Lucius Beebe, foreign imports like Ludwig Bemelmans and Joseph Wechsberg, or exports to France like Samuel Chamberlain. But until Claiborne, only James Beard and M. F. K. Fisher had crossed the lines of sexual apartheid in a significant way to make both actions of cooking and eating bisexual. After Claiborne, food was unisex, food was beyond sex, because Claiborne for the first time put food in headlines on the front

---

page of the newspaper least likely to sandwich affairs of the palate between wars and affairs of state. For Americans, Claiborne made food news news of the world.

And through food, he took us around the world to become, with him, an international connoisseur. By combining cooking in with eating out, he was the first to systematically let us in on the secrets of famous chefs, to take us behind the scenes of restaurants we'd never dreamed of visiting, to tease us into sampling exotica like Nuoc Mam Sauce that we could cook before we could pronounce, to brave on our behalf the contumely of famous maître d's, and to judge, on our behalf, the quality of their costly tables. He became our surrogate palate and kingmaker, who could make or break the world's most renowned or most obscure kitchen by rewarding or withholding our stars. Through this unassuming, unobtrusive little man, who had so few distinguishing features that he seemed to blend into the silverware, we tasted power.

It was power to the people, all right, and from a revolutionary source: food power, an untapped natural resource in the great American social climb. In 1962, with Claiborne's first dining out guide, the doors of New York's snobbiest restaurants were opened, all unknowing, to a Mr. Anonymous with a limitless expense account and no social or commercial ax to grind. *The Times* was proud enough and rich enough to afford the luxury of objective judgment. "I was never bedeviled, nor beseeched, nor implored, nor had any contact with the advertising department," Claiborne says. Such freedom enabled him to initiate honest restaurant reviewing in this country comparable to the impeccable honesty of the *Michelin Guide* in France. New York chefs went into shock. Headwaiters scurried to locate photos of the man but, even with his mug posted in the kitchen, the man was too unnoticeable to be noticed. He frequently found himself at one of the "bad" tables, where he was doused with soup, beaned by rolls, where silverware was knocked from his hands, and plates removed before sampled. These were the years when he ate every single blessed meal out, including breakfast.

Through him, we took our revenge. In the solid middle-class way of the *Michelin,* he made price a factor of pleasure. Outdoing *Michelin,* he made the quality of the food, rather than the service, the sole criterion. "The restaurants in this volume are judged with a single question in mind," he wrote in the foreword to the first revised edition of the *1964 New York Times Guide to Dining Out in New York.* "How does the quality of the food and its preparation measure up to the cost?" These standards put one of the most pretentious spots in town, The Forum of the Twelve Caesars, on equal one-star footing with a Chinatown joint like the Joy Luck Coffee Shop. Across the country, Americans who had never been near New York bought Claiborne's *Guide* for the simple joys of image bashing. Our money was as good as anybody's, even at the imperial Forum where, instructed by Claiborne, we might find Caesar's pottage wanting.

Claiborne was uniquely equipped to become our surrogate palate. Despite his disclaimers that he never took his restaurant reviewing as seriously as his readers did, he spoke with authority. He was the first of our native major food writers to have any formal training in the preparation and service of food. For formal training, apart from industry geared classes on the one hand or private maid-and-cook classes on the other, Americans had to go to Europe. Claiborne had to go to Switzerland, but how he got there is part of that Walter Mitty persona that made him a spokesman for all us rubes and hayseeds confronted by urban sophisticates at home and abroad.

Claiborne, even more than Fisher, echoed the country drawl of Mark Twain because he was born on September 4, 1920, to a Craig and a Claiborne in Sunflower, Mississippi. His was "one of those incestuous type Southern Families," Claiborne remarks, where cousins intermarried and reproduced names like Fredibelle Claiborne and Claiborne Craig. His was also one of those southern families that were land rich and dirt poor. His father was a gentleman farmer by birth, an accountant by trade, a teetotaling Methodist by conviction, and fifteen years senior to the woman who married him and always called him "Mister C." While his father knew about food as a farmer, raising his own chickens, smoking his own sausages, it was his mother, Mary Kathleen Craig, who was the cook. And it was his mother who turned her skill to a profession, during hard times, by running boardinghouses. Claiborne, like Beard, was the product of a cooking mother who ran the ranch as well as the range.

They moved to Indianola and from then on from house to house, where his mother would sublet and take in paying guests. They moved so often, Claiborne recalls, that when anyone in Indianola saw a wagon load of furniture going down the street they'd holler, "Shut the door! Here come the Claibornes." It began "a lifelong series of humiliations" for a small sensitive round-faced boy with an elfin grin who is haunted still, he says, by fears of failure and shame. He remembers his mother shaming him for having proudly won second place in a spelling bee instead of first. He remembers the math teacher who teased him for being a sissy and scared, forever after, numbers from his head. He remembers his father who was ashamed of his own man's body. He remembers the humiliation of being arrested and thrown in jail for drunken driving in East Hampton and of calling *The Times* for help. His recent autobiography is the story of a Bad Little Boy saved by Big Daddy. The second Big Daddy was *The Times*. The first was the navy.

When he saw that he was flunking his premed course at Mississippi State, he says, he switched to the School of Journalism at Missouri University and majored in advertising. Graduating in 1942, he joined the navy to avoid the draft. "I've always been a little bit of a snob," he confesses, and for a Sunflower kid the navy had class. "I lived in some style from the first day I put on a navy uniform to the day I got out—during two wars." In the navy he learned to travel and to eat, for they were both sides of the same coin. While he had grown up in a kitchen, it was the kitchen of Negro mammies like Aunt Catherine, who did both the real cooking and mothering. He grew up on field peas and hog jowl and hot tamales and fried chicken and chess pie and grits and once a year a chit'lin' supper. His affection for southern fare remains, but he didn't convert to Food Hedonism until, as a yeoman, he ate his first couscous in Casablanca, at a restaurant aptly named La Comédie.

The man who has done most to introduce into the American kitchen dishes from around the world sampled them first in the navy. As secretary to Admiral John Leslie Hall, Claiborne stayed in North Africa for nearly a year. "A sweet life," he says. "All I did was type and sightsee." After a stint of NROTC at Notre Dame, he took his "typewriter and tourism" to the Pacific and to the action of Hawaii, Okinawa, and Guam. With the end of the war, he marked time in Chicago doing public relations for radio ABC and Don McNeill's *Breakfast Club* before suffering his next culinary epiphany. That took place aboard the *Île de France* when he tasted a classical *turbot à l'infante* and had a spiritual *extase* that led him to ask the waiter for the recipe. Claiborne's French was so minimal that when the waiter said the sauce was based on a *fumet de poisson* Claiborne thought he had eaten smoked fish.

Both his French and his knowledge of ingredients improved on that first postwar trip abroad when he hit Paris and had his first passionate affair with a city. On his return to Chicago, he was happy to rejoin the navy at the outbreak of the Korean war. By 1953, after eating his way through Hawaii and points farther East, he knew he was destined for food. With the GI bill, he enrolled in the École Hôtelière in Lausanne and spent half a year learning to serve, half a year learning to cook, and another six months working in hotels. It was as good as the navy. From then on he had a single ambition, as he remembers it: "to be food editor of *The New York Times.*"

How he got to *The Times* is one of those fables in which the hapless geek wins the princess. Seeking his fortune in New York, he got a job as receptionist with *Gourmet* and then yet another public relations job with Procter & Gamble. As a PR man, he knew how to con, he says, so he asked Jane Nickerson, food editor at *The Times,* how she would like to interview a Mississippi boy who'd just graduated from "the best cooking school in the world." As a PR man, he knew the use of superlatives, not to mention the value of a Mississippi barefoot-boy image. When Nickerson retired, she had Claiborne meet another Mississippi boy, Catledge Turner, then executive editor at *The Times.* When Turner found that Claiborne had roomed at Polecat Alley during his years at Mississippi State, the editor hired him on the spot. "I hadn't roomed there," says Claiborne, "but I knew *he* had."

*The Times* was almost better than the navy. "I would not leave *The Times* for $100,000, not for $200,000," said the man who, after two decades of eating out, told *The Times* in 1978, "Give me my benefits, I'm quitting this place." The power of the restaurant critic had finally got to him and he had lost too many friends. "Things got to the point where I couldn't go to a restaurant at night," he told an interviewer, "unless I came home here and had at least four Scotch and sodas and four martinis." He had either to quit or to become a total alcoholic. He went to Kenya to dry out, went bankrupt trying to put out a restaurant newsletter called "The Craig Claiborne Journal," and in two years returned to *The Times* with relief.

He returned with the proviso that someone else review restaurants. As it happens, he was threatened with a lawsuit by a restaurant only once. "A terribly cheap Italian place in Greenwich Village," he recalls, "where the veal was dreadful." Claiborne reported that the meat had been tenderized with a claw hammer. The irate owner claimed he had *never* used a claw hammer: "We put our meat through a machine."

What Claiborne liked to report was interesting people cooking interesting foods, in what became a twenty-year series of food profiles that helped turn the Women's Page into the Living Section. He was the first to write in detail about exotic Szechuan, Vietnamese, and Thai cooking and to document them with recipes. The recipes, a total of some 11,500 by now, were the blood and guts of his copy because they allowed everyman to become his own armchair traveler by way of the stove. We, too, could sample the Sussex Pond Pudding cooked for Craig by Jane Grigson in Swindon, England, or the Plantain Fritters served up by Governor and Mrs. Romero in Puerto Rico. On our own mainland, we, too, could search out the infinite variety of our ethnic mix, eating at one time a Matzo Meat Pie at a Sephardic-Ashkenazic Seder and at another a Hoppin' John from Mrs. Wilkes's Boarding House in Savannah, Georgia.

We, too, could play host to the world's great chefs and learn Chinese cooking from Virginia Lee, Italian from Marcella Hazan, Indian from Madhur Jaffrey, Mexican from Diana Kennedy. We could test out the latest and trendiest fancy French against establishment French, here and elsewhere, because for years Claiborne had described, translated, and mediated the recipes of chefs like Roger Fessaguet, René Verdon, Jean Vergnes, Gaston Lenôtre, Paul Bocuse, Jean Troisgros, Michel Guérard, not to mention Pierre Franey. We could travel first class on the S.S. *France* and cook in the kitchens of Henri Lehuédé. Claiborne was our medium through which we got the message.

He answered our mail, some fifty letters a week, when we queried the origin of the word "salsify," or protested the killing of live lobsters. He cheerfully shared our prejudices, listing his Loves and Loathes. Loves:

breakfasts, off-color jokes, Kasanof's Jewish Caraway Rye Bread, picnics and covered-dish suppers, caviar, truffles, champagne, hamburgers, corn on the cob, and chili con carne—"conceivably America's greatest contribution to the world's cuisine." Loathes: gluttony and excess, iceberg lettuce, tepid soup, cigars, maraschino cherries, dinner plates on laps, and guests who use books for coasters, pour on soy sauce before tasting, "help" with the dishes.

He made us aware of the way we eat, in restaurants or at home. He made dining alone a social event by setting the table as elaborately for himself as for a guest, everything "meticulously laid out—placemat, silver, china and wineglass." He critiqued the domestic manners of the Americans, calling us "a nation of culinary schizophrenics" freaked out on diets while binging on junk foods, driven to paranoia by "the fright merchants" of cholesterol, driven to gluttony by guilt over the starving Bangladesh. Fastidious about his own weight—158 in the morning and 162 at night—he found obesity immoral and "Eat Less" a categorical imperative. Himself a salt freak, he made salt-free meals a virtue after acute hypertension drove him to construct a Gourmet Diet. A snob about elegance, he deflated snobbery about foods: "It's harder to make a good hamburger than it is to make an ordinary soufflé."

It was his snobbery about elegance that led to the perfect marriage of two country boys, the one from Sunflower, Mississippi, and the other from Thunder ("Tonnerre"), France. It was Claiborne's story on "The Decline of Elegance in New York Restaurants" that took him to Le Pavillon and the arrogant Henri Soulé, described by Claiborne as "the greatest restaurateur that ever came to this country." Soulé had come to run the French Pavilion at the 1939 New York World's Fair, and among the team of chefs was a young assistant, the eighteen-year-old Pierre Franey. The story of how Franey teamed up with Claiborne and became, in his own right, *The Times'* "60-Minute Gourmet" is a French version of small-town boy makes good.

Franey began his apprenticeship at thirteen in a Paris restaurant, where he started as a scullery boy and spent the next five years working twelve hours a day, six days a week, to climb snail-like from the vegetable station to "second commi" at the fish station. The New York trip was a break and, caught by the war, Franey stayed on with the rest of the team to become head chef at Le Pavillon. Looking back on his long apprenticeship, Franey today feels that while the training was thorough, some of it was a waste of time. "I honestly feel that I wasted two or three years of my life peeling potatoes and cleaning fish and poultry when I was more than ready to handle more adventurous tasks." Eventually Franey found a more adventurous task than enduring Soulé's temper and became a vice-president at Howard Johnson's, where his young assistant was Jacques Pépin.

Meanwhile, Franey and Claiborne had become a cooking-writing team and near neighbors in Gardiners Bay. Every weekend since 1964 they have cooked together, trying out dishes on Franey's family and their mutual guests. Their annual New Year's Eve party became as famous as their Fourth of July picnic, like the picnic of hamburgers and truffles celebrated by the poet Phyllis McGinley. Claiborne's books of signed menus attest to the quality, variety, and champagne merriment of the chefs who have participated in these annual rites. "The Franeys are my family, their children are my children," Claiborne has said. When Pierre's daughter Claudia was married, 170 guests were fed by half a dozen of New York's finest, who labored with love for Craig and Pierre—in Craig's home kitchen.

Craig's kitchen, about fifteen minutes from Pierre's, in the house he calls "my Taj Mahal, my Xanadu," is as unlike Fisher's or Beard's as it is like an American's need to cook at home. Claiborne lives at Three-Mile Harbor near East Hampton, past Springy Bank and Hand Creek Road, on Clamshell Avenue. Walls of windows overlook pines, sand, and bay.

But the action is in the kitchen, a professional restaurant kitchen of stainless steel and glowing copper, of banks of burners and ovens, so complete that a marble pastry counter is cooled by a built-in refrigerator, a Tandoori oven is built into a wall, a Chinese roast-pork smoker waits near the battery of omelet and crêpe pans. Imagine a typical workday, repeated three to five times a week, in this unique recipe factory. Franey in blue apron rolls out empanadas, Cornish pasties, Texas turnovers, poaching some, frying and baking others, tasting, reshaping. Lou, a Hampton bartender, assists. A black Labrador named Luke and a spotted dog named Kiki lounge, waiting for tidbits. At one end of the massive central counter, Claiborne, in yellow shirt and orange-striped Adidas, stands at his electric typewriter and plays it like a console. "Was that one-quarter or one-eighth of a teaspoon of curry powder, Pierre?" Pierre is as casual and relaxed as an American. Claiborne, pacing restlessly between telephone, reference cookbooks, hi-fi set, and typewriter is as "nerveux" as a Frenchman. Bach's "Goldberg Variations" drifts through the loudspeakers. Outside the sun is sparkling on the bay.

"The whole point is that I believe in hedonism," Claiborne says, remembering his Methodist upbringing and the once-a-year eggnog exemption at Christmas. Flowers on the table, good silver, and crystal, these are his passions—and music. He has typed out the recipe for his funeral, in step-by-step ingredients. First, Verdi's "Requiem." Second, no weeping. Third, everyone drinking champagne while Pierre cooks. Fourth, a pilot friend who will throw his ashes into Gardiners Bay when the "Requiem" hits the first note of "Tuba Mirum." "Eating is one of the three greatest pleasures of my life," Claiborne says with his Huck Finn grin. "I love music and sex and food, and outside of that, forget it."

I hope the sea wears Parisian ruffles when his ashes go over the side.

## JULIA McWILLIAMS CHILD

*Sauce Mother to Millions*

# _Julia Child_

"Julia," as the world knows her, changed we happy few to we happy millions by taking the la-dee-dah out of and putting the hee-haw-ho into French cooking. "She's a natural clown," Paul Child says, watching her tape five shows in two hours in the television studios of ABC for *Good Morning, America.* "I'm Jim Hartman," her host says on camera. "And I'm Julia Child," says Julia, as if we didn't know.

For the past twenty years she's been clowning in our living rooms, burlesquing the high priests of gastronomy by clashing pot lids like cymbals, carving whole suckling pigs with a rubber knife, dropping monster monkfish on the floor like an animated cartoon of the old radio cooking comedian, Tizzie Lish. In a world of frozen sets, dehydrated jokes, and canned laughter, Julia is so spontaneous, freewheeling, relaxed, and utterly real that many Americans are convinced she's either loony or drunk. She throws the British for a loss. The BBC decided not to run her original French Chef series, after a trial run, because they were deluged with calls asking "what on earth a drunken or demented American woman was doing on the Third Programme."

An American woman she is. Drunken or demented she is not. She's one of the most totally organized persons I've ever met, which is why the clowning works. No matter what catastrophes ensue in the anarchy of her kitchens, we know she will wheeze, chortle, and hoot her way through with the imperturbability of a Bugs Bunny or Woody Woodpecker. No one has better exposed the secret of her comedy than Dan Aykroyd on *Saturday Night Live* in a Julia parody in which he hacks off a finger while boning a chicken, applies chicken livers to the wound, and, falling to the floor in a pool of blood, hurls a last defiant "Bon appétit!" Behind her antic comedy, she is cool, controlled, "utterly unflappable," as Paul says. And had she not become a major woman television comic second only to Carol Burnett and Lucille Ball, she might have become our first woman astronaut.

She is not only the top comedian of the food world, she is also its most systematic engineer. It is her high-tech instincts for cooking that have made her books as popular with professional men as leisured women. "We've produced some fine well-educated cooks in the last two or three years who've been to Harvard, Berkeley, et cetera," Julia tells me, while she sets up the cooking props for her first tape. "They've found it's creative and more fun than banks. They like the handwork, management, control." Are men more interested now than before? She refuses the sexual gambit. "People," she replies, "we say people like to cook. A lot of us feel that America will end up being the food capital of the world."

If America does, Julia will be more responsible than anybody because through the newest mass media she has brought home-cooking back into the American home. That she snuck it in with a French accent is tribute to the cunning of this master showman. Good cooking "happened" to have begun in France, she says, so that the techniques of cooking are French in language and form, much as the techniques of music are German and Italian. Now that Americans have become far more sophisticated in cooking and eating, French terminology and French structures are less relevant. Actually, Americans are more fanatic cooks than Frenchmen, who do not take up cooking as a hobby as we do, and whose kitchens are not nearly "so nice to work in." The French, in fact, are now imitating Americans in breaking open their "very rigid tradition" of classicism. "I think we invented *nouvelle cuisine* before the French," she explains, "and now we're beginning to get confidence in ourselves as a cooking culture."

From the beginning, Julia and her French collaborators, Louisette Bertholle and Simone Beck, addressed their *Mastering the Art of French Cooking* to an ecumenical readership, "those who love to cook." They disclaimed French ingredients and French-movie atmosphere—"cobwebbed bottles, the *patron* in his white cap bustling among his sauces, anecdotes about charming little restaurants with gleaming napery"—for the here and now of basic techniques that anyone could master with the basic ingredients of a supermarket. They suggested, in fact, in their foreword, that "the book could well be titled *French Cooking from the American Supermarket.*" Where good materials are available, technique is all that matters, technique that can be taught and learned American style by doing it yourself. "Train yourself," Julia advised us. "Keep your knives sharp. Above all, have a good time." What could be simpler?

Interestingly, in the five volumes Child has written since the 1961 volume I of *Mastering,* she has become ever less French and ever more

American. After *The French Chef Cookbook* of 1968, she drops French for Julia. In 1975, it is *From Julia Child's Kitchen*. In 1978, it is *Julia Child & Company* and, in 1980, *Julia Child & More Company*. Significantly, it is the American-born Frenchman Jacques Pépin who titles his books *La Technique* and *La Méthode*. With Julia, technique is a means to the end of having a good time with good company. "Cooking with friends is such *fun*," she says, sweeping her arm to embrace the dozen or so cooking helpers who ready her show, the cameramen and directors, and those invisible millions who find cooking with *Julia* such fun.

"We took her to our hearts," journalist Chris Chase says of the woman who first taught us how to master the French "Mother Sauces," as they are called, and in the process became our live-in Sauce Mother, cajoling us, giving us confidence, cheering us on, freeing us from fear of disasters. She makes food a living thing that shares in the pleasure of her company. "Food is in some way human to her," one journalist says. "She mothers and respects it." Holding an egg in front of the cameras, Julia explains the technique of egg poaching. "Swing the shells WIDE open and DROP them in," she says, as she swings and drops the egg into vinegared water. "If you happen to live near a hen, you can have fresh eggs like this instead of a nasty stale egg like THIS (holding up another egg in a saucer) where the white is relaxed and the yolk is practically naked." "Beautiful," the producer whispers. "Takes your breath away."

" 'If you happen to live near a hen'—did you hear that?" Paul laughs aloud. "I never heard her say that before." She flubs a line. "Get it right, Julier," she says, talking to herself and the cameras, whom she also mothers and respects.

Under the glare of spots and the ganglia of their cables, against a decorator wall of painted casseroles and plastic bouquets, "Julier" is "realer" than life. At six feet, one inch, she looms over the kitchen counter in a bright purple shirt with her familiar jutting jaw, the crinkly blue-green eyes focused by a frown line between her brows and lit by an F.D.R. grin that speaks volumes about contained energy, relaxed control. The counter conceals the surprising elegance of her long legs, just as the camera flattens her imposing height. She skews our sense of scale.

Beside her, Paul, ten years her senior and thirty-six years her partner, plays straight man to her clown but carries equal weight as a comic team. "We decided from the beginning to be a couple," says the man who designs their kitchens, photographs their food, whispers the time at their lectures and demonstrations ("Julia has not a good instinct for timing"), and helps carry props in the Sacred Bag of implements. "We always do everything together," Paul says. He is her best audience, constantly amused and amusing. He wears tweedy professor clothes, a blue cashmere sweater to match his eyes behind the thick-lensed spectacles, but his red tie and cream and blue striped shirt are natty. His nose and chin are strong. He speaks with authority. "I'm a person who has to be filled with something creative," he says. "I love writing, wood carving, painting, photography. There are all sorts of things behind my belly button." All sorts of things include a black belt in Judo, a teaching knowledge of French, a talent for mimicry, and a delight in telling stories.

While Julia performs on camera, he performs, between takes, the story of their romance in several languages. They met in Ceylon during the Second World War when they were both in the OSS. He had become expert in designing War Rooms and brought the same instinct for visual presentation to the charts and diagrams of Lord Mountbatten's Room in New Delhi that he would later apply to the pots and pans of Julia's kitchen in Cambridge, Massachusetts. Julia was in charge of the Registry, a document center for messages, in which she developed the organizational skills that would eventuate in a wall of cooking files worthy of a research institute. Sent to Chungking at the same time, they courted in Chinese restaurants, where the food was as wonderful as the people were fascinating. Sent home at the war's end, they met again in Maryland to check each other out in civvies. They liked what they saw and decided to get married but almost got killed instead. The day before the wedding, their car was struck by a truck without brakes. Julia went through the windshield and got twenty-seven stitches in her head. "We were married in stitches," Paul says, "me on a cane and Julia full of glass."

The convergence of their twain was partly wartime luck but mostly a shared adventuresomeness—"the romance of the OSS"—and a liberated individualism. Born a twin in New Jersey, Paul was raised in Boston by his mother, Bertha Cushing Child, who taught singing. With little money and no formal education after Boston Latin School, Paul worked on farms, taught school here and in France, and educated himself in his three major passions—photography, Judo, and English literature.

Julia was born on the other end of the country and the other side of the tracks. Julia Carolyn McWilliams was born in Pasadena on August 15, 1912, "such a long baby," her mother noted in Baby's Happy Days, "that her feet usually stuck out of her long clothes." She became a long child, towering over her younger brother Johnnie and sister Dorothy. Family photo albums show a freckle-faced girl with long legs, a big grin, and a shock of wavy blonde hair. She seems half clown and half deb, whether mugging on top of a birdbath or in cat makeup and whiskers for the Junior League's *Bells of Brittany,* or sprawled at ease in lawn chairs with cool drinks, riding horses at Ojai, skiing at Sun Valley, yachting at La Jolla, or eating barbecued steer at the Reading Ranch.

In 1930, when she went East to Smith (where her mother had enrolled her at birth), she didn't know whether to be a basketball player or a novelist. After three years with the advertising department of W & J

Sloane in New York, she returned to Pasadena, where "I had a very good time doing virtually nothing," she says. With the war on, she took a typing job in Washington and escaped its drudgery by volunteering for overseas duty with the OSS.

Not until her marriage and Paul's assignment, in 1948, to the USIS office in Paris did the lightning strike. It struck at La Couronne in Rouen, where the Childs had stopped for lunch, driving an old Buick from Le Havre to Paris. It struck in the form of a Sole Meunière, "a whole big fat sole for the two of us . . . handsomely browned and still sputteringly hot under its coating of chopped parsley, and around it swirled a goodly amount of golden Normandy butter," she recalled. "I was quite over-whelmed." It was the beginning of her second lifelong romance.

Ensconced in a Left Bank apartment, Julia fell in love with everything she saw and, as with any affair of passion, it took her years to get over the infatuation. With typical thoroughness, she struggled with the French language and the strange new language of cooking by going to school. She enrolled at the Cordon Bleu under a trio of classic chefs—Max Bugnard, Claude Thillmont, and Pierre Mangelatte—and found there the company who would join her in starting their own École des Trois Gour-mandes.

What happened next, as Julia fans know, is the Cinderella story of the book nobody wanted. Julia's thirst to learn was equaled only by her hunger to explain. After six years of research and 800 pages devoted to chicken and their sauces, the manuscript was turned down by Houghton Mifflin, which had paid a $250 advance. Five years and several desperate revisions later, during which Julia taught herself "with help from Paul and one or two other people" to write, Knopf published the first volume of *Mastering* in 1961. Claiborne gave it a smash review in *The Times* that helped make it a bestseller of the kind cookbook publishers have been dreaming of ever since.

When the Childs came to New York, Beard took them in hand—"We were nobodies from nowhere"—and introduced them to the New York food world. Julia's celebrityhood did not take off, however, until her first appearance, in 1962, as the French Chef on Boston's noncommercial station WGBH. By then they had settled into a comfortable 1880 house, on Irving Street in Cambridge, owned once by the Harvard philosopher Josiah Royce. For the next decade Julia worked twelve hours a day taping four shows a week. They were twenty-minute sessions done in a single take and almost no editing to avoid expense. Her ability to improvise was a TV gold mine that exploited the suckling pig that refused to be carved, the pot holder that caught fire, the fish that fell, the desserts that melted.

"I came at the right time," Julia has said of the astonishing success of her television shows. "There was a new interest in food, the Kennedys were in the White House, everyone was traveling to Europe. Food became chic. Now it's not just French food that's chic."

But the clue to Julia's success is that she is anti-chic. "No fakery, no pretense," Paul says admiringly, "very free, natural, the same off screen as on." "We're middle-class Americans, we're not fancy," Julia explained to a visitor watching her at work in her Cambridge kitchen. "You don't have to live up to the Joneses or down to the Joneses or ANYTHING. It's just a completely free life." They were free to break all the rules and they did. They shocked the fastidious by smoking cigarettes between courses and drinking highballs before. They shocked the meticulous by cooking up a storm rather than cleaning up the mess. When viewers accused Julia of cooking sloppy, she replied, "I don't find it sloppy. . . . they're prissy people and to hell with them." They shocked the trendy by not following fashion. Of *nouvelle cuisine* Julia has said, "I don't really like it because the food looks FINGERED. It doesn't look foody to me." They shocked earnest dieters by refusing to knuckle under. "I would rather have one spoonful of Chocolate Malakoff than two bowls of Jell-O," Julia says. "Wouldn't you?"

Julia shocked television audiences by her reality. She ambled around her studio kitchen as if it were her own. Her own, of course, is just what you'd expect—the big central table, potted geraniums by the sink, copper pots by the black Garland stove, pegboards with utensils outlined so that each can be returned to its own place in the culinary scheme of things. The cupboards and walls are green, the tablecloth blue. A framed artichoke is painted on a blue ground. Julia wears a blue apron over green trousers. Paul wears a green shirt and blue tie. Attention has been paid to detail.

Paul talks of the cottage he designed and got built in Provence, halfway between Cannes and Grasse, by fighting it out with the French builder who wanted a palazzo. "I finally got what I wanted," Paul says. "I'm tough and I speak perfect French." Julia talks while she runs up an eggnog for the first course of our lunch and chops eggs and dill for the main dish of braised celery with anchovies, and fresh dark rye bread. She talks and works with the same economy of word and action that enables her to create a fish soup on television in four minutes or to cut down the timing on pork and beans. "I won't dry off the meat," I had remembered her saying to her TV director. "Takes another second. We don't want to waste."

With the same neat efficiency, she types up the lunch recipes after we eat. She types upstairs at a U-shaped desk walled in by books and files with complete notes on every dish she's ever tackled. Paul's study is next to hers, with complete photographic files and a lifetime of canvases. Now they are packing for Santa Barbara in California, where they have just bought a condominium to escape Cambridge's mean winters. "We rather enjoy it, the snowing," Paul says. "We get out our shovels, we each have one." I can picture them shoveling snow, side by side, in matching mufflers.

Together they have taken the one-upmanship out of marriage as well as out of cooking and together they embody what cooking is about and what cooking is for. "Julia Child & Company" includes us, whoever we are, in the circle of friends who share mutual respect in performing a common task. Julia Child is the mother we always hoped to find in some ideal kitchen in the sky, cooking up an American *cassoulet,* as she calls it, "or plain old pork and beans." She is also the teacher we always hoped to find, making us laugh, involving us in her craft, pushing us in our own directions. "A natural rightness rather than a pedantic correctness is my goal in cooking," she wrote in *Julia Child & Company.* Her mastery of French cooking freed her from the pedantry and correctness of the French to speak in the pure American accent of Emerson and Thoreau. "One turns with relief from words to realities," she concludes. There is only one word for her reality and that is "Julia."

# AND ALL
# THOSE OTHERS

*All American ladies should know how to clear-starch and iron: how to keep plate and glass: how to cook dainties: and, if they understand the making of bread and soup likewise, so much the better.*

—Harriet Martineau
Society in America *(1836)*

All Victorian English ladies, such as Harriet Martineau and Mrs. Frances Trollope, were clear about the priorities with which they ruled the conduct of their own lives and the lives of others. Even fronting the wilderness, a true lady kept her linen starched and her glassware shined and left base sustenance, insofar as she could, to servants and other savages. English ladies, whenever they emigrated to the New World, brought with them Ladies' Cookbooks that were, from their beginning in the sixteenth century, guides to conduct. Such books, written first by men and only later by women, instructed *The English Hus-Wife,* as Gervase Markham did in 1615, in "The inward and outward vertues which ought to be in a compleat woman. As, her skill in Physicke, Cookery, Banqueting-stuffe, Distillation, Perfumes, Wooll, Hemp, Flax, Dayries, Brewing, Baking, and all other things belonging to an Houshould."

In the days of the colonies, the American "hus-wife" found her model for the compleat woman in the great tradition of English homemaking, with its emphasis on empirical good sense and practicality and the benevolence of a long line of Lady Bountifuls. "Receipts" were transmitted through family manuscripts in noble households and one such manuscript was given to Martha Washington on her first marriage, to Daniel Custis, in 1749. The largest part of this *Booke of Cookery,* based on seventeenth-century recipes, was devoted to "A Booke of Sweetmeats." Recipes for bread and soup were as nothing to the hundreds of ways for making Paste of Eglantine or Candy of Angelico or Sirrup of violets, and other lady-like dainties.

This was the tradition of English homemaking detailed by Hannah

Glasse in 1747 in her *Art of Cookery* and furthered by English housewives in the nineteenth century who became famous for their cookbooks. Such were Eliza Acton, whose *Modern Cookery for Private Families* appeared first in 1845, and Isabella Beeton, whose *Book of Household Management* followed in 1861. Even American orphans might aspire to this tradition, and Amelia Simmons in her 1796 *American Cookery* paved the way, dismissing "the art of dressing viands, fish, poultry and vegetables" in a phrase in order to get on to the dainties, "the best modes of making pastes, puffs, pies, tarts, puddings, custards and preserves, and all kinds of cakes, from the imperial plumb to plain cake."

This was the tradition promulgated by a host of American lady cooks like Mrs. T. J. Crowen in her *American Lady's Cookery Book* of 1847. Her 1,200 recipes included the preparing of everything from soups to a voluminous number of fancy desserts, together with the etiquette of the dinner table and every variety of dinner party, "The whole being a Complete System of American Cookery." American ladies were keen on Complete Systems. A very few, like Mrs. A. L. Webster in *The Improved Housewife* of 1845, focused on French systems. A great many focused on economy, like Lydia Maria Child in *The American Frugal Housewife* of 1832: Dedicated to Those Who Are Not Ashamed of Economy. Some focused on clarity, like Eliza Leslie in her 1837 *Directions for Cookery, in Its Various Branches.* Some on regional methods, like Mary Randolph in *The Virginia Housewife or Methodical Cook,* in 1824. Toward the end of the century, while Mrs. Porter in her *Southern Cookery Book* and Mrs. Parloa in her *Appledore Cookbook* had emphasized the regional, housewives like Marion Harland and Sarah Tyson Rorer emphasized the complete, systematically, in volume after volume.

Housewives isolated in sod houses and prairie wagons pooled recipes as a form of social bonding that reaffirmed the values of starched linen. Women's Leagues attached to churches and synagogues became Women's Clubs and Junior Leagues, productive of vast numbers of communal cookbooks, such as the *Buckeye* cookbook of 1883. The need for conversing about clear-starch and dainties accounted for the success of a horde of ladies' magazines at the turn of the century and for later corporate inventions of cookbookery like Betty Crocker.

The desire to systematize household economy and the new science of dietetics and nutrition in the 1880s brought in the cooking school, which refocused the interests of the American lady. Science supplanted art and intellectualized homemaking when Mrs. Mary Lincoln instructed Boston ladies in the chemistry of foods. Fannie Merritt Farmer, when she took over the instruction of the Boston Cooking School, initiated, with her first book in 1896, the age of the cookbook industry. The genteel role of the lady housewife, by definition an amateur, was colored by a new professionalism, modeled on factory efficiency.

The French tradition of cookery was, from the beginning, in the hands of male professionals: namely, the chefs who served first royalty and then princely merchants. French cookbooks were written by men and, from the eighteenth century on, for commercial enterprises like catering and restaurants. This was the tradition of Antonin Carême that was transmitted to Americans by Pierre Blot in his *Hand-Book of Practical Cookery* in 1867. The same tradition was fostered by Oscar Tschirky of the Waldorf in 1896, by Charles Ranhofer of Delmonico's, and by a number of French chefs transplanted to America in the twenties and thirties: cookbook writers like Louis Diat, Louis De Gouy, Joseph Donon, all of whom followed the precepts of Auguste Escoffier.

The French had also founded a line of gentlemen gastronomers, epitomized by the casual jottings of Brillat-Savarin in his *Physiologie du Goût*. These were men who became arbiters of taste and manners in the art of fine dining and wining. American gastronomers, mixing French with English manners, were men like Frederick Stokes in his prescriptions for *Good Form: Dinners, Ceremonious and Unceremonious* in 1903, and Theodore Child in his *Delicate Feasting* of 1890. It was a tradition furthered by George Rector, Joseph Wechsberg, Alexis Lichine, Julian Street, Lucius Beebe, A. J. Liebling, and Waverley Root, almost all of whom looked to Europe as the heart of civilized life. It was a tradition finely rendered in 1952 by Samuel Chamberlain in *Bouquet de France: An Epicurean Tour of the French Provinces,* rendered by camera and drawing pencil more than by recipe.

The traditions of Central Europe, particularly the German-Jewish tradition of rich pastries and other sweet dainties, were first acclimatized in America by Mrs. Simon Kander in her 1901 *Settlement Cook Book,* published in Minneapolis. The coupling of middle Europe with the Midwest was to produce more fruitful progeny in the work of Irma von Starkloff, who became the Mrs. Rombauer of the *Joy of Cooking.* In 1931, to occupy her widowhood, Mrs. Rombauer published her book herself and mailed copies from her St. Louis apartment to immigrant housewives hungry for instruction and for reminders of home. They responded so fully with letters and requests for more recipes that Mrs. Rombauer's daughter, Marion Becker, joined her in revising the format and in finding a commercial publisher for the next edition in 1936, the first of many for the happy Rombauer family. But even here, the *Joy of Cooking* belonged to those guidebooks for the conduct of a compleat lady, reflected in the book's first dust jacket, which portrayed a medieval lady subduing a dragon with pot and broom.

The same year, 1936, saw the publication of *June Platt's Party Cookbook,* the product of a painter, wife, and mother, who knew good food from a childhood in England and France and who brought a new sophistication to the recipes she wrote for *House & Garden.* A year later, in 1937, Fisher took the same tradition of lady cookbooks and cross-fertilized it with the male line of gastronomic writing that deceived her first readers into believing she was one of the boys. By the 1940s, the gastronomic germ was sufficiently planted for Mary Laswell to burlesque it in *Mrs. Rasmussen's Book of One-Arm Cookery* in 1946.

An important transitional figure for women cooks was Dione Lucas, who bridged the amateur and the professional. She abandoned her aspirations to be a jeweler and then a cellist and became instead a student at l'École du Cordon Bleu in Paris, founded in 1880 "for the daughters of upper- and middle-class French families." When she founded a branch of the École in New York, along with a Cordon Bleu restaurant, she preached the message that cooking was a lady's art as well as a man's profession. In 1947, her *Cordon Bleu Cookbook* was for many American housewives their first introduction to a fully French cuisine. Lucas paved the way for the intensified French of Julia Child.

In the fifties and early sixties, other important women's cookbooks came from Helen Evans Brown, a *confrère* of James Beard, who wrote one of the best regional books in *The West Coast Cookbook* in 1952. And from Paula Peck, in *The Fine Art of Baking* in 1961 and *The Art of Good Cooking* in 1966. The 1960s also saw the pioneer work of Grace Chu in introducing Americans to the arts of Chinese cooking, a tradition that has been richly developed by Florence Lin and Joyce Chen and Virginia Lee. The Italian tradition was slower to take hold, possibly because Americans thought of Italian cooking as peasant food washed down by Dago red. But Ada Boni changed that notion with her *Italian Regional Cooking* in 1969. And Marcella Hazan canonized Italian cuisine in *The Classic Italian Cookbook* of 1976.

Also during the sixties, the success of Beard and Claiborne encouraged Time-Life Books to invest in a twenty-six-volume series entitled *Foods of the World,* which Claiborne has recently called "the most important collection of international cookbooks ever assembled in America." Responsible for the quality of the recipes was an advisory staff of three Americans who became influential in the food world through their books or classes. Richard Olney, in *The French Menu Cookbook* of 1970 and *Simple French Food* of 1974, was a purist whose devotion to French food led him to live permanently in France. Michael Field, a pianist, cooking teacher, and restaurant chef, was as eclectic in his tastes as in his careers, and he spoke for a sophisticated internationalism in *Michael Field's Cooking School* of 1965. John Clancy, whose style was distinctly American, became known first for his classes in baking and recently for his fish restaurant in Greenwich Village.

The seventies saw an extraordinary diversity as we discovered more and more cuisines through restaurants, travel and—most important— cookbooks. We found India through Madhur Jaffrey's *An Invitation to*

*Indian Cooking* in 1973. We found Morocco through Paula Wolfert's *Cous-cous and Other Good Food from Morocco* in the same year. We found Mexico through Diana Kennedy's *The Cuisines of Mexico* in 1972, and Japan through Shizuo Tsuji's *Japanese Cooking: A Simple Art* in 1980. We even found England in Elizabeth David's *English Breads and Yeast Cookery* in 1977.

We became specialists, at the same time, in the latest trends of French cooking, French hardware, and French restaurants through the media and merchandise-blitzing of France's celebrity chefs. *The Escoffier Cook Book* was crowded out by the translated works of Paul Bocuse, Michel Guérard, Raymond Oliver, Jean and Pierre Troisgros, Roger Vergé. Child's collaborators, Simone ("Simca") Beck and Louisette Bertholle, published separate works. Claiborne's collaborator, Pierre Franey, reached a new audience with his *60-Minute Gourmet.* A young transplanted chef, Jacques Pépin, taught French techniques through photographs in *La Technique* and *La Méthode.*

But because we were Americans, so much French jazz was bound to provoke resistance. The Second World War that caused so many to turn to France and Europe for visions of old-world civility caused others to retreat to the wilderness. Away with starched linen and irons. Away with plate and glass and dainties of all kinds. Where Nature was God the making of bread and soup was not an ancillary accomplishment of a lady but the daily routine of the commune. Nature had its own pedantries: The bread must be whole grain and the soup must be vegetarian. And the table must be a plain pine board. Cookbooks were still guides to conduct as men and women sought to be "compleat," but inward and outward virtues were defined by skill in vitamins and minerals, herbs and simples, yogurts and tofus, and the whole battery of cooking for health and the higher purity.

The tradition was as old as Thoreau, of course, but it received new impetus after the war in the Back to the Whole Earth movement that produced "cookbooks" such as Euell Gibbons' *Stalking the Wild Asparagus* in 1962. It also produced "gospel books," such as Adelle Davis' *Let's Cook It Right,* which many took as text for the New Jerusalem envisioned earlier by Gaylord Hauser in *Eat and Grow Beautiful.* While some looked to the complete system of nutrition in guides like *Laurel's Kitchen,* others looked to Zen mantras in *The Tassajara Bread Book.* Vegetarians went bananas over sophisticated guides like *The Vegetarian Epicure.*

In California, ecotopia seemed to be just around the corner when organic gardeners began to leak their produce into gourmet food shops and into the kitchens of a new breed of restaurateurs. California had always bred a wide variety of communes and cults, along with lettuce and artichokes and garlic and wine grapes. And now its various strains came together in the restaurant of Alice Waters, whose *Chez Panisse Menu Cook-*

*book* of 1982 bred hope for the future. Waters' book was the first American Ladies' Cookbook to be written by an American lady chef, and it was notable for the quality and abundance of her breads and soups rather than her dainties. It was notable, too, for transforming native materials in the alembic of French art. As national and sexual divisions have melded, so, too, have the distinctions between amateur and professional. New revolutions are in the making, not the least of which is the understanding that good bread and fine soup are the best base on which to found a Complete System of American Cookery.

# HOW TO READ A RECIPE

❦

*Recipe for New England Pie*

*To make this excellent breakfast dish, proceed as follows: Take a sufficiency of water and a sufficiency of flour, and construct a bullet-proof dough. Work this into the form of a dish, with the edges turned up some three-fourths of an inch. Toughen and kiln-dry it a couple of days in a mild but unvarying temperature. Construct a cofer for this redoubt in the same way and of the same material. Fill with stewed dried apples; aggravate with cloves, lemon peel and slabs of citron; add two portions of New Orleans sugar, then solder on the lid and set in a safe place till it petrifies. Serve cold at breakfast and invite your enemy.*

—Mark Twain
A Tramp Abroad *(1897)*

Fisher has said in "The Anatomy of a Recipe" that all recipes are divided into three parts: name, ingredients, and method. Seems simple enough, rational, and even scientific. But to these three we must add a fourth, which is seldom overt and is often subversive, as above, in the New England Pie (name) of bullet-proof dough and petrified apples (ingredients) that are toughened and kiln-dried and soldered in place (method) for a particular end—to exterminate your enemy. So the aim or purpose or end of the recipe is the fourth crucial part that may subvert the whole. Inside every fat recipe there is an anti-recipe trying to get out, and for the very good reason that all recipes are a kind of hoax perpetrated by the recipe-maker on some unsuspecting victim of his labor.

The very word "recipe" suggests a giver and a receiver in a transaction noted by a "receipt," whether medical, economic, or magical, the sort of thing jotted down in household accounts and kept together in the same book as a reminder of how to do whatever it was you had in mind. Say you had in mind the same end as the medieval recipe-maker of the "phisical receipt" which Fisher chose to anatomize as an outstanding example of *The Recipe:*

**Name:** To Drive a Woman Crazy
**Ingredients:** 1 or more nutmegs, ground
1 left shoe, of
1 woman

---

> **Method:** Sprinkle small amount of nutmeg on left shoe every
> night at midnight, until desired results are obtained
> with woman.

What could be simpler, clearer, or more methodical? The only problem is that we don't know whether the desired results are to drive the woman crazy with love or to drive her crazy out of the house.

And until we know the desired end, we don't know whether the recipe is a cure, nostrum, restorative, remedy, or panacea for an aching heart, mind, or body—or all three at once? As with bullet-proof dough, the end is everything. When for centuries people carried knowledge of such things in their heads because writing or reading was not for every man, the end of a recipe was often named directly, as in "To Barrell Oysters Yt They Shall Last 6 Moneths." The name was often prescriptive shorthand, like an Rx today, for ingredients and methods generally understood. Exact measurements or detailed processes were unnecessary when recipes referred to knowledge shared but easily forgot, as when Amelia Simmons reminds her readers in *American Cookery* to wash off the snails and caterpillars when they come "To Boil All Kinds of Garden Stuff." For centuries recipes suggested actions rather than substances. To get this, do this. To drive a woman crazy, buy a nutmeg and steal her left shoe and stay awake until midnight.

Not until the beginning of the industrial revolution and the age of science did ingredients begin to take precedence over aim. In 1816, an English chemist, Dr. William Kitchener, decided that collections of cooking receipts would profit by measuring ingredients exactly and by listing them in order of use. Dr. Kitchener introduced scientific method into cookery in his *Apicius Redivivus,* bowing politely to older methods only in his subtitle, *The Cook's Oracle.* Enterprising household cooks adopted his innovation when they came to publish their own receipts. In 1845, Eliza Acton added the refinement of exact timing as well as exact measurements in her *Modern Cookery.*

Mrs. Isabella Beeton, in 1861, applied these newfangled methods in a comprehensive way to her entire *Book of Household Management* and unscrupulously took credit for them when others followed, others like Mrs. Mary Lincoln and Fannie Farmer.

In America the new science of domestic economy did not become voguish until the turn of the century, through the cookbooks of Mrs. Lincoln's Cooking School in Boston and Mrs. Sarah Tyson Rorer's in Philadelphia. Until then, the shape and form of the cooking recipe in American cookbooks was usually a single solid paragraph, like Lydia Child's recipe for Egg Gruel in *The Frugal Housewife* (1832):

This is at once food and medicine. Some people have very great faith in its efficacy in cases of chronic dysentery. It is made thus: Boil a pint of new milk; beat four new-laid eggs to a light froth, and pour in while the milk boils; stir them together thoroughly, but do not let them boil; sweeten it with the best of loaf sugar, and grate in a whole nutmeg; add a little salt, if you like it. Drink half of it while it is warm, and the other half in two hours.

But new ways have crept in even here. The name of the recipe is not its function but suggests its major ingredients. The purpose is part of the paragraph of explanation: a food and medicine for dysentery.

A century later, recipe organization has changed radically. Recipes have so interbred that they can be distinguished only by main ingredient and its variations: Eggs Scrambled, Poached, Sautéed, Deviled, Curried, with Pineapple, Onions, Anchovies, etc. Not only are ingredients measured exactly, they are set apart—by typography, by placement, or both. They may be interspersed with method, as in Mrs. Rombauer's *Joy of Cooking,* in a step-by-step vertical ordering. Or they may precede method, first the ingredients, then their combination, as in *Fannie Farmer.* The real focus, however, is on the exactitude of the measurement, implying that the formula is as precise as any chemical or physical experiment designed to attain predictable results.

The French tradition has been very different, the noted English food writer Elizabeth David remarks, in comparing French vagueness about quantities and temperatures to American scientism. "American cookery writers are inclined to err in the other direction," she finds, "specifying to the last drop and the ultimate grain the quantities of salt, sugar, powdered herbs, spices, and so on, leaving absolutely nothing to the imagination or discretion of the cook."

David wrote this in 1960, at the dawn of the American cookery explosion. Twenty years later cookery writers and their recipes have so proliferated that not even cooking has been left to the cook. The unsuspecting victim is now the recipe reader whose time and attention are so consumed by the specificity of both drop, grain, and process (and often in the name of speed or ease, as in the the Quick and Easy Way to Make Croissants in 125 Simple Steps) that to read about it is enough. To actually cook it would be superfluous. In our multiplying cookery magazines, the simplest operation has become as elaborate as a recipe for making a basement spaceship or atom bomb. Process, maybe, is the point. As cooks we no longer see ourselves as Dr. Louis Pasteur, fiddling with test tubes, but as Colonel John Glenn checking out the control panel of *Mercury-Atlas I* before takeoff.

Nothing is too minute or insignificant for inspection. Take, for example, a recipe that might a century ago have been named "To Boil an Egg."

## Oeufs à la Nage

| | |
|---|---|
| 2 fresh extra-large eggs, brown preferable* | ½ teaspoon salt** |
| | ⅛ teaspoon pepper*** |
| 4 cups fresh water (50 to 60 degrees) | 1 tablespoon unsalted butter, optional |

Equipment: one 1-quart saucepan, 1 electric or gas burner****
Shopping materials: 2 eggs, salt, pepper, butter (optional)
Calories: 75 per egg
Nutritional content: per egg—6 grams protein, 32 calcium, 112 phosphorus, 1.5 iron, 64 potassium, 600 Vitamin A.

*Available in gourmet stores and some supermarkets.
**Sea salt or kosher salt, preferable. For salt-free diet, substitute ¹⁄₁₆ teaspoon cayenne pepper.
***Freshly ground in pepper grinder.
****Microwave oven or electric skillet not recommended for this dish.

All this before the reader learns what to do with the ingredients, or non-ingredients, once he has got them, or not got them.

What has happened to the recipe is that the aim is not named as such because the aim is not "To Boil an Egg." The aim of the recipe, beneath its technical lingo, is the aim of a magical potion compounded of French romance, rural nostalgia, consumer choice, and domestic security to secure health, knowledge, and power. You may not have more than an egg at the moment, but at least that egg is completely in your power.

We all get into trouble with recipes, I think, unless we can see through the expressed form and shape of a particular recipe, or group of recipes, to its assumed, covert, subversive, or simply unacknowledged aim. For some people any recipe is trouble. The wife of a famous physicist told me that she hated recipes, never used them, couldn't follow them. "I have to put in either more or less." I asked why. "Perversity," she said. "I don't want anybody telling me what to do." For her, the covert aim of all recipes was to dictate and she rebelled. For her, the recipe itself was the enemy, the one you invite to breakfast to dine on bullet-proof pie, rather than a helping friend who gives you a tip or two or reminds you of what you've just forgot. I remember Fisher describing how she checks through Julia and Mrs. Rombauer and *Larousse* to see what they all say, "And when I don't agree, then I do it my way."

Some get into trouble with one kind of recipe because they expect it to be a different kind and make the wrong demand of it. If an aspiring cook goes to Julia for quick instruction in how to boil an egg, he may toss volumes I and II into the disposal in his rage and frustration. He will find out instead that a six-minute boiled egg is a possible substitute among the many variants that take up eight pages in her discussion of the Poached Egg. He will also learn about the different cooking qualities of whites and yolks, he will learn what the French names are for various poached-egg dishes, and what to sauce them with and what to serve them with. He may get curious about the mind and imagination of the maker of these recipes, whose aim is to condense a ten-year course of instruction and experimentation into a single volume, organized by master recipes and their spin-offs. He may become so distracted that he'll forget about boiling an egg and will gobble a Ring-Ding instead. But it would be a pity if he never looked in Julia because she doesn't tell him how to boil an egg.

The hungry breakfaster who goes to Fisher for the same information will find a three-page discussion, in *How to Cook a Wolf*, of "How Not to Boil an Egg." He may snarl at her conclusion: "Probably the wisest way to treat an egg is not to cook it at all." In the meantime, however, he will have discovered a great deal about the peculiar nature of eggs and of Fisher and of her children and of the last Great War and of Prairie Oysters and Fried Eggs and Eggs Preserved in Water Glass and Dishonest Eggs and Eggs Obstulacos. If he simply had the boiling of an egg in mind, however, he has come to the wrong kitchen.

The still-starving breakfaster might get by on the information supplied by Claiborne in his first *New York Times* volume in the brief paragraph on Hard and Soft-Cooked Eggs. But he would likely be deflected by the exotic names and ways that excite the true interest of this recipe-maker and find himself scanning the ingredients and numbered steps of Madras Egg Curry or Eggs à la Tripe.

If, after all this, the breakfastless reader is stubbornly set on boiling an egg, his only recourse among our four masters is Beard. As the only continuing cooking-class teacher of the four, his aim has always been to teach the basics of good cooking in the simplest form. In his first general cookbook, he outlines briefly Egg information: selection, grading, color, storing, cooking utensils, and cooking suggestions. The reader now fainting with hunger can, however, go directly to Boiled Eggs: Soft and Hard. For straight cooking information, Beard's books are the most practical.

Because form determines content, the way each recipe-maker shapes his recipes reveals not only the nature of the cook but his relation to that unsuspecting victim, his reader, or potential fellow cook. Child structures her recipes on the sequence of use, so that ingredients are often repeated in the quantities needed as used, rather than totaled at the beginning. The ingredients form a gloss on the left of the page with methods in paragraphs on the right. Her method demands patient and thorough study for its benefits to pay off, but anyone yielding to those demands will find a comprehensive knowledge about principles and techniques, aided by diagrams, charts, and photographs, that is not available in any other form as condensed and yet clear as Julia's two volumes of *Mastering*. Her organizational genius is at work in each division and subdivision of her genealogical tables. The danger, of course, is overkill, as in her infamous twenty-two-page recipe that might have been titled "How to Almost Clone a Loaf of Genuine French Bread in 30 or 40 or 50 Not at All Easy but Rather a Lot of Fun Steps."

Fisher's recipes are essentially literary, like Coleridge's ballads or Shelley's dramas. They are meant to be read rather than performed. They are full of a scholar's lore and an artist's quick eye and a mother's sure advice, but they are not served best by an actual pot on an actual stove, despite the simple straightforward listing of ingredients, followed by a paragraph of clear directions, that lull the unwary. She is perfectly candid about the undoing of the unwary if they want to know, for example, how to fry an egg.

> . . . in spite of what people tell me about this method or that, I continue to make amazingly bad fried eggs: tough, with edges like some kind of dirty starched lace, and a taste part sulphur and part singed newspaper. The best way to find a trustworthy method, I think, is to ask almost anyone but me.

Claiborne, on the other hand, lays out his recipes with the sequential tidiness and economy of a good newspaper columnist. If he was not the first to divide up the method paragraph into numbered step-by-step units, he has certainly been the most influential recipe-maker to do so, and the measure of his cookbook success has been in large part the result of the instant visual clarity of his recipes. We know where we are and we can see where we are going simply by counting the number of steps.

Beard's arrangements are the most traditional, as they are usually the briefest. He will put explanations into an introduction to a section rather than into the recipe itself. The advantage of his shorthand is that the reader can get a quick fix on any particular recipe and see whether he's got the right stuff for it and the right know-how to make it. The disadvantage is that he may not know enough to make it work, because more has been assumed than he knows. The advantage of Beard over an encyclopedic basic book like Rombauer's *Joy* or the revised *Fannie Farmer* (revised by a student of Beard's) is the advantage of selection and taste. Beard's overt and covert aim is to make simple food taste good and his methods produce it.

Different recipes for different occasions. There are as many ways to exterminate an enemy by means of a breakfast pie as there are ways to drive a woman crazy by means of a nutmegged shoe. Cookbooks are as varied as any other kind of literature, or shorthand manuals of life, and we can have the pleasure of them the more we relish their infinite variety, or our own.

# HOW TO USE THIS BOOK

❦

*Look frequently to the pails, to see that nothing is thrown to the pigs which should have been in the grease-pot.*

> —*Mrs. Lydia Child*
> The American Frugal Housewife
> *(1832)*

T he domestic grease pot is not unlike the national melting pot. What other countries throw out, America tends to take in and make something of. Our language, our peoples, our culture, our cooking—would be where without the synthesizing grease pot? Synthesis describes our past and our present and the body language of our food. Food, in addition to nourishment, the late French mythographer Roland Barthes has said, is "a system of communication, a body of images, a protocol of usages, situations, and behavior." Food is commemorative and enables each of us to partake of our national past.

Americans with their hunger for the new are apt to show off their latest blossoms and ignore their roots, having come from so many different stocks, so many successive graftings and transplantings. In cooking, we run for the latest trend, the newest new, throwing to the pigs our national past instead of savoring it, day by day, in the simmering pot. In recipes we look for "originality," "individual creativity," believing with Brillat-Savarin that "the discovery of a new dish does more for human happiness than the discovery of a star."

But as M. F. K. Fisher is quick to point out, Brillat-Savarin's aphorism was not original. He was quoting a friend's. Nor did the master claim as his own "inventions" the dishes he described. They were instead simply "his own methods for carrying out timeless patterns," Fisher writes, "whose origins were lost in the smoke and steam of unknown and occasionally mythical kitchens." And in the pails tipped now to the pigs and now to the grease pot. Such dishes and the recipes for them, the wisdom of the kitchen and hearth, belong to that shared knowledge passed somehow from generation to generation, sometimes by word of mouth only and sometimes scribbled on the back of laundry lists or envelopes or wine labels handed from friend to friend.

With recipes there are no inventions, the inventive Paul Bocuse once said; there are only "marriages." Better yet, in our current jargon, there are only "relationships." One moves out, another moves in—for a quick melding—before making new arrangements, some better than others, some more lasting than others. "Roasting and boiling and baking have gone on for centuries," Fisher reminds us. It is only the tools that have changed and even they have changed but little. There are closed ovens instead of open hearths and controlled egg production and synthetic packaging, which still does not alter the original packaging accomplished with unimprovable economy by the hen. We have yet to "invent" an egg.

As the continuing tidal wave of cookbooks might suggest, nobody can lay claim to a set of ingredients or methods and possess them, by copyright, as his personal property. He can copyright only the particular arrangement of words by which he has expressed one or another fragment of a body of public knowledge available by rights to all. For this same reason, nobody can plagiarize a recipe unless he publishes it exactly word for word in the same order as his printed source. A common device of journalists pressed for time (and what journalist is not?) is to alter a detail or two, change ¼ teaspoon here and ½ teaspoon there of this or that spice or flavoring, and then publish the recipes as their "own." A common device of chefs pressed for time (and what chef is not?) is to lift recipes bodily from earlier and now forgotten texts and recast them to make cookbooks of their "own." Lawyers don't shout "Plagiarism!" Only moralists do, or epistomologists innocent of those thousands of centuries during which father passed to son the knowledge of how to start a fire and mother passed to daughter the knowledge of how to make water hot. Knowledge about the food we grow and cook and eat is public property in the oldest and best sense. The better we understand and act upon that knowledge the more our tables will reflect in the present their ancient civilizing function of sharing, among family, friends, and even guests who are strangers, the nourishment of our hearths.

What is left to the individual cook in the way of personal inventiveness and imagination? Everything that counts—all those particularized marriages, relationships, one-night stands. With food as with sex, the particular moment is unique no matter how common its performance. And with either, a missing "secret ingredient," hoarded by some chef or lover, is a myth to explain the inevitable gap between what's in our mind or memory and what is actually laid out before us on table or bed. If we have hit upon ¼ teaspoon of this or that or a nutmegged shoe at midnight, the chances are that somebody else, looking for the same desired results, has hit upon it, too. The perceptions of our bodies and our taste buds are not infinite. Our tasting palate is squared by a quadrant of sweet, sour, bitter, and salt. Variations that seem to be infinite are curved, like space, reflecting the taster as much as the tasted.

I'm going the long way round to explain how and why I have created the recipes you find in this book. What I have done is to make a synthesis of the four masters, as I have called them, because their ways of handling food are what I have synthesized over the last thirty years in my own actual grease pot. Anyone who cooks a lot cooks after a while by osmosis, absorbing new ideas and details as instinctively as a sunflower sops up the sun. Indebtedness is automatic. Indebtedness is my point. Indebtedness is the point of any good teacher as well, and certainly the point of these particular four good teachers.

All of them are revolutionists who are also radical conservatives, who point to the traditions out of which they have created their individual styles. We understand M. F. K. Fisher's uniqueness by understanding the shock of Campbellite Puritans thrown into the fleshpots of Marseilles. We understand James Beard's uniqueness by understanding the battle of the saucepans waged by an English mother and a Chinese cook in a corner of the American Northwest. We understand Craig Claiborne's uniqueness by understanding the amazement of a Mississippi River boy let loose in the ports of Said and Singapore. We understand Julia Child's uniqueness by understanding the romance of la-dee-dah Paris for a girl of the golden West.

Their "inventions" are reinventions, their "creations," recreations. Nothing is thrown to the pigs that might be worked in some way into the common grease pot. Because, unlike French cooking, our cooking is always changing, always *nouvelle*, we cannot codify a Master List of the kind Escoffier laid down for the French. To do so would be un-American. But during the last three decades, there has been a striking consensus about principles—about quality of ingredients, honesty of presentation, and the liberation of pleasure and fun. Less striking but no less important is a kind of consensus about what dishes are American by virtue of acclimatization and popular acceptance rather than by regional origin. We recognize Walter Cronkite's voice as distinctively American even though it bears no regional accent. In the same way, we are beginning to recognize a distinctive American voice in cooking that is different from collective regionalisms and that might be called "federal grease pot."

The dishes I have chosen to represent here by the recipes I have synthesized in my own way, in my own kitchen, for my own family, are obviously selective. Others would choose differently. My basis for selection is that these are the ones that occur most frequently or most interestingly among our four recipe-makers and transmitters. With soups, for example, we eat more and better French Onion Soup than the French do, or at least we did a decade ago, when we were still discovering the dish and making it our own. Vichyssoise, on the other hand, was created for an American restaurant by a French chef, when he decided to serve a hot leek-and-potato soup cold. Does that make Vichyssoise American and French Onion not?

Wherever possible, I've tried to suggest that our recent discoveries are rooted in traditions of our own that reach into the eighteenth century and on back into the smoke and steam of unknown and occasionally mythical American kitchens. My method has been to look backward as well as ahead. I have tried to make a synthesis of our basic methods as well as of our basic dishes within the range of home cooking which is what we have always done best. Therefore, I have not included a dish as American as pizza because most of us do not yet, anyway, make it at home but eat it out (in increasingly fancy restaurants, it is true, because they have pizza ovens and we do not). I have also avoided dishes that have become so clichéd in the last decades through overuse that I simply cannot face making them anymore. That includes old favorites of mine, such as quiche, which may be somebody else's newest discovery. Fine. Just don't serve me one when I come to dinner. As I say, my selection of dishes for this book is as personal as my taste. And while the recipes should suggest a kind of mini-history of the origin, rise, and flowering of our current taste revolution, the history is sketched in watercolors, not cast in concrete.

As to the form of recipes, I have added my own ¼ teaspoon of this or that by including a note on proportions at the beginning of each recipe so that a reader can see at a glance the essentials of the dish. I have always been irritated at the atomistic listing of every ingredient to the last grain and drop and would personally rather leave herbs, aromatics, and spices to the imagination and discretion of the cook. But since exactitude in these matters belongs to the historical moment, and to the cooks I am covering, I have tried to represent their methods fairly and accurately. Therefore, remember that not only salt and pepper are "to taste," but any seasoning is. Let your tongue guide you. I have also tried, whenever possible, to simplify directions. One result of our revolutionaries is that today we can take far more cooking and eating knowledge for granted and our recipes can be shorter. But, no matter how short a recipe is, remember to read it through completely before you start to make the dish to know exactly what the procedure is going to be. You will then avoid having to butter a cake pan while the batter falls or to turn on an oven which should be already hot.

I hope readers *will* find many of these recipes too short. I hope such readers will go directly to the sources, to investigate the books of these four writers and the books they in turn refer to. I hope readers will learn to look to the past with the same kind of pleasure with which they now look to the future. I hope cooks will become readers and will look to books for knowledge the way they now look to classes. Even in a city as food manic as New York, with millions of dollars' worth of charcuteries and caterers and cooking classes and kitchen boutiques, there is but a single bookstore specializing in cookbooks and that is a new one. We need more and more Eleanor Lowensteins, the late bibliophile whose Corner Bookstore on Fourth Avenue was for so long an important ingredient in our shared cooking knowledge.

Cookbooks belong first in the kitchen, and only second in private libraries for scholars or bibliophiles. James Beard has acted on that principle by leaving his personal papers to the University of Wisconsin, but not his magnificent collection of American cookbooks. Cookbooks are to cook by as well as to read, and as Americans we have always learned best by doing. So I would like my book to be cooked by as well as to be read. I would like readers to see through these recipes my covert and subversive aim. I would like them to see through the high visibility of our current food stars the humblest and least known of those who, generation after generation, looked to the pails and the grease pot. I would like them to hear behind the voices of our current articulators of taste the now unheard shouts of a fish peddler like Clyde "Kingfish" Smith, who once sung his wares on the streets of New York, crying:

> Yo, ho, ho, fish man!
> Bring down your dishpan!
> Cause fish ain't but five cents a pound!

I would like them to feel that the real living tradition is at the hearth and in the pot, not on the printed page, which can only note, like the scrawl on a cave wall, a moment when people shared fire and pot to keep bodies and souls together.

# A NOTE ON
# THE PROCESSOR

B ecause I have found that many more people own a processor than use one, I have used the processor wherever possible in the recipes which follow in order to show how often and how much the machine can lend a helping hand. For the woman who does her own work, a processor is like a live-in kitchen slavey, one who never sulks or takes a day off or gets pregnant, but is ever obedient to your command. You must, as with any helper, know what it can and can't do, and you must not abuse it by violence or filthy habits. Treated nicely, the machine will gratify an amazing variety of whims and will give you the freedom to experiment without undue cost in labor.

For those who don't own and don't want to own this modern kitchen helper, anything you can do with a processor you can obviously do by an old-fashioned hand if it has not withered from disuse. There are many for whom cooking is a pleasant and meaningful way to consume time and to reenact the ancient rites of chopping, blending, kneading, and beating. For these, the processor is quite rightly an excrescence which should be banished from their kitchens. But please don't banish it from mine. Of the many electric tyrants in my kitchen, the processor is the one I most willingly submit to and would be most loath to part from.

# PART THREE

# DRINK AND DRINK FOOD

### Vegetable

Guacamole with Corn Crisps · 81
Eggplant Caviar with Homemade Melba Toast · 83
Stuffed Garlic-Butter Mushrooms · 84

### Pastry

Nut-Cheese Wafers · 85
Cocktail Puffs with Tarama Filling · 87
with Creamed Crab Filling · 88
*Tapenade* "Pizza" · 89

### Seafood

Scallops Seviche · 90
Shrimp Butter · 91

### Meat

Peasant *Foie Gras* · 92
Country Pâté · 94

*All but the desserts in this book goes good with the beer . . . an' speakin' o' beer, you can stir up most o' these dishes with one arm an' hold a beer in the other.*

—*Mary Laswell*
Mrs. Rasmussen's Book of
One-Arm Cookery *(1946)*

Nothing has changed American food habits more than the change in American drinking habits brought about by the Second World War. In the decade before the war, our heads were still splitting from Prohibition, when the tea-party and church-supper crowd were not on speaking terms with the bathtub gin and cocktail set. For the moral majority, cocktails meant tomato or grapefruit juice, shrimp or canned fruit. The beverage of your choice meant coffee, tea, Sanka, Postum, iced water, milk, or soda pop—and, above all, Coca-Cola.

Coca-Cola, the soft drink with a kick, seemed to bridge the gap between Wets and Drys, as it bridged the gap between hard-hat beer guzzlers and white-gloved tea drinkers. Coke came of age in the 1930s as the socially correct drink for all ages, sexes, and conditions, under the aegis of such commercially sponsored cookbooks as Ida Bailey Allen's 1932 *When You Entertain.* For the cocktail set, she suggests ice-cold Coca-Cola with pineapple and cheese canapés; for the tea-party set she recommends well-chilled Coca-Cola bottles opened individually and poured into glasses sprigged with mint.

The closest rival to Coca-Cola was milk. Milk was the favored beverage of the Depression because, when rickety children walked the streets, milk was a sign of health, affluence, and hope. Milk, like Coke, was a meal in itself, a liquid casserole flavored with chocolate or Ovaltine or malt, or with ice cream and syrup in a milk shake. We drank milk with everything as we once, in the early nineteenth century, drank rum, whiskey, and hard cider: a dram or two at every meal for every man, woman, and child, to the tune of 4½ gallons per person per year.

That was our "Gothic Age of drinking," as H. L. Mencken called it, before the temperance movement reared its head in the 1830s to feminize men and to ruin housewives trained to make their first duty the brewing of cider, beer, and wine. That was the age of our colonial forefathers, who distilled molasses and rye and corn into kindred "ardent spirits," who turned cowslips and turnips and birch bark into table wines, and who mixed concoctions called possets and shrubs and those bitter slings that became known as cocktails, from having been brewed (according to legend) in eggcups called *coquetiers.* That was also the age when the tables of Jefferson and Franklin and William Penn were set with fine wines from France.

Our Baroque Age of abstinence was a late development and a sure sign of decline, related to the discords of the First World War. It took a Second World War to shake us loose from our binary categories of wet and dry, hard and soft, wicked and innocent, bitter and sweet, vulgar and high-falutin'. At the beginning of the second war, beer wasn't what went good with everything but dessert. Beer was what you chug-a-lugged with the boys out of brown quart bottles. To consider beer in the context of food was as revolutionary as it was comic, and Mrs. Rasmussen in her *One-Arm Cookery* makes clear that the cookin' and eatin' are designed to interfere minimally with the drinkin'.

At the beginning of the second war and even after, *Fannie Farmer* might daringly include a recipe for eggnog or champagne punch, but mostly the beverage section advocated teetotaling euphemisms like "Chocolate Chip Bracer." For M. F. K. Fisher to advocate homemade vodka and to rhapsodize over "the safe, the perfect, and the intimate (and therefore pluperfect)" gin martini, and to supply recipes for the same as if drink belonged to food, was shocking. Even a decade after the war, Claiborne startled readers of his *New York Times Cook Book* with instructions on the drinking of wine and with recipes for drinks formerly limited to bar manuals—the Bloody Mary, the Manhattan, the Old-Fashioned.

The war had made beer and hard likker not only respectable but necessary to America's fighting blood. The war had also brought America's fighting men in contact with cultures where only pigs drank milk. Humans drank wine and beer. They drank wine and beer, moreover, in relation to food, for both nourishment and taste. Beer and wine, Louis De Gouy had to instruct the readers of his 1947 *Gold Cook Book,* were beverages and *foods* that elsewhere had always been used in cooking. And he meant not wines labeled "cooking wine" or "cooking sherry," but the real stuff that was meant for drinking.

We needed a lot of instruction in what wines to drink and how to drink them and how to cook with them. But we were not about to let our new interest in wine with dinner interfere with the cocktail hour (or two or three) that preceded dinner. Even in the 1930s, with temperance cocktails of spiced apricot juice, hostesses knocked themselves out over platters of "appetizers and canapés" more likely to suppress appetite than provoke it. These were finger-food nibbles and tidbits (a Puritan euphemism for "titbits," as M. F. K. Fisher notes) which *Macy's 1932 Cookbook* called "Those smart morsels that are coming more and more into favor." Beard, who began his cooking career in 1938 as a caterer for cocktail parties and his cookbook career with *Hors d'Oeuvres & Canapés,* called such dibbles and dabbles "doots." If he was revolted by the idea of drinking milk— "a loathsome emetic"—he was appalled by the idea of eating "concoctions fabricated by pastry bag and tube on small bits of soggy bread or toast."

What characterized Coke as a drink characterized our food in general, but especially those smart morsels I've called "drink food." Americans like food and drink, as French critics have observed, that is "sweet, soft, and colored." Tastes die hard, and even after our taste in drink shifted from sweet to dry, as we displaced rum-and-coke or rye-and-ginger with gin and vermouth, our taste in drink food was slower to change. The craze for the martini cocktail party after the war was accompanied by a craze for the gooey cocktail-party dip.

The most ubiquitous was a dip made from canned clams, packaged cream cheese, and commercial onion-soup powder, served with a ring of Ritz crackers. This was an instant canapé that did not interfere with the need of host or guest to dip with one hand and hold a martini glass in the other. Instead of altering the taste, we altered the names to vary the monotony and came up with names like Bean-Bacon Chip-Dip, Saucy Crab-Clam Dip, Blue-Cheese Chili Fluff, and Pink Devil Dip-n-Dunk. Down with such dips, Fisher once exploded: "Down, down to hell itself with dips."

The dip was only one of a number of standard fixtures necessary to the cocktail party. There was also the cheese log, soft and bland and colored and rolled in nuts. There was the pickle wrapped in bacon and skewered with a toothpick. There was peanut butter spread on a Trisket and topped with bacon. There was Edam cheese scooped out, mixed with sweet port or sherry, and served in its waxy shell. And there was the fancy fun-time cabbage, impaled with Vienna sausages and set aflame with Sterno.

But our hearts and heartburn were in the right place, and our revolutionaries slowly turned us from the sweet and soft toward the salt, crisp, and fiery. Beard had provided such drink food during the war for United Seamen's Service Clubs in various parts of the world. Claiborne had imbibed such food as a seaman stationed in Morocco and Okinawa. Fisher had concocted such food from a spice shelf unhampered by wartime shortages. And Child had discovered such food during her service with the OSS in China and Ceylon.

They replaced our dips with nippy cheeses spiced with cayenne, fish or meat pastes liquored with brandy, salty mixtures of olives and anchovies, or fiery mixtures of chilies and curries. They explored ethnic diversity, mixing Mexico with the Middle East, Italy with Spain, Jewish with French. Beard called for honest rugged "highball sandwiches" of roast beef with horseradish, eggs stuffed with caviar, deep-fried onion rings. Claiborne moved toward the elegant: "fresh caviar, genuine *foie gras,* cold lobster, smoked salmon, and thin slices of fine ham, such as that of Paris, Parma, Westphalia, or Bayonne."

As we learned that a meal might come in several courses, appetizers became interchangeable with the first course, which we might eat standing or sitting. As we began to explore wines, we learned that wine might be drunk before the meal, interchangeably with sherry or gin. We discovered that wines need not be as sweet as Manischewitz or Liebfraumilch or Sparkling Burgundy or Blue Nun. We discovered that some wines were hard and some were dry and that they came in colors other than red, white, or pink.

About the time that the hard-core cocktail set was giving up gin for vodka, the advance-guard of wine explorers was giving up both for wine-based aperitifs. Instead of such palate-killers as Pernod or Scotch, white wine with a dash of soda for a spritzer or a dash of Cassis for a kir became the mark of the sophisticate. White wine in jugs had the additional advantage of being cheaper than either the hard stuff or the latest soft stuff, a French unsweetened soda pop called Perrier.

Because few of us knew much about wine, we were obsessed with rules. White was for fish, we were told, and red was for meat. White should be chilled, and red should be at room temperature. Both colors should be stored in a wine cellar, preferably inherited from a father or rich uncle. Neither color should be shaken. Red, if it was old, should be opened early "to breathe" and decanted to avoid sediment. Those who had memorized baseball scores in their youth now memorized vintage charts and kept score. We put away childish things such as old Chianti bottles dripping with candle wax. Instead, we steamed off labels and kept notes and discussed *sommeliers* and increased our vocabulary with words like "fruity" and "full-bodied" and "steely" or "soave." We learned to distinguish by silhouette the hunched shoulders of a Bordeaux from the sloping shoulders of a Burgundy. And just when we'd learned to apply textual criticism to the reading of labels in order to distinguish the region from the maker and the shipper of a score of French wines, the French threw out all the rules and said, "Drink Beaujolais, chilled, with everything."

We had to start all over with California wines. Now the talk was of "varietals," and of Pinot Chardonnays and Cabernet Sauvignons (how to remember which was red and which was white?) and of Zinfandels, which were entirely different. Labels, shapes, colors, prices multiplied so rapidly that it was hard to keep up. Our masters tried to be helpful but, considering the possibilities, Child was often reduced to a generic spread that would cover a baseball diamond: "You should really serve an Alsatian Riesling with it, but a strong dry white wine like a Côtes du Rhône would do, or a *rosé*, or even a big pitcher of beer." This was for a dish of black beans with braised pork and sauerkraut, which Child labeled Haricots Secs Garnis à l'Alsacienne, while admitting that the dish wasn't Alsatian at all, but if the Alsatians had black beans this is what they might do with them. So much for food-and-wine rules.

As we became more adventurous about wines, and as French table wine deteriorated and California varietals improved, we learned that the only rule about wine is that there is no rule. We found that we could drink red wine with fish and white with meat, depending not only on the wine and the food but on our mood, the state of our budget, even the state of our health. We found that we could drink what we liked, with impunity, throughout the meal. Serious wine drinkers and bargain-hunters became versed in Italian, Spanish, Portuguese, Australian, Greek, and Hungarian wines. The best French and German wine-makers set up shop in the wine valleys of California to produce "Champagne" from Napa and "Johannisberg Riesling" from Sonoma. Wine shops became supermarkets with prices that rose and fell like the stock market. Wherever wine grapes were available, as in California and New York and Michigan, families once again turned to making wine at home, as they would have done a hundred years ago. Soon, no doubt, we shall return to making "weed" wines and consult on what's the best food to serve with dandelion or elderberry wine.

What has happened with wine has also happened with beer. GIs occupying Germany after the war discovered that the beers of the enemy were far superior in variety and quality to the soft and bland brews of the beer industry at home. Beer was no longer a monolithic Bud or Schlitz. Stateside customers demanded, and were willing to pay for, bitter, sharp, pungent, and hefty beers—Löwenbräu from Germany, Heineken from Holland, Guinness from Great Britain. At our local supermarket today, we can choose beer from Mexico, Japan, Thailand, Canada, and even regional beers from the United States. We began to learn why an unpasteurized beer, such as Coors, has more taste than pasteurized brands, processed like bread and cheese for longevity. Who knows? Brewing may once again become the first duty of huswife and husbandman. This is not what Mrs. Rasmussen had in mind in her *One-Arm Cookery*, but she aimed us in the right direction. And if the beer tastes good enough, who needs desserts?

The drink food I've included here is all hearty enough to go well with beer or wine and to survive the inroads of harder liquor. All four of our master cooks are refreshingly unsnobby and unpedantic about alcohol and tobacco. They drink what they like, often whiskey or gin, and smoke if they please. The Puritan spirit of admonitions and prohibitions is not in them. Theirs is the Cavalier spirit that says Make Merry, for there *shall* be ale and ginger shall be hot i' the mouth.

# GUACAMOLE WITH CORN CRISPS

"Americans are greater consumers of raw vegetables than any other people," Beard has said in describing the big platter of raw vegetables ubiquitous at the cocktail hour. Beard, from first to last, has pushed the raw vegetables that the French call *crudités,* but that seem American as all get-out in displaying the largesse of a land that produces tiny artichokes, asparagus spears, green onions, red and green peppers, broccoli buds, cauliflowerets, radishes, and mushrooms, not to mention mountains of carrot sticks.

Raw vegetables suit the American need to eat, drink, and diet, *all at once.* Raw vegetables support the dieter's illusion that he is drinking few calories because he is eating few. Raw vegetables also support the eater's illusion that the dunk into which he has dipped his carrot stick is as non-caloric as the carrot. The only trouble with raw vegetables is that the dips and dunks are so often dull. Mayonnaise, sour cream, cream cheese, variously combined and flavored—there is hardly any thick emollient we didn't try during the cocktail craze. And when we tried thinner more exciting dunks like the Italian hot olive oil with anchovies called *bagna cauda,* they usually dripped down our own and other people's fronts.

One solution to the dunk problem is to use one of the best of America's raw vegetable-fruits, the avocado, as a dunk for vegetables. Dieters can feel virtuous in forgoing Fritos or taco chips and drippers can feel secure in avoiding spotted fronts. One of the best forms of avocado is that south-of-the-border import, guacamole. Guacamole has finally spread from West to East and is now almost as common and as variable as gazpacho. Where guacamole was once eaten as salad (both Beard and Claiborne list it as such in their first books), it now appears as dip or spread or cocktail, but definitely as a drink food.

Whatever category applies, mashed and spiced avocado is as venerable as the Aztecs who called the pear-shaped native fruit *ahuacatl.* The spices depend on the spicer. Claiborne suggests chili powder and onion, Beard a jolt of black pepper. Mrs. Rasmussen in her *One-Arm Cookery* liked a teaspoon of garlic vinegar. Child recently suggested potato mashed with cream and olive oil to make an avocado *brandade.* In the recipe below, I've omitted chopped tomatoes, a frequent addition, and increased fiery hot pepper to make a seasoned dunk for unseasoned raw vegetables.

## Proportions

for 4 to 6 servings, 1 large avocado, 1 clove garlic

1 large ripe avocado
1 clove garlic, minced
1 tablespoon minced onion
1 tablespoon or more lemon
  or lime juice
1 teaspoon minced hot green
  or red chili pepper, or a few
  drops *salsa picante,* or red
  pepper flakes to taste

½ teaspoon minced fresh
  cilantro (Chinese parsley)
Salt and freshly ground
  black pepper to taste
Raw vegetables, taco chips,
  or Corn Crisps (below)

1.   Cut the avocado in half around the central pit. (If the skin is thick, scoop the pulp from the shell and save half the shell to use as a serving bowl for the guacamole.) Put the pulp in a bowl and mash it with a fork, or purée it in a blender or food processor. (If you use the blender or food processor, the purée can be made either very smooth or chunky.)

2.   Add the garlic, onion, lemon juice, and seasonings and mix well. (If the avocado is not richly ripe, you will need more seasonings to give it taste.)

3.   Heap the purée in the reserved avocado shell and surround it with the prepared raw vegetables or with taco chips or homemade Corn Crisps.

*Note:*   To keep the guacamole in the refrigerator without the top turning brown, squeeze lemon juice over the top and cover tightly with plastic wrap.

# CORN CRISPS

An excellent homemade corn crisp of taste and character, known before Fritos were born, was furnished by Helen Evans Brown in her *West Coast Cook Book.* I've adapted her recipe below.

## Proportions

for 25 to 30 crisps, about 1 cup of cornmeal to 1 cup of water

1¼ cups white cornmeal, or ⅞
  cup yellow cornmeal
1 cup boiling water

3 tablespoons melted butter
1 tablespoon salt

1.   Put the cornmeal into a bowl, gradually pour in the water, and stir until smooth. Add the butter and salt and mix well.

2. Drop the mixture from a teaspoon onto a buttered baking sheet. Flatten each mound with the bottom of a jar or glass, so that the mound is ¼ inch thick and 1½ inches in diameter. Bake at 350 degrees for about 35 minutes, or until the edges are nicely browned. Remove and cool on a rack. Store the crisps in an airtight can.

# EGGPLANT CAVIAR WITH MELBA TOAST

"Peasant Caviar," Fisher calls it, while admitting that she's never known a peasant who ate it. As we raid Mexico for avocado dishes, so we raid the Middle East for eggplant dishes. Because cooked eggplant flesh is as easy to mash as raw avocado, eggplant dips and spreads have been popular under various names for a decade or two.

Fisher supplied us with a trio of recipes for her peasant caviar: the first "cheap and easy," the second "finicky," and the third "fancy-fine." The seasonings remain roughly the same—onion, garlic, oil, and vinegar. What differs are the methods of cooking the eggplant: boiling, baking, or stewing.

So familiar has puréed eggplant become that Claiborne in one of his most recent books calls it by its Turkish name, Baba Ghanouj. Child, in *Mastering II*, devised a French name for it, La Tentation de Bramafam, and included walnuts, ginger, and allspice. Later, adding sesame paste, she redubs it Caviar d'Aubergine. Beard, attributing the popularity of the dish to the magic of the word "caviar," included a recipe for it in his *American Cookery* and pushed it toward Morocco by adding cinnamon and mint.

In my recipe below, I have tried to reproduce the tastes of a peasant caviar I ate once in Istanbul at the hands of an Ottoman princess, who roasted her eggplant on a fork over a single-burner gas stove. The charred skin produced a flavor as delicious as the charred skin of roasted green or red peppers. Instead of olive oil, she used yogurt and a little cream. We ate it on pita bread and washed it down with *raki,* the anise-flavored drink the Greeks call *ouzo.* Her entire menu was drink food, she explained when she said, "We will drink *raki* throughout the meal."

## Proportions

for 4 to 6 servings, 1 medium-sized eggplant, 2 cloves garlic

| | |
|---|---|
| 1 medium eggplant (about 1 pound) | ¼ cup yogurt |
| 1 tablespoon sesame paste | 2 tablespoons sesame seeds, toasted |
| 1 to 2 tablespoons lemon juice | Salt and freshly ground black pepper to taste |
| 2 tablespoons heavy cream | |
| 2 cloves garlic, minced | 1 tablespoon minced parsley |

1. Puncture the eggplant skin with a fork so that it will not explode. Broil the eggplant under high heat for 20 to 30 minutes, turning it to blacken skin and cook the interior pulp evenly.

2. When the skin is cool enough to handle, peel it off and mash the pulp by hand or in blender or processor.

3. Thin the sesame paste with the lemon juice and cream so that it will mix in easily. Add to the eggplant pulp with the garlic, yogurt, toasted seeds, and salt and pepper. Taste carefully for seasoning. Heap into a bowl and sprinkle with minced parsley. Improves if left to ripen an hour or more at room temperature and keeps for days in the refrigerator.

*Serve with toasted pita bread, homemade Melba toast (below), crisp crackers, or thin slices of plain or toasted French bread.*

# HOMEMADE MELBA TOAST

To make Melba toast, cut the crusts from diet-thin sliced white bread. Cut the slices in half lengthwise or on the diagonal. Lay on an unbuttered baking sheet and toast in a 325-degree oven for about 7 minutes on each side. The toast will keep crisp if stored in an airtight can.

# STUFFED GARLIC-BUTTER MUSHROOMS

A finger-food vegetable as popular as Italo-American menus is stuffed mushrooms. Since the white button mushrooms of our supermarkets know as little of seasons as they do of woods, they can be a drink-food staple year round. Size is important. The smallest are best marinated in oil, lemon, and spices, to be speared with toothpicks. The largest are best for entrée vegetables or garnish. Only the middle size are just right for bite-sized drink food that can be popped into the mouth without dribbling juice.

Child's recipe for Champignons Farcis in *Mastering I* invigorated those of us who had never tasted a mushroom stuffed with anything but bread crumbs. Beard suggested a stuffing perked up with Tabasco sauce and chives. Claiborne offered a trio of stuffings, one based on chicken livers and cream cheese, another on chicken, ham, or shrimp, and a third on canned snails in garlic butter. The garlic butter without the snails is an even better stuffing. Redolent of snail butter, the mushrooms reveal their kinship to their fellow creatures of the dark earth.

## Proportions

for 20 mushrooms, ¼ pound butter, ½ cup bread crumbs, ¼ cup parsley, ½ cup Parmesan cheese

| | |
|---|---|
| 20 mushroom caps, about 1-inch in diameter | ½ cup fresh bread crumbs (see Note) |
| ¼ pound (1 stick) butter | ¼ cup minced parsley |
| 3 tablespoons minced shallots or green onions | Salt and freshly ground black pepper to taste |
| 1 large clove garlic, minced | ½ cup grated Parmesan cheese |

1. Wipe the mushrooms, if necessary, and remove the stems. Chop the stems fine.

2. Melt half the butter and brush the caps inside and out. Put the caps hollow side up in a roasting or broiling pan.

3. Heat the remaining butter and sauté the stems quickly over high heat for 1 to 2 minutes. Add the shallots, garlic, bread crumbs, and parsley. Taste carefully for seasoning. Fill the caps with the stuffing and sprinkle with the grated cheese.

4. Bake in a 375-degree oven for 5 to 10 minutes, depending on the size of the mushrooms. The tops should be browned and the mushrooms should be cooked through but still firm, not wilted. Test with a toothpick for doneness.

*Note:* Bread crumbs must be fresh. To make them, simply cut off the crusts of 1 or 2 slices of bread, tear the bread into pieces, and process in a blender or processor.

*These appetizers also make a good garnish for steaks or a good first course.*

# NUT-CHEESE WAFERS

Since the twenties, Americans have been partial to salty crackers, with or without cheese, under classic brand names like Nabisco, Trisket, Cheez-It, Pepperidge Goldfish, and Ritz. For decades Ritz crackers encircled a dip as inevitably as Indians a fort. Because the Ritz taste was as distinct and uniform as Bottled Ketchup, all dips tasted the same. The idea of making cheese crackers from scratch was as novel as the idea of making mayonnaise. As long as the recipes looked quick and easy, we leaped at the chance. Some recipes, however, were quicker and easier than others.

The ideal cheese wafer turned out to be a pastry rather than a cracker. The point was to make a bite-sized round as crisp and buttery as possible, with a minimum of flour and a maximum of cheese. Too much butter and the dough would crumble when baked; too much flour and the wafers would be dull or tough; too much cheese and the wafers would stick to the baking sheet. Homemade wafers required more craft than cheese.

Child's masterly analysis of pastry of various types and uses provided a breakthrough on the pastry front. Once the principles were understood, proportions could be varied for a cheese-wafer recipe that used hard cheese rather than soft. In her Galettes au Fromage, she used "just enough flour" (¾ cup) to bind 2 cups grated Swiss cheese to 1 cup butter, but warned that softer cheese would require more flour. Beard simplified the formula by using equal amounts of flour, Cheddar cheese, and shortening (¾ cup of each). Claiborne avoided the problem by starting with leftover pastry dough, which he spread with grated cheese, folded, rolled out, and cut into straws and rings. Fisher defaulted with a recipe for Questionable Cheese Crumpets made with Bisquick, Parmesan cheese, and a few enrichers like butter, egg, and cream. "They are dishonest," she confessed, "and gratifying."

My recipe suggests half hard and half soft cheese to get the best cheese flavor. I have also added nuts for crunch and, consequently, reduced the butter. The wafer is fragile but as crisp and buttery as you could want.

## Proportions

for 60 half-dollar size wafers, 2 cups cheese, 1 cup flour, ¼ pound butter, 1 cup walnuts

¼ pound (1 stick) butter
1 cup flour
2 cups grated cheese (half sharp Cheddar or Swiss, half chèvre or Monterey Jack, mixed with blue or Parmesan)

1 cup walnuts, chopped medium fine
Salt and freshly ground black pepper to taste
Pinch of cayenne pepper

1. Cut the butter into the flour by hand, or use a processor as in making pastry. Mix in the cheese, nuts, and seasonings, and press together into a ball.

2. Cut the ball in half. Lay each half on a sheet of plastic wrap or wax paper. Shape the dough by hand into two cylinders about 1½ inches in diameter. Wrap them in the plastic wrap and refrigerate for at least 30 minutes to firm up the dough.

3. Cut the cylinders in ¼-inch-thick slices and place 2 inches apart on well-buttered baking sheets, as the dough will spread. Bake in a 350-

degree oven for 10 minutes. Let cool for a minute or two before loosening the wafers carefully with a spatula, because they crumble easily. Store in an airtight can.

# COCKTAIL PUFFS
# (WITH TARAMA FILLING OR
# CREAMED CRAB FILLING)

At the height of the cocktail craze, at least one hot and fancy drink food among the dips and spreads was a must. One "hot and fancy" showed your guests that, in the language of the fifties, you were committed—you cared. Child introduced us to cocktail-party cream puffs and taught us that they were as easy to make as they were useful for drink food, instead of for dessert food.

In practice, while bite-sized puffs were easy to make, they were time-consuming to fill. They could be filled ahead, frozen, and reheated, but if the hostess were careless in her timing, the buttery hot shells could conceal a nasty cold surprise. One way to avoid this problem is to freeze the empty puffs, reheat when ready to fill, and then fill at the last moment when ready to serve.

---

## Proportions

for 30 small puffs, 1 cup flour, 1 cup water, ⅓ cup butter, 4 eggs

| | |
|---|---|
| 1 cup water | Pinch of cayenne pepper |
| 6 tablespoons (⅓ cup) butter | 1 cup flour |
| 1 teaspoon salt | 4 large eggs |
| ¼ teaspoon freshly ground black pepper | 1 egg yolk plus 1 teaspoon water |

1. Heat 1 cup water with the butter and seasonings until the butter has melted. Remove from the heat and add the flour all at once, beating vigorously with a spoon. Beat over high heat 1 to 2 minutes, or until the mixture forms a ball, but be careful not to scorch it.

2. Remove the pan from the heat, make a well in center of the dough, and beat in the eggs one at a time, until they are absorbed. (With the processor, put the cooked dough in the bowl with a metal blade and add the eggs one at a time through the opening in the lid.)

3. Drop the paste from a teaspoon onto buttered baking sheets. Or transfer the paste to a pastry bag with a ½-inch-wide opening and squeeze mounds 1 inch in diameter, ½ inch high, and 2 inches apart.

4. To make a glaze, beat the egg yolk with a teaspoon of water and

---

brush each mound lightly on top, being careful not to drip glaze down the sides onto the pan or the dough may not rise well.

    5.   Bake in a 425-degree oven for 15 to 20 minutes. Turn the oven off. Remove the puffs and pierce the side of each puff with a knife point to let out the steam. Return to the oven for 10 minutes, leaving the door slightly ajar, to cook the interior of the shells. Cool the puffs on a rack before filling or freezing.

    6.   To fill, put the filling in a pastry bag and pipe into each puff, or slit the puffs open and fill them with a teaspoon. The best fillings are both creamy and intense, like an anchovy cream, the carp-roe spread called *tarama* by the Greeks, or a deviled crabmeat moistened with heavy cream and seasoned with mustard and hot pepper. Only smooth creams like the tarama (below) are suitable for filling with a pastry tube. Textured mixtures, such as crab, need the puffs slit open and filled.

# TARAMA FILLING

## Proportions

to fill 30 puffs, 1½ cups filling (½ cup tarama, 3 slices bread, ¼ cup each of olive oil and cream)

| | |
|---|---|
| **3 slices white bread, or 1 English muffin** | **¼ cup olive oil** |
| **½ cup tarama (salt carp roe, available in specialty food stores)** | **¼ cup heavy cream** |
| | **3 to 4 tablespoons lemon juice Freshly ground white or black pepper to taste** |
| **1 clove garlic, minced** | |

    1.   Remove the crusts from the bread, put the slices in a bowl, and cover with water until well soaked. Squeeze out most of the water and put the bread in a blender or processor.

    2.   Add the tarama, garlic, oil, cream, lemon juice, and pepper and process until creamy. If the mixture is too thick or too salty (from the salt carp), add more cream. If it is too thin, add more soaked, squeezed-out bread.

# CREAMED CRAB FILLING

## Proportions

to fill 30 puffs, 2 cups filling (1 cup cream, ¾ cup crabmeat, ¼ cup mushrooms)

| 1 cup *crème fraîche* or sour cream | ½ teaspoon grated fresh gingerroot |
| ¾ cup lump crabmeat (if frozen, fully thawed and drained) | ½ teaspoon lemon juice<br>Salt and freshly ground white pepper to taste |
| ¼ cup fresh mushroom caps, slivered | Pinch of cayenne pepper |

Mix all the ingredients together well and taste carefully for seasoning. The mixture should taste delicately of crab. Fill room-temperature puffs at the last moment to avoid sogginess.

# TAPENADE "PIZZA"

For the masters of the American palate, all roads lead eventually to the Mediterranean, where the sun cures olives on the trees, ripens garlic in the fields, and crusts the brine of anchovies in barrels in the streets. One of the spreads furthest removed from processed soft and bland dips distills the Mediterranean by melding olives, garlic, and anchovies in a mixture called *tapenade*. The *tapenade* of Provence, an ancient remedy for head colds and numbed taste buds, is one solution for the cocktail pizza problem.

Since the war, pizza has become as American as pumpkin pie and, as it is a finger food by nature, it should be an ideal drink food—but it isn't. For the nibbler, the dough is too filling and the cheese topping too gooey. For the server, the dough is too unwieldy to cut into small pieces. Child's solution has been to make a rectangular "pizza" of piecrust dough and to spread it with the stewed onions, anchovies, and olives typical of the French pizza that the people of Nice call *pissaladière*.

A simpler solution, however, is to spread a prebaked crust with *tapenade* and to warm the "pizza" just before serving. In this way you have the best of both worlds: a crisp crust and an intense topping. The spread is another of those mixtures in which the processor has supplanted the mortar. Oil-cured black olives are the chief ingredient, and while Fisher allows for the American canned and pitted kind, only the desperate would comply. Canned olives in brine deny the depth of flavor of this Marseillaise mix that tastes, as Fisher says, "as subtly ancient as Time itself can taste."

## Proportions

for 2 cups *tapenade* to make 20 appetizers, 1 cup olives, ½ cup anchovy fillets, ½ cup tuna

| 1 cup (20 to 30) black olives, pitted and chopped | 4 tablespoons olive oil |
| 2 cloves garlic, minced | 2 tablespoons brandy |
| 1 tablespoon drained capers | 1 tablespoon lemon juice (optional) |
| 1 small (3¼-ounce) can tuna in oil | Double recipe of Butter Crust (page 348) |
| ½ cup (about 15) anchovy fillets | |

1. Mash all the ingredients together in a bowl. If you are using a processor and want a slightly chunky texture, chop the olives first and set them aside. Purée the remaining ingredients until smooth, remove from the processor, and add the olives. Taste carefully before adding the lemon juice, as it will cut the oil but increase the saltiness.

2. Pack the *tapenade* in a covered crock or jar. It will keep for weeks in the refrigerator.

3. To make a cocktail "pizza," spread the *tapenade* on the Butter Crust which has been formed and prebaked in a buttered 11- by 17-inch jelly roll pan. (If you have trouble rolling the dough for this large a pan, simply press the dough into the pan with your fingers.) Just before serving, warm the *tapenade* in a 400-degree oven for 2 to 3 minutes, then cut into small squares.

# SCALLOPS SEVICHE

Until the seventies, much of America knew fish only on Fridays and then only batter-coated and oil-fried. For many such the idea of raw fish was repellent. But as Claiborne pointed out when he introduced Sea Scallops Seviche in his first cookbook, the same folk who shuddered at eating fish raw, gulped down raw oysters and clams without a qualm. Food tastes, like so much else, begin in the mind and filter down to the body.

The Spanish way, called "seviche," of marinating raw fish in acid is quite unlike the Japanese way, called "sushi," of serving fish raw to be dipped in mustard and soy. Seviche is a method of cold cooking, because the fish changes color and texture in an acid bath of lemon or lime juice as it would under heat. Fisher tells us that the Tahitians call the method "I'a Ota" and that after marinating the fish, they serve it up in coconut milk flavored with onions.

The Tahitian method is a good one to use with scallops, because scallops are too fragile and self-effacing for the usual Spanish marinade accompaniments of chopped onions, peppers, chilies, cilantro, and Tabasco sauce. Coconut milk, on the other hand, cuts any lingering acid from the marinade and makes the scallops milky white. Sea scallops are better than bay scallops for marinating, for the tiny ones can be as easily overcooked by citrus juice as by heat.

## Proportions

for 8 cocktail servings, 1½ pounds scallops to ⅔ cup lime juice to 1 cup coconut milk

1½ pounds (about 2 cups) sea scallops
4 tablespoons minced onion
2 tablespoons minced parsley
⅔ cup lime or lemon juice (about 6 limes)

⅛ teaspoon mace
¼ teaspoon cardamom
Pinch of cayenne pepper or dash of Tabasco sauce
1 cup coconut milk (see Note)

1.   Rinse the scallops and cut any large ones in half to make bite-sized morsels. Mix with the onion and parsley and cover with lime juice. Refrigerate, covered, for 1 or 2 hours. (Longer than 3 hours is apt to "overcook" them.) Drain and reserve the scallops.

2.   Mix the mace, cardamom, and pepper into the coconut milk and pour over the scallops. Taste for seasoning. The natural sweetness of the scallops should complement the tartness of the lime or lemon. Refrigerate until ready to serve. Drain and serve with toothpicks or skewers.

*Note:*   To make coconut milk, puncture the "eyes" of the brown husk with a hammer and ice pick and drain off the liquid within. Bake in a 400-degree oven for 20 minutes to crack the husk. Remove the husk and hammer the coconut under a towel to break it into pieces. Pare off the brown skin from each piece. Cut the white meat into small pieces and put in a processor or blender with 2 cups of boiling water. Process until the coconut is finely shredded. Pour through a strainer into a bowl, pushing as much liquid as possible through the strainer. If you can buy unsweetened grated dried coconut instead of fresh, steep 1 cup in a cup of boiling water for 15 minutes, then strain. You can freeze leftover coconut milk to use later in sauces or soups or desserts.

# SHRIMP BUTTER

Now that the shrimp in our local fish markets is no longer local but may have come by way of Bombay or Tampico, and now that fresh means freshly thawed, one of the best ways to avoid a soggy shrimp is to purée it. And one of the best ways to preserve a puréed shrimp is in butter. The English have done so for centuries and have called it potted shrimp.

Shrimp, butter, and lemon are the only essentials in Fisher's recipe for

Potted Shrimps Hyde Park, although she elaborates the mixture with onion, mustard, and brandy for a Shrimp Pâté. Maybe the reason potted shrimps are not as universally popular in America as in England is a matter of language rather than seasoning. Where *pâté* suggests the food, "potted" suggests the drinker as well as the pot.

In any case, shrimp is complemented by so many flavors that the only way to go wrong is to skimp on the shrimp. "Never skimp on anything," Beard says. Do not spread but *heap* the shrimp, potted or pâtéd, onto thin slices of crustless toast. In the recipe below, I've added tarragon to flavor the shrimp butter, but many other herbs or spices could be used, ranging from dill to curry and coriander.

## Proportions

for 2 cups purée to make 16 to 20 appetizers, 1 pound shrimp, ½ pound butter, ⅛ cup of lemon juice

| | |
|---|---|
| 1 **pound cooked shrimp, shelled and deveined** | 2 **tablespoons fresh tarragon, or ½ tablespoon dried** |
| ½ **pound (2 sticks) butter** | **Salt and freshly ground** |
| 2 **minced shallots or green onions** | **black pepper to taste** |
| 2 **tablespoons lemon juice** | **Pinch of cayenne pepper or mace** |
| 1 **tablespoon dry sherry** | |

1.   Chop the shrimp by hand or in a processor. Melt 2 tablespoons of the butter, add the shallots, and cook until soft. Put the shallots, shrimp, lemon juice, sherry, and seasonings in the processor.

2.   Melt the remaining butter and, when hot, pour all but ¼ cup through the opening in the lid while the machine purées the shrimp mixture. Taste carefully for seasonings as the cold purée will lose some of its flavor.

3.   Pack the purée in a bowl or crock and pour the remaining ¼ cup melted butter over the top. When the butter has cooled, decorate with a tarragon leaf and cover with plastic wrap. Refrigerate for 1 or 2 days to ripen. It will keep well for at least a week. Serve with homemade Melba toast (page 84) or a good English cracker.

*Note:*   Instead of shrimp, various smoked fish, such as smoked trout, whitefish, salmon, or haddock, make an excellent butter.

## PEASANT *FOIE GRAS*

Chopped chicken livers have been as much a part of Jewish-American cooking as chicken soup and matzo balls. Puréed chicken livers, on the other hand, immediately suggest France and the unctuous pâtés of duck and goose that have made Strasbourg famous. Once upon a time, the livers of French geese were fattened forcibly by peasant hand to fatten the livers of French diners. But now that peasant hands are as scarce as hens' or geese's teeth, and as costly, all kinds of livers appear under the label *foie gras,* including the humble chicken liver.

When Fisher gave a recipe for Doro's Chicken Liver Spread, she recalled the Orthodox Jewish godmother who had served it to "an ecumenical crew of Presbyterians, Episcopalians, Orthodox Greeks, Catholics, atheists, and back sliders . . ." The ingredients were similar to those in Child's recipe for Mousse de Foies de Volaille. The distinction was more linguistic than culinary. But, as our cooks know well, with food and drink the name is the thing.

Once again blender and processor make short work of what was once done by sieve and spoon. Modern methods also allow us to buy chicken livers by the pound instead of chicken by chicken. If we are lucky, we can sometimes buy duck livers as well. Chicken fat has been out of favor in recent years, but its flavor and binding qualities are particularly useful in puréeing chicken livers and, in the recipe below, I've suggested using half butter, half chicken fat. Madeira, sherry, or Cognac are all good flavor enhancers with liver paste, but Calvados is especially complementary to both chicken and duck. If you have it, use it.

## Proportions

for 2 cups to make 20 to 30 appetizers, 1 pound chicken (or duck) livers, ¼ pound butter (or chicken fat), ¼ cup of cream

1 pound chicken and/or duck or goose livers

¼ pound (1 stick) butter, or ¼ cup butter and ¼ cup melted chicken fat

4 tablespoons minced shallots or green onions

2 tablespoons Calvados or Cognac, etc.

¼ cup heavy cream

½ bay leaf, crumbled

⅛ teaspoon cinnamon

⅛ teaspoon allspice or cloves

Pinch of mace or nutmeg

Salt and freshly ground black pepper to taste

1.   Cut the chicken livers in half. Melt 4 tablespoons of the butter and add the shallots and chicken livers. Sauté until the livers stiffen on the outside but are still soft and pink inside (3 to 4 minutes). Transfer to a processor or blender.

2.   Pour the Calvados into the sauté pan and scrape up any juices. Add to the processor with the remaining softened or melted butter (and/ or chicken fat, if you have it, that has been rendered by slow heat in a

skillet or double boiler). Add the cream and seasonings and purée until smooth. Taste carefully for seasoning.

3. Pack into a jar or crock. Cover tightly with plastic wrap and refrigerate. Once used, to avoid a green discoloring from oxidation, smooth the surface of the purée and cover with a little melted butter or fat.

*Serve with slices of toasted French bread or homemade Melba toast (page 84).*

# COUNTRY PÂTÉ

During the hard times of the Depression, a meatloaf covered with a layer of ketchup and sprinkled with cornflakes was considered a treat. Many of us Depression children were pleasantly surprised to discover the meatloaf that the French called pâté and that substituted thin strips of pork fat for ketchup and ground veal for beef and Cognac for cornflakes. Many of us could hardly get enough of this surprising French meatloaf.

So we were particularly grateful to Claiborne, whose opening act in his first cookbook was to go all the way with pâtés, from turkey galantine to pâtés truffled, livered, Cognaced, creamed, spiced, and jellied. Claiborne brought them straight from Paris, with a little help from Paula Peck. Child, too, was heavy on pâtés, and for a decade no cocktail buffet table was complete without one or more Claiborne or Child pâtés.

American butchers, unaccustomed to complicated orders for ground meats lean and fat, ground their teeth as customers demanded fresh ("no, not salted") pork fat. American hostesses hoarded fat to make the classic white wrapping that they sported like merit badges as testimony both of intensive study in Claiborne and Child and of a benevolent butcher. Child's Pâté en Croûte, shaped by a hinged tin mold and lined with paper-thin fat, was the equivalent of Eagle Scouthood. Such a *croûte,* lined additionally with a pig's caul, was the equivalent of the *Légion d'Honneur.*

Pâté, which was the most spectacular of drink foods, was also the most hazardous to slice and eat. The effect of decorative checkerboards of veal, tongue, and chicken, studded with truffles and pistachios, was lost on drinkers who wanted finger food. Plates and forks were obligatory and pâté was a lot easier to eat sitting down. Then fat-free diets became voguish and richly lubricated meats were avoided. Pâtés turned from meat to fish, in which fat could be disguised as cream. At the same time, French-food charcuteries were sprouting in American cities in such numbers that it seemed easier to buy complicated pâtés than to make them.

The pleasure of a French meatloaf made at home, however, is that it is truly a *pâté maison,* in which you can combine whatever flavors you like with whatever meats. The essential point is to provide enough fat or liquid to the ground or chopped meats to lubricate them during their slow cooking and to keep the cooked loaf from drying out. The pâté below uses pork fat, eggs, cream, and Cognac to moisten and flavor a mixture of veal, pork, and ham in a purée of chicken livers. What makes the pâté "country," instead of "city," is the garlic and roughly diced meat, mixed together simply, instead of layered, as if it were a humble American meatloaf.

## Proportions

for a 9-cup loaf to serve 20 to 24, about 4 pounds meat to 3 eggs to ¾ cup of liquid

| | |
|---|---|
| 1 **pound pork fat for lining pan (see Note)** | 3 **cloves garlic, minced** |
| 2 **tablespoons butter** | ¼ **cup heavy cream** |
| ½ **cup minced onion** | ⅓ **cup Cognac** |
| 1½ **pounds ground veal** | 1½ **tablespoons salt** |
| 2 **pounds ground pork shoulder (1¼ pounds lean to ¾ pound fat)** | 1 **teaspoon freshly ground black pepper** |
| | 1 **tablespoon dried thyme** |
| ½ **pound smoked ham, cubed** | 1 **teaspoon allspice** |
| | ½ **teaspoon ground bay leaves** |
| ½ **pound chicken livers** | ½ **teaspoon cardamom** |
| 3 **eggs** | |

1. Freeze the pork fat, then thaw it just enough to cut it in as thin slices as possible. Line a 9-cup loaf pan with the slices, reserving some for the top.

2. Melt the butter and cook the onion until soft. Mix the onion with the ground veal and pork and cubed ham.

3. Put the livers, eggs, garlic, cream, Cognac, and seasonings in a blender or processor and purée until smooth. Mix together with the meats. (The easiest way is to use your hands.) Sauté a small spoonful of the mixture to test the seasoning and adjust accordingly.

4. Put the mixture into the lined pan and cover with the remaining strips of pork fat. Cover tightly with foil. Put the loaf pan in a roasting pan and fill the roasting pan halfway up with boiling water. Bake in a 350-degree oven for 2 to 2½ hours, depending on the shape of the meat pan. The interior temperature of the meat should register 155 to 160 degrees.

5. Remove the pan from the water and weight the loaf to firm it by fitting a small board or piece of heavy cardboard over the loaf and putting heavy cans or jars on top of it. Refrigerate when cool. Invert when ready to serve. The pâté should be allowed to ripen for 2 or 3 days and will keep well for 10 days to 2 weeks in the refrigerator.

*Note:*  You can accumulate pork fat by trimming uncooked pork roasts and freezing the trimmings.

*As meat pâtés are solid protein and richly substantial, they make a good first course garnished with a sprig of parsley and a French cornichon. To make into finger food, slice the pâté, cube the slices, and spear the cubes with toothpicks.*

# SOUPS

*To take a soup with a noise, or indeed to make a needless sound with the mouth while eating or drinking anything, is unrefined. To be candid, it is vulgar.*

—Frederick A. Stokes
Good Form: Dinners,
Ceremonious and Unceremonious
*(1903)*

" 'Can' is not a synonym for 'Soup,' " James Beard has said. The postwar revolution in cooking and eating began with the dethronement of the Can, and in particular that Soup Can that had replaced Mom's Apple Pie with Campbell's Cream of Tomato as a symbol of the American way of life. When John T. Dorrance first canned soup concentrates in 1897, the can was a synonym for man's progress and woman's liberation from cooking. In the First World War, the can was a synonym for patriotism, in such slogans as "We Can Can Vegetables and the Kaiser too." But during the Depression and the Second World War, the can suffered a change of image. For the hoboes by the track, for Rosie the Riveter home from the factory, for GIs abroad with their K-rations, the can became a synonym for rock-bottom subsistence.

To recapture the meaning and pleasure of eating and cooking, our revolutionaries mounted a joint offensive against the can. The strategy of Claiborne in his first cookbook in 1961 was to quote M. F. K. Fisher and then to supply 1,500 recipes to refute her dictum that American cuisine is based on "the flavor of innumerable tin cans." While the author of *Fannie Farmer* was exhorting women to "Experiment with canned soups to improve the flavor and give a 'homemade' taste," Beard and Child were opting for the real thing. "A good homemade soup in these days of the can opener," Child wrote in her first cookbook, "is almost a unique and always a satisfying experience." To a generation born to bottles and weaned on cans, the return to old-fashioned homemade soup stock had the force of revelation.

The rediscovery of homemade soup stock signaled a return not only to civilian life but to civilized life. Soup has always been a touchstone of what we eat, how we eat, and what we eat for. Because soup requires a heated vessel rather than a stick held over a fire to turn some raw bird or root into a cooked one, soup represents the first giant step from raw to cooked and the foundation, thereby, of cooking and culture. Soup demands a pot; a pot demands a potter. Civilization—the transformation of nature by art—begins with soup.

When our first hairy ancestor tossed some gnawed bones, a couple of roots, and a handful of spicy leaves into a pot of spring water to boil over a fire of twigs, he was creating the first pot on the fire, the *pot-au-feu,* or stockpot. In returning to home cooking, each of our four modern masters begins at the beginning with the "stock" that is the trunk and stem of cooking in English, or the *fond de cuisine* in French, because it represents the transformation of bone and root into artful flavor and nourishment.

James Beard's first general cookbook in 1959 was so basic that he began with how to boil water. He began, in other words, with the soup principle, which is how to flavor liquid, whether it is the illusory flavor of Stone Soup in folk tale or the costly flavor of Consommé aux Truffes in *nouvelle cuisine.* The whole range of food boiled in a pot, from sauces to stews where liquid is essential, can be charted on a grid of the liquid's flavor and texture. What is the source and intensity of the flavor? What is the texture: thin or thick, smooth or chunky? And if thick, what is the source of the thickening? Flour and butter, cream and egg, or some solid ingredient like a puréed vegetable?

The simplest way to categorize soups is by texture: thick or thin. That is the English way that, until the Second World War, dominated American menus, methods, and manners, including the Edwardian insistence that "a gentleman never has soup for lunch but *always* has soup for dinner." When soup was served 365 nights of the year, choice was simple. "Thick or thin, sir, thick or thin?" In his 1910 *Delicate Feasting,* Theodore Child expostulated: "Are there, then, but two soups in the world?"

The French way is to make simple division complex by introducing a class distinction between crude and refined. In *Mastering I,* Child adopts the French distinction between *soupes* and *potages. Soupe* is vulgar, *potage* is refined. French *soupe,* with its shared English roots in "supping" and "supper," suggests the "sop," or crust of bread dipped by hand into whatever liquid filled the bowl. French *potage,* like English "pottage," with shared roots in "pot" and "pod," suggests the container of the liquid and its contents. For the French, the noblest of all liquids is that distillation furthest removed from the lowly sop—a clear consommé, suggesting heavenly consummation by its name.

"Broth is to good cooking what wheat is to bread," émigré Pierre Blot advised Americans in his 1867 *Hand-Book of Practical Cookery.* But the French method of producing broth was under dispute among American cookbook authors in the nineteenth century. The traditional method "To Make French Pottage" was cited in *Martha Washington's Booke of Cookery* as follows: "Four hours before you goe to dinner or supper, hang over ye fire a good pot of water, with a pritty piece of beef and let it boyle an hour." French thrift, however, gave rise to the myth that any old table scrap would do as well as beef. Nonsense, said Miss Eliza Leslie in her 1837 *Directions for Cookery.* While confessing that "there is much *bad* soup to be found in France," Miss Leslie states that *"good* French cooks are not, as is generally supposed, really in the practice of concocting any dishes out of the refuse of the table." Miss Leslie divided her own soups between Rich Brown Soup, made of six pounds beef and six glasses claret, and Rich White Soup, made of a pair of large fat fowls.

Miss Leslie also devised a lengthy recipe for Portable Soup, beginning with the quantities of calves' shins, knuckles, and feet needed to be "made first into jelly and then congealed into hard cakes, resembling glue." She ended with her personal footnote: "If you have any friends going the overland journey to the Pacific, a box of portable soup may be a most useful present to them." The recipe so delighted Beard that he quotes it in its entirety in *American Cookery,* recognizing it as equivalent to our meat glaze or a properly made bouillon cube. Miss Leslie herself delights Beard because she is knowledgeable, forthright, and practical.

If there is any single thing that distinguishes our American masters from the French, it is the Yankee willingness to toss out theory that doesn't square with the facts. The facts of American life, as recognized by Miss Leslie, are that Americans are always on the move and the overland journey is a long way across. Portable food is necessary, in cube or can. Contemporary Americans are also always in a hurry and don't have time to watch an eternally bubbling stockpot on the back of a stove they may be commuting to and from. If our postwar revolutionaries were anti-can, they were also anti-doctrinaire. When a can serves, they said, use it.

For city commuters, the simmering stockpot is "foolish and outmoded," Fisher warns us, "and will make fuel bills rise and apartments smell." In his latest book, *The New James Beard,* Beard advises us on how to make such traditional soups as Lady Curzon or Boula-Boula with canned turtle soup. Even while extolling the virtues of homemade stock, Child always included canned substitutes for chicken, beef, or fish stock. She taught us to avoid canned consommés for their sweetness and bouillon cubes for their weak flavor and salty additives. But she also taught us how to improve canned broth by vegetables and herbs or bottled clam juice by wine and vermouth.

Flexibility and continued experimentation in ingredients, methods, and function turned our revolutionists into evolutionists. They have all worked to simplify stock as they have all worked to lighten their thickened liquids, to use less flour, butter, cream, or egg and more vegetable purées. They have replaced the food mill with the food processor for puréeing. They have increasingly suggested soups as hearty main dishes, the center of supping, instead of the opening stimulant. As they were the first to break through the code of English gentility and let in the heady aromas of Mediterranean Europe, so they have moved on to the exotic fragrances of the Far East.

By reinvigorating our native heritage of the stockpot, they introduced many of us for the first time to the strong particularities of immigrant stocks that have created our national palate. We savored French civility by means of French Onion and Sorrel Soup. We savored Russian and Polish earthiness by means of Borsch, or Spanish fire by means of Gazpacho. Returning to the roots of cooking meant returning to ethnic roots, roots that retained their unique flavor even while transforming and being transformed by the liquid in the common pot.

The soups that follow, arranged from thin to thick, constitute a brief list of soups that have been domesticated and integrated into American cooking and eating. On the overland journey from Atlantic to Pacific, the choice is no longer simply between Campbell's Cream of Tomato or Campbell's Chicken Noodle. For the backpacker, there are dozens of dehydrated or freeze-dried portable soups. For the commuter, there are dozens of ways of improving the flavor of the can. But far more of us have now discovered the unique and satisfying experience of returning to our primitive roots by putting herbs and bones in a pot on the fire to make soup a synonym for good cooking and eating.

# MIXED STOCK

The principle of stock is simple: to extract by slow heat the essence of bones, root vegetables, and herbs in order to flavor a liquid. The process requires time: time for simmering (4 to 5 hours), time to degrease (preferably by chilling overnight), and time to concentrate flavor by reducing liquid. The resulting stock can be as thin as broth or as thick as meat glaze if the liquid is reduced to a syrup (3 quarts of liquid to make 1 cup of glaze).

The only way to reduce time and fuel cost is to increase the proportion of meat to bone, since meat will give up its flavor more quickly. The ideal proportion for flavor, however, is half bone and half meat. The ideal cut of beef, therefore, is beef shin or shank, with veal knuckles and pork rind for body and marrow bones for richness. Best of all for gelatinous body are calves' feet, but few today can heed Child's directive in *Mastering I* that "they can usually be ordered from your butcher, and come skinned and cleaned." Beard suggests using chicken gizzards to produce a gelatinous chicken stock and advises the use of oxtails for a fine-bodied beef stock.

For those without time, canned beef or chicken broth, such as that put out by College Inn, can be improved by simmering with fresh vegetables and herbs. Canned broth is most useful as a base for cold soups when a jellied stock is not wanted.

Child's analysis of stocks in *Mastering I* is formidably comprehensive, classified by Simple, Brown, and White, Clarified for consommé, and Jellied for aspic. Beard's stock recipes are simpler, classified by Beef, Fowl, and Fish, and they tend to be heartier. My Mixed Stock recipe below aims for the rich flavors of a traditional *pot-au-feu,* which combines beef for heartiness, pork for succulence, and chicken for delicacy. Here flavor is all, purity nothing, and the greater the variety of flavors the better, as long as they mix and meld.

"There is excitement and real satisfaction in making an artful good soup from things usually tossed away," Fisher writes, "the washed tops of celery stalks, stems of parsley, skeletons of fowl, bones of animals." Thrift is another virtue of the Mixed Stock that can absorb whatever skeletons and bones you may have artfully saved in your freezer: chicken, duck, turkey carcasses; beef short ribs; leftover lamb and pork bones from chops and roasts. Vegetables, too, like mushroom stems, watercress stems, tomato paste squeezings, potato peelings, broccoli stems. As long as you know that a little lamb, pork, watercress, or broccoli will go a long way, you'll find that almost anything goes.

A few important points: Use cold water to cover because it extracts flavor better than warm. Use little salt because you may want to reduce your liquid considerably. Bring the liquid to the simmer without boiling to avoid muddying the waters. Remove scum three or four times during the first 10 minutes of simmering. To degrease, after simmering, drain the liquid through a colander into a pot that will fit into your refrigerator. You can easily lift the fat from the surface as soon as it has congealed. Reheat the stock and taste for flavor, reducing it as much as you need for concentration or for space saving. Pour into plastic bags for freezing. You should boil up unfrozen stock every 3 or 4 days to avoid spoilage. You can clarify stock by simmering it gently with a whipped egg white and crushed eggshell and then straining it carefully through several layers of wet cheesecloth. You can enrich stock by adding Madeira or brandy.

## Proportions

to get 2 quarts of medium-strength stock, use 4 pounds of bones and 4 cups of vegetables to 6 quarts of water (or enough to cover)

4 **pounds meat and fowl scraps and bones (including, if possible, a veal knuckle, beef marrow bones, ½ pound chicken gizzards)**
¼ **pound pork rind**
3 **large onions, chopped**
2 **large carrots, unpeeled but chopped**

3 **celery stalks with tops, chopped**
1 **leek, washed and chopped**
1 **turnip, chopped**
3 **cloves garlic, unpeeled but chopped**
1 **tablespoon salt**
1 **bay leaf**
1 **teaspoon thyme**

| | |
|---|---|
| 8 sprigs parsley | 4 whole cloves, or 6 Szechuan |
| 1 sprig rosemary | peppercorns |

1. Put the bones, scraps, and rind in a roasting pan. Add the chopped onions, carrots, and celery and roast in a 450-degree oven for 30 minutes, turning them to brown evenly.

2. Transfer them to a large stockpot (8 to 10 quarts) and cover with cold water. Deglaze the meat juices in the roasting pan with a little boiling water and add to the pot.

3. Bring to a simmer slowly and skim three or four times while the coagulated juices turn to scum. Add the chopped leek and turnip, garlic, and seasonings.

4. Partly cover the pot and simmer gently for 4 to 5 hours. Strain and chill the liquid. Remove the fat, reheat the stock, and taste for seasoning and strength. If the flavor is too weak, reduce by boiling the stock rapidly.

# POULTRY STOCK

## Proportions

to get 2 quarts stock, use 4 pounds chicken parts to 3 quarts water (or water to cover)

A good combination is 2 pounds necks, backs, wings, and carcasses, plus 2 pounds gizzards. Use the same vegetables and seasonings listed for Mixed Stock, but omit the turnip and add 6 crushed black peppercorns. Simmer for 2 to 3 hours.

# FISH STOCK

## Proportions

to get 2 cups fish stock, use 2 pounds of fish to 1 quart of liquid

| | |
|---|---|
| 2 pounds fish heads, skeletons, or small whole fish | 1 slice lemon |
| | Pinch of salt |
| 3 cups water (or to cover) | 6 parsley stems (leaves darken |
| 1 cup dry white wine | the stock) |
| 1 onion, sliced | 6 crushed white peppercorns, |
| 1 celery stalk with top, chopped | or 8 fennel seeds |

1. Wash the fish thoroughly and remove the gills on the fish heads (to avoid any bitter taste).

2. Put the fish in a saucepan, cover with water and wine, and skim when the liquid comes to a simmer. Add the chopped vegetables and seasonings, and simmer for 30 minutes. Longer simmering does not improve the flavor.

# FRENCH ONION

"It is the soup of soups," Fisher quotes the American Ambrose Heath in extolling the French soup that above all others symbolized the Europe we longed to get to after the Second World War. Essentially, French Onion Soup is a beef stock flavored with onions and fortified by a bread sop crusted with cheese. But how varied those essentials can be is evident in a recipe Fisher cites that calls for dry champagne, whipped eggs, half a Camembert, and thirty skinned walnuts, to "eat between 3 or 4 A.M. for optimism."

Despite the watery dilutions that now desecrate its name, French Onion was, and is, the classic peasant soup that nourishes and restores. As such, it was savored by all our masters, at dawn, among the workers of Les Halles or at the bars of the old transatlantic French Line or at the end, says Fisher, of "second-rate balls in French Switzerland." As such, it is worth the time it requires. "Count on 2½ hours at least," Child advises, because it needs a long, slow simmering to develop its flavor.

"More important than onions in a good onion soup," Claiborne adds, "is the beef stock with which it is made." If you begin with a canned beef broth, you may need to reduce it first (adding a few chopped vegetables) to intensify the flavor. If you begin with a good homemade stock, you may want to enrich it with stronger brews. Child calls for dry white wine. Beard calls for red wine or sherry or port. The heartier the liquid, the better. Child recommends further a "spirited finish" of egg yolks beaten with port or Madeira or a deluxe fillip of Worcestershire sauce, egg yolk, and Cognac.

Reversing the current trend toward simplicity, Child in her latest cookbook, *Julia Child & More Company,* has evolved a richer, thicker, crustier dish than ever. Here she ladles the liquid into a tureen between a top and bottom layer of French bread topped with mixed Swiss cheeses. In the recipe below, I have aimed for a simpler version that takes less time but still focuses on a highly spirited broth.

## Proportions

for 6 to 8 servings, use 6 cups onions to 10 cups of liquid, plus 1⅓ cups cheese

| | |
|---|---|
| **6 cups sliced yellow onions** | **1 tablespoon olive oil** |
| **6 tablespoons butter** | **½ teaspoon sugar (optional)** |

| | |
|---|---|
| 8 cups beef stock or broth | ¼ cup Cognac |
| 2 cups red wine (Beaujolais or Bardolino type) | Salt and freshly ground black pepper to taste |

### For the Crust

| | |
|---|---|
| 6 to 8 slices French bread | ⅓ cup grated Parmesan cheese |
| 1 cup grated, mixed Emmenthaler and Gruyère cheese | |

1. Sauté the onions gently in the butter and oil until they are wilted. *EITHER* sprinkle the onions with sugar and caramelize them over a high flame, turning constantly to avoid burning *OR* bake the onions for 1 hour in a slow oven (290 degrees) to get the same effect without sugar.

2. Combine the stock and wine, heat, and pour over the onions. Partly cover and simmer gently for 30 minutes. (If you want a slightly thickened broth, purée ½ cup of the cooked onions with a little stock in a blender and return the purée to the pot.) Add the Cognac and taste for seasoning.

3. Toast the bread on both sides in a 425-degree oven for a total of 5 to 7 minutes. Ladle the soup into a large oven-proof tureen or individual soup bowls. Float the bread on top, covered with the grated Swiss cheeses and topped with Parmesan. Bake for about 30 minutes in a 425-degree oven, or until the crusts are nicely browned and the cheese has melted.

*This is best as a meal in itself, served with a simple green salad and a hearty red wine.*

# SLAVIC BORSCH

Some like it hot. Some like it cold. Some like it in the pot with beef, cabbage, and onions. Some like it as a deep crimson consommé. "It can be hot, cold, thick, thin, rich, meager—and still be good," writes Fisher in praise of "one of the best soups in the world."

Claiborne offers a pair of thick hearty stews, Ukrainian and Russian, calling for beef, pork, and a variety of root vegetables. Beard also favors a soup that makes a one-dish meal with black bread and butter. Fisher offers a cold summer consommé and a hot winter vegetable soup and a thickened raw-beet soup she calls A Little Borsch, which is "Polish if you are Russian, Russian if you are Finnish, and so on." Child offers a cold soup with puréed cucumber for a variant. The only constants are beets, fresh or canned, and stock, chicken or beef.

But the essence of borsch is the opposition of sweet and sour, the sweetness of the root countered by vinegar or lemon or sour cream. Proportions are as variable as any of its ingredients and the degree of sweet and sour depends on personal taste, as well as ethnic origin. Color varies, too. You can intensify the redness of beetroot by adding freshly grated beets at the last moment. Or, you can turn crimson to magenta, deep rose, or pink by adding increasing amounts of yogurt or sour cream.

The version below is a fairly thick vegetable purée with a slightly chunky texture, in which color and acid are intensified by the addition of tomatoes, and in which horseradish counters the sweetness of both beets and leeks. For a thinner soup, merely add more stock. For a tarter soup, more vinegar. For a richer soup, more cream. This is a soup that is as good cold as hot and does well cold with yogurt, in addition to sour cream. It also does well with canned beets which, of course, are easier to use.

# Proportions

for 6 to 8 servings, use 5 cups of liquid to 3 cups of vegetables

| | |
|---|---|
| 2 cups cooked and grated beets | 2 tomatoes, peeled, seeded, and chopped |
| 4½ cups beef or chicken stock | Salt and freshly ground black pepper to taste |
| ¼ cup red wine vinegar or fruit vinegar | ½ cup sour cream, or ¼ cup yogurt and ¼ cup sour cream |
| 8 beet tops | |
| 1 small fresh beet (optional) | |
| 2 tablespoons butter | 2 tablespoons freshly grated horseradish, or 2 tablespoons chopped fresh dill |
| ¾ cup chopped leeks or onions | |

1.  Wash the beets gently. Cut the stalks off 6 inches above the beets to save the maximum juice. Either bake the beets in foil in a slow oven (290 degrees) for 1 hour, or simmer them in the beef stock 30 minutes. Drain, saving all liquid, and remove the skins.

2.  Grate the beets by hand or in a processor and marinate them in vinegar for 2 hours, if possible. Blanch the beet tops for 1 minute in boiling water and set aside for garnish. Peel the small fresh beet, grate it, and put it aside for garnish.

3.  Melt the butter and cook the leeks until soft. Add the tomatoes and cook for 3 or 4 minutes.

4.  In a saucepan, combine the beets and their liquid with the vegetables and the stock. Simmer gently for 15 minutes, or until all the

vegetables are tender. Taste carefully for seasoning, adding salt and pepper if needed and more vinegar if the soup is too sweet.

5.   Purée in a processor or food mill for a chunky texture, or in a blender for a completely smooth liquid. Add sour cream, or a mixture of sour cream and yogurt, to make a creamy texture and to help blend the flavors.

6.   Pour into bowls and put a dollop of sour cream in the center of each. Sprinkle with grated horseradish and grated raw beet. Add a green beet top, whole or shredded, for a striking color contrast.

*Note:*   To deepen the sour taste, add lemon juice. To deepen the sweet taste and red color, add port, Punt et Mes, or even Cassis.

*This is a filling soup, best complemented by a salad and slices of good rye or pumpernickel bread.*

# AMERICAN BLACK BEAN

"One of the greatest of all American soups," Beard calls it, in giving the recipe of Leon Lianides, whose Coach House Restaurant in New York has long featured the mellifluous purple-black purée that distinguishes this from all other bean soups. Child made the white bean soups of the French familiar to us, as Claiborne did the split pea soups of the Dutch. But these are country soups, halfway to *cassoulets* and the New England bean pot.

American Black Bean, on the other hand, is strictly a city soup, suave and urbane. It's an American example of the French distinction between a *soupe* and a *potage*. Whereas pork and beans make a *soupe*, puréeing the beans and cutting their creaminess with lemon juice and sherry or Madeira are methods appropriate to a *potage*. This particular *potage* is so rich that a small cup will suffice to begin a meal and a small bowl will make a meal by itself.

I have simplified The Coach House recipe, which calls for flour and beef bones, along with the essential elements of black beans, vegetables, some kind of pork, and some kind of fortified wine. The beans are usually flavored by ham hocks or shanks, but I find that pork rind alone supplies the melting smoothness one is after.

## Proportions

for 8 servings, use 2 cups beans and 2 cups of vegetables to 6 cups of liquid (or more to cover)

| | |
|---|---|
| 2 cups dried black beans | 1 small minced hot pepper, or |
| 1 6- to 8-inch square of pork rind | ¼ teaspoon cayenne pepper |
| 2 medium onions, chopped | ⅓ cup dry sherry or Madeira |
| 2 cloves garlic, chopped | ¼ cup fresh lemon juice |
| 3 to 4 celery tops, chopped | 8 slices lemon for garnish |
| 1 bay leaf | 4 tablespoons minced parsley |
| 2 whole cloves | for garnish |

1.   Prepare the beans by the quick-soak method. Cover with cold water. Bring to a fast boil and boil for 1 minute. Remove from the heat, cover, and let stand for 1 hour. Drain and discard the liquid.

2.   Put the pork rind in the bottom of a pot with the beans, chopped vegetables, bay leaf, cloves, and hot pepper. Cover with cold water. Bring to boil and simmer gently for 2 to 3 hours, or until the beans mash easily.

3.   Remove the pork rind. Add the sherry and lemon juice to the beans and purée in a blender. If the mixture is too thick, add boiling meat stock or broth to get the texture you want.

4.   Garnish each bowl with a thin slice of lemon, sprinkled with minced parsley. This soup improves with heating, but let it barely simmer to keep the lemon juice fresh tasting. This soup also freezes well and can be frozen almost as a concentrate to which you add boiling stock.

*A small cup is a good prelude to a steak or roast or similar meaty entrée.*

# RED PEPPER AND TOMATO

Nothing has radicalized homemade soups more than the food processor that has replaced the food mill for making purées—especially vegetable purées. Where the blender liquefied vegetables and turned soups into baby pap, as Child complained in her first book, the processor commands the full spectrum of chunky to smooth and has opened up a new world of vegetable combinations and textures.

Nowhere is this more evident than in the switch from traditional cream soups to soups using vegetable purées instead of cream. Take an American soup cliché like cream of tomato, canned by Campbell and cloned by Warhol. There are many ways to redeem its bad name, by using fresh ripe tomatoes instead of canned and by adding new unlikely flavors like sage, as Beard suggests, or concentrated orange juice and thyme.

But better yet is to get rid of the blandness of cream altogether and to revitalize tomato purée by another vegetable purée. *The New James Beard* has a good section on Basic Cream Vegetable Soup in which Beard suggests the use of instant mashed potato with vegetable purées for thickening if the vegetables have a high water content. Vegetables in different combinations can be used to thicken each other as well as to flavor each other.

In the recipe below, I have combined tomatoes with red peppers for both texture and flavor. And I have heightened the combination by marrying two favorite Italian-American tastes: a rich tomato sauce and roasted sweet red peppers. While either the sauce or the peppers, puréed separately with stock, make a good soup, together the acidity of the tomatoes is countered by the sweetness of the peppers and by the underlying flavor of roasted and charred skin.

You can also vary the stock. With a meat stock as base, the soup evokes a rich gazpacho. With a fish stock, the soup suggests a bouillabaisse. This is a soup that is as good cold as hot because the color and flavor are intense.

## Proportions

for 6 to 8 servings, use 2 cups of tomato sauce and 2 cups of puréed peppers to 4 cups of stock

| | |
|---|---|
| 3 cups ripe tomatoes, quartered and seeded | 2 tablespoons minced fresh basil, or 1 tablespoon dried |
| 1 medium onion, chopped | 1 bay leaf |
| 1 carrot, chopped | ¼ teaspoon thyme |
| 1 celery stalk with top, chopped | 6 sprigs parsley |
| 3 cloves garlic, crushed | Pinch of cayenne pepper |
| 2 tablespoons butter | Salt and freshly ground |
| 4 tablespoons olive oil | black pepper to taste |
| ½ cup beef stock | 4 sweet red peppers |
| | 4 cups meat or fish stock |

1. To make the tomato sauce, sauté the chopped tomatoes and other vegetables in the butter and oil until soft. Add ½ cup beef stock and the basil, bay leaf, thyme, parsley, cayenne pepper, salt, and pepper. Cover and simmer for 10 minutes. Uncover and simmer for about 20 minutes, or until the tomato liquid is reduced and the flavors have blended.

2. Roast the peppers under a hot broiler for about 10 minutes, turning them to blacken the skin on all sides. Put them in a paper bag for a few minutes to steam and loosen the skins. Remove the skins and seeds (under cold water if too hot to handle).

3. Purée the tomato sauce in a blender with 1 cup stock, in order to pulverize the tomato skins. Chop 3 of the peppers and purée them in

a processor. Combine the peppers and tomatoes, and gradually add the stock to make the soup thick or thin. Simmer for a few minutes to blend the flavors.

4. Cut the remaining pepper into thin strips (julienne) for garnish. Serve the soup either very hot or very cold.

*This is a piquant appetizer to precede a hearty entrée of meat or fowl or a cream-sauced pasta.*

# GREEN SORREL

Although sorrel, the cultivated offspring of a family of wild sour grasses, is native to America as well as to France, when Claiborne introduced Cold Cream of Sorrel Soup in his first cookbook, its associations were entirely French. Here were yolks and cream to thicken a broth of pale green, flavored by a puréed leaf more sour by far than watercress or spinach. Child gave sorrel as a variant of Cream of Watercress, citing its French names, *Potage Crème d'Oseille* or *Potage Germiny.* In those days, most of us first encountered sorrel in a can, labeled *oseille* and imported from France.

Today, many of us grow sorrel in our gardens and curse its weedy spread, since it grows even faster than the number of uses *nouvelle cuisine* cooks have found for it, from soups to sauces and salads and even desserts. Its associations remain French, even though it appears often in early American cookbooks as one of the ingredients of a green garden soup. Fisher, in fact, gives a garden soup based on sorrel and lettuce (named *Potage Else,* for a friend) that is halfway between a mixed vegetable cream soup and the classic French version that uses sorrel alone.

Our tolerance for the distinctive sour of sorrel seems to have grown, since Claiborne's early proportions of ½ pound sorrel to 5 cups broth and 2 cups cream are very different from Beard's recent proportions of 1 pound sorrel to 3 cups broth and 1 cup cream. The major variable with sorrel is the leaf itself that becomes more sour the bigger and older it gets. Half a pound of young sorrel will be very delicate in comparison to half a pound of old sorrel. The best way to sweeten the disposition of the old is to wilt the leaves, stripped from their stems, in butter for 5 to 10 minutes before puréeing. The purée can then be frozen, if desired, for later use in soup and sauce.

## Proportions

for 4 to 6 servings, use ½ to 1 pound sorrel (depending on age, old or young) to 5 cups of thickened liquid

½ to 1 pound sorrel leaves (to
make ½ to 1 cup purée)
4 tablespoons butter or peanut
oil
4 cups chicken stock
¼ teaspoon white pepper

Pinch of cayenne pepper
Salt to taste
1 cup heavy cream
4 egg yolks
Fresh chervil sprigs for
garnish

1.   Taste the sorrel and, if it is quite sour, wilt it for 1 or 2 minutes in melted butter in a covered pan. If the sorrel is very sour and the leaves are very large, cut them in strips and wilt for 5 to 10 minutes.

2.   Purée the sorrel in a blender with 1 cup of stock until the liquid is absolutely smooth. Return to the pan, add the remaining stock, white pepper, cayenne, and salt and simmer for 5 to 10 minutes to blend.

3.   Beat the cream and egg yolks together and add gradually to the hot stock. Let the mixture thicken gently a minute or two just below a simmer. Return the mixture to the blender to smooth it further. Serve very hot or very cold. Garnish, if possible, with a sprig of fresh chervil, a tiny sorrel leaf, or a drop or two of beet juice swirled into each cup, just before serving, for a marbled effect.

*Note:* A good gelatinous stock will solidify when cold as the jelly sets. To liquefy, put the mixture in a processor or blender just before serving.

Instead of the usual chicken stock, try a fish stock, which alters character by altering association and evokes those creamy green sauces often served with salmon or bass.

*The tartness of sorrel makes it a good provocative for a fish or chicken entrée. Because of the rich cream, it's best to avoid a cream sauce on your main dish.*

# HOT VICHYSSOISE

The idea of a *hot* Vichyssoise is somewhat but not entirely perverse. *Fannie Farmer* of thirty years ago gave two recipes for Vichyssoise, one cold and one hot. Even thirty years ago, the ersatz French label was what gave the soup class, far more than its humble ingredients of leek and potato or the method of chilling invented as a bit of show business by Louis Diat for New York's Ritz-Carlton hotel in 1910. Even twenty years ago, Claiborne was still complaining that "someone should start a campaign to instruct Americans that vichyssoise is not pronounced veeshy-swah . . . It is veeshee-swahze." So the credentials of veeshee-swahze are a bit hokey to begin with.

At one time, according to Fisher, the "gastronomical voodoo" associated with this soup was as rigid as the ritual martini: cream of 24 percent fat content, brought to a 196-degree Fahrenheit simmer, seasoned by $\frac{1}{16}$ teaspoon ground mace. At one time, as in Beard's first recipe for it, the proportions were as fat-making as 2 cups vegetable broth to 4 cups heavy (or sour) cream.

But today's voodoo puts a watery prefab desecration on the menu of every roadside diner. Today Vichyssoise, however Americans pronounce it, demands as much revitalization as Campbell's Cream of Tomato. In *The New James Beard*, the master varies the cold cream of potato soup he originally sold at his shop, Hors d'Oeuvre, by adding chopped raw apple, or cooked carrot, turnip, or watercress to replace some of the leeks, or a garnish of caviar along with the chives. He even rings in a Scotch Vichyssoise made of leek and potato puréed with smoked finnan haddie.

However named or varied, the marriage of leek and potato is too good and too permanent to founder on a cliché and one way to reinvigorate it is to return to the idea of a hot purée. Today's voodoo no longer requires that the purée be strained twice through a "tammy" (fine-meshed) sieve. The processor will produce a nicely textured purée and the blender a perfectly smooth one. Because potatoes provide thickening as well as flavor, the kind and proportion of liquids used will vary according to your need for a thick or thin soup.

## Proportions

for 6 to 8 servings, use 6 cups of vegetables to 6 to 8 cups of stock and cream

| | |
|---|---|
| 3 tablespoons butter | Pinch of cayenne pepper |
| 3 cups sliced leeks (or half leeks and half onions) | Pinch of mace or nutmeg |
| | Salt to taste |
| 3 cups diced potatoes | 1 cup heavy cream (or half |
| 6 cups boiling chicken stock | sour cream or half yogurt) |
| ½ teaspoon white pepper | Chopped chives for garnish |

1. Melt the butter in a large saucepan, add the leeks, and cook gently until soft. Add the potatoes and pour in the boiling stock. Add the white pepper, cayenne, mace, and salt and simmer, partly covered, for about 30 minutes, or until the vegetables are tender.

2. Purée the mixture in a processor or blender and return it to the pan. Thin the purée with cream to get the texture you want. Heat the mixture to just below a simmer (to avoid separating the sour cream or yogurt, if used) and pour into individual cups. Garnish with chopped chives.

*The soup is rich from the cream and potatoes, but a small cup is a good prelude to a main dish, such as a broiled chop or fish.*

# CREAM OF MUSSEL

America is rich in mussels but poor in uses for them, so that most of our recipes for this delectable seafood reflect the influence of France. Steamed mussels, like steamed clams, consist of two equally good parts: the broth and the seafood whole. In her first book, Child teaches us how to steam mussels with wine in the French way called *moules marinière* and how to turn the broth into a soup by thickening it with egg and cream. She furnishes another traditional Soupe aux Moules in *Julia Child & More Company* by adding leftover whole mussels to a robust vegetable soup based on a curried cream sauce. In both, the thickening comes from some other ingredient than the mussels.

The most renowned cream of mussel soup on these shores was created by the transplanted French chef Pierre Franey, for the Pavillon in New York, in its days of greatness under Henri Soulé. As Diat renamed cream of potato Vichyssoise, after a French resort, Vichy, so Franey renamed cream of mussel Billi Bi, after a tin tycoon, William B. Leeds. The soup and its creator achieved instant fame when Claiborne called the former "the most elegant and delicious soup ever created," and the latter "one of this nation's greatest chefs." It could be said that we owe the subsequent achievements of the Claiborne-Franey team to a whimsically named mussel soup.

Franey uses whole steamed mussels only for garnish, since it's the broth he's after, thickening it with 1 egg yolk to 2 cups heavy cream. Beard adds another egg yolk in his recipe for Billi Bi to make the broth even richer.

In my version below, I've puréed some of the whole mussels themselves to intensify the flavor while thickening the broth. You can omit the egg yolk entirely this way, if you like, but you'll get a creamier texture if you use 1 yolk and a little cream. The result is halfway between a cream soup and a bisque, such as oyster or clam, that uses a minimum of fatty cream.

The only problem with mussels is the cleaning. French fish stalls often have electric machines that clean by hydraulic abrasion and eject, in a matter of minutes, shiny black sandless shells. Here, unfortunately, we must still scrub the shells in cold water (I use a dish brush with metal bristles), pull off any weedy beards, and then soak the shells in a sink or bucket of cold water with a little flour to get rid of any final sand. Boring, but necessary.

## Proportions

for 4 to 6 servings, use 1½ quarts (2 pounds) mussels to 1 cup wine and 3 cups fish stock

| | |
|---|---|
| 1½ quarts (2 pounds) well-cleaned mussels | 2 sprigs parsley |
| 2 shallots, minced | ¼ teaspoon thyme |
| 1 small onion, minced | 1 bay leaf |
| 1 clove garlic, minced | Pinch of cayenne pepper |
| 1 tablespoon butter | Salt and freshly ground black pepper to taste |
| 1 cup dry white wine | 1 egg yolk |
| 3 cups fish stock or clam juice | ¼ to ½ cup heavy cream |

1.   Put the cleaned mussels in a large pot with the chopped vegetables, butter, wine, stock, parsley, and seasonings. Cover tightly, bring to a quick boil, and steam for 4 to 7 minutes, or until the shells open.

2.   Remove the mussels from the shells when they are cool enough to handle. Strain the broth carefully through a double thickness of cheesecloth to avoid any residual sand.

3.   Purée 6 to 8 mussels in a blender with 1 cup broth. Pour into the remaining broth and bring gently to a simmer.

4.   Beat the egg yolk with the cream and add slowly to the purée, thickening it gently just below a simmer. Return the soup to the blender to make the cream absolutely smooth. To thin, add more stock or cream. To thicken, purée 1 or 2 more mussels. Garnish each bowl with a single whole mussel.

*It's good to follow an intense fish soup, such as this, with a contrasting meat or fowl, because the soup acts as a fish course.*

# LOBSTER BISQUE

Bisque was originally a rich soup made by boiling down game birds, and only later did it become associated with crayfish and finally lobster and crab. Whatever beast is used, bisque connotes a soup that is rich, thick, and intense. In a lobster bisque, intensity of flavor and of color derives from the cooked shells.

Child's lobster bisque, in *Mastering II,* begins with an anatomy lesson on the lobster so exquisitely detailed and illustrated that soup-making is swallowed up in the arts of surgery. Her soup is a baroque production calling for 3 to 4 live lobsters to make 6 to 8 servings. Thrift enters by using only the chests and legs for the bisque and reserving the tails, claws, and liver for a lobster dish like Homard à l'Américaine.

In bisque recipes, the proportion of lobster to serving varies radically since flavor is extracted from the shells rather than the meat, which is used for garnish. The thriftiest bisque, then, uses shells only, as in a Claiborne-Franey recipe that makes soup from 3 lobster carcasses. The recipe below is a compromise in which I've used 2 carcasses to 1 live lobster. Whenever I serve lobster, I freeze the shells afterward for soup. But if you have no carcasses on hand, you simply use another live lobster. In addition to its shell and meat, the live lobster also provides juice and the interior liver (the green tomalley) and coral (the pink eggs, if the lobster is female). The flavor is strongest in these inner trappings.

The deep orange of the bisque is further intensified by tomatoes, in the form of pulp and sometimes paste. Liquid is usually a combination of wine and stock, spiked by Cognac. Thickening is traditionally provided by rice rather than flour and enrichment is provided by cream. This is a soup that depends far more on process than ingredients: The point is to squeeze flavor by every possible means from the obdurate shell.

## Proportions

for 6 to 8 servings, use 2½ pounds lobster shell and meat to 2½ cups of vegetables and 8 cups of liquid

| | |
|---|---|
| 1 1- to 1½-pound live lobster | 1 small red or green hot |
| 2 lobster carcasses | pepper, or ¼ teaspoon |
| 2 tablespoons oil | cayenne pepper |
| 6 tablespoons butter | Salt and freshly ground |
| ¼ cup Cognac | black pepper to taste |
| 1 small onion, diced | 1½ cups dry white wine |
| 1 carrot, diced | 2 cups boiling beef or |
| 2 celery stalks, diced | chicken stock |
| 1 clove garlic, mashed | ¼ cup raw white rice |
| 1 to 2 cups chopped fresh | 3 cups fish stock (or half |
| tomatoes | clam juice) |
| 1 bay leaf | ½ to 1 cup heavy cream |
| 1 tablespoon dried tarragon, | |
| or 2 tablespoons chopped | |
| fresh tarragon | |

1.  Kill the lobster by severing the chest from the tail. (A quick thrust with a sharp knife will sever the spinal cord.) Cut up the lobster over a bowl to save all juices. Cut off the tail in one piece. Cut straight up the underside of the chest to remove the small stomach pouch at the top of the shell and the long dark vein that runs from the pouch to the tail. Scrape the green liver and any pink coral that may be inside the shell into a bowl. Cut off the legs and claws and crack the claws with a hammer or lobster cracker.

2.  With heavy shears or lobster shears, cut up the live and leftover lobster carcasses in small pieces (except for the tail of the live lobster,

which is to be used for garnish). Heat the pieces in the oil and 3 table-spoons of the butter over high heat for about 5 minutes, or until all the pieces have turned bright orange. Pour the Cognac over them and ignite (by match or flame from a gas burner).

3. Melt the remaining butter in a separate pan. Add the chopped vegetables and cook until soft. Add to the lobster pieces. Add the bay leaf, tarragon, hot pepper, salt, and pepper. Pour in the wine and bring to a boil. Partly cover and simmer for 20 minutes.

4. When the shells are cool enough to handle, remove the meat from the tail and claws and set it aside. Cut up the tail shell in small pieces and put the shells, except for the claws, into a blender with a cup or more of boiling beef stock. Do only a few pieces at a time to avoid clogging the machine and add enough stock each time so that the machine can move. Begin slowly and gradually increase speed to pulverize the shells as much as possible. Strain the mixture through a sieve, pressing the shells and scraping the bottom of the sieve to extract as much liquid as possible. Add to the remaining beef stock.

5. Boil the rice in 1 cup of fish stock in a covered pan for about 20 minutes. Put the rice in the blender, along with the reserved liver, coral, and any juices and blend until smooth. Add to the rest of the fish stock.

6. Combine the liquids, bring to a slow simmer, and add the cream. Taste carefully for seasoning. Add more Cognac if the flavor is thin and more cayenne if bland. Garnish each bowl with a piece of lobster meat from tail or claw that has been heated gently in a little butter and Cognac.

*This is a fine main dish because it is a hard act to follow, except by a salad and an elegantly classical dessert, such as a fruit tart or a soufflé.*

# COD AND CLAM CHOWDER

Even though chowder gets its name from the big stew pot called *chaudière* on the French side of the Atlantic, on the American side a pot of clams, pork, potatoes, and onions seems quintessentially Yank. Fisher confesses that she was astonished, and a little put out, to find the best "New England chowder" she ever ate served up in Madame Prunier's restaurant in Paris. Somehow Yankee chowder so evokes foggy coasts and hungry fishermen that it ought to taste better the closer to salt air and sea.

For Beard, a chowder made of razor clams evokes the entire seascape of his childhood on Oregon's coast. In *The New James Beard,* he gives yet another version of My Clam Soup That Cures. Hot milk, enriched with a little cream and butter, and flavored intensely by clams, is a combination that cures by soothing troubled memories as well as appetites.

Because razor clams are available only in the West, most of us must be cured either by the hard-shelled clams called little necks or the soft-shelled clams called big necks. The names are misnomers, since the necks aren't necks at all but siphons that work like vacuum cleaners to suck up food for the clam. Worse yet, hard-shelled clams are renamed according to size: "littlenecks" for the smallest, "cherrystones" for the middle-sized, and "quahogs" for the biggest. Soft-shelled clams, of whatever size, are renamed "steamers."

Traditionally, quahogs have been the staple of clam chowder because chopping and stewing was the best way to make their toughness tender. But any kind of clams can be used as the essence of flavor is in the clam broth. Whatever else goes in—sometimes corn instead of or in addition to clams and sometimes a heretical tomato from Manhattan—pork, onions, and hot milk are essential, says Fisher, "for reasons of gastronomical, regional, and even national honor and integrity."

To these essentials I have added a solid white-fleshed fish, such as cod, to give the stock more body and to make the soup a fuller meal. The result is a fish chowder in which the flavor of clams dominates but in which all danger of rubbery clam meat is avoided by using the clams whole instead of chopped. This is a soup that tastes best made a day ahead and reheated after the flavors have ripened.

## Proportions

for 6 to 8 servings, use 2 pounds of fish and 2 dozen clams to 3 cups of vegetables and 7 cups of liquid

| | |
|---|---|
| 2 **pounds cod, halibut, or haddock fillets** | 2 **thick slices salt pork, diced** |
| 1 **teaspoon thyme** | 1 **large onion, sliced** |
| **Salt and freshly ground black pepper to taste** | 1 **clove garlic, minced** |
| | 2 **baking potatoes, diced** |
| 2 **dozen small hard-shell or soft-shell clams** | 1 **bay leaf** |
| | **Pinch of cayenne pepper** |
| 4 **cups fish stock** | 2 **cups hot milk** |
| | 1 **cup heavy cream** |

1. Cut the fish fillets in 2-inch squares, season with thyme, salt, and black pepper, wrap in plastic, and refrigerate for 2 hours or more so the seasonings will permeate the flesh.

2. Scrub the clams thoroughly to remove all sand. If using soft-shells, add ½ cup cornmeal to a pail of water to help the clams purge themselves before scrubbing them.

3. Steam the clams open in a covered pot, using 2 cups of the fish stock for liquid. When cool enough to handle, remove the clams from the

shells and set them aside, keeping them moist with a little broth. Strain the broth carefully through a double layer of cheesecloth to eliminate any trace of sand.

4.   Sauté the diced pork in a soup kettle. If the pork is very lean, you may have to add a little butter. If it is very fat, pour off all but 1 tablespoon of fat. Add the onion, garlic, potatoes, clam broth, remaining stock, bay leaf, and cayenne and bring to a boil. Add 1 cup of *hot* milk and the cream and simmer until the potatoes are barely done (about 5 minutes). Use the remaining cup of milk to thin the liquid if needed.

5.   Remove from the heat and add the fish to the hot soup. If made a day ahead, the soup should be refrigerated immediately to prevent the fish from cooking. Next day, let the soup sit at room temperature before reheating gently, just before serving. The point is not to overcook the fish. For the same reason, add the reserved clams just before serving so that they will warm through but not toughen.

*This is a filling and satisfying main dish, particularly good for Sunday suppers since it's best made a day ahead and left to ripen.*

# MINESTRONE

"If Italy can be said to have a national soup," Claiborne wrote in his first book, "minestrone is it." Over the last twenty years minestrone has become as Americanized as pizza, partly because of the trend toward vegetables and partly because of the trend toward one-dish meals. The vegetable chowder that the Italians call minestrone and the French call *soupe au pistou* eminently fulfills the idea of a vegetable main course that is as simple as soup.

What separates a simple garden soup from minestrone is the presence of beans and pasta for full nourishment and of basil and cheese for full flavor. The heartiest form of minestrone combines three soups in one: a bean soup, a vegetable soup, and a soup based on the garlic, oil, and basil sauce that the Italians call *pesto* and the French *pistou*. The minestrone recipe in *The New James Beard* omits the *pesto* but is exemplary of the number and kinds of vegetables that can go into the pot, including Swiss chard and cabbage. Beard's recipe also illustrates how American the soup has become, since he attributes this version to the most recent embodiment of *Fannie Farmer*, Marion Cunningham.

The character of a minestrone will depend on what vegetables are in season and what tastes you prefer. In my version, I have chosen vegetables that are light and crisp and have bound them with a rich *pesto*, omitting the macaroni or spaghetti to keep the soup lighter with garden produce. To make the soup lighter still, omit the *pesto* altogether and add basil leaves fresh or dried without the garlic and oil.

# Proportions

for 6 to 8 servings, use 5 cups of vegetables to 8 cups of liquid, plus ½ cup of *pesto*

½ cup dried beans, such as Great Northern, white pea beans, lima beans, or French flageolets
2 tablespoons olive oil
1 small onion, chopped
2 tomatoes, peeled, seeded, and chopped
8 cups hot chicken stock

1 cup green beans
1 small zucchini, diced
1 small yellow squash, diced
8 to 12 snow peas or sugar-snap peas
A few fresh green leaves of spinach, watercress, or turnip

## *Pesto* Sauce

1½ cups basil leaves
2 cloves garlic, chopped
¼ cup olive oil
2 tablespoons softened butter
¼ cup pine nuts (optional)

Salt and freshly ground black pepper to taste
½ cup grated Parmesan cheese

1. Prepare the beans by the quick-soak method. Cover with cold water, bring to a boil, boil for 1 minute, and remove from the heat. Cover the pot and let sit for 1 hour. Drain. Cover with cold salted water and simmer gently for 1 hour, or until the beans are just tender.

2. Heat the oil and cook the onion until soft. Add the tomatoes. Cover with hot stock. Add the vegetables in order of cooking time, beginning with the green beans, then the squashes, then the peas and the chopped green leaves at the last minute. The vegetables should keep their crunch. Combine with the cooked and drained dried beans If you want a thicker stock, add some of the bean liquid.

3. To make the *pesto*, pack the basil leaves in a blender with the garlic, oil, softened butter, and pine nuts. If the mixture is too thick for the blender, add enough stock to blend. Adjust seasoning with salt and pepper. Reserve the *pesto* in a bowl and stir in ¼ cup Parmesan cheese.

4. Pour the soup into serving bowls and swirl a large spoonful of *pesto* into each bowl. Sprinkle with the remaining cheese or pass it separately. Serve the soup immediately to prevent the vegetables from wilting in the hot broth.

*As this soup does not include pasta, pasta-lovers can follow it with pasta as a main dish, washed down with plenty of Chianti.*

# GAZPACHO

In his *American Cookery,* Beard indicates how long ago this Spanish soup emigrated to America, by quoting Mrs. Mary Randolph's recipe in *The Virginia Housewife* of 1826 for "Gaspacho, a Salad." Her recipe called for soft biscuit or bread covered with fresh tomatoes, cucumbers, and onion in a liquid of tomato juice, mustard oil, and water. Half salad, half soup.

And so it has remained in its myriad variations. Claiborne called it "a liquid salad," in his first book, and puréed it in a blender with raw eggs, tomato juice, and olive oil. In *Julia Child & More Company,* it is a picnic salad made decorative in a glass bowl by layering alternately red, green, and white diced vegetables. Fisher, eschewing a blended salad as a "basically unattractive mess," recalls a freakish version that a friend named "Guzpatchee," from its ingredients of raw vegetables, hardtack, and bottled mayonnaise. After experiences such as these, Fisher confesses that in her search for the "true" gazpacho she gracefully admitted defeat.

Now that gazpacho is as common as Vichyssoise, and often as awful when served for an exotic name rather than substance, its true nature is more than ever ambivalent. The only certainties are that it is always cold, mostly raw, and usually bound by a mixture of oil and vinegar. The virtues of this hybrid are obvious in that you can make it thick or thin, chunky or smooth, mild or fiery hot. You can spoon it or drink it. You can make it a meal or a cocktail, by adding vodka, gin, or Pernod, to end with a Bloody Mary salad.

Beard's California Gazpacho (in *American Cookery*) is relatively classic in its ingredients of garlic, tomatoes, cucumbers, green peppers, and onions in a liquid of tomato juice, seasoned by olive oil, vinegar, and Tabasco sauce, and garnished with croutons and ice cubes of frozen tomato juice. You simply chop the vegetables fine and stir them into the juice.

My version is more complicated only because I like a darker, thicker, richer liquid than puréed raw tomato provides. Consequently, I add wine and meat stock to the juice and reduce it somewhat to intensify flavor. I also like the liquid, once it is icy, to be peppery hot and so prefer a *salsa picante* to Tabasco. The pleasures of the "true" gazpacho lie in just such contradictions as an icy-hot salad-soup.

## Proportions

for 6 to 8 servings, use 3 cups of vegetables to 6 cups of liquid. To change soup to salad, omit the liquid, retaining only the oil and vinegar dressing

| | |
|---|---|
| 1 **cup red wine** | 2 **cups meat stock** |
| 3 **cups tomato or vegemato juice** | 1 **clove garlic, mashed** |

2 tablespoons wine vinegar or
  fruit vinegar
3 large tomatoes, peeled,
  seeded, and diced
1 large cucumber, peeled and
  diced
1 green bell pepper, diced
1 red bell pepper, diced
1 celery stalk, minced

4 green onions, minced
⅓ cup olive oil
2 tablespoons minced parsley,
  or 1 tablespoon minced
  cilantro (Chinese parsley)
  Dash of *salsa picante* or
  Tabasco sauce
  Salt and freshly ground
  black pepper to taste

## Garnish

½ cup bread cubes
2 tablespoons olive oil

1 clove garlic, minced

1. Mix the wine with the juice and stock in a saucepan. Add the garlic and simmer uncovered for 5 to 10 minutes. Add the vinegar and chill until ready to assemble the other ingredients.

2. Prepare the raw vegetables by dicing them into small uniform cubes, about ¼ inch square. Add to the chilled juice. Stir in the olive oil and seasonings. Taste carefully. If you want a thicker liquid, purée a cup of the vegetables in a blender or processor and add to the rest. Chill until ready to serve.

3. Prepare the croutons for garnish by frying the bread cubes in hot oil for 2 or 3 minutes, tossing them to brown evenly, and adding the garlic at the last minute. Garnish each bowl with a handful of croutons.

*Gazpacho, because it connotes informality, is especially good for backyard barbecues on hot summer nights when beer is the going drink.*

# SAUCES

*To put any kind of sauce—be it the best in the world—on such a dish as fresh sole or salmon, steak or chop is as unpardonable as it would be to pour cologne over a bunch of fragrant violets.*

—Henry T. Finck
Food and Flavor *(1913)*

S auce is the key to the cooking of any culture. The Far East has its salted and fermented soy, India its hot curries, Mexico and Spain its *salsa picante*, England its bread sauce and America its bottled ketchup. But France is different. France has 200 or more named sauces. Whether you regard sauce as a foppish perversion of nature, as Henry T. Finck did, or as the summit of gastronomic art, French cooking is synonymous with sauce.

In the territory of the sauce our cooking revolutionists had to battle on two fronts. They had to fight an Anglo-American prejudice against French cooking as snobbish, phony, and pretentious. The art of French cooking, said an eighteenth-century English gentlewoman appropriately named Anne Cook, is "the art of making *bad meat edible.*" The art, in other words, of "the sauce." Many an American, from Henry Thoreau to Calvin Trillin, has condemned the sauce as not only overkill but cover-up. If the meat is good, why muck it up with all those rich, heavy, fancy French perfumes?

On the other front, our revolutionists had to fight an Anglo-American prejudice for the bottled sauce (H-P, Worcestershire, mustard, ketchup) and for a glutinous, lumpy, gray-brown library paste called gravy. American Red-Eye Gravy, made from ham fat, flour, and boiling coffee, was too often a form of Depression Gravy, designed to make inedible gristle at least swallowable. A bottled sauce like Heinz ketchup was designed to make any kind of gunk taste at least of ketchup. Talk about cover-up. If American soup was synonymous with the can, American sauce was synonymous with the bottle.

The strategy of our revolutionists was to debunk the mystique of French sauces in order to introduce their variety and quality into home cooking. "Sauces are the splendor and glory of French cooking," Child told us in *Mastering I,* "yet there is nothing secret or mysterious about them." She spoke in response to Theodore Child, who warned that the splendor of French sauces was beyond the reach of the home cook: "In a modest household it is impossible to make them; they require professional skill, expensive materials and extensive apparatus." Or in response to Irma Rombauer, who warned readers of her 1943 *Joy of Cooking* of the mystique of mayonnaise: "Don't try to make mayonnaise if a thunderstorm threatens or is in progress, as it simply will not bind."

The difference between gravy and sauce is like the difference between *soupe* and *potage*. At its best, gravy suggests the natural pan juices of meat, fish, or fowl returned to the beast that lost them in the process of cooking. Pan Gravy used to be called Drawn Gravy because the juices were stretched or drawn out by water or wine to make stock. In the origins of Western cooking, "gravy" referred to a white dressing created by stretching a broth with almond milk. "Sauce," on the other hand, meant something heavy with salt, like the rotted fish entrails called *garum* that Romans splashed on their food like ketchup. Sauce got into English by way of the brine and vinegar used in pickling sows, as in a receipt in *Martha Washington's Booke of Cookery*, "How to Souce a 2 or 3 Shilling Pig." Nowadays, sauce in contrast to gravy suggests something with class, something French.

If civilization begins with soup, it evolves with sauce. As soup requires a pot to transfer flavor from bone to liquid, so sauce requires a pan to distill and concentrate flavor. If soup is flavored liquid, sauce is liquid flavoring. It appeals to one or more of the four sensations of taste, combining them variously—salt, sour, bitter, sweet. At one end of the spectrum, sauce liquefies into soup and at the other end solidifies into relishes and condiments. No wonder sauce defines the nature of cooking as the sauce-maker defines the art of cooking.

The sauce has two functions: to flavor and to bind. What distinguishes French sauce is that both flavor and binding are based on butter. The original mother of all the French "Mother Sauces" is the butter drawn out by flour and milk to make Sauce Béchamel. Typically, the name is royal, honoring one of Louis XIV's stewards, the Marquis de Béchamel. The French method is to cook a paste of butter and flour before adding liquid to make it thick or thin. Properly understood, the process is simple, but until Child's masterly anatomy of the French family of sauces, American housewives were intimidated by fear of the lump. "The most difficult step for a beginner," *Fannie Farmer* warns in 1948, "is to make a perfectly smooth sauce."

A perfectly smooth sauce became easier for a beginner once the French wire whisk replaced the rotary egg beater or kitchen spoon. A perfectly smooth sauce became child's play once the blender and finally the processor became standard kitchen fixtures. Technology ended the sauce mystique as it dispelled fear of curdle and lump. Better yet, these mechanical arms opened up a new range of sauces by thickening liquid with puréed vegetables, fruits, and cheese. Flour-based sauces diminished once we understood how mushrooms, onions, garlic, basil, parsley, peaches, bananas, ricotta, or chèvre could be both flavorers and binders, solids and liquids. We could get rid of sieves along with egg beaters. Sauces became lighter, smoother, wilder in their combinations of bitter and sweet, salt and sour.

The difficulties of binding butter to egg, as in hollandaise, or oil to egg, as in mayonnaise, were no longer formidable. Salad dressings did not have to come from a bottle because they were so easy to make. There were fewer midnight calls like the one I got from a panicked teenager who asked, "Look, if you're out of mayonnaise, is there any way to make it?" Technology coincided with a change in taste that replaced the English or German boiled dressing with the homemade mayonnaise of the French. Fisher's "almost painful craving for mayonnaise" in later life she attributes entirely to her grandmother's insistence on Boiled Dressing, composed of cider vinegar, flour, and salt, boiled until done and served over wet shredded lettuce.

Our revolutionists changed the meaning of "French Dressing" in America from a bright orange bottled liquid composed of sugar, vinegar, flour, and food coloring to a transparent emulsion of olive oil and vinegar called French vinaigrette. They displaced sugar and vinegar with fresh lemon juice, cheap salad oils with quality olive. They broke through the Garlic Barrier and made garlic as respectable as green and yellow onions. They experimented with exotic soy sauces and hot peppers and curries. They even changed the meaning of native American ketchup by making fresh tomato purées and hotted-up barbecue sauces. They restored the good name of gravy by making it the quintessence of sauce. And they accustomed red-blooded Americans to the notion that a sauced salmon, steak, or chop could be as honest and sincere as a naked one. They even persuaded some that the art of the sauce was the art of making good meat better.

# PAN JUICE

Since the principle of sauce is to intensify the flavor of a major ingredient, either by adding more of the same or by complementing it with another flavor or texture, sauce begins with recycling juices extracted by heat. The simplest way of retrieving those juices is to deglaze a roasting pan or skillet with a little boiling water in order to loosen any particles of juice or meat stuck to the pan. The best way, however, is to deglaze a pan with boiling *stock* (and/or wine), by adding fish stock to a pan of fish, meat or poultry stock to a pan of meat or poultry.

The first step is to remove as much fat as possible, after tipping the pan so that the fat will rise to the top as the juice drops to the bottom. The second step is to loosen particles with a spatula as you pour in the hot liquid. The third step is to reduce the liquid by boiling to concentrate flavor.

There are two difficulties here. One is that pan gravy requires last-minute work at the least convenient time if you're serving up a dinner party. The other is that there may not be enough juice to go around, so that any added liquid must supply its own flavor. Dry vermouth, Madeira or sherry, white or red wine, canned chicken or beef broth or clam juice —whichever is appropriate—are better additives than tap water. Fisher confesses to using Kitchen Bouquet, if nothing else is handy, and under the exigencies of wartime even "one of those frightening, efficient cans of 'rich brown *meat* gravy.' " But when mere survival is not at issue, Kitchen Bouquet, Bovril, Maggi, and such are worse than a crushed bouillon cube because of their permeating factory flavor.

The best solution is to make pan gravy ahead, from a previously cooked roast or fish, or from meat trimmings or fish stock. If you're preparing a roast turkey, for example, you can make a stock of the giblets and neck the night before, degrease it by chilling and reduce it the next day. The juices from the cooked turkey you can then degrease, deglaze, and reduce at leisure, to save as meat glaze for the next pan gravy. It's what the Chinese do in adding continuously to a "Master Sauce," into which all saved juices are poured to form a flavoring essence for the next sauce.

# BUTTER SAUCE

The French refinement of pan juice is the butter sauce. Butter added at the last minute to pan juices enhances flavor and creates the liaison characteristic of good sauce. Until recently, no self-respecting French steak would appear naked on a plate without its butter pat. The French treat butter as if it were meat juice twice removed, and it is a form of natural sauce if thought of as condensed cow juice.

Because butter absorbs flavors readily, it is a nearly perfect neutral medium for stronger flavors. In the simplest hot butter sauces, butter becomes an emollient for an acid like lemon juice or vinegar, as in *beurre blanc,* or a peppery condiment like mustard, or a salt like anchovy paste, or a green herb like parsley or tarragon. Butter, heated until it is brown, takes on a nut-like character of its own.

During the postwar years of affluence, our cooking masters taught us that there is no substitute for butter. Margarine is worse than nothing because its flavor and texture are ersatz. Margarine was to butter what the can was to soup and the bottle to sauce. Beard, in particular, liberated Americans from stingy butter hands by calling for sticks of butter instead of tablespoons, and for two or three at a time. Subsequent cholesterol panic countered liberation somewhat, but the lesson had been learned. There is no substitute for butter because there is no substitute for quality. The message was use less if you must, but don't try to fake it.

One way to use less butter is to flavor it with stronger but less caloric agents, so that less will be more. In the fifties, American taste began to change from the bland to the beautiful by way of garlic. Garlic, once a separator of WASP sheep from immigrant (namely, southern Mediterranean) goats, is now distinctively all-American, as Gilroy, California, has become the garlic capital of the world. In the fifties, garlic mixed with butter seemed almost as exotic as the snails curled in pools of it or as the fork and tong used to extract them from it. Now garlic has become one of the most useful of all flavorers and beats Kitchen Bouquet any day, as in the all-purpose meat, fowl, or fish sauce below.

# GARLIC-PARSLEY BUTTER SAUCE

## Proportions

for ⅓ cup of sauce, ¼ cup of liquid plus flavorings

1 large clove garlic
4 tablespoons butter (or half meat or fish juice)
1 to 1½ teaspoons anchovy paste

⅓ cup packed parsley leaves
Freshly ground black pepper to taste

1.  Mash the garlic clove with the side of a knife and mince. Melt the butter and add the garlic to warm it. Stir in the anchovy paste.

2.  Chop the parsley leaves in a processor or mince them. Add to the butter mixture and taste for seasoning. With a processor this sauce takes no more than a minute.

*Use the sauce for mushrooms, snails, fresh vegetables, boiled beef, grilled fish, hard-boiled eggs, toasted French bread, or hot potato salad.*

# WHITE WINE SAUCE

So basic is the white sauce béchamel or velouté to sauce making that all four masters begin with a recipe for a medium-thick one. The usual proportions were 2 tablespoons each of butter and flour to 1 cup of liquid, milk and/or stock. Child lightened these proportions somewhat by suggesting 1 tablespoon butter and 1½ tablespoons flour to 1 cup liquid. She also demonstrated that the basis of a classical soufflé is no more than a thick white sauce, in the ratio of 3 tablespoons flour to 1 cup liquid. She explained how to thin a sauce by adding more liquid or how to thicken a sauce by the traditional French trick of a butter-flour paste *(beurre manié)*, whipped in a bit at a time while the sauce cooks. A teaspoon each of butter and flour, mixed together and added to a cup of liquid, will thicken rapidly under heat.

There are four simple steps in creating a foolproof smooth sauce:

1. Cook the butter and flour together for 2 or 3 minutes.
2. Heat the liquid separately and add it all at once.
3. Whip the mixture vigorously off the heat until smooth.
4. Simmer the sauce for 5 minutes after it comes to a boil.

Of course you could put all the ingredients in a blender or processor to begin with, but cooking the flour first produces a far better flavor than heating flour-thickened liquid.

Originally, béchamel was based on veal stock as well as milk and cream. The function of the Mother Sauces of classical cuisine was to "quintessence" the flavor, as Theodore Child would say, of the most savory and succulent of quadrupeds, fowl, or fish, by sacrificing costly materials and by simmering for days and sometimes nights. Julia Child cut the time for white sauce to 5 minutes, but cautioned that the sauce was only a base for flavors and enrichments. Those are what give the sap its savor.

I find the most useful white sauce to be one that begins with the mixed flavors of wine and stock, to which a little milk or cream is added for smoothness. Fish, poultry, or mixed stock can be used for fish dishes, but fish stock is better reserved for fishy purposes unless the dish mixes—in the manner of *nouvelle cuisine*—shellfish with chicken or veal or other white flesh. Because the wine and stock are reduced by simmering together, the final sauce has a blended taste lacking in a quick white sauce.

## Proportions

for 1 cup of medium sauce, 1 tablespoon each of butter and flour to 1½ cups of liquid

| | |
|---|---|
| ½ cup stock | 1 tablespoon flour |
| ½ cup dry white wine | Salt and freshly ground |
| ½ cup milk or cream | black pepper to taste |
| 1 tablespoon butter | |

1. Heat the liquids together in a saucepan. Melt the butter in a separate saucepan. Add the flour, mix well, and cook gently for 2 to 3 minutes.

2. Remove the butter and flour mixture from heat and add the hot liquid all at once, whipping vigorously with a wire whisk.

3.   Return to the heat, stirring constantly, and simmer for 10 minutes or more, or until the liquid has reduced to the texture wanted. Taste carefully for seasoning. If the mixture seems too bland, add a few drops of lemon juice, a drop or two of vinegar, or a pinch of cayenne pepper.

*A white sauce is a base for all kinds of flavorings: puréed onions, mushrooms, tomatoes, cheese, parsley, tarragon, curry powder, garlic. White sauce made of fish, fowl, or meat stock has a homologous relation to fish, fowl, or meat, but of course the added flavor is also good for eggs and cheese dishes and for creaming all kinds of vegetables.*

*A basic white sauce that replaces stock and wine with milk or cream, and replaces salt and pepper with sugar, becomes the base for dessert soufflés or tart fillings.*

# CREAM SAUCES

Enrichment by cream makes the liaison of a white sauce richer and smoother. Enrichment by cream and egg yolk makes the liaison richest of all. The French have a different name for every variant in the escalation from a simple *sauce crème* to *sauce suprême.* In plain American, the addition of 1 or 2 egg yolks to the White Wine Sauce above creates a Super Rich Cream Sauce.

Unfortunately, after we had experienced the velvet smoothness of a liaison produced by egg, the cholesterol panic banned the egg, and saucemakers looked for alternatives. Sour cream, *crème fraîche,* and yogurt came into favor. Each of these thickened milk products is good for binding but unreliable under heat. All of them will thin out and separate under heat, except for *crème fraîche* when thickened with buttermilk rather than sour cream. The safest method is to stir in these enrichers at the last moment, off heat. Another method is to use them with another thickener like cornstarch, arrowroot, or potato starch, mixing the powder with some of the cream before adding to the hot liquid.

The flavor and texture of *crème fraîche* are so good and the cream keeps so well under refrigeration, far longer than sweet heavy cream, that I keep a large jar of it on hand specifically for sauces. *Crème fraîche,* of course, is not "fresh" at all but ripened, like cheese, by natural fermentation. It is kin to the English clotted cream made in Devonshire and named for the area. Americans cannot duplicate the French or English product unless they have access to raw (certified but not pasteurized) milk products, because the thickening of the cream takes place from the natural lactic acids and bacteria that develop the butter fat.

Americans can, however, make a very good thickened cream by a number of methods. Child introduced a formula for it in *Mastering I,* supplied by her colleague Simca, that called for 1 teaspoon buttermilk to 1 cup heavy cream. Beard's formula calls for 2 tablespoons buttermilk to 1 cup cream. The larger proportion of buttermilk works faster but results in a more sour product. Child came up with another formula in *Mastering II* that called for 2 parts heavy cream to 1 part sour cream (1 cup to ½ cup). It ripens quickly and keeps well but thins out more under heat. The method is to stir the souring agent into the cream and leave it in a covered jar at room temperature until it thickens. At 70 degrees, the cream may take 8 to 12 hours. Refrigeration halts the fermenting process.

Another egg alternative is cheese, particularly the mild creamy goat cheese called chèvre, or a freshly made farmer's cheese. Ricotta was a favorite in *nouvelle cuisine* recipes translated for American products, but now that chèvre is being made and made well domestically, its mild but distinctive flavor is ideal for sauces made in the processor or blender for quick smoothing.

The trio of sauces below suggests how useful *crème fraîche* is as a binder of flavors from tart to sweet, for meats, fish, salads, and desserts.

# BALSAMIC CREAM SAUCE

## Proportions

for 1 cup of sauce, 1⅓ cups of liquid

⅔ **cup poultry, fish, or mixed stock**

⅔ **cup** *crème fraîche*

1 **teaspoon lemon juice**

2 **to 3 drops balsamic or other excellent vinegar**

1. Reduce the stock with ⅓ cup of *crème fraîche* by about one-third.
2. Stir in remaining *crème* and season with lemon and vinegar.

*The sauce is especially good with poached chicken or fish, eggs, vegetables, stuffed crêpes.*

# CHÈVRE CREAM SAUCE

## Proportions

for 1 cup of sauce, ¼ cup of cheese to 1 cup of liquid

1 **tablespoon minced shallots or green onions**

2 **tablespoons fresh tarragon or chervil, or 2 teaspoons dried**

¼ **cup white wine vinegar**

½ **cup dry white wine**

¼ **pound creamy goat cheese**

¼ **to ½ cup** *crème fraîche*

**Salt and freshly ground black pepper to taste**

1.  Boil the shallots and tarragon in vinegar and wine until the liquid is reduced to about ½ cup. Crumble the cheese and stir it into the liquid.

2.  Put the mixture in a processor or blender with the *crème* and process. Taste carefully for seasoning as the goat cheese will be salty. Can be reheated gently.

*Particularly good with a delicate fish, such as flounder, sea trout, striped bass.*

# CIDER CREAM SAUCE

## Proportions

for 1 cup of sauce, 1 cup of cream to 3 cups of apple cider

**3 cups apple cider**                    1 cup *crème fraîche*

1.  Boil the cider to reduce it to 2 cups.
2.  Add the *crème* and continue to boil until the liquid has reduced to 1 cup. The result is a thick caramel-colored cream that is remarkable warm or cold as a topping for apple pies, tarts, or other fruit desserts. If you have slightly fermented cider, use it.

# TASTY BROWN SAUCE

Traditionally, white sauce is used for white meats, such as chicken, veal, and fish. Brown sauce is used for red meats, such as beef, lamb, turkey, duck, game. But more and more those divisions are blurred. Classically, the French brown sauce is simply browned white sauce or pan gravy raised to its highest powers. The single aim is to darken flavor, color, and taste by almost any means available, including Beard's suggestion to use burnt sugar or caramel to achieve that wanted rich brown color. Best is to use meat glaze for both look and taste.

If you have no glaze, you need to inject flavor by other means. Child suggests beefing up stock or canned broth by simmering it with diced ham, tomato paste, carrots and onions, meat trimmings and bones. In other words, you need an intense stock, but her method is time-consuming. Beard suggests a Quick Brown Sauce that beefs up canned broth with green onions stewed in butter, simmered with dry red wine, and thickened with a butter and flour paste added last.

My recipe is a compromise between the two. I begin by browning the flour and butter and reducing canned beef broth if I have no good meat stock on hand. What I add next depends entirely on the taste or lack of it of the stock. Here's where a Master Sauce proves its worth. Anything goes that turns the flaccid to something tasty, but I have found the ingredients below relatively foolproof.

# Proportions

for 1 cup of sauce, 1 tablespoon each of butter and flour to 2½ cups of liquid before reducing

½ cup red wine
2 cups beef broth
1 tablespoon butter
1 tablespoon flour
1 teaspoon tomato paste
½ to 1 teaspoon anchovy paste

¼ teaspoon thyme
Dash of Worcestershire sauce
Pinch of cayenne pepper
Freshly ground black pepper to taste

1.   Combine the wine and broth and boil to reduce to 1 cup.
2.   Melt the butter in another pan and add the flour. Cook slowly until golden brown. Stir in the tomato paste.
3.   Add the hot liquid all at once and stir vigorously off the heat with a wire whisk.
4.   Taste carefully for seasoning and add seasonings according to desired saltiness and hotness. Simmer for 5 to 10 minutes, or until flavors have blended.

*Use with roast meats or game of all kinds.*

## Variations

1.   **SAUCE DIABLE:** To 1 cup of brown sauce, add ¼ cup red wine vinegar, 1 teaspoon dry mustard, and 1 tablespoon fresh tarragon, and increase amount of black and cayenne peppers. Particularly good for pork roasts and chops, for lesser cuts of beef, such as flank steaks, or for mixed seafood grills.
2.   **SAUCE PIQUANTE:** To 1 cup of brown sauce, add 1 tablespoon drained capers, 1 tablespoon chopped sour pickles, and 1 tablespoon chopped anchovy fillets. A traditional sauce for boiled beef or tongue, but also good with lamb.
3.   **SAUCE ROBERT:** To 1 cup of brown sauce, add 2 tablespoons minced green onions or shallots, cooked in butter until soft, and 2 tablespoons Dijon mustard. Complements roast pork, ham, calves' liver, kidneys, or broiled fowl like squab.
4.   **MADEIRA SAUCE:** To 1 cup of brown sauce, add ⅓ cup Madeira and reduce by a third. Stir in 2 tablespoons of butter. A classic sauce for beef fillet, chateaubriand, tournedos, and for a fine roast veal.

# TOMATO PURÉE

After White Sauce and Brown Sauce, the third major sauce is Red. Tomatoes are another ingredient like butter that both flavors and thickens. Of all the vegetable purées, tomato is the most common and the most useful because it is tart, colorful, and thick. A tablespoon of it in a béchamel creates *Sauce Aurore,* as rosy as the dawn. It can be made hearty with garlic, elegant with cream, fiery with mustard or hot peppers, rich with cheese. But alas, the canned paste with its unmistakable metallic tinge has given the purée a bad reputation. To begin at the beginning, with either fresh tomatoes in season or with canned Italian plum tomatoes out of season, is to reenact the shift from distrust to delight that many Americans experienced on first confronting the tomato early in the nineteenth century when it was still called the "love apple."

If you have freezer space, the only time to make tomato purée is at the height of the summer season when ripeness is all. Otherwise, use a good brand of Italian canned tomatoes, because the purée will never be better than the quality of the original tomato. From the many recipes for fresh purée supplied by our master chefs, I have synthesized a formula that omits flour and sugar, that is best with fresh tomatoes but that still works with canned.

## Proportions

for 1 cup of sauce, 2 cups of fresh tomato pulp with seasonings

2 tablespoons olive oil
1 tablespoon butter
2 tablespoons minced green onions, shallots, or yellow onions
1 clove garlic, minced
2 cups fresh peeled, seeded, and chopped tomatoes, or 3 cups canned

1 tablespoon minced fresh basil (or other herbs fresh or dried, such as oregano, thyme, fennel, saffron)
Salt and freshly ground black pepper to taste

1. Heat the oil and butter, add the onions, and cook for 2 minutes. Add the garlic, tomatoes, and seasonings, cover, and cook for 2 minutes so that tomatoes will exude their juice. Simmer, uncovered, for 10 minutes to reduce the liquid until it is thick.

2. Purée the sauce in a blender or processor to make it smooth. (A blender with a full range of speeds will liquefy tomato seeds if there is enough liquid, but it's a bit neater to seed the fresh tomatoes to begin with.)

*Use on pizzas and pastas of all kinds. Also good with chicken, fish, and mixed vegetable sautés.*

# ONION SAUCE

Traditionally the French call a sauce made of puréed onions, thickened further by a white sauce, a *soubise.* But you can omit a flour-base entirely and use onions for both thickening and flavor, as in the other vegetable purées. The result is a stronger but lighter sauce. In the following recipe, if you want a light-colored sauce, use cream. If you want a brown sauce, omit the cream and use a meat stock, as in French Onion Soup.

## Proportions

for 1½ cups of sauce, 2 cups of onions to 1 cup of liquid

2 **cups chopped yellow onions**
3 **tablespoons butter**
½ **cup stock**
½ **cup heavy cream**
¼ **teaspoon each nutmeg and cardamom for a white stock**

**Pinch of cayenne pepper for a brown stock**
**Salt and freshly ground black pepper to taste**

1. Cook the onions in butter until they are wilted. Purée in a processor or blender with a little stock.
2. Heat the remaining stock with the cream. Add the onion purée and simmer for at least 5 minutes. Taste carefully for seasoning.
*Note:* The sauce is even better if you use a little *crème fraîche* to counter the natural sweetness of the onions.

*Good for the white flesh of veal and chicken and fish, such as cod, haddock, or halibut.*

# MUSHROOM SAUCE

The mushroom purée that the French call *duxelles* and that many of us learned to make when first encountering Child's Veau Prince Orloff makes a rich and flavorful sauce base. As with onions, the mushrooms act as the major thickener, without flour. The processor can give you a slightly chunky texture or a perfectly smooth one. Because mushrooms give a good earthy undertaste to meat sauces, the addition of a table-spoon of purée to a rich brown sauce will make it richer. You can freeze the purée as you would tomato purée to have it on hand. The only trouble with mushrooms for a white sauce is color. They can turn white a dingy gray instead of a fashionable beige. Nonetheless, you can work on your color palate as you would your taste palate, bleaching with lemon juice and cream, darkening with meat glaze or a bouillon cube or a drop of Worcestershire.

## Proportions

for 1 cup of sauce, 1 cup of chopped mushrooms to ¾ cup of liquid

¼ **cup minced onion**
2 **tablespoons butter**
1 **tablespoon oil**
1 **cup chopped mushrooms, or**
   ¼ **pound mushrooms,**
   **chopped**

½ **cup mixed stock**
¼ **to ½ cup heavy cream**
**Salt and freshly ground**
**black pepper to taste**
**A few drops lemon juice**

1.   Cook the onions in butter and oil for 2 minutes, or until soft. Turn the heat high, add the mushrooms, and cook rapidly, stirring to brown on all sides.

2.   Purée in a processor to the smoothness wanted. Add a little stock if necessary to make the purée completely smooth.

3.   Heat the purée with the stock and cream, either thinning the mixture with more cream or reducing it by slow simmering. Simmer for 5 minutes to blend the flavors. Add a few drops of lemon juice and taste carefully for seasoning.

*Good with veal, chicken, fish, turkey, meat patties, and pastas.*

# GREEN HERB SAUCE

Like vegetables, herbs can serve both to flavor and to thicken, as in the ubiquitous *Pesto* Sauce based on liquefied basil. Now that herbs have come into their own, along with processors, herb-based sauces have proliferated because mincing is no longer an arduous time-consuming task. Those who grew up with mortar and pestle may take, along with Fisher, "some atavistic pleasure from their primitive functioning." She still prefers the rough texture of a *pesto* pounded in a mortar with garlic and salt to make a paste thinned by oil. But long before the food processor hit the market, she had admitted defeat. "Blenders are almost as omnipresent as death and taxes," she wrote in 1968, and gracefully offered a blender recipe for A Hot-Cold Green Sauce composed of half basil, half parsley, half butter, half oil, heated and then cooled.

My recipe below is another version of a mixed herb sauce that can be varied according to what herbs may be in the market or in your garden. Tiny dandelion leaves, mustard greens, watercress leaves, arugula leaves, young sorrel leaves—all can be mixed with a combination of basil and parsley or parsley alone. The one necessity, however, is to strip the leaves from the stems before adding them to the processor.

## Proportions

for 1 cup of sauce, 1½ cups of herbs to ¾ cup of liquid

1½ cups mixed green herbs (parsley, basil, watercress, sorrel)
¼ cup olive oil
⅓ cup (6 tablespoons) melted butter

2 to 3 tablespoons *crème fraîche* or sour cream
Salt and freshly ground black pepper to taste
A few drops lemon juice

1. Put the leaves in the processor and mince.
2. Heat the oil and butter, add to the processor, and process again. Add cream in order to smooth the mixture and seasonings in order to flavor it according to the types of herbs used.

*This sauce is particularly good with fish, such as poached salmon or grilled salmon steaks, shad or other whole baked fish, and also with cold meats, such as boiled beef.*

# GARLIC PURÉE

Beard loves to astound, and one of his most astounding dishes when he first introduced it in the fifties was a chicken cooked with forty cloves of garlic. Little did we know that garlic works on the principle that more is less, provided that it is cooked and cooked slowly. More and more, garlic is now being treated as a vegetable, a whole head baked and served like a potato with a roast. Garlic has long been a flavorer for the cold mayonnaise called *aïoli* and for the hot mayonnaise called *bourride*. But we are just beginning to see how useful a garlic purée is as both flavorer and thickener for a wide range of sauces. Now that California is producing huge sweet cloves of elephant garlic, the pungent root may become a staple of health and diet in America as it has been in Europe since the time of the Greeks and Romans.

Because garlic keeps so well, it's convenient to have some purée on hand in the refrigerator to add to cold or hot sauces when wanted.

Particularly for those on salt-free diets, garlic is a good alternative or addition to other salt substitutes like lemon, vinegar, and pepper.

## Proportions

for 1 cup of sauce, 1 head of garlic to 1 cup of liquid

1 **head of garlic (12 to 15 cloves)**
1 **cup chicken, fish, or meat**
  **stock**
1 **to 2 tablespoons heavy cream**
  or *crème fraîche*

**Salt and freshly ground black**
**pepper to taste (if desired)**
**A few drops lemon juice or**
**balsamic vinegar**

1.  Separate the garlic cloves and simmer them, in their husks, for about 45 minutes in the stock in a covered pan.

2.  Pour the stock through a strainer and set it aside. When the garlic cloves are cool enough to handle, squeeze the garlic from the husks. Put in a blender or processor with the stock and process until smooth. Taste carefully for seasoning and add cream and seasonings as desired. The cream will enrich the sauce and smooth it out, but the garlic itself makes a creamy paste and, for diet purposes, garlic in broth alone can't be beat.

*We are now using garlic with everything, from eggs, fish, and chicken to beef and lamb. This sauce is especially good with a sturdy white fish, such as cod, or a plain pork roast.*

# FRESH PEACH SAUCE

The idea of puréed fruit is as old as applesauce or cranberry sauce and once again the home processor has allowed us to experiment with various kinds and combinations of fruits in season as they pass through the spectrum of tart to sweet. It was our cooking masters who insisted on our always using the freshest and the best. It was the health freaks and young vegetarians who insisted on using fresh fruits in ever more imaginative combinations and textures.

The recipe below for peaches can be adapted to a wide range of fruits. For a major ingredient, I have used honeydew melon, cantaloupe, blueberries, strawberries, ripe skinned plums, etc. The one essential is that the fruit be truly ripe because the other flavors are there to intensify the taste of fruit. An unripe peach in such a sauce is no better than cornstarch. A canned peach is possible (use cling rather than freestone), but as the major flavor even of the drained peach is sugar syrup, eliminate the sugar and increase the lime or lemon juice.

Because the sauce is delicate, it is particularly good poured over fresh fruit, such as more peaches, pears, bananas, and other light-colored fruits.

## Proportions

for 1 cup of sauce, 2 peaches to ½ cup of liquid

2 **ripe peaches**
¼ **cup sugar or to taste**
⅓ **cup heavy cream**
2 **teaspoons lime or lemon juice**

1 **to 2 tablespoons Grand Marnier, or ½ teaspoon vanilla extract, or ¼ teaspoon almond extract**

1.   Skin the peaches, cut up the fruit quickly, and purée in a blender or processor. If the peaches are really ripe, their skins will slip off easily. If less ripe, they can be dipped into boiling water before peeling.
2.   Add the sugar, cream, lime juice, and flavoring and process again. Taste carefully for sweetness and sourness and adjust.

# FOOLPROOF HOLLANDAISE

One of the glories of the French butter sauce is hollandaise and more than any other it has suffered from the French-sauce mystique. Never make it in humid weather, Irma Rombauer warned in 1943, unless you use clarified butter, or it will never take hold. The method then was to make the sauce in a double boiler over hot, not simmering, water and to beat it for 30 minutes, or until your arm fell off.

Hollandaise, however, is simply another drawn butter sauce thickened by egg yolk and flavored by acid. Beard and Child explained its principles and demonstrated that its only secret ingredient was patience. The magical processors did not eliminate that ingredient but they certainly reduced the quantity needed.

Proportions vary according to desired richness and tartness. Beard suggests 4 egg yolks to 1 stick of butter to 1 to 2 tablespoons lemon juice. Child prefers a lighter sauce of 3 egg yolks to 1 stick butter to 1 tablespoon of lemon and 1 of cold water. The water helps to stabilize the emulsion, just as it does with a mayonnaise. Where Beard likes to spike his sauce with a dash of Tabasco, Child likes a pinch of white pepper.

With either proportion, the sauce is foolproof made in blender or processor, provided that
1. you add the butter when it is bubbling hot and
2. you add the butter slowly in a thin steady stream.
The processor is easier to use with this sauce than the blender because it beats in more air and does not clog when the emulsion is thick. The great boon of explainers such as Child and Beard is to remove the fear

of failure. They both demonstrate ways of rescuing a turned or curdled sauce. If the sauce starts to separate, beat in a tablespoon of cold water or an ice cube. If that trick doesn't work, start over by beating together a fresh egg yolk with a teaspoon of lemon juice and beat in the turned sauce gradually, by spoonfuls, until the emulsion takes hold.

The proportions below are for a medium-thick sauce spiked with a little vinegar, as in a béarnaise.

## Proportions

for ¾ cup of sauce, 3 eggs to ¼ pound of butter

| | |
|---|---|
| **3 egg yolks** | **½ teaspoon salt (or less)** |
| **1 tablespoon lemon juice** | **¼ pound (1 stick) butter** |
| **1 tablespoon tarragon white wine vinegar** | |

1. Put the yolks in a processor with the lemon juice, vinegar, and salt. Process for 10 seconds. Heat the butter until it starts to bubble and, while it is still bubbling, pour it through the opening in the lid in a slow steady stream, processing until the sauce is thick and smooth.

2. To keep the sauce warm, set it near a pilot light on your stove or set it over a pan of lukewarm water. Leftover hollandaise is delicious as a cold butter spread or hot sauce enricher.

*A classic sauce for asparagus, artichokes, fish, Eggs Benedict, but also wonderful for chicken breasts.*

# FOOLPROOF MAYONNAISE

While mayonnaise suggests by its name a French origin, its roots are more ancient and more primitive. Its stiff creamy texture is a refinement of the universal garlic-oil sauce of the Mediterranean—the *aïoli* of the French, the *ali-oli* of the Spanish, the *olio-aglio* of the Italians, the *skordalia* of the Greeks.

But instead of thickening oil with garlic, mayonnaise thickens it with egg and flavors it with acid. Mayonnaise involves the same principle as hollandaise but because it is a cold emulsion rather than a hot or warm one, it lasts longer and can be used more variably.

To my generation mayonnaise was entirely a bottled product which, opened, kept forever on a refrigerator shelf next to the ketchup. While Americans were addicted to the bottle, lavishing its contents on everything from hamburgers to canned pear and cottage cheese salads, homemade mayonnaise was like a homemade bomb—fraught with hazard. Our cooking masters replaced fear with craft and technology. By experimenting, Claiborne discovered early on that the blender required not only a whole egg, instead of yolks, to provide more liquid, but also an initial dollop of oil, unlike the method of hand beating. His trick was to add ¼ cup olive oil to 1 egg, lemon, mustard, and salt at the *beginning* of mixing and then the remaining ¾ cup slowly.

Now, the slower speed of the processor has made homemade mayonnaise even simpler, provided you follow three simple rules for binding egg to oil:

1. Make sure the eggs and oil are warm not cold, warm as in room temperature. (If the eggs come from the refrigerator, put them in warm water for 5 minutes.)
2. Beat the eggs first, to lighten them.
3. Add the oil slowly, in a steady stream of droplets, until the sauce really thickens.

Proportions vary according to the richness and thickness wanted. Child bases her recipe on the safe proportions of ½ cup oil to 1 U.S. large egg yolk, flavored by ¼ teaspoon salt, ⅛ teaspoon dry mustard, and 1 teaspoon vinegar or lemon juice. Beard prefers a stiffer sauce of ¾ cup oil to 1 egg yolk, flavored by ½ teaspoon coarse salt, ¼ teaspoon Dijon mustard, and ½ tablespoon lemon juice. The differences are a matter of taste, not science.

My recipe below is a compromise that reduces the proportion of oil to make a quicker sauce that is creamier and less stiff in texture than the bottled product. Claiborne suggests stabilizing homemade mayonnaise that you wish to preserve in the refrigerator by adding a teaspoon or two of water at the end, but I have never found that step necessary with a blender or processor. As Beard points out, the machines can make a stabler and firmer sauce than beating by hand. To those who consider the machine a cheat, Beard gives short shrift: "I think that anyone who spurns the modern methods is either a fanatic or a masochist."

## Proportions

for 1¼ cups of sauce, 1½ eggs to 1 cup of oil

| | |
|---|---|
| 1 whole egg | ¼ teaspoon salt |
| 1 egg yolk | 1 tablespoon fresh lemon juice |
| ¼ teaspoon Dijon mustard | 1 cup olive oil |

1. Make sure the eggs are at room temperature. Whip the eggs in a processor with a metal or plastic blade for 30 seconds before adding the mustard, salt, and ½ tablespoon lemon juice.

2. Pour the oil through the opening in the lid, while the machine is running, in a steady stream of drops until the mixture thickens (usually 3 to 4 minutes).

3. Taste carefully for seasoning. If too bland or too thick, flavor and thin with the remaining lemon juice. Or add a tablespoon of heavy cream or yogurt. If the sauce is too thin, add more oil, up to ⅓ of a cup.

4. If not used immediately, transfer the mayonnaise to a bowl and cover tightly with plastic wrap to avoid surface skin, or put in a jar with a tight-fitting lid, and refrigerate. May keep 3 or 4 weeks or more.

*Mayonnaise is classic for masking cold dishes of eggs, vegetables, or fish, but it also works well with hot or warm chicken, veal, and other light meats. For specific uses, see Classic Potato Salad (page 164), Crab Louis (page 167), Papaya, Orange, Avocado, and Duck Salad (page 168), and Salmon and Scallop Salad (page 172).*

# BASIC SALAD DRESSINGS

To the young who were weaned on huge bowls of mixed greens, it may come as a shock to learn that many prewar American tables had never served a salad other than Jell-O, with a blob of mayonnaise on top. Those who had were apt to serve a wedge of iceberg lettuce with a bottled sweetened dressing, ranging in color from orange to dingy white. The one essential was sugar. *Fannie Farmer*'s 1948 French Dressing called for 2 parts oil to 1 vinegar, plus a little sugar. Her Cooked Dressing called for a white sauce, enriched by egg, soured by vinegar, and sweetened by a little sugar. The principle of the dressing was something thick, sour, and *sweet*.

Imagine the shock of reading Beard's list of Don'ts for Salad Dressings in his first cookbook. Don't use sugar. Don't use prepared herbed vinegars. Don't mix the dressing hours ahead. Don't store it in the refrigerator. And his Do's. Do keep it simple—oil, vinegar, salt, and pepper. Do make it fresh. The European vinaigrette that gently cloaked each varied leaf with oil and perfumed it with lemon startled our palates with its refreshing quality and simplicity. From then on a sweetened dressing was as passé as Depression Gravy.

Once basic ingredients were established, proportions could be varied to taste, but the essential proportion was at least 3 oil to 1 acid. Child's basic vinaigrette suggests 1 to 2 tablespoons vinegar or lemon juice to 6 to 8 tablespoons oil, flavored by ¼ teaspoon salt, ¼ teaspoon dry mustard, pepper, and herbs. Beard goes for a saltier dressing of 1½ to 2 tablespoons vinegar to 6 tablespoons olive oil, flavored by 1 teaspoon kosher (or coarse) salt and ½ teaspoon pepper. Because all four masters specified freshly ground black pepper, instead of the commercial powdered product, the European pepper mill came in with the vinaigrette.

Both oils and vinegars have vastly improved in quality and range from the days when the only readily available oil was Wesson and the only readily available vinegar was cider. Although many standard brands of olive oil have deteriorated over the last decade, the taste for a rich and fruity olive oil had to be introduced on a broad scale before mass marketing could corrupt it. Now, if we can pay for it, we can choose between walnut oils, sesame oils, and extra-virgin cold-pressed oils from Tuscany and Provence. We can choose between grades of vintage balsamic vinegar from Modena, aged in the cask, or vinegar made from the best sherry or flavored with fresh raspberries or blueberries. Nowhere has the American palate improved more radically than in its taste for the simplest emulsion of oil and acid. Like a basic black dress, the function of the dressing is to show off the quality of what it covers.

Use not only to dress salads but as a marinade for fish, fowl, and meats.

---

# Proportions

for ½ cup of dressing, 2 tablespoons of acid to 7 tablespoons of oil

| | |
|---|---|
| 1 tablespoon lemon juice | 2 tablespoons walnut oil or |
| 1 tablespoon wine vinegar | sesame oil |
| ¼ teaspoon salt | Freshly ground black pepper |
| ¼ teaspoon Dijon mustard | to taste |
| 5 tablespoons olive oil | |

1. Beat the lemon juice, vinegar, and salt into the mustard.
2. Add the oil and beat vigorously with a fork or shake in a jar with a tight-fitting lid. Add the pepper and taste carefully, adjusting salt, lemon, or oil.

## Variations

**ROQUEFORT DRESSING:** Add ¼ cup Roquefort or other good blue cheese, by crumbling it and puréeing in a blender or processor.

**CREAMY YOGURT DRESSING:** Add ¼ cup yogurt and blend in a processor.

**SUNFLOWER SEED DRESSING:** Instead of walnut or sesame oil, purée ¼ cup toasted sunflower seeds with the other ingredients in a blender.

**CREAMY TOFU DRESSING:** Add ¼ cup tofu to other ingredients and purée in a blender.

**MUSTARD DRESSING:** Increase the Dijon mustard to 1 tablespoon (see 1-2-3 Bean Salad, page *163*).

*Any of these dressings are good with cold pasta or vegetables, at room temperature or cold. (See SALADS for specific uses: Jerusalem Artichoke and Spinach Salad, Greek Salad, Caesar Salad, Salade Niçoise, Cobb Salad, Wilted Greens.)*

---

# GREEN AVOCADO DRESSING

One of the best of American invented dressings is the one created by the Palace Hotel in San Francisco for George Arliss when he was starring in a famous play of the twenties, *The Green Hat.* The dressing was called Green Goddess and was a kind of green mayonnaise, colored by parsley, chives, and tarragon, and salted by anchovy fillets. Claiborne provided a good recipe for it in his first cookbook, calling it a sauce rather than dressing, and lightening the mayonnaise base with sour cream.

Because it is a California dressing and because of its name, for years I assumed that the name honored what must be its central ingredient, that green goddess of California produce, the avocado. Disillusion was easily remedied. Since avocado tastes and acts like green butter or oil, it is another vegetable-fruit that purées so well in the processor that it can be treated as an oil substitute. With lime or lemon as an acid, anchovy for salt, onions for flavor, yogurt or sour cream as a substitute for egg yolk, you can quickly blend or process an excellent dressing that at last tastes the way Green Goddess sounds. If you serve it to California purists, omit all reference to Green Goddess and harp on the virtues of Avocado Green.

## Proportions

for 1 cup of dressing, ½ avocado to ½ cup of liquid

½ ripe avocado, peeled and pitted

1 tablespoon minced onion or shallots

1 anchovy fillet, or 1 teaspoon anchovy paste

1 tablespoon lime or lemon juice

⅓ cup yogurt, sour cream, or *crème fraîche*

Chop the avocado and put it in a blender or processor with the onion. Add the anchovy, lime juice, and yogurt. Purée until smooth. Taste carefully for seasoning.

*This is a rich colorful dressing not only for salad greens but also for sliced red tomatoes and other raw vegetables, such as peppers, cucumbers, red onions. Also good for hard-boiled eggs or cold poached fish or chicken or pasta salad.*

# HOT BARBECUE SAUCE

Nobody has done more to elevate the All-American Bottled Catsup than Fisher, who cited Mark Twain, as we have seen, to justify her own lifelong lust for an impossibly vulgar combination—Mashed Potatoes *with*

Catsup. What American does not know the satisfactions of the sweet thick blood-red coagulation called catsup or ketchup, depending upon the brand, or the frustrations of coaxing the coagulate from the bottle to the food?

Strictly speaking, ketchups are condiments rather than sauces, originating in the *katjaps* and *kechaps* of Southeast Asia, based on salted fish rather than salted tomatoes. Until recent times, ketchups were based variously on oysters, mushrooms, walnuts, and almost anything else that could be preserved in vinegar or sherry or salt. Spice was traditional but sugar was not.

Like mayonnaise, once the bottled product took over, no one thought of making ketchup at home and only old wives told tales by the chimney corner of unsweetened and untomatoed concoctions. If they spoke of tomatoes, they remembered Miss Eliza Leslie's formula for Tomata Catchup, flavored exotically of mace, cloves, mustard, and pepper with not a drop of sweet. But as the old ways were forgotten, new ways were devised to use the sweet-sour purée as a base for sauces ranging from very sweet to hot and peppery. Among a half dozen good marinating and basting sauces in his *New York Times Menu Cook Book,* Claiborne offers a good recipe for turning bottled ketchup into a Barbecue Sauce by adding onions, garlic, parsley, thyme, bay leaf, Worcestershire sauce, hot pepper, vinegar—and sugar. In his first general cookbook, Beard hots up straight tomato purée, flavored similarly with onions, Worcestershire sauce, mustard, and herbs—and sweetens it with ½ cup honey.

But more recently the American sweet tooth, aided by natural decay and excess flesh, has moved further from sweet and closer to fiery, as the hot peppers of China and Malaysia and Mexico have become more familiar. In the recipe below, I have used no sweetening but plenty of pepper to recall the great catsup days of the nineteenth century.

## Proportions

for 2 cups of sauce, 2 cups of cooked tomatoes, ½ cup of sherry or vinegar, and ½ cup of onions

3 cloves garlic, minced
½ cup minced onion
2 tablespoons olive oil
2 cups cooked fresh tomatoes or canned Italian plum tomatoes
1 tablespoon Worcestershire sauce
1 tablespoon Dijon mustard
¼ teaspoon ginger
¼ teaspoon cloves
¼ teaspoon mace
1 small hot red pepper, or ½ teaspoon red pepper flakes
Salt and freshly ground black pepper to taste
½ cup sherry or fruit or wine vinegar

1.  Cook the garlic and onion in the oil until they are soft. Add the tomatoes and seasonings and simmer for 1 hour, uncovered, so that the mixture will reduce.

2.  When the mixture is thick, add the sherry and simmer for 15 minutes longer to blend the flavors. Taste carefully for seasoning. Will keep for weeks in the refrigerator.

*Some folks put barbecue sauce on everything, but traditionalists limit its use to broiled and grilled meats and birds, such as spareribs and chickens and hamburgers and hot dogs. It's also good with jumbo shrimp grilled in the shell, to be unshelled at the table and dipped one by one into the sauce.*

# SOY-HONEY MARINADE

Any barbecue sauce, thinned, can be used as a marinade and basting sauce for grilled meat, fowl, and fish. The thick tomato sauce once *de rigueur* in America for almost all barbecued meats is now often replaced by the soy-based sauce restaurants call "teriyaki" and use everywhere because it makes tough meats tender and gives flavorless meat flavor. The soy bottle, in fact, often replaces the ketchup bottle nowadays in homes as well as restaurants.

Soy sauce, or *shoyu,* is far more ancient than ketchup and came to England from the Orient over three centuries ago, to become domesticated in such typically English condiments as Worcestershire sauce. Or so it is rumored. A typical form of Japanese soy sauce is made half from soybeans and half from barley or wheat, which is then added to an equal weight of salt and fermented. The soybean displaces the fish entrails of the Roman *garum.*

To Beard, who was raised by a Chinese cook and an English mother, soy sauce was as much a staple of his childhood kitchen as mayonnaise was of mine. And because he has always had a special feeling for barbecued foods, providing us with the first American cookbook devoted exclusively to its methods, he has experimented with a wide range of marinades and basters. In my adaptation of his Oriental Sauce below, I have included, this time, the sweetening he suggests because the thickness of the honey provides the meat with a nice even glaze that takes on a golden-brown color.

## Proportions

for 1½ cups of sauce, ¼ cup of soy sauce to 1 cup of other liquids

¼ cup soy sauce
½ cup peanut or vegetable oil
¼ cup dry sherry
¼ cup honey
2 to 3 tablespoons minced
fresh gingerroot

2 cloves garlic, minced
3 Szechuan peppercorns,
crushed
1 small red pepper, or ½
teaspoon red pepper flakes

1. Put all ingredients in a blender and process until smooth. To make a really thick paste, add a few whole shelled peanuts to the blender.

2. Marinate the meat for at least 2 to 3 hours at room temperature and baste the meat with the liquid while grilling it over charcoal or under a broiler.

*This marinade is particularly good with chicken or duck, cut in pieces suitable for grilling. It's also good with pork, cubed for kebabs or rolled in a boneless roast.*

# SALADS

### Raw

Green Garden Salad · 151
Jerusalem Artichoke and Spinach Salad · 153
Cucumber-Yogurt Salad · 154
Chinese Coleslaw with Boiled Dressing · 155
Spiced Orange and Onion Salad · 156

### Composed

Greek Salad · 158
Caesar Salad · 158
Salade Niçoise · 160
Cobb Salad · 161

### Cooked

Wilted Cold Greens · 162
1-2-3 Bean Salad · 163
Classic Potato Salad · 164
Chicken Salad Chinese · 166
Crab Louis · 167
Papaya, Orange, Avocado, and Duck Salad · 168

### Jellied

Raw Vegetable Aspic · 170
Salmon and Scallop Salad · 172

*Only bear in mind, good ladies, that if you do wish to eat lettuce salad with your fingers you must mix the salad with oil and vinegar, and not with that abominable ready-made white "salad-dressing," to look upon which is nauseating.*

*—Theodore Child*
Delicate Feasting *(1890)*

Nothing provokes our tastemakers more quickly or more vehemently to passion than the subject of salads and their dressings. It may be that the very "rawness" of the salad green threatens the cook because it is in constant danger of escaping his "dressing" to revert to the savage and naked wild. Or it may be that the salad and its dressing are sexually loaded. The hard-core anti-salad minority that still condemns salad greens as "rabbit-food" is male. Salads threaten the committed American male carnivore with effeminacy. To him, salads are for California health nuts, hippy weirdos, religious kooks, women, and children. Down with them.

His is a losing cause. The spreading salad bar has become not only a standard fixture of Surf 'n Turf restaurants of all kinds, but the salad is often recognized even by red-blooded males as the best part of the meal. Americans, Beard claims, have become "the greatest salad-eaters in the world." And, Beard might have added, the most dictatorial about how to make salads and how to serve them and how to eat them. About salads we seem to have as many mixed assertive feelings as the greens in the bowl or the ingredients in the dressing.

Here is Beard himself laying down the rules on the fine art of salad-making in his *American Cookery:*

> The greens must be fresh, crisp, and cool. They should not sport a drop of moisture when they are placed in a bowl. They should be broken into bite-size pieces or left in large pieces to be cut at table. The salad should not be tossed till just before eating. The perfect dressing should be neither oily nor acid. Sugar has no place in the dressing.

Here is Fisher laying down the law in *With Bold Knife & Fork:*

A green salad, I firmly believe, should *follow* the main course of a meal, at noon or night, and should be made almost always and almost solely of fresh crisp garden lettuces tossed at the last with a plain vinaigrette.

Here is Claiborne in *The New New York Times Cookbook* uncharacteristically laying down the law about nutrition:

Salads are part and parcel of good nutrition and, with rare exceptions, should have a place in almost every major meal year in and year out.

From Mrs. Rorer we expect such prescriptive grammar as "every well regulated table should"—serve a salad 365 times a year. From a man like George Ellwanger, in *The Pleasures of the Table* in 1902, we expect dictatorial terms: "To serve cheese with the salad is a syncretism, besides being a great injustice to the roast to which the salad rightly appertains."

But from our ordinarily tolerant, freewheeling, improvising current revolutionaries we do not expect "rules." I can only explain their invoking them as a response to the peculiar Salad Controversy and its Rituals that developed in the 1930s. It was then that salad became a sexual issue.

A century earlier, salad was merely a health issue. In the 1830s, the Swiss-born Delmonico brothers were supposed to have introduced Americans to the idea of fresh green salads at the very time the Eastern cholera epidemic frightened city councils into forbidding fresh raw anything. But Americans were not nearly as ignorant of salad greens as they've been discredited with. The seasonal garden salad was commonplace wherever there was leisure to cultivate a kitchen garden. "To have this delicate dish in perfection," Mrs. Webster suggests to *The Improved Housewife* (1845) in search of a salad, "pick your lettuce, peppergrass, chervil, cress, etc., early in the morning." And what the garden didn't provide, the wild wood might.

Even *The Buckeye Cookbook* of the Midwest suggested a sophisticated variety of greens for salad—lettuce, chicory, celery, asparagus, cabbage, dandelion, purslane, watercress—to be shredded with the fingers instead of a knife. Most important, the greens were to be dressed with oil, vinegar, salt, pepper, and mustard, all of the best quality. No nauseating salad dressing here.

The nauseating Boiled Dressing so dear to Fisher's midwestern grandmother belonged to the English tradition of Mrs. Beeton and her followers. It was Mrs. Beeton who tempered vinegar with "pounded" sugar and salad oil with a little milk. The boiled dressing thickened with flour and egg yolk became the white dressing as common then as mayonnaise now and much easier to make and keep. It was the kind of dressing in which sugar *did* have a place when it doused the cold and hot slaws that the

Dutch and Germans made of cabbage wherever they went. So you might say that we owe the boiled and sugared dressing to the north of Europe, and the plain oil and vinegar to the south. Mrs. Beeton herself is careful to distinguish the sugarless sauce she calls French Salad-Dressing from the basic sugared dressing she calls Excellent.

By the turn of the century the division between French and English dressing increased as garlic became associated with the French. "To make French dressing," Mrs. Rorer instructs, "rub the bottom of the bowl with a clove of garlic or onion." Now the bowl will become an essential ingredient of the dressing. Now garlic will divide the men from the girls. And now a salad bowl, the wooden bowl rubbed with garlic and never washed until it acquires, as George Rector says, "the patina of a Corinthian bronze and the personality of a hundred-year-old brandy" will become the special prerogative of the man. So much did salad belong to a man's world, Rector said in his 1934 *Dine at Home with Rector,* that in his father's restaurant "in the old days" customers kept their own salad setups on the premises—like shaving mugs at the barber shop.

And what was a woman's prerogative in the salad line? Sugary fantasies of fruits and flowers with fancy names like Frou-Frou, Lollipop, and Marshmallow Dream, said Rector, all peers of a salad he once met "consisting of fresh violets and whipped cream." While men, under the duress of Prohibition, were comforted by salads of garlic, women, evidently, were comforted by salads of canned fruit, Jell-O, and ginger ale. Irma Rombauer in her 1943 printing of *Joy of Cooking* calls her "Ginger Ale Salad" of peeled grapes, orange, grapefruit, canned pineapple, ginger, gelatin, lemon juice, and ginger ale, with mayonnaise dressing, "about the best molded fruit salad given."

The thirties was a period of women's clubs and women's lunches and women's magazines and women's salads. It was a period of intensive advertising of the latest fabricated food, like sweetened gelatin powder in the form of Jell-O, like solid gelatin in the form of marshmallows, like packaged cream cheese, like syrupy canned fruits, like bottled soda pop and bottled mayonnaise dressing. It was a period of "company" give-away cookbooks that put it all together on the plate—the same plate—as a salad. It was a period for garnishes of cream cheese balls and stuffed prunes and tomato aspic of lemon Jell-O and topiary fruits labeled "Bunny" or "Sunbonnet." It was a period in which the *pièce de résistance* in *Fannie Farmer* was the Frozen Pear Salad consisting of a can of frozen Bartlett pears, sliced or cut in squares, sprinkled with paprika, garnished with cherries and cream cheese rosettes and served with French Dressing. No garlic please.

The Second World War, fortunately, took the battle of the sexes into larger fields and postwar cookbooks burgeoned with unisex salads, tossed in wooden bowls rubbed plentifully with garlic and dressed simply with vinegar and oil. Both sexes learned to eschew the bottled French Dressing that was replete with sugar and was colored orange. While the rules of the new masters differed in detail (*always* wash your wooden salad bowl, Claiborne instructed), they agreed that the best salad for both sexes was the classic one of fresh crisp greens, coated with the best fruity olive oil, seasoned with the best wine vinegar, and at the furthest possible remove from any abominable ready-made salad dressing to look upon which was, and remains, nauseating.

# GREEN GARDEN SALAD

The only major controversies today over the "rules" of salad are when to serve it and whether iceberg lettuce should be banned from it. Beard is one of the few defenders of the commercial iceberg designed to be as sturdy as a basketball for packing, long hauling, and longevity. Provided it is broken by hand and not cut, says Beard, its flavor and texture are good. Others are less kind in their assessment, although Fisher does recall a hot potato salad in which hunks of iceberg had been buried among the steamy potatoes, salt pork, onions, and vinegar to such effect that it has kept her "quietly loyal to such a wretched vegetable."

For a time, iceberg so monopolized the lettuce market that its hard compact head was all you could buy. Romaine, or cos lettuce, ran it a close second, however, because it too had staying power. Then there was chicory, or curly endive, the toothy bitter leaves of which seemed as permanent under mastication as on the plate. A typical restaurant of the fifties added to the above chunks and curls some sliced red cabbage and a segment or two of plastic tomatoes and called it a "mixed green salad." Dressings were no longer bottled mayo or bottled French but bottled Russian, Thousand Island, or Roquefort. The point of the dressing, beyond its permanence, was that it be thick enough to blanket the leaves and sweet enough to mask the vinegar.

Today, a typical restaurant salad bar of the eighties doesn't offer much more in the way of greens and dressings, but it has added a great variety of condiments and garnishes, many of which are fresh. The major revolution of the salad bar, however, is that it has established the salad, at least in mass steak house restaurants, as a first course. Until the last decade or so, salad first was a quaintly California custom, an extension, Fisher suggests, of the Italian habit of eating something raw before the pasta. More likely, it was an extension of the old-fashioned relish dish of pressed or cut glass supporting strips of celery, carrots, and black olives embedded in ice.

Because the function of salad, whatever its position in the menu, is "to excite the digestion," as Theodore Child would say, salad first is as logical as soup first. The French habit of salad last, to awake the appetite for dessert, runs counter to the theory that a vinaigrette kills the taste of a good wine. By that theory, to serve salad with cheese is, if not the "syncretism" of which Ellwanger complains, at least a contradiction of the experienced fact that salad and cheese and wine go good together. So much for French "rules" that are contrary in any case to the improvisatory nature of American eating habits. Most of us will eat salad when we feel like it and serve it the same way unless we are being Frenchly formal.

The best thing about the green salad today is that better greens are available at the greengrocer. Today even supermarkets boast counters of soft lettuces such as the tender heads known in the East as "Boston" and in the West as "butter." Curly leaf lettuce appears in reds and greens and copper colors. Tiny Bibbs line up next to watercress, fat white Belgian endive, Italian arugula, Oriental bean and alfalfa sprouts. And more seeds are available to the home gardener, who can grow 5 kinds of the corn or field salad that the French call *mâche,* or as many varieties of spinach or escarole or cress, dandelion, parsley, and chives. The line between herbs and greens disappears in the summer salad sprinkled with basil or burnet, sorrel or peppergrass.

Washing greens is still a labor, particularly the weedy leaves picked fresh from the garden, but drying them is now a snap. What the processor is to chopping, the salad-dryer is to drying, a labor-saving device as essential to a salad lover as a sharp knife to a butcher. Instead of patting leaves dry with paper or kitchen towels or whirling them in a wire cage, we can now whisk them dry in seconds before putting them in a plastic bag to crisp in the refrigerator until ready to use.

The basic salad dressing today is, happily, French or Italian, meaning oil and vinegar, seasoned with salt and pepper. Proportions have changed slightly, increasing the ratio of oil from 3 oil to 1 acid, to 4 to 1. The change may be less a matter of taste than of product. Where vinegars have gotten better, olive oils have gotten worse. Standard brand olive oils are so dilute as to resemble corn and peanut and other neutral vegetable oils. Increasingly one has to buy an expensive, classy olive oil—cold virgin pressed—to get any flavor at all.

In these latter salad days, a recipe for a garden salad seems redundant, except for a couple of new suggestions. One is a decorative note from *Child & Company,* where Child depicts a salad arranged by her friend "Rosie the Salad Whiz." If you have a large perfect head of Boston or butter lettuce, arrange the washed leaves in a salad bowl to "reconstitute" the head, opened like a full-blossomed rose. Then pour the dressing carefully over the top so that you won't have to toss the leaves. Another is a taste note from *The New James Beard,* where Beard suggests an all-parsley salad of mixed Italian or flat-leafed and curly parsley with a garlic vinaigrette. For 3½ cups mixed parsley sprigs, he suggests a dressing of 8 tablespoons oil, 2 tablespoons vinegar, 5 to 6 minced garlic cloves, and

½ cup grated Parmesan cheese, tossed in after the dressing has been poured on.

My own suggestion in the salad way is to arrange greens by color in a round salad bowl or plate. When a variety of leaves are available, don't mix them all together, but alternate concentric rings of dark with light. For dark there is spinach, romaine, curly endive, copper leaf lettuce, Bibb, watercress, arugula. For light there is Boston lettuce, Belgian endive, bean sprouts, and the center of escarole. You can "compose" greens as you would cold vegetables to remind eaters that art had a hand in nature's gifts.

# JERUSALEM ARTICHOKE AND SPINACH SALAD

One reason for the popularity of the spinach and mushroom salad is that the contrast of white and green looks as good as the contrast of bland mushroom and tart leaf tastes. A similar pleasure can be had from the contrast of spinach and the unfortunately named Jerusalem Artichoke. The French call this knobby tuberous cousin of the sunflower *Topinambour,* which sounds interestingly exotic. Californians have renamed the tuber "Sunchoke," in the hope of improving its current image. But Jerusalem Artichokes they have been since the seventeenth century when Samuel de Champlain is said to have named them after he found Indians growing them on Cape Cod and thought their flavor reminiscent of artichoke. But why Jerusalem? Some speculate that Jerusalem was a corruption of the Spanish word for sunflower, *girasol.* Others that Jerusalem resulted from the early European confusion of the New World with the East. But Champlain may simply have been an ironist, suggesting to other adventurers the kind of dinner they might expect among savages as heathen as the Saracens.

Comparisons are odious, but if the tubers were called Western Water Chestnuts they might fare better in our current vogue for things Oriental. Beard laments their neglect and attributes it largely to innocence of what they are and what to do with them. All through the nineteenth century, cooks sauced them and pickled them and served them for salad in a vinaigrette. But in the twentieth century, the labor of hand peeling them may have done them in. More's the pity because, as Beard points out, "They not only taste delicious but are extremely low in calories."

Child suggests treating them *à la grecque,* cooking them lightly in a spiced liquid of lemon and oil to be served cold with other vegetables. But I find their uncooked crispness and nuttiness particularly appealing. All they require is patience to peel.

## Proportions

for 4 servings, 8 to 10 Jerusalem artichokes to 1 pound of fresh spinach to ½ cup of basic salad dressing.

**8 to 10 Jerusalem artichokes**
**1 pound fresh spinach leaves,**
**as small as possible**

**½ cup basic salad dressing**
**(page 141)**

1.   Peel the knobs with a vegetable peeler and drop into cold water to which a teaspoon of lemon juice has been added to prevent discoloring.

2.   Wash the spinach leaves thoroughly to get rid of any sand. Tear the leaves from the stems and whirl the leaves dry in a salad-dryer or pat dry and put in a salad bowl. Slice the artichokes thin, either by hand or with the slicing attachment of a food processor. Heap the slices in the center of the bowl and immediately pour the dressing over the whole.

*Spinach is especially complementary to eggs, fish, and fowl, and because this salad is crisp and simple, it can be served before, with, or after a rich dish like Baked Shad with Roe and Sorrel (page 205) or Baked Cod in Garlic Mayonnaise (page 204).*

# CUCUMBER-YOGURT SALAD

One of the best imports from Greece and the Levant is what the Turks call *cacik* and the Greeks *tzaziki*. We can call it plainly cucumber and yogurt, seasoned with garlic and lemon and, if the fancy takes us, fresh mint. It's one of the most refreshing of summer salads and a good salad to serve with fish year round. You can substitute sour cream for yogurt and chives for green onions. Or you can leave out the garlic and call it by an East Indian name, *maste khiar*, as Claiborne did in his first *Times* book. However called, it belongs to the Yogurt Belt that now encircles the globe.

## Proportions

for 4 servings, 2 medium cucumbers, 2 cloves garlic, to 1 cup of yogurt

**1 cup yogurt**
**1 tablespoon lemon juice**
**Salt to taste**
**¼ teaspoon freshly ground**
**black pepper**
**2 medium cucumbers, peeled,**
**seeded, and chopped**

**2 cloves garlic, minced**
**2 to 3 tablespoons chopped**
**green onions**
**2 to 3 tablespoons chopped**
**fresh mint, for garnish**

Season the yogurt with the lemon juice, salt, and pepper and mix with the vegetables. Taste carefully before salting because of the lemon juice. Refrigerate until ready to use. Serve on lettuce leaves or in a glass bowl, sprinkled with mint.

*While cucumber is a traditional complement to fish, the yogurt salad will best accompany plain poached or grilled fish or simple sautés, such as scallops or flounder.*

# CHINESE COLESLAW WITH BOILED DRESSING

As many Americans say "cold slaw" as "coleslaw," since we've had a couple of centuries to Anglicize fully such European words for cabbage as Dutch *kool*, German *kohl*, Spanish *col*. In the illogic of language, we've made Dutch *sla* for salad mean any shredded cabbage, usually cold but sometimes hot. Shredded cabbage in a boiled dressing was certainly a favorite salad of nineteenth-century cookbooks for the good reason that cabbage would keep well in the winter where leafier greens would not. The variations were mostly in the dressings and Beard brings together a number of them in his *American Cookery*. He cites with special fondness Mrs. Crowen's 1847 recipe for shredded cabbage wilted with butter and vinegar and served hot. An even finer version, I think, is Mrs. Harland's of 1893 when she adds a little sour cream just before serving. "This is a very nice preparation of cabbage, and far more wholesome than the uncooked," she says. "Try it!"

Another favorite of Beard's, which he repeats in *The New James Beard*, is the coleslaw of his childhood prepared by a Chinese cook named Billy. His dressing is a version of boiled dressing made with flour, sugar, and vinegar, enriched with cream and egg yolk. Rather than steaming the cabbage briefly in the hot dressing and serving the salad hot, Billy served it cold after the cabbage had wilted slightly by marinating in the dressing. The method was an old one but his dressing was richer than most. I have found the dressing, in a less thick and more mustardy version below, even more delicious on the curly leafed Chinese cabbage that is now a familiar part of our supermarkets. Because there is more stalk than leaf in the Chinese cabbage, the shredded head remains crisper. The slicer or the steel cutting blade of the food processor makes the shredding of it quick work.

Beard lists a dozen variants of a Quick Chopped Coleslaw, adding green onions, red and green peppers, carrots, radishes, and seafood such as tiny shrimp. Child suggests adding celery and apple. For conventional dressings, you can make a quick mayonnaise in the same processor, or combine mayonnaise with yogurt or sour cream and such variants as mustard or celery seed or caraway. Still, there's something about that old-fashioned boiled dressing that takes one back to the days when a Dutchman and a Chinese might rattle the pots with hot and cold words but smile together over the same hot cold slaw.

## Proportions

for 4 to 6 servings, 1 medium head Chinese cabbage to 2 cups of boiled dressing

| | |
|---|---|
| 1 **medium Chinese cabbage** | 2 **tablespoons sugar** |
| ½ **cup olive oil** | ½ **cup wine vinegar** |
| 1 **tablespoon flour** | **Dash of Tabasco sauce** |
| 2 **tablespoons Dijon mustard** | 1 **cup heavy cream** |
| 1½ **tablespoons dry mustard** | 2 **egg yolks** |
| ½ **teaspoon salt** | |

1.   Wash the cabbage and cut off the butt end. Cut in half crosswise and lengthwise, then in half again to fit a processor. Put through the slicer, then chill while making the dressing.

2.   Heat the oil in a saucepan, then stir in the flour, Dijon mustard, and dry mustard and blend well. Stir in the salt, sugar, vinegar, and Tabasco until the sugar dissolves. Beat the yolks with the cream, stir in a little of the hot sauce, then add the whole to the mixture. Cook over low heat until the sauce is well blended.

3.   Pour sauce over the prepared cabbage and toss well. Refrigerate when cool or serve at room temperature.

*Coleslaw, Chinese or otherwise, is a classic companion to baked hams and fried fish and chicken and any barbecued meats.*

# SPICED ORANGE AND ONION SALAD

Mixing fruit and vegetables in salad is at least as old in America as the Waldorf Salad introduced by Oscar Tschirky of the Waldorf in the 1880s and quickly adopted by any cook with any pretense to style. But other parts of the world had mixed fruits and vegetables, in sweets and sours, for centuries with no sense of violating botanical decorum. Wrapping fruits and vegetables in a mayonnaise, however, as opposed to a vinaigrette, may have been Oscar's particular contribution to the salad world and it was not universally approved. Mrs. Rorer applauded his mixture of apple and celery only when served with French dressing. On the subject of mayonnaised fruits, Mrs. Rorer was firm: "Fruits mixed with mayonnaise dressing, and served as a salad are unsightly, unpalatable and a little nauseating." At the turn of the century, dressings seemed peculiarly apt to provoke nausea.

The molded salads of the 1930s have perhaps made us cautious about what goes with what, remembering the days of anything goes. In olden days, a typical Luncheon Aspic Salad of the *Joy of Cooking* combined in the same gelatin bath capers, cooked asparagus, canned grapefruit, and shrimp. And who over the age of fifty does not remember the ring mold of cranberries, celery, nutmeats, cabbage, and crushed pineapple that was the delight of the buffet table? But the heaped salads of health fooders and vegetarians, along with the chic combinations of *nouvelle* France, have broken through the classicism of our late middle age. It is possible once again to consider more daring combinations than apple and celery and nutmeats, minus the mayonnaise of course, but perhaps with a touch of yogurt to cream the dressing.

The combination of orange and onion is really a classic of its own that shouldn't be forgotten in the rush for more exotic congress. The fruit and the vegetable are each sweet and tart and juicy, alike yet different, in ways that refresh the mind as well as the palate. Beard puts them together with shrimp. Claiborne adds anchovy fillets. An older combination is thin sliced hot beets, with blanched tops for the greens. Now that we're more familiar with Moroccan ways, a newer touch is to add an Eastern spice like cumin and, if the season is right, some chopped and fragrant mint.

## Proportions

for 4 servings, 4 navel oranges to 1 red onion

| | |
|---|---|
| 4 navel oranges | ⅛ teaspoon cayenne pepper |
| 1 large red onion | Salt and freshly ground |
| ⅓ cup olive oil | black pepper to taste |
| 1½ tablespoons lemon juice | ¼ cup chopped fresh mint |
| ½ teaspoon cumin | |

1. Peel the oranges and cut away any white pith. Slice ¼ inch thick and cut the slices into quarters. Remove the outer layer of skin from the red onion and slice the onion as thin as possible.

2. Mix together the oil, lemon juice, and seasonings and pour over the oranges and onions. Serve chilled or at room temperature. Garnish with the fresh mint.

*The mingled sweet and sour make this salad good for roast duck or pork or grilled squab or a rich fish such as bluefish.*

# GREEK SALAD

Any bowl with feta cheese in it is apt to be called Greek nowadays, but in fact the salty hunks of this white goat cheese are far preferable to the rubbery cubes of processed Cheddar or the bland cream cheese balls of yesteryear. When the tomatoes are ripe, the cucumbers crisp, the onion sweet, the cheese creamy, and the olives pungent, it is one of the best "composed" salads.

Even though the Greek island of Cos gave its name to a variety of lettuce, lettuce is a rarity in Greece's rocky isles where tomatoes are not. The salad is more "Greek" when layered in a bowl or on a platter without the bedding of green that usually surrounds it in a restaurant Greek salad in this country. The real essentials are the combined salty tang of cheese and olive.

## Proportions

for 4 servings, 4 tomatoes, 1 onion, 1 cucumber, 1 bunch radishes, ½ pound feta cheese, 2 dozen Greek olives, to ½ cup of basic salad dressing

4 **ripe tomatoes**
1 **large red onion, peeled**
1 **medium cucumber**
1 **bunch radishes**
½ **pound feta cheese**
24 **Greek olives, such as kalamatas or the oil- or dry-cured wrinkled Mediterranean types**

½ **cup basic salad dressing (page 141)**
2 **tablespoons chopped fresh dill**

Slice the tomatoes and onion as thin as possible. Peel, seed, and dice the cucumber. Trim the radishes and slice thinly. Arrange the vegetables on a platter and top with the crumbled cheese and pitted olives. Pour the dressing over and garnish with fresh chopped dill.

*Easily a meal in itself, but also a good first course for a grilled fish or fowl to follow. The Greeks serve it with the array of appetizers they call* mezedes, *but Americans are more apt to use it to replace a luncheon or supper Chef's Salad.*

# CAESAR SALAD

Claiborne cites the legendary Caesar Salad as one of the first of our "exotic" imports. It is legendary because its origins from the beginning were obscured by Hollywood hype. Apparently it came from south of the border, probably from Tijuana and possibly from the restaurant of a

Caesar named Cardini. Hollywood stars in search of booze during Prohibition are said to have made the salad popular by the frequency of their border trips. The legend is plausible enough, since the climax of the salad is the breaking into its heady mixture of garlic and anchovy a raw or nearly raw egg. It's the kind of nourishment that appealed to the Prairie-Oyster set and the garlic croutons guaranteed its appeal to strong men braving the border patrol with strong breath.

While no longer exotic, it is still a good salad and a period piece of restaurant entertainment when it is assembled and performed by an earnest and often pompous uniformed waiter. Think of it as a set piece like a Busby Berkeley musical number, and then the ritual dousings and squeezings and tossings may begin to please rather than annoy the diner who wonders what the fuss is all about.

Heeding Helen Brown's admonition in her *West Coast Cook Book* to keep the ingredients simple, Beard gives a fairly classic version of the Caesar in his *American Cookery.* "Like any salad of this kind," Brown says, "the artist adds (or subtracts) as he goes along," but the essentials are a sturdy green, garlic croutons, anchovies, an oil-egg-lemon dressing, and Parmesan cheese. The one ingredient missing from the recipe books, however, is a shot of tequila, on which everything else depends but which is best taken on the side.

## Proportions

for 4 servings, 1 head romaine lettuce, 1 cup garlic croutons, 1 can anchovies, ¼ cup grated Parmesan cheese

| | |
|---|---|
| 1 **head romaine lettuce** | 1 **can anchovy fillets** |
| ½ **cup olive oil** | **Salt and freshly ground** |
| 2 **cloves garlic, crushed** | **black pepper to taste** |
| 1 **cup bread cubes** | 1 **whole egg** |
| 1 **tablespoon lemon juice** | ¼ **cup grated Parmesan cheese** |

1.  Wash the romaine and break up the leaves into a large bowl.

2.  Heat 2 tablespoons of the oil in a skillet, add the crushed garlic and bread cubes, and shake and stir the cubes so that they will brown on all sides.

3.  Add the remaining oil to the romaine leaves and toss thoroughly to coat each leaf. Add the lemon juice and the anchovies and their oil, toss well, and season with salt and pepper. Add the croutons. Break an egg into the bowl, either raw or coddled for 1 minute. Toss until the egg is thoroughly mixed in. Add the grated cheese and toss again.

*The general richness of the sauce and all those garlic croutons make this a good prelude to an ungarnished beefsteak or other red-blooded meat.*

# SALADE NIÇOISE

In her first cookbook, Child included only "composed" salads as part of a cold buffet devoted largely to aspics and molds. Her focus reveals the French attention to "composition," no matter what the material at hand. The difference between French and English gardens characterizes also the difference between the produce of those gardens when laid out in salads on a buffet. The French insist on an artful look, the English on a "natural" one. As Americans have become more familiar with French ways, we have relied less on the virtues of sheer natural abundance and more on the pleasures of visual design. As we've taken to French clothes, so we've taken to French salads, and one of the first to gain common currency was the mixed vegetable Mediterranean salad called "Niçoise" for the bustling port of Nice.

While the French were accustomed to use a vegetable salad for an appetizing first course, as Le Snack-Bar became popular in postwar France, Salade Niçoise became a quick entrée like the omelet and entrecôte. Certainly it is hefty enough to make a good one-dish meal and the inclusion of tuna and anchovy guarantees a quota of protein. Because tuna salad is one of those old-fashioned reliables in American luncheons or suppers, the Niçoise can be thought of as a tuna salad raised to Francophilian heights.

## Proportions

for 4 servings, 1 can each of tuna and anchovies, 2 cups each of green beans, potatoes, and tomatoes, 1 head of lettuce, 1 cup of basic salad dressing

1 **cup basic salad dressing (page 141)**
2 **cups warm sliced boiled potatoes**
2 **cups green beans**
1 **head Boston or romaine lettuce**
1 **can tuna in oil**
3 **tomatoes, quartered**
3 **hard-boiled eggs, quartered**

½ **cup pitted black Mediterranean olives**
½ **cup sliced pimiento-stuffed olives**
1 **can anchovy fillets**
**Salt and freshly ground black pepper to taste**
2 **tablespoons chopped fresh parsley or basil**

1.  Pour ¼ cup basic salad dressing over the potato slices while they are still warm.
2.  Trim the beans and blanch them in boiling salted water for 3

to 5 minutes only, in order to keep them crisp. Drain and run under cold water to stop their cooking.

3. Arrange the lettuce leaves around the edge of a bowl or platter. Put the boiled potatoes in the center on one side and the beans on the other. Arrange the chunks of tuna in a line between them. Alternate tomatoes and eggs around the edge. Sprinkle the tomatoes and eggs with the black and green olives. Arrange the anchovy fillets like the spokes of a wheel on top of the potatoes and beans. Salt and pepper lightly, because the anchovies are salty. Pour the remaining dressing over all and sprinkle with chopped fresh herbs for garnish.

*If used as an appetizer, the salad should be followed by a simple main dish, such as a broiled steak or chop. If used as a main dish, the salad does not preclude thoughts of a good fattening dessert like a fruit tart or chocolate cake.*

# COBB SALAD

California, America's Salad Bowl, has appropriately given us a number of salads other than Caesar, including the Cobb. Said to have originated in Hollywood's Brown Derby restaurant, where it was served in glassware that looked like wide-mouthed brandy snifters, the Cobb is something like a Club Sandwich in salad form. The essential ingredients are chicken breast, bacon, hard-boiled egg, tomato, lettuce, and avocado. But the distinguishing method is that all ingredients are chopped fine and layered.

In *Julia Child & More Company,* Child photographs a decorative version where the ingredients are layered in stripes across a large glass bowl. If you are patient and determined, you can do the same striping in individual glass salad bowls. But you'll need patience in any case to do all that dicing. This is one place where the hand is better than the processor, because the look is everything and the dice will be more uniform by hand than by machine.

## Proportions

for 6 servings, 2 bunches greens, 2 chicken breast halves, 6 slices bacon, 3 eggs, 2 tomatoes, 1 avocado, 1 cup of basic salad dressing

1 bunch watercress or arugula
½ head iceberg lettuce
½ head romaine or equivalent amount of Bibb lettuce
2 chicken breast halves, poached
6 slices bacon, fried
3 hard-boiled eggs

1 avocado
Lemon juice
2 tomatoes, peeled, seeded, and chopped
2 tablespoons chopped chives
1 cup basic salad dressing (page 141)

1. Wash the greens, spin dry, wrap in paper towels inside a plastic bag, and refrigerate. Dice the cooked ingredients first, then the fresh ones. Cut the chicken breasts in strips lengthwise, then crosswise. Crumble the bacon. If you have an egg slicer, cut the eggs in one direction, then another. Keep the ingredients separate as you go. Dice the avocado last and squeeze lemon juice over it to prevent discoloring.

2. Shred the greens lengthwise as for slaw, then crosswise, so that the greens are diced, too. Line the bottom of a large glass salad bowl with a bed of the mixed greens. Put a wide stripe of chicken breasts in the middle with crumbled bacon on top. On either side put a stripe each of tomatoes, eggs, and avocado. Sprinkle the chives on top. Pour the dressing slowly over the mixture.

*This is the kind of salad that calls out for a slice of Apple-Pecan Pie (page 370) afterward or a fruit ice or ice cream.*

# WILTED COLD GREENS

The simplest kind of cooked salad is a plate of wilted greens dressed with lemon and oil. Many Americans are partial to greens, some are dubious and others can't abide 'em. I am partial. Those who like the rusty iron taste of spinach are apt to love the peppery zing of mustard greens, the tang of dandelion, the dark zap of collards, the sweetness of turnip, and the gentleness of beet. There's no accounting for the variety of greens or even the quantity we consume—some 240 million pounds a year, Beard says, of cultivated greens alone. There must be some primal appeal in their dark taste and chewy texture.

Even lettuce greens of various kinds—chicory, endive, escarole, romaine—take on this dark taste when wilted or braised. It's a good way to vary the daily garden salad and a good way to make tender any greens that have passed their first youth. Mixing greens is also a satisfying way to contrast textures and degrees of assertiveness, particularly when the summer garden is bursting with produce and each leafy top is clammering for attention. The best way to shut them up is to pick them while still too young to holler, give them a good cold bath, strip leaves from stems, and take the starch out of them by a steamy sauna of oil and occasionally garlic. Once cooked, they will rest comfortably for days in the refrigerator until you are ready to quiet them for good with a squeeze of lemon and a good grind of black pepper and lots more soothing oil.

For a long time our cookbooks ignored greens as if they were too peasanty or too southern regional or too close to the poverty line to be mentioned in polite society, but recently they've been given more serious attention. Child has a good photograph of collards, kale, and mustard greens in *Child & More Company* for those puzzled by the variety of leaves in the grocery store. And Beard has a good descriptive bibliography of greens in the concordance at the back of *The New James Beard.* The best way as always is simply to touch and taste unfamiliar greens, when you find them, since the cooking is simple and the risk small.

## Proportions

for 4 servings, around 2 pounds of greens to ½ cup of basic salad dressing

| | |
|---|---|
| 2 pounds greens, such as turnip, mustard, beet, dandelion, collard, etc. | Salt and freshly ground black pepper to taste |
| 2 to 3 tablespoons olive oil | ½ cup basic salad dressing (page 141) |

1.   Wash the greens thoroughly to remove any trace of dirt or sand. Unless the greens are very young and tender, strip the leaves from the stems. Put in a large skillet, or in a wok, with the olive oil.

2.   Sprinkle lightly with salt and pepper, cover, and wilt over moderate heat. Toss once or twice to cook evenly. (Moisture in the washed leaves, plus the oil, will keep them from sticking to the pan.) Cooking time will vary according to kind and age of green, anywhere from 5 to 15 or 20 minutes.

3.   When the greens are wilted, drain well in a colander and chop as you would spinach. Dress with the salad dressing and more salt and pepper if wanted. A crushed clove of garlic during the wilting is particularly good with the greens. Serve the greens cold or at room temperature.

*The tongue-coating astringency of greens has a chemical affinity for the oil of fish, as in tuna, mackerel, bluefish, and for meat laced with fat, as in bacon, sausages, and other pork products.*

# 1-2-3 BEAN SALAD

Because there are almost as many kinds of beans as greens, mixing cooked beans together with a little chopped egg and onion is another old-time favorite. The bean choice is limited only by time, season, and cans on the shelf. Here's one place where the canned kidney bean or chick-pea comes into its own. A mixture of canned with freshly cooked beans, however, will persuade your guests that you have taken some trouble over them after all, and I can't think of any bean that isn't the better for company.

Tiny limas dried or fresh, black turtle beans, black-eyed peas, the Italian fava beans inside their pink streaked pods or the American cranberry beans flecked with red and green or the delicate French flageolets

—all or any can go into the pot. But for an exemplary choice, let's pick two canned and one fresh bean, the former with a soft texture, the latter with a crisper one, each a different color and shape.

## Proportions

for 6 servings, 3 cups of mixed beans, 2 hard-boiled eggs, ½ cup of onion to ½ cup of mustard dressing

| | |
|---|---|
| 1 cup canned red kidney beans | 2 hard-boiled eggs, chopped fine |
| 1 cup canned chick-peas or garbanzos | Salt and freshly ground black pepper to taste |
| 1 cup fresh fava beans, shelled and cooked | ½ cup mustard dressing (page 142) |
| ½ cup finely chopped yellow or green onions | 2 tablespoons chopped parsley |

Drain the canned beans well. Boil the shelled beans for 8 to 12 minutes in salted water and drain well. Mix with the chopped egg and onion, season to taste, and pour mustard dressing over all or use the boiled dressing for Chinese Coleslaw. Garnish with chopped parsley. Serve the beans at room temperature rather than cold, although they may be marinated well ahead of serving time.

*For vegetarians, this is a one-dish meal of solid protein, but it is also a good accompaniment for cold meats or birds.*

# CLASSIC POTATO SALAD

Considering the standardized potato salad of most delicatessens today, the quality and variety of potato salads of the past, remembered or mis-remembered from hundreds of church socials or family picnics, are surprising. Mrs. Rorer furnishes a classic French type when she suggests slicing the hot boiled potatoes directly into a bowl of French dressing to marinate until cool. Mrs. Harland furnishes a more Anglo-Saxon type with mashed potatoes "rubbed through a cullender" and mixed with cabbage, pickle, and egg in a boiled dressing.

The split between French and Anglo dressings continues in current recipes, with Child listing a classic American mayonnaise type in *Child & Company,* Claiborne revising Grandmother's mayonnaise with a French dressing in *The New York Times Cook Book,* and Beard bridging the gap in *The New James Beard* with both an Old-Fashioned Oregon Potato Salad and a French Hot Potato Salad.

What old-fashioned Oregon means to Beard is a mixture of potato with onions, celery, and carrots, doused in vinegar, coated in mayonnaise, and garnished not only with the usual eggs but shredded nasturtium leaves. Old-fashioned American to Child means potatoes with onion, celery, eggs, and pickle, slavered in mayonnaise and garnished with pimiento. The classic French way, which Child first gave us in *Mastering I,* is to douse the hot slices with wine, then marinate in oil, mustard, and vinegar, adding chopped herbs when cool.

The salad Child has recently labeled Rosie's Great Potato Salad after her friend Rosie, the Salad Whiz, combines the best of both worlds. She marinates the warm potatoes in vinegar and chicken broth (instead of white wine), then folds them when cool into homemade mayonnaise, along with the crisp and chunky bits of onion and celery and pickle and pimiento that remind me of the Fourth of July more than sparklers or firecrackers. For a spark of red, I prefer fresh red sweet peppers to canned pimiento. And I like to use enough eggs to completely cover the top with circles of yellow and white. That spells old-fashioned American to me.

## Proportions

for 6 to 8 servings, 3 pounds of new potatoes to 6 eggs to ¾ cup of mayonnaise

| | |
|---|---|
| 3 pounds new potatoes (or other good boiling potatoes) | 1 large celery stalk, diced |
| | 1 small dill pickle, diced |
| | 1 sweet red pepper, diced |
| ½ cup chicken broth | 6 hard-boiled eggs |
| 2 tablespoons white wine vinegar or cider vinegar | ¾ cup homemade mayonnaise (page 139) |
| Salt and freshly ground black pepper to taste | 2 tablespoons minced chives |
| 1 medium onion, diced | |

1.   Boil the potatoes in their skins in salted water until barely tender. Drain well and return to the dry pan, covered, to sit for 5 minutes before peeling and slicing. Peel the skin while the potatoes are still warm (unless the potatoes are so new that the skin almost disappears) and slice the potatoes ½ inch thick into a bowl. Pour on the broth and vinegar and sprinkle with salt and pepper.

2.   Dice the other vegetables and add them to the potatoes. Slice the hard-boiled eggs in rounds, putting aside enough of the best circles to cover the top of the bowl. Dice the white ends and imperfect slices and add them to the vegetables.

3. Fold the mayonnaise into the vegetables, smooth the top, and lay on the slices of hard-boiled egg. Sprinkle the chopped chives over the eggs. Cover with plastic wrap and refrigerate until ready to use.

*Potato salad, like potatoes, can go with just about any fish, fowl, or flesh, but for picnic suppers it is usually flanked by cold ham or turkey, fried chicken, or barbecued ribs.*

# CHICKEN SALAD CHINESE

When Claiborne gave us Chicken Salad à la Chinoise in his first cookbook, the Chinoise part was canned bean sprouts and a dash of soy sauce mixed into the traditional chicken, celery, and mayonnaise. A mere twenty years later, the Chinese revolution has permeated so far into Western cooking methods that Claiborne's description of a chicken salad prepared by the renowned French chef Jean Troisgros is essentially that of a Chinese stir-fry garnished with truffles. He calls it Salade de Poulet Troisgros, but it is really a sophisticated Chicken Salad Chinese.

Chef Troisgros' method is to slice raw chicken meat, pound the slices flat, dice them fine, and then brown them quickly in peanut oil in a skillet (read wok), before adding to mixed salad greens and herbs flavored with scallions, vinegar, and—a thoroughly French touch—truffles and their juice. Another sophisticated Chinese salad that is easier and less costly to prepare is given by Beard in *The New James Beard*. Here the chicken is roasted before shredding the meat and tossing it with Chinese seasonings like sesame seeds and the Chinese parsley known elsewhere as cilantro. Beard beds the chicken in shredded iceberg lettuce, but as there is no liquid dressing for the chicken, I think the dish looks better and more Chinese without the bed.

## Proportions

for 6 to 8 servings, 1 roasting chicken (4 to 5 pounds), 1 bunch of Chinese parsley, 1 cup of sesame seeds

1 4- to 5-pound roasting chicken
1 cup sesame seeds, toasted
4 tablespoons dry mustard
½ cup cold water
1 tablespoon Szechuan peppercorns or cracked black pepper

½ cup sesame oil
2 tablespoons light soy sauce
1 bunch green onions, chopped
1 bunch Chinese parsley (cilantro), chopped

1. Poach or roast the chicken (see pages 229 or 215). When it is cool, skin, remove the meat from the bones, and shred it. The white meat will shred easily with your fingers; the dark meat may require a sharp knife. Toast the sesame seeds in a 350-degree oven for about 5 minutes and set them aside.

2. Dissolve the mustard in cold water and let it sit for 15 minutes. Heat the peppercorns for a few minutes in the sesame oil to release their flavor. Mix with the soy and mustard to make a dressing. Toss the chicken shreds in the dressing to coat evenly.

3. Add the sesame seeds, green onions, and chopped parsley. Taste carefully for seasoning. Serve at room temperature.

*Because the salad is Chinese in flavor, you might accompany it with a mixed vegetable stir-fry and follow it with fresh orange slices or baked bananas.*

# CRAB LOUIS

Another California contribution to the salad world is a dish sanctified, as usual, by a foreign name to validate a local product, in this case the West Coast Dungeness crab. According to Helen Brown's *West Coast Cook Book,* Crab Louis was already operative as early as 1914 in Solari's restaurant in San Francisco. Beard found it in the Bohemian restaurant of his native Portland and it's not hard to account for its popularity. First, crabs were as plentiful then as coolie hands to dig out the meat. Second, bottled chili sauce was new enough to make exciting a pink chunky mayonnaise called Thousand Island Dressing, of which the Louis sauce is a spicy version.

Nobody has ever said a word against California's native crab, and most would agree that it's the best in the country; so good, in fact, that it shouldn't be sullied with anything but fresh mayonnaise. But in the days when crab was cheaper and more plentiful than now, a variant mayonnaise was the spice of life, and a pink one, lightened by cream and spiked with onion and green olives, added tone. There are still disputes over what properly belongs to a Louis dressing. Claiborne added Worcestershire sauce, horseradish, chives, and even a little French dressing to the mayonnaise in his Crab Louis of the first *New York Times Cook Book.* Beard in his *American Cookery* cites the simple version of the old Bohemian and the fuller one of Solari's as outlined by Helen Brown.

I, too, have followed Helen Brown, with the added suggestion that a homemade chili sauce as well as a homemade mayonnaise allows the contemporary cook to get rid of the sweet in favor of the hot. Good crabmeat is much harder to find today than a good dressing, but when the two come together in a delicate blend of pink and white we can celebrate the unlikely convergence of a Dungeness with a Louis.

## Proportions

for 4 servings, 2 large crabs or about 3 cups of crabmeat to 2 cups of sauce

| | |
|---|---|
| 1 **head Boston lettuce** | 4 **hard-boiled eggs, quartered** |
| 3 **cups quality crabmeat,** | 4 **ripe tomatoes, quartered** |
| **cooked** | |

### Sauce

| | |
|---|---|
| 1 **cup fresh mayonnaise** | ¼ **cup minced green onions** |
| ¼ **cup heavy cream** | 2 **tablespoons diced green** |
| ¼ **cup homemade chili sauce** | **olives** |
| ¼ **cup minced green pepper** | **Lemon juice to taste** |

Arrange the washed lettuce leaves on a plate. Heap the crabmeat in the center. Combine the sauce ingredients and pour them over the crabmeat. Garnish with eggs and tomatoes.

*The salad makes a fine luncheon dish, followed by a Lemon Meringue Pie (page 374) or Orange-Almond Sponge Cake (page 378) for the hungry, or by a fruit ice (page 392) for the abstemious.*

# PAPAYA, ORANGE, AVOCADO, AND DUCK SALAD

To make any salad or first course *nouvelle* French, all one has to do is cube some *foie gras,* dice some truffles, or sliver a roasted duck. Or so it seems. Of these three trademarks, only the duck is readily affordable and post-*nouvelle* restaurants have used duck in far more imaginative ways, hot and cold, than ever before. Roasted duck *à l'orange* hot has now become duck-and-orange salad cold.

Even though the gamy taste has been bred out of duck, the dark meat still has an affinity for the sweet and tart of fruit. And even though fat has been bred in or rather on duck, we can strip the meat of fat and supply a complementary richness in less costly ways than *foie gras* by using avocado. As for truffles? Think of them as the vulgar ostentation of the expense-account set and you'll never miss them. Better, far better, to use as garnish the crisp cracklings of duck skin that many believe is the best part of the duck.

But why papaya? For color and shape. One of Beard's favorite salads is papaya, avocado, and other curvilinear shapes like shrimp. The alternating strips of pale orange and pale green are as pleasing to the eye as the alternating soft and firm textures are pleasing to the palate. This makes a spectacularly dressy salad without a hint of truffle or *foie gras*.

## Proportions

for 6 to 8 servings, 1 duck, 2 papayas, 4 oranges, 2 avocados to 1 cup of orange-mustard mayonnaise

**1 duck, roasted (page 221)**  **4 seedless oranges**
**2 ripe papayas**              **1 head romaine lettuce**
**2 ripe avocados**             **1 lime or lemon**

### Sauce

**1 cup homemade mayonnaise**   **Grated rind of 1 orange**
**(page 139)**
**1 to 2 tablespoons Dijon**
**mustard**

1.  When the duck is cool, remove the skin and any trace of fat from the meat; remove the meat from the bones. Slice the breast lengthwise as thin as possible. Do the same with the thighs and legs, though the pieces will be scrappier. Strip the excess fat from the skin and cut the skin in narrow strips to make cracklings. Put the cracklings in a pan in a 400-degree oven for 30 to 40 minutes, pouring off the fat once or twice as it accumulates. Drain the cracklings on paper towels.

2.  Peel the papayas and avocados and cut in uniform slices lengthwise. Grate the rind of 1 orange before peeling and put the rind aside for the dressing. Peel the remaining oranges and break them into sections, removing the inner membranes.

3.  On a large platter arrange the romaine leaves in a circle with stalks toward the center, green tips outward. Alternate slices of papaya and avocado in a large circle. Sprinkle with a little lime juice. Arrange the orange segments in a circle within the outer ring. Put the scrappiest slices of duck in the center on the bottom and cover with the sliced breast meat. Outline the circle with a row of cracklings.

4.  To a cup of mayonnaise add the Dijon mustard and the grated orange rind. Serve the sauce separately.

*The salad is a full rich meal best followed by black coffee or tea and noth-ing more.*

# RAW VEGETABLE ASPIC

When the electric refrigerator came in big in the 1930s, so did the jellied salad mold. Tomato aspic, as a generic type, was entirely a creature of the newfangled machine that could keep gelatin from melting on a hot summer day even when the iceman failed to come. Before, tomato jelly had meant fruit jelly, like marmalade, sweetened with sugar and thickened if need be with cornstarch. Afterward, tomato jelly meant gelatin and the aspic took over. The 1943 *Joy of Cooking* gives five tomato aspic recipes in climactic order, ending with Frozen Tomato Aspic, in which tomato juice and gelatin are whipped with egg whites and frozen in refrigerator trays to make cubes for salad.

The Victorians, of course, were devoted to jellied molds of elaborate shapes, but usually for desserts or set-pieces for the grand buffet. In *Mastering I,* Child's salad section is a subdivision of the Cold Buffet consisting largely of Aspics and Molded Mousses. But now that we have moved away from formal showpieces even for our buffet tables, we find that Child's "Buffet for 19" in *Child & Company* sports oysters on the half shell, a turkey casserole, and a simple salad of fresh green beans with watercress and diced tomatoes. Not an aspic in sight.

Few who were alive in the thirties will regret the passing of tomato aspic. Few who first learned to make a flawlessly clear aspic from Child's instructions in *Mastering I* will regret the passing of aspic of any kind. But the aspic has its place even in today's informal scene because it looks good and tastes good and can be made quickly even without a pair of calves' feet or veal knuckles. Child's formula for turning stock into aspic by means of commercial gelatin is to add 1 package of gelatin to 2 cups of liquid. For lining a mold, she increases the proportions of gelatin: 1 gelatin to 1½ liquid.

Because gelatin is tasteless, the taste must come from the broth or stock, the more intense the better. If you're using canned chicken broth, reduce it or add pork rind or chicken gizzards to give it body and flavor. A little tomato juice will help the flavor but Madeira or Cognac is better still.

Once fat is removed from the stock, you still need to clarify it to make it transparent and sparkling. The method is peculiar but magical, or at least alchemical, because you must muddy the liquid to make it clear. The coagulating properties of egg white and eggshell do the trick. Add a frothed egg white and a crushed eggshell to the hot liquid, beat it with a whisk until the liquid boils and the white rises to the surface as scum. Remove the pan from the heat and let the liquid settle for 5 minutes. Then pour without stirring through a damp linen towel or layers of wet cheesecloth lining a sieve or colander. The towel or cheesecloth wrung out in cold water traps fat particles as well as strains out the impurities caught by the egg scum. Sounds nasty but it works. Then taste the stock and add what it needs: a little lemon, some Madeira, or sherry?

A vegetarian can make a vegetable aspic entirely of vegetable juice, of course, with gelatin to set it. But you'll get a better flavor with chicken or mixed stock. You can use any variety of vegetables, as in the Cobb Salad, but you may surprise your guests by showing how good raw corn is when complemented by other summer flavors. The prettiest way is to layer the vegetables one at a time. The fastest way is simply to mix the vegetables in a mold or bowl and pour in the stock.

## Proportions

for 4 to 6 servings, 4 to 5 cups of diced vegetables to 6 cups of liquid

| | |
|---|---|
| 4 packages gelatin | 1 cup peeled, seeded, and |
| 6 cups chicken stock |   diced cucumber |
| 2 tablespoons lemon juice | ½ cup diced sweet red onion |
| 1 cup diced raw zucchini | 1 cup raw corn kernels |
| 1 cup peeled, seeded, and | Parsley or watercress sprigs |
|   chopped tomatoes |   for garnish |

1.   Prepare the aspic by first softening the gelatin in 2 cups of cold stock, then stirring it into remaining stock and heating until the gelatin is entirely dissolved. Remove from the heat, add lemon juice to taste (it's good quite tart), and refrigerate until it becomes syrupy.

2.   Meanwhile, prepare the vegetables for layering and keep them separate. If your gelatin is flavorful enough you will not need to salt or pepper your raw vegetables.

3.   Put a layer of aspic in the bottom of a mold (a charlotte mold or a plastic refrigerator container is good) and chill quickly until set. Add a layer of zucchini and aspic to cover. Chill again. Continue adding vegetables and liquid in layers. (Reheat small amounts of the aspic as you go and rechill it over cracked ice to get it syrupy again. Layering is work but the results are worth it.)

4.   Refrigerate until ready to use. Unmold by immersing the container briefly in warm water and inverting it on a serving platter. Surround the base with sprigs of parsley or watercress.

*Good with cold meat like a Boeuf à la Mode or chicken or veal, plain or sauced.*

# SALMON AND SCALLOP SALAD

A whole fish poached and molded in its own jelly is a joy for eyes and salivating glands, but it's not always easy to serve. One solution is to arrange boned pieces of salmon with white poached scallops for an attractive taste and color contrast that also reassures eaters of boneless bites. It is easy to skin and bone salmon steaks once they are cooked and scallops are an added dividend. Covering the whole with a clear fish jelly keeps the fish from drying out, besides giving a nice glossy finish.

You'll get the best flavor if you poach the salmon in a court bouillon of wine and water (see the Fish Stock, page 103), but Beard, in *The New James Beard,* suggests a simple poaching in salted water flavored with slices of lemon and sprigs of dill. Or you can wrap the salmon in foil with lemon and dill, or other herbs, such as tarragon, and "poach" by baking in a low oven (325 degrees). Either way, cook for 10 minutes per inch of thickness if the fish is at room temperature.

## Proportions

for 4 servings, 4 salmon steaks, 12 sea scallops, 2 cups of fish aspic to 1 cup of yogurt mayonnaise

| | |
|---|---|
| 4 **salmon steaks, 1-inch thick** | 4 **cups court bouillon** |
| 12 **sea scallops** | 1 **package gelatin** |

### Sauce

| | |
|---|---|
| 1 **cup homemade mayonnaise (page 139)** | **Watercress and lemon for garnish** |
| ½ **cup yogurt** | |
| 2 **tablespoons chopped fresh herbs** | |

1.   Poach the salmon steaks in the court bouillon and drain well. Do not overcook. Salmon should be fork tender but not fall apart (see page 188). While the steaks are still warm, remove the outside skin and all bones. Cover with plastic wrap.

2.   Poach the scallops gently for 2 to 3 minutes in the same salmon liquid and drain well. Strain the liquid and reduce to 2 cups. (Clarify by simmering gently with 1 beaten egg white and crushed shell.) Soften the gelatin in ¼ cup cold water. Add to the hot stock and stir until the gelatin is dissolved. Refrigerate immediately.

3.   Arrange the steaks in a row on a serving dish, placing 3 scallops between the forked ends of the steaks. When the aspic is syrupy and beginning to set, spoon it quickly over the steaks in a protective layer. Chill until ready to use. Finish decorating the plate by placing a bunch of washed watercress at either end and a row of lemon slices across the top and bottom. Serve the sauce of yogurt mayonnaise separately.

*Asparagus before, fruit and cheese afterward would make this a classic luncheon or dinner on a hot day. The salad is also visually good for a buffet table and it is easy to serve.*

# EGGS

*To guess (I do not say determine) whether an egg is good, shut one eye; frame the egg in the hollow of the hand, telescope-wise, and look at the sun through it with the open eye. If you can distinctly trace the yolk and the white looks clear around it, the chances are in favor of the egg and the buyer. Or, shake it gently at your ear. If addled, it will gurgle like water; if there is a chicken inside, you may distinguish a slight "thud" against the sides of the egg.*

—Marion Harland
Common Sense in the Household
*(1893)*

After man first ate the apple, he learned—from the serpent—how to suck an egg. The most universal of foods, it is also one of the most ancient because it can be drunk or eaten in its own pot. An egg, in fact, is a liquid bird that comes in its own container. Because that container holds all the major nutrients necessary to life, the current bad reputation of the egg as an artery clogger is as unfair as its earlier reputation as a sexual provocative. While the egg does contain substances that clog arteries, it also has substances that unclog them. And while the egg has doubtless nourished countless lovers, it has also nourished centuries of invalids and infants.

Americans have tended to underrate the egg. In imitation of the English, they have valued eggs principally as a breakfast food—raw, poached, boiled, baked, fried, or scrambled. Eggs were too common and cheap to be valued. Not until the Second World War, when dried and powdered eggs became the fighting man's breakfast, did a "fresh" egg become the subject of libidinous dreams.

"Fresh," of course, is a term more relative with the egg than with almost any other of our staple foods. Mrs. Harland's discriminating ear might not hear gurgles and thuds in her local supermarket egg today, but she could determine—not guess—that the egg had dropped at least a week earlier from its feathered container to its cardboard one. While today the chances of getting an addled supermarket egg are small, the chances of getting a freshly plucked egg are nil.

If our cooking masters could not restore the days of a chicken in every yard, they could show us how better to use the eggs we had. They could explain the principle of the egg as binder, stabilizer, thickening agent, leavening agent, and clarifier. They could explain the first principle of egg cooking: Start with room temperature eggs (warm refrigerated eggs for a few minutes in hot water). They could explain the second principle of egg cooking: Be gentle, be slow, and keep the heat low—unless, of course, you are making an omelet.

They could explain in pedantic detail the intricacies of the French rolled omelet, along with the American fluffed, Italian flat, and Chinese sliced. As we discovered that mastering the French omelet was easier than we had thought, we also discovered that mastering simple scrambled eggs was harder. A perfectly scrambled egg is one of the rarest of dishes, Beard claims, because the egg is generally overcooked until hard and lumpy. One must push the curds slowly in butter and must "know when to stop," since eggs will continue to cook with their own heat once removed from the stove.

We learned that the principle of the scrambled (sautéed or stir-fried) egg, which must cook gentle, slow, and low, is opposite to the principle of the rolled egg, which must cook fast and hot to make an omelet. From Claiborne we learned to make omelets by step-by-step photographs, an innovation in cookbooks in 1961. From Child we learned by copious illustrations the look of the omelet pan we must buy: a Number 24 chef's iron pan of 7 inches that is seasoned, wiped clean, and never washed. We also learned, by illustrative arrows, the movements we must make back and forth and round and round to create an omelet by the scrambling method. To create an omelet by the rolling method, we learned to jerk the pan at a 20-degree angle, one jerk per second, increasing the angle until the eggs began to roll. We practiced, as Child suggested, in the backyard, with a cup full of dried beans. Our yards were full of beans if not of chickens laying eggs.

Poaching was another process to be mastered. Those of us who had grown up on steamed eggs, made into perfect rounds by metal molds placed over boiling water, learned for the first time how to drop an egg directly into a simmering bath. And we learned the binding properties of eggs with milk and cream. We learned that not all custards were sweet and not all custard pies were desserts. We learned this when Child inaugurated the Era of the Quiche. We learned that custards might contain bacon, onions, spinach, leeks, cheese, crab; that they might be cold as well as hot; that they might be eaten with the fingers as well as with forks. Restaurants and delis learned the lesson of the quiche so well and rapidly that today quiche in assorted flavors takes its place beside tuna-and-egg salad and chopped chicken livers at deli counters everywhere. Today the quiche lesson is also a moral fable: There is nothing so good that it can't be ruined.

In learning the leavening properties of eggs, we also discovered we could master the soufflé. Once we learned the principles of the egg white, we were no longer traumatized by visions of the Fallen Soufflé. We practiced the wrist action for whipping whites as we had practiced the wrist toss for rolling omelets.

Claiborne's photographs and Child's drawings de-mystified the process by which egg yolks were first thickened by sauce, and then leavened by beaten and folded whites. From Child we learned to adjust proportions precisely for molds of varying size. From Beard we learned to improvise our equipment: The copper bowl and balloon whisk were no more necessary for beating than a rubber spatula for folding. You could fold by gentle hand.

Finally, we learned from all to try more daring combinations: to poach, scramble, bake, and fry with hot peppers and tomatoes, Mexican style. Or to deep fry in a sausage coating, Scotch style. Or to make the Italian omelets called *frittatas* of not only zucchini but, as Fisher said, "Alla Anything-At-All." Honors for eclecticism would always go to Fisher. How universal was the egg she showed us in Eggs Sino-Aixois, as she called it, a scandalous but delicious marriage between Chinese and Provençal that scrambled eggs with black olives, oil, and garlic, and nested them in Chinese rice. The combination would have startled Mrs. Harland, perhaps, but it might represent a final solution to the problem of the indeterminately fresh egg.

# EGGS BENEDICTINE

The beauty of a poached egg is its plump rounded shape, achieved in one of three ways: by dropping the egg into a whirlpool of simmering water (not easy), by trimming the ragged white once the egg is poached (easy), or by using a metal egg poacher (very easy). "As for poaching, I cheat," Fisher confesses, remembering too many skillets and skimmers and free-floating whites.

The texture, however, of an egg dropped into vinegared water, which helps coagulate the white quickly, is entirely different from that of an egg dropped into a little metal hat to steam. To me the machine-tooled uniformity of texture and shape lacks the excitement and idiosyncrasies of the free-floaters. Real poaching is more fun.

Beard's directions for real poaching call for 2 or 3 inches of water, salted and vinegared (½ teaspoon each), and brought barely to the boil in a flat-surfaced pan or skillet. Break each egg first into a small cup in order to slide the egg easily from cup to water. Then invert the cup over the egg for a few seconds in order to keep the white from spreading. When all eggs (no more than 2 or 3 per skillet) are in, remove pan from heat and baste tops with the hot water for 3 or 4 minutes until whites are set and yolks are filmed. Remove with slotted spoon and drain eggs on paper towels. If whites are ragged, trim them quickly with a knife or shears.

The beauty of a plump rounded egg is that it's right for nesting in something to replace the shell it has lost. Round muffins or square toast provide flat nests. Spinach nests, as in Eggs Florentine, provide green ones. Mashed potatoes provide white ones. One of the best nesting materials comes from the French version of Eggs Benedict, the richer and heartier and utterly satisfying Eggs Benedictine, nested in the purée of codfish, garlic, oil, and cream called Brandade de Morue. The advantage of Benedictine over Benedict is that the egg melds with the nest in a way impossible to layers of ham and toast and sauce. A dividend is that the cod purée is so rich and intense that a single nest with a single egg constitutes a meal. A bonus is that the cream and oil make an added sauce unnecessary.

## Proportions

for 4 servings, 4 eggs, 1 pound salt cod to 1½ cups boiled potatoes to ½ cup each of olive oil and cream

| | |
|---|---|
| **1 pound cooked salt cod** | **½ cup olive oil** |
| **1 large potato, boiled and chopped** | **½ cup heavy cream** |
| | **A few drops lemon juice** |
| **2 cloves garlic, minced** | **Freshly ground black pepper** |
| **4 poached eggs** | **to taste** |

1.  To cook the dried cod, soak it overnight in cold water, changing the water two or three times to remove the salt. Drain, rinse well, and bring to a boil in cold water to cover. Immediately reduce the heat and simmer for 10 to 15 minutes. If you boil it, the cod will be tough and stringy. Drain and put in a processor with a hot boiled potato and the minced garlic.

2.  Poach the eggs and slip them into a bowl of warm water. The heat of the purée will warm the eggs after they are in their nests.

3.  Gently heat the oil and cream in separate pans. Shred the cod in the processor and, while the machine is running, add the cream and oil alternately until the purée is smooth and thick. Taste carefully for seasoning and add lemon juice and pepper to taste.

4.  Scoop the purée onto 4 plates. Make a hollow in the top of each mound and fill with a drained poached egg. Grind a bit of black pepper on top.

*Serve for brunch or lunch or Sunday supper with a crisp green salad and nothing else.*

# BAKED EGGS WITH SMOKED SALMON

As easy as poaching eggs is baking (or shirring) them in heat-proof ramekins that substitute for shell or nest. Child advises setting the ramekins in a pan of boiling water to guarantee even heat, but she specifies ramekins about the size of custard cups, 2½ to 3 inches in diameter and 1½ inches high. Wider and flatter ramekins don't require the water bath because the eggs will lie flat like fried eggs. No water makes baked eggs quick and easy work.

To conceal beneath the eggs a thin layer of something unexpected and delicious, like sliced mushrooms, sliced duck or chicken livers, puréed spinach, a slice of pâté, or a slice of smoked salmon, as in the recipe below, is to turn one of the simplest of dishes into one fit for a champagne supper. Instead of topping simply with butter or cream, you can top the eggs with any kind of complementary sauce that won't curdle under heat. Or, if you long for the taste of a hollandaise or béarnaise, you can simply add the sauce after removing the eggs from the oven.

The only trick is not to overcook, as the eggs will continue to cook in the hot ramekins outside the oven. The best way is to remove them when the whites are barely set and still trembly. The yolks should be runny, not hard.

## Proportions

for 3 to 6 servings, 6 eggs: for each egg, 1 teaspoon butter, 2 tablespoons heavy cream, 1 slice of smoked salmon

| | |
|---|---|
| 2 tablespoons butter | Salt and freshly ground |
| 6 slices smoked salmon | black pepper to taste |
| 6 eggs | Lemon juice |
| ¾ cup heavy cream | |

1. Melt 1 or 2 teaspoons of butter in each ramekin in a 350-degree oven, which warms the ramekins as well as coats them. Remove from the oven and put a slice of smoked salmon in each. Break one or two eggs into each ramekin, on top of the salmon. Pour heavy cream over the top and sprinkle lightly with salt and pepper.

2. Bake on the top shelf of the oven for about 7 minutes, or until the white is just set. Remove and sprinkle with a drop or two of lemon juice to complement the salmon. Serve immediately with toast points (see Melba toast, page 84).

*One egg apiece makes a good first course. Two eggs apiece make a good main dish for lunch or supper. Serve with a cold white wine.*

# FOOLPROOF FRENCH OMELET

For years the word omelet conveyed to Americans a puffy pan-fried soufflé, often sweet, in which whites and yolks were beaten separately so that the whites would rise. The classical French omelet, however, is really an egg pancake, rolled instead of puffed or scrambled. As anyone knows who has made a feast of a simple omelet in a humble bistro anywhere in France, texture and shape are everything. The trick of the pancake is to keep the inside creamy while making the outside firm enough to shape.

There are two major ways of doing this. Only Child bothers to give instructions for the hard way of rolling an omelet onto itself by shaking the pan with a series of synchronized jerks. For most of us the scrambled way is safer and, with a little practice, foolproof once we understand the principles. The first principle is to get the right kind of pan and to keep it right by not washing it, if it is seasoned, and by not cooking anything else in it that might stick. When Child recommended "the French type of plain iron pan ⅛ inch thick," to cook anything other than omelets in it was hazardous. But with the recent developments of nonstick pans like Teflon and Calphalon, the omelet-maker's task is easier and he need not hide his omelet pan from the rest of the household.

The second principle is to get the pan and its lubricating butter to the right temperature before throwing in the eggs for a quick shake, roll, and turn out. The butter should foam up but not brown. That is the moment to add the eggs and to start shaking them back and forth, stirring continuously with the back of a fork, while they thicken. They will do this in 3 or 4 seconds. If the eggs seem to be cooking faster than you can stir, you can control the temperature by lifting the pan off the heat. Now is the time to add any filling by sprinkling it in quickly.

The third principle is to roll the pancake away from you so that it can roll from the pan to the plate. That is why the sides of the pan must be nonstick, so that the egg will slip easily from the pan. If the shape on the plate is less than perfect, you can always tuck the edges under with a fork.

For a plain omelet, the ingredients are as simple as butter, eggs, salt, and pepper. Only Beard suggests a tablespoon of water (not milk or cream which toughens) to 2 eggs, to help the blending of yolk and white. The others prefer, as I do, not to dilute the egg. So popular have omelets become in recent years, particularly in restaurants, that a plain omelet unstuffed with mushroom, cheese, herb, avocado, sour cream, or anything else that sounds good on a menu, is becoming as scarce as an egg fresh from the hen. For this reason, I have left the omelet below unstuffed, unsavored, uncreamed with anything but its delicate golden creamy self.

## Proportions

for each serving, 2 large eggs, 1 tablespoon butter, in an 8- to 9-inch pan

**2 large eggs**                    **1 tablespoon butter**
**¼ teaspoon salt**
**Freshly ground black pepper
to taste**

1.  Beat the eggs and seasonings together in a bowl with a fork. Heat the omelet pan over high heat with the butter until it begins to foam.
2.  Swirl the butter around and quickly add the eggs. Shake the pan forward and backward with one hand while stirring the eggs with the back of a fork with the other. In 3 or 4 seconds, the bottom will be set, so if you want to add a filling, do it now.
3.  Tilt the pan away from the handle end and with a fork push the egg pancake to roll it toward the far end of the pan directly onto the plate.

*Garnish with a sprig of parsley or watercress and serve with a green salad and a bowl of ripe fruit.*

# ITALIAN *FRITTATA*

A flat egg pancake that is not rolled but stuffed with mixed vegetables, meats, or whatever happens to be in your refrigerator that egg can bind, is the peasant omelet the Italians call *frittata.* Garnished with tomatoes, onions, and peppers, the Basques of Spain and France call it *pipèrade.* Garnished with celery, mushrooms, and bean sprouts, the Chinese call it Egg Foo Yeung.

The dish has as many names as possibilities because the egg functions like bread in a sandwich to hold together what would otherwise fall asunder. That is one reason a *frittata* is as good cold as hot and is far easier to carry and eat on a picnic than a layered sandwich glued tenuously by butter and mayonnaise. Filled with potatoes, onions, and ham, it can be as hearty as a soup or stew. Filled with sliced fresh black truffles, as I had it once in a suburban American kitchen immortalized by it, it can be a meal for kings.

To call it an Italian *omelet,* however, is misleading because the cooking method is opposite to that of a French omelet. Slow and gentle heat is required to cook the eggs through from bottom to top without rubberizing the bottom layer. A quick run under the broiler seals the top. As with a rolled omelet, the right pan is essential, ideally a 10-inch cast-iron pan that will retain a slow and even heat, but that can also be put under the hot broiler.

## Proportions

for 6 servings, 8 eggs to 2⅓ cups of filling

| | |
|---|---|
| 2 **tablespoons olive oil** | ⅓ **cup grated Parmesan cheese** |
| ½ **cup thinly sliced onions** | **(see Note)** |
| 1 **cup grated zucchini** | 4 **tablespoons butter** |
| ½ **cup shredded prosciutto** | 2 **tablespoons finely chopped** |
| 8 **eggs** | **Italian parsley** |
| **Salt and freshly ground** | |
| **black pepper to taste** | |

1. Heat the olive oil and cook the onions until soft. Squeeze the grated zucchini to eliminate excessive liquid and add to the onion, along with the shredded prosciutto. Remove the pan from the heat so that the contents will keep warm but will not cook.

2. Beat the eggs in a bowl with the salt and pepper. Add the vegetables and prosciutto and fold in the grated cheese.

3. Melt the butter in a heavy skillet and, when it foams, add the eggs. Sprinkle with the parsley. Turn the heat very low and cook slowly until the eggs are set, but the top is still runny (20 to 25 minutes).

4. Run under the hot broiler to set the top quickly. Beard advises "not less than 30 seconds nor more than a minute."

*Note:* 2 tablespoons of grated Swiss or cubed mozzarella can replace 2 of the Parmesan for a good variation.

*A good filling dish for lunch, supper, or picnic spread.*

# FOOLPROOF CHEESE SOUFFLÉ

The alchemical magic of egg whites has quite rightly produced the mystique of the soufflé. How a nasty viscous jelly can transform itself and other heavies into airy castles of foam is cause for wonder. It's worth buying a glass-windowed oven for this magic show alone. Child, in her lengthy analysis in *Mastering I,* did not take the magic out of the soufflé by explaining its methods. Rather, she enabled us all to become skilled magicians in our own kitchens.

Because of the ability of an egg white to incorporate air, it can hold in suspension, like a bridge, elements far heavier than albumen or air. Even without air, the white within an uncooked shell holds afloat an entire potential chicken. Tasteless itself, the white is nonetheless the cause of taste in others and the sole support of a large family of foods from *quenelles* to macaroons.

A soufflé can be looked at two ways: either as egg white and air flavored by sauce, purée, or syrup; or as sauce, purée, or syrup expanded and semi-solidified by egg white and air. Either way the magic combines lightness with flavor. The classic soufflé, as in Child's master recipe, chooses the elemental flavor of cheese.

In America, the cheese soufflé that was once a staple of ladies' luncheons and of restaurants with minor pretensions has suffered a decline now that showier flavors have taken over, flavors such as crab, lobster, smoked salmon or salmon roe, spinach, zucchini. The cheese soufflé may have suffered from one too many ladies' luncheons in which thrift dictated substitutes, such as the puffed cereal Fisher once recommended for stretching a soufflé of three eggs to serve four people. As she later glossed, ". . . at least three of whom, I feel impelled to add, you dislike intensely and hope never to see again."

The way to restore the dignity of the cheese soufflé, still one of the simplest and best of flavors, is to serve it with an unctuous sauce like a creamy chèvre or hollandaise or a mousseline of tomato or sorrel or shrimp butter. The way to make a foolproof soufflé, with a soft interior and a golden-brown surface, is to treat the egg white with respect and all the rest will follow.

The proportions are those of Child and Beard, calling for one more egg white than yolk and for a mixture of Swiss and Parmesan cheeses. Claiborne's basic cheese soufflé in his first book calls for Cheddar and Worcestershire sauce, which suggests how far we've moved in twenty years from English toward French.

## Proportions

for 4 servings from a 6-cup mold, 3 tablespoons each of butter and flour to 1 cup milk, 4 egg yolks, 5 whites, and ¾ cup cheese

| | |
|---|---|
| 3 **tablespoons butter** | **Pinch of cayenne pepper** |
| 3 **tablespoons flour** | 4 **egg yolks** |
| 1 **cup milk, scalded** | 5 **egg whites** |
| **Salt and freshly ground** | ¾ **cup grated Swiss and** |
| **black pepper to taste** | **Parmesan cheese, mixed** |

1. Prepare the soufflé mold by buttering the inside well with additional butter and by sprinkling additional grated cheese on the bottom and sides to form a coating. (You can use any baking dish for a soufflé mold, but best is a dish that is two-thirds as deep as it is round.)

2. Melt the butter in a saucepan and add the flour. Cook together for about 2 minutes, stirring, without browning. Remove from the heat and add the scalded milk all at once. Stir vigorously until smooth. Add the seasonings and return to the heat for 1 or 2 minutes, beating constantly. Remove from the heat and beat in the egg yolks one at a time.

3.  Beat the egg whites with a balloon whisk or an electric mixer. (A copper bowl is in no way necessary. Adding ¼ teaspoon of cream of tartar creates the same chemical reaction of stabilizing the albumen by acid that copper does, and far less expensively.) The whites should be stiff but not dry. A simple test for stiffness is to turn the bowl upside down, or to try to. If the whites shift, they're not stiff enough.

4.  Stir one third of the egg whites into the sauce, along with most of the cheese. Reserve 2 tablespoons for sprinkling over the top. Then fold in the remaining egg whites gently but quickly with a rubber spatula or with your hands, cutting straight down and turning over until few white spots are left. Don't overfold or the whites will lose air.

5.  Turn out quickly into the prepared mold, sprinkle with the remaining cheese, and bake in a 400-degree oven for 20 to 25 minutes. (Larger molds should cook at 375 degrees after the initial 400-degree heat to avoid browning the outside before the interior is cooked.) If you want a soufflé with a dry interior rather than a moist one, cook 5 to 10 minutes longer. (You can test the interior by shaking the mold slightly or by inserting a long straw.) Many, like myself, prefer a wet inside and a crisp outside. Serve at once because the puffed top will begin to fall almost immediately. It will fall more while cutting or spooning it out onto plates.

*Serve as a first course for 4 or as a main course for 2. Especially good for vegetarian friends nostalgic for meals with a little pizazz. Both white and red wines go well.*

# FISH AND SHELLFISH

*Fish is eaten with an ordinary fork, with as much dexterity in the evasion of bones as can be commanded with such an inadequate instrument, and a bit of bread as an aid.*

—*Frederick A. Stokes*
Good Form: Dinners Ceremonious
and Unceremonious *(1890)*

At the turn of the century, fish for the well-heeled diner was an obligatory second course that followed the soup and preceded the roast. An 1892 book of menus, instructing young housekeepers in what to order cook and butler to prepare, suggests for a week's worth of dinners a soufflé of salmon with white sauce, fried smelts with tartar sauce, lobster à la Newburg, boiled striped bass with white sauce, fillet of bluefish with anchovy sauce, kingfish with butter sauce, and halibut steaks with cream sauce.

While methods of cooking fish were as varied as kinds, there were three constant hazards: the white sauce, the overcooking, and the bones. The fishbone that had escaped the dexterity of the fork to stick in the throat until dislodged by a bit of bread was a constant subject of jokes. One of the most popular ballads of 1855 was composed by a fish-eating Latin professor from Harvard who described the dilemma of a diner who asked the waiter for a bit of bread after ordering "One Fishball."

The waiter roars it through the hall:
"We don't give bread with one Fishball!"

During the nineteenth century, only the poor ate fish regularly as a main course on nights other than Fridays. With increasing numbers of Catholic immigrants from Ireland and the Continent, fish began to stink of popery as well as poverty, and in the first part of the twentieth century, fish fell into ill repute. It was common enough for fish to stink on its own since, unlike beef, fish did not improve with age on cross-country journeys. The problem then, as now, for non-coastal regions was how to get fish fresh and, once got, how to keep it "fresh." Once railroads developed the refrigerator car in the 1850s, however, barreled oysters packed in ice were commonplace in the Midwest from then on, and even Maine lobsters were available in Chicago "as fresh as could be desired."

But fish salted, dried, smoked, or canned was the most common solution to the fish problem. Recipes in Kansas cookbooks were devoted largely to ways of dealing with only two fish: codfish salted or salmon canned. Oysters were the only common shellfish and they were dealt with in two ways: scalloping them in bread or cracker crumbs for a main dish or pickling them in vinegar for a condiment.

The first major change in fish consumption in America came in the mid-1930s when Clarence Birdseye sold his quick-freezing process to General Foods. Now fish could be boned, preserved, and even breaded all at once. After the war, fresh fish became synonymous with fresh-frozen. The frozen fish fillet proved to be a commercial bonanza for mass restaurants and fast-food chains. As local fish markets declined, frozen fish at the supermarket was often fresher than the "day's catch" leftover from perhaps several days before at the fishmonger's. As local fishing fleets declined, fish was frozen aboard the trawlers to be sold to wholesale fish markets, so that the distinction between "fresh" and "frozen" lost meaning.

By the early sixties, frozen fish was so ensconced that Child gives instructions for telling good fish from bad in two forms: the unfrozen and the frozen kind that may have been thawed and refrozen several times between sea and supermarket. Beard as early as 1954 in his *Fish Cookery* gives equal time to instruction on how to tell a fresh fish and how to thaw a frozen one. Fisher summed up the resigned acceptance of many when she admitted, "But I do use *frozen* fish, which I myself can pick up like bleak logs now and then in the markets. They tease my inventiveness."

By the 1970s, however, the status of class fish—and above all shellfish—rose in direct proportion to its scarcity. As the world market for fish increased and supply diminished, shellfish became the most expensive and, therefore, the most valued item on a menu, with fish second and beef often third. Because shellfish is boneless and is, in effect, a fast finger food, it is the world's favorite form of fish. But with the increasing use of air transport, a great variety of fish once frozen or wholly unavailable is shipped to restaurants and markets in a matter of hours, so that genuine fresh Dover sole can be found more readily in a costly restaurant in New York than in a dockside restaurant in Dover.

With the return of fresh unfrozen fish, Americans have rapidly replaced English boiled with French poached, Chinese steamed, and Japanese raw fish. Through the recent proliferation of Japanese *sushi* and *sashimi* bars, Americans have left behind the dry overcooked fishballs of canned cod and salmon for slices of raw tuna, conch, octopus, and sea urchin roe, with hardly a flutter of their chopsticks.

At the same time, we are discovering the plenitude of remarkable fish and shellfish untasted on our own shores. Crayfish from the American South have begun to make inroads on the frozen bleak logs of lobster tails from South Africa. Whitefish roe from the Great Lakes, under the label "American caviar," has begun to displace inferior grades of sturgeon roe labeled "Russian" and "Iranian" caviar. Fresh salmon trout from our inland waters have begun to replace frozen blocks of rainbow and brook trout at the fish market. Supermarkets are installing lobster tanks for fresh lobsters. Oysters are being eaten year round, the superstition of summer malaise having given way to knowledge and appetite. New kitchen hardware like shrimp deveiners and food processors have opened up new methods of preparation, so that many housewives have turned their hands to exotic fancies like mousselines and *quenelles*. We are even learning once again to cook fish on the bone as well as to bone our own. It's a long way from the day of "One Fishball."

# FISH TIPS

1. *To choose fresh fish:* Look for bright not sunken eyes, bright pink or red gills, shiny scales, firm flesh that springs back when pushed by forefinger, and no strong odor.

2. *To keep fish fresh:* Remove from wrapping and place in a fresh plastic bag on ice in refrigerator until ready to use. Renew ice twice a day and, at 30 degrees, the fish will keep for a couple of days, according to Child. Fisher prefers to coat fish with soy sauce which helps to seal the skin. Keep frozen fish frozen and, when possible, do not thaw before cooking.

3. *To cook fish without overcooking:* Beard's formula of 10 minutes per inch of thickness, whatever the cooking method, is a very rough guide. Fish less than 1 inch at the thickest part must be watched carefully. A ½-inch-thick fillet may take only 2 to 3 minutes, a ¼-inch-thick fillet may take no more than a minute.

4. *To open shellfish the easy way:* Put mussels, clams, or oyster shells under a preheated broiler until the shells open enough to insert a knife blade (about 2 or 3 minutes usually, depending on size and kind). Flesh will be warm to hot. Serve in shell with a little melted butter, lemon juice, and pepper or a dash of Tabasco sauce.

5. *To keep oysters:* Scrub shells well under cold running water and refrigerate, covering them with damp paper towels and foil. Store the oysters convex side down. They will keep safely for as long as a week.

# MARINATED MACKEREL

In recent years we have learned not only *not* to overcook fish, we have even learned to eat it raw. The popularity of *sushi* bars and restaurants in our big cities is eloquent of the numbers of Americans who have learned to eat raw fish in postwar Japan. The popularity of raw or "green" herring, salmon, tuna, and mackerel, either ground fine as in steak tartare or marinated as in gravlax or gravad makrel, testifies to the numbers of Americans who have sampled the raw fish of Northern Europe and Scandinavia.

Now that fresh unfrozen fish is again available in this country, the simplest way to eat it is to slice it thin or grind it fine, to season it with salt, pepper, lemon, fennel or dill, mustard or soy, and to serve it up on black bread, buttered toast, or cold rice and seaweed. The next simplest way is to marinate it overnight in a mixture of salt, sugar, pepper, and dill in order to cure it slightly without cooking, either by acid or by heat. The Swedes call this method "gravad," when they marinate lox, or salmon, to make gravad lax or gravlax. The Danes marinate mackerel in the same way. But we don't need to evoke Scandinavia for a method of curing as basic and universal as salt and sugar. Miss Eliza Leslie used the same marinade (minus the dill) in 1828 as a way "To Keep Fresh Shad."

Although gravlax has become a restaurant fashion recently, Beard supplied a basic recipe for it as long ago as his 1954 *Fish Cookery*. He called then for a whole salmon of 4 or 5 pounds and also for saltpeter, when the fear of poisoning by bacteria was stronger than the fear of poisoning by chemicals like nitrites, of which saltpeter is one. While salmon is the fish most commonly cured in this manner now that salmon fillets are easy to come by, mackerel is far cheaper and is particularly receptive to a salt curing that cuts its oiliness.

---

## Proportions

for 4 to 6 servings, 2 mackerel to make 4 fillets, 4 tablespoons salt, 3 tablespoons sugar, 1 large bunch dill

2 **mackerel (about ¾ pound each) for 4 fillets**
4 **tablespoons salt**
3 **tablespoons sugar**

1 **tablespoon freshly ground black pepper**
4 **cups coarsely chopped dill**

1.   To fillet the mackerel, cut off the head. With a sharp knife cut along the back of the fish from head to tail. Keeping the knife flat along the rib bones, cut the flesh in one piece from the back to the belly. Turn the fish bone side down and repeat on the other side.

2.   Mix the salt, sugar, and pepper together and rub the mixture into the flesh side of each fillet.

3.   Spread 1 cup of the dill on a platter. Place 2 fillets on the dill, skin side down. Sprinkle each fillet with ½ cup dill and cover with the remaining 2 fillets, matching head to tail. Cover with the remaining dill

and lay a board or flat plate on top, weighted down with a heavy can or two. The salt will draw out the moisture and the weight will press the moisture from the flesh.

4.   Refrigerate for at least 12 hours and preferably 24, turning the paired fillets once. May be left for 3 or 4 days. When ready to serve, scrape all seasonings from the fillets and slice very thin, cutting slanting slices from the bottom skin in the manner of smoked salmon. Arrange the slices by overlapping them on a serving plate. Garnish with dill. Serve with small slices of buttered bread.

*Good for a buffet table or for a first course, followed by a substantial meat or bird main dish.*

# BOILED LOBSTER

Traditionally, Americans have either boiled or broiled the armored beasts that the Pilgrims found in abundance in the cold waters of the Northeast and learned to cook from the Indians. How long the Indians steamed their lobsters and corn, smothered in seaweed over hot stones, is not recorded; but the recipe books of the early nineteenth century suggest to housewives, cooking over wood stoves, an unpromising half hour to an hour at a rolling boil. Many also warn against eating "the lady in the lobster," which turns out to be the stomach sac near the head, and to "eat but little" of the meat.

Today, we eat as much of the meat as we can afford, but how long to cook the beast is still a matter of controversy. Claiborne advises 12 minutes for a 1-pound, 15 minutes for a 2-pound lobster. Child originally suggested 20 minutes for a 2-pound lobster but has since reduced the time slightly to read 10 minutes for 1 pound, 18 minutes for 2 pounds, 25 minutes for 5 pounds. Beard has consistently called for much shorter times: 5 minutes for the first pound, 3 minutes for each additional pound. All of them, however, specify significantly less time than the minimum of 20 or 30 minutes suggested by the 1940s editions of *Fannie Farmer* and *Joy of Cooking.* All of them also agree that restaurant lobsters are generally overcooked. As usual, the problem is that one man's "over" is another man's "under." "Under" and the flesh is not yet tender. "Over" and the flesh is tough and stringy. For me, lobster is just right cooked 8 minutes for 1 pound, 11 or 12 for 1½ pounds, 15 for 2 pounds. It's good to remember that we could eat lobster raw, if we fancied, as we do other shellfish.

Traditionally, Americans have boiled lobsters rapidly in heavily salted water as a substitute for the sea water we do not usually have on hand. The French, however, simmer lobsters in court bouillon, or a quick broth of wine and herbs that one can later reduce to a good stock.

Traditionally also, Americans are more squeamish than the French about killing live lobsters. Plunging a lobster head down into boiling water brings death within 15 seconds, according to latest scientific count. But as Beard says, "They do wiggle," and it would be thoughtful of American fish dealers to imitate the French and tie the beasts with string. When it is necessary to cut up a live lobster before cooking, the quickest way is to sever tail from body in a single blow, "without hesitation or remorse," as one Frenchman has put it.

The lobster is one index of change in Americans' increasing sophistication with seafood and in the increasing split between frozen and fresh. The bad news is that restaurants and supermarkets are still flooded with imported frozen rock-lobster tails from the spiny lobster that the French call *langouste* to distinguish it from *homard.* The spiny lobster, abundant in the warm waters of South Africa and our own American South, deserves a better break than the treatment it gets in Surf 'n Turf restaurant chains across the land.

The good news is that the true Maine lobster has come into its own as one of the sweetest of meats, provided it is simmered tenderly in its protective armor, before shedding it for a quick butter dip. Time was when you had to wrestle a cook to the floor to prevent him from slicing the lobster in half, stuffing it with half a loaf of stale bread and ravaging it under the intense heat of a broiler. While it is easy enough to overcook boiled lobster, no matter what your definition of "over" and "under," your chances of overcooking *broiled* lobster are close to 100 percent.

## Proportions

for 2 servings, 2 quarts of liquid to 2 1½-pound lobsters in a deep kettle, or liquid to cover

| | |
|---|---|
| 1 quart water | ½ teaspoon thyme |
| 1 quart dry white wine | ½ teaspoon freshly ground |
| 2 large onions, chopped | black pepper |
| 2 carrots, chopped | 1 small dried red pepper |
| 2 celery stalks with leaves, | 1 teaspoon salt |
| chopped | 2 (or more) 1½-pound lobsters |
| 1 bay leaf | 1 lemon |
| 6 sprigs parsley | ¼ pound (1 stick) butter |

1. Make a court bouillon by combining the water with the wine, vegetables, and seasonings. Simmer in a covered kettle for 15 to 20 minutes.

2. Bring to a boil and plunge each lobster head down into the kettle. Cover and bring back to a boil as quickly as possible. When the court bouillon is boiling again, lower the heat and simmer, covered, for 8 to 12 minutes.

3. Remove the lobsters, hold with pot holders, and put the lobsters on their backs in order to split them in half, head to tail, with a heavy knife. Discard the "lady" or stomach sacs in the heads, together with the long dark intestinal tubes. Crack the claws with a mallet or lobster cracker.

4. Have ready ¼ cup melted butter per lobster and a half lemon cut in two. Serve immediately while the lobster and butter are hot. (Later, reduce the court bouillon by half to use as stock for cooking other fish.)

*Since lobsters are all-involving, serve something simple before and after. Other shellfish like oysters or clams on the halfshell are good before. A green salad with French bread and cheese is good after.*

# POACHED STRIPED BASS WITH FENNEL

Before fish got classy, you had to fight the fishmonger, if you could find one, to leave the head and tail intact and to merely gut and clean a fish you wanted whole. Supermarket fish were uniformly guillotined, as though open mouths and glassy eyes would repel potential fish buyers. Gone were the days when a cod's head and shoulders could be prepared by Miss Eliza Leslie's instructions, or a cod's cheeks and tongue by Fannie Farmer's, even as recently as 1948. Salmon cheeks are still a delicacy prepared by Beard, although he admits they are no longer easy to come by unless you happen to live near a salmon cannery.

Today, however, you can continue your eyeball confrontation with the fish in the shop at home on stove and table. The advantage of cooking a fish whole is that the bones and gristle of head, spine, and tail give flavor to flesh as they give flavor to stock. The advantage of serving a fish whole is aesthetic. A fish is a natural work of art for eye, nose, and tongue, and the best way to reveal the beauties of a perfectly fresh fish is to poach it whole.

Fortunately, poaching has replaced the word boiling in our cookbooks. Poaching suggests that the liquid is kept just below the simmer, whether the liquid is contained in an elongated fish poacher equipped with a rack or a skillet or an improvised container of aluminum foil. The virtue of poaching is that it treats the fish as gently as possible while flavoring it with herbs and aromatics.

The trouble with most fish poachers, however, is that the size you have may not fit the fish you have. Unless the poacher is equipped with a rack, it is difficult to lift the fish and drain it (even helped by a layer of cheese-cloth or foil), without the fish breaking apart. One way around the problem is to "poach" the whole fish by steaming or braising it in a wrapping of foil in the oven. Another way is to steam the fish directly, in the Chinese manner, in a basket or colander over boiling water. Size again determines what method to use. For a really large fish like a 7- to 10-pound bass or salmon, the foil wrap may be the only possible one.

Claiborne's Whole Salmon Baked in Foil, in his first book, provides a good compromise between traditional poaching in a court bouillon and braising in foil with a small amount of liquid. He suggests reducing ¾ cup of dry white wine by simmering it for half an hour with thyme, basil, tarragon, rosemary, shallots, lemon, and celery leaves. After making an envelope of foil for the fish, you pour in the wine mixture and seal the edges of the foil tightly, as you would for cooking fish *en papillote*, or in heat-proof paper. The foil then goes into a large baking pan to catch any leaking juices.

An even simpler method is to omit the liquid and to spread the foil with olive oil or melted butter, then add whatever fresh herbs you want by strewing them on the foil, within the cavity of the fish, and on top of the oiled fish before sealing the foil. A fish like striped bass, one of the glories of American fishery, because of its delicate and firm flesh, lends itself to a great variety of herbs and spices, from Chinese ginger and chilies to French fennel and Spanish saffron. Such a fish, subtly spiced, calls for a rich subtle sauce like hollandaise or the white butter sauce called *beurre blanc*. Braising a whole bass in blanched lettuce leaves has become a fad of France's *nouvelle cuisine*, which makes a colorful variation for wrapped fish but lends more moisture than flavor.

I have chosen fennel for the bass below because you can "wrap" the fish in the chopped leaves, serve it with the fennel bulb, chopped and sautéed, and sauce it with a hint of Pernod to complete the taste and fragrance of anise.

## Proportions

for 6 servings, a 6- to 7-pound whole striped bass plus 2 large bulbs of fennel

| | |
|---|---|
| 1 **6- to 7-pound whole striped bass (or other whole fish)** | ½ **teaspoon salt** |
| ¼ **cup olive oil** | ¼ **teaspoon freshly ground black pepper** |
| 3 **cups chopped fennel leaves and stalks** | 3 **cups chopped fennel bulbs** |
| | 4 **tablespoons butter** |

# White Butter Sauce with Pernod

½ cup fish stock, or ¼ cup white wine plus ¼ cup clam juice

2 tablespoons white wine vinegar

2 tablespoons Pernod

4 tablespoons minced shallots

3 sticks (¾ pound) butter

Freshly ground black pepper to taste

Lemon juice to taste

1.  Heat the oven to 375 degrees while preparing the fish. Measure the fish at its thickest part and allow approximately 10 minutes per inch, provided the fish is at room temperature.

2.  Place the fish lengthwise on a long piece of foil and oil the fish thoroughly on all sides, including head and tail, so that nothing will stick to the foil.

3.  Sprinkle with the fennel leaves, salt, and pepper, and stuff the cavity with fennel leaves and stalks. Wrap the fish tightly in foil, sealing the edges on themselves so that no juice can escape. Place in a large baking pan or another piece of foil with turned-up edges in case any juice leaks.

4.  Bake while preparing the sauce. Turn the fish once so that both the top and bottom of the fish will be in contact with the metal pan or extra foil, which will transmit heat faster.

5.  Cut off the bottom of the fennel bulbs and slice by hand or in a food processor. Sauté gently in butter until tender but still slightly crisp, about 5 to 8 minutes.

6.  Prepare the sauce by reducing the stock, vinegar, and Pernod with shallots until the sauce is about ¼ cup. Cut each stick of cold butter into 8 slices and beat the butter into the saucepan 2 slices at a time with a balloon whisk, beating vigorously. The trick is to warm the butter and make it creamy without letting it melt or get oily. Lift the pan from the heat if the butter appears to melt. Add pepper and lemon juice to taste. Time the sauce so that it is done when you expect the fish to be done. You can let the sauce stand off the heat while you remove the fish from the oven and foil and slide it onto a serving plate. (Test for doneness with a fork inserted into the flesh at the thickest point.)

7.  To serve, cut the fish along the center bone, from head end to tail, and lift the flesh from the ribs on each side to cut into large serving pieces. Sauce each piece or pass the sauce separately and accompany with sautéed fennel for vegetable garnish.

*Steamed White Rice (page 307) is another good accompaniment for both fish and sauce. Because the sauce is rich, follow with a tart, light dessert, such as lemon ice.*

# BROILED SWORDFISH STEAKS

In this century, broiling has been America's most popular way of cooking fish, possibly because fish steaks suggest meat instead of fish. Now that the status of fish has risen and that of meat has dropped, the dried-out tough and stringy paprika-covered slab labeled "broiled fish of the day" on restaurant menus is no longer the only fish to be got.

Broiling is truly quick and easy, but it is also a quick and easy way to overcook and render tasteless. A dense compact flesh like swordfish or an oily flesh like tuna or salmon will fare best under high heat. But a gas or electric broiler imparts no flavor, only heat. A swordfish, that has good texture but mild flavor, will benefit from a quick marinade before and during cooking.

Both Claiborne and Beard list dozens of ways to broil different kinds of fish with different kinds of flavors, but they agree on the affinity of swordfish and rosemary. You can press dried rosemary into the flesh on both sides, as you would crushed peppercorns into a meat steak for a steak au poivre. Or you can add rosemary to a marinade, as I have done below.

Timing depends on the thickness of the steak, the proximity to the source of heat, and the "precooking" done by a marinade with acid. You will get best results if the steak is between 1 and 1½ inches thick and if it is placed about 2 inches below the heat. To get more even heat, place an oiled sheet of aluminum foil on the broiling pan and heat it before you put the steaks on top of it. This will seal the bottom of the steaks.

Beard's rule-of-thumb of 10 minutes to an inch changes with a marinade, since marinating with acid reduces the time by a minute or two. Test after the steak has cooked 3 minutes on each side. Use a fork to open slightly the interior of the steak as you would cut into a meat steak with a knife. The pink of swordfish should have just turned to white.

One problem with oven broilers is that the oil in the broiling pan may catch fire as it sputters upward. Flames are no more damaging to the fish than they would be on a charcoal grill but they may produce anxiety in the cook and any spectators. If you can't pull out the pan, you can turn off the broiler for a minute or two. One way to prevent flaming, particularly when you continue to baste the steaks with an oil marinade, is to puncture the foil on each side of the steaks so that some but not all of the liquid will drain into the pan below. This is particularly useful with salmon, which seems to give off a lot of fat in the cooking.

## Proportions

for 4 servings, 2 pounds steaks to ¾ cup of marinade

1 or 2 swordfish steaks 1-inch
  thick, totaling 2 pounds
½ cup olive oil
¼ cup lemon or lime juice

1 tablespoon rosemary
Salt and freshly ground
black pepper to taste

1.   Marinate the steaks at room temperature in the combined oil, lemon, rosemary, salt, and pepper for at least 30 minutes. (A good way is to put the fish and the marinade together in a plastic bag and seal it.)

2.   Cover a broiling pan with a sheet of foil and oil it lightly. Place below the broiler and preheat the broiler and pan.

3.   Put the steaks on the foil and broil for 3 minutes. Baste the steaks with the marinade and turn. Broil for 3 minutes on the other side. Test the interior with a fork and cook a minute or two more if needed. The marinade will serve as a sauce.

*Fish steaks, like meat steaks, are so classical that they are good preceded by a soup and followed by a salad. A green vegetable, such as sautéed snow peas, is a good companion.*

# GRILLED WHOLE BLUEFISH

Nothing is more frustrating to the backyard barbecuer than to throw a freshly caught whole fish onto the grill and to watch it disintegrate into bits of skin, flesh, and bone, irremediably stuck to the metal of the grill. The rest of the world has solved this problem by soldering cheap metal into a hinged grill that holds the fish between the two sides so that it can be turned at will over the coals. A cheap iron that will season is far preferable to stainless steel that will stick to the delicious crackly skin when you remove the fish from the grill.

Grilling the fish in foil is a fainthearted evasion, since the point is to achieve a crisply charred skin that imparts its flavor to the whole fish. With a large fish it is also difficult to cook the interior before the outside layers fall apart. One compromise is to combine charcoal grilling with oven broiling. You can char the skin quickly on both sides with a hinged grill and then transfer the fish to the slower contained heat of a broiler. A strong oily fish like the bluefish takes particularly well to this method since there is little danger of the bluefish drying out and its dark flesh is complemented by the smoky taste of charcoal. Mesquite charcoal, long used in Mexico and imported now by way of America's Southwest, imparts the best flavor of all.

## Proportions

for 4 servings, a 5- to 6-pound bluefish

1.   Light the charcoal and heat the coals until the flames have died and the coals are ashy and glowing. Brush a hinged grill well with oil and oil the skin of the fish well. Place the fish in the hinged grill and hold as close to the coals as possible so that the oil flames up. When the skin is crisp on one side, turn the fish over and crisp the skin on the other side.

2.   Transfer the fish carefully to oiled foil on a broiling rack. If the top of the fish is 3 to 4 inches from the flame, rather than closer, the interior of the fish will cook more evenly.

3.   Base timing on 10 minutes per inch and turn the fish over halfway through. Test for doneness by poking a fork along the backbone to see if the fork pierces the flesh easily. To serve, make a lengthwise cut down the center and lift the fillets from either side of the central bone. Garnish with a sprig of fresh thyme, rosemary, or parsley. If you like, serve with an herbed vinaigrette of lemon juice, olive oil, and seasonings.

*A rich oily fish like the blue does well with acid accompaniments, such as sliced fresh tomatoes or a spinach soup or salad or cucumber-yogurt garnish (page 154).*

# SIMPLE SAUTÉED SCALLOPS

Of all sea creatures, the one most violated by being breaded or battered and dumped in hot oil is the moon-white tender scallop. The scallop has become the darling of home and restaurant cooks because it is the easiest of all shellfish to prepare. It comes to the fish market sans sand, sans shell, sans everything but its sweet, naked, and defenseless self.

Because its flavor is so delicate, the less it is treated or tarted up the better. The French like to serve their slightly different scallop, in the shell, bearing a crescent of orange roe and "swimming" in a little broth, as Coquilles St. Jacques à la Nage. Our scallop breed is most itself swimming in a little butter, perfumed by chopped scallions or shallots, and accented by minced parsley. Claiborne suggests also sautéing scallops in garlic butter, or with cucumbers in a tomato-cream sauce. Beard suggests tarragon and chives, in addition to parsley, or a curried cream sauce. The scallop will adapt itself to any number of flavors, but it is also easily overwhelmed by them. While it is delicious paired with mushrooms in a wine-cream sauce and heaped into shells to be served as Coquilles St. Jacques, or paired with pecans or pine nuts and served with fresh pasta, still the simple scallop is most eloquent when most alone.

## Proportions

for 4 servings, 1½ pounds bay or ocean scallops, ¼ pound butter

| | |
|---|---|
| 1½ pounds bay or ocean scallops, halved or quartered | 2 tablespoons minced shallots |
| Salt and freshly ground black pepper to taste | 2 tablespoons *crème fraîche* (optional) |
| ¼ pound (1 stick) butter | 2 tablespoons minced parsley |
| | Lemon wedges |

1.  Wash the scallops to remove any bits of shell and dry with a paper towel. Sprinkle with salt and pepper.

2.  Melt the butter in a skillet and sauté the shallots for about 1 minute. Add the scallops and cook quickly, shaking the pan so the scallops cook evenly until just tender (about 2 minutes, depending on size). Overcooking turns them tough and rubbery.

3.  If desired, quickly stir in a little *crème fraîche.* Sprinkle with parsley and serve with lemon wedges.

*Scallops make a good first course, as well as a main dish. They might be followed by a hefty meat like a Steak au Poivre (page 252), or accompanied by a colorful vegetable like Carrots Glazed with Orange (page 286). White rice or bread will soak up the butter.*

# OYSTER LOAF

Fisher first encountered the Oyster Loaf from her mother's descriptions of forbidden midnight feasts in the dormitories of ladies' seminaries in the 1890s. The loaf was wrapped in a napkin at the baker's and smuggled under a chambermaid's cape to a clutch of famished, giggling, sinning girls. Later she found a recipe for it in *Sunset's All-Western Cook Book* and included it in her 1941 excursion into oysterhood titled *Consider the Oyster.*

I first encountered the Oyster Loaf in Mrs. Rasmussen's *One-Arm Cookery Book,* which described the loaf as the best of all midnight feasts to accompany several cases of beer. Later I discovered that the loaf was traditional in many nineteenth-century American cookbooks and was traditionally associated with midnight wickedness. According to Beard, the loaf was often a peace offering brought home by the guilty intemperate to placate a waiting wife.

We can no longer bring home an Oyster Loaf from the bakery any more than we can bring home a schooner of beer from the bar, but we can hollow out our own loaves and fry up our own oysters to make a guilt-free feast for lunch, supper, drink time, or picnic time. The point of the Oyster Loaf is that it is transportable and so particularly amenable to movable feasts. The lidded loaf is a casserole to keep the oysters warm, with the added advantage that after the oysters are eaten you can eat the buttered and toasted and oyster-flavored container.

---

## Proportions

for 4 servings, 2 dozen oysters, 1 white loaf, ¼ pound butter

**2 dozen oysters, shucked**
**1 loaf unsliced bread, French,**
**Italian, or American white**
**¼ pound (1 stick) butter**
**Salt and freshly ground**
**black pepper to taste**

**1 cup fresh bread crumbs**
**(from the hollowed-out loaf)**
**½ cup heavy cream**
**Lemon wedges**

1. Rinse the oysters and pick out any shells. Cut the top from the bread to make a lid. Hollow out the remaining loaf, leaving a wall ½ inch thick around the sides and bottom. Toast in a 300-degree oven for 20 to 30 minutes, or until golden brown.

2. Melt the butter in large frying pan. Brush some of the butter onto the interior of the toasted loaf. Make bread crumbs of the hollowed-out bread by tearing in pieces and putting in a processor.

3. Sprinkle the oysters with salt and pepper, dip them into the cream, and then into the crumbs. Sauté quickly in the remaining hot butter (add more butter if needed), turning each oyster to brown the crumbs nicely. The oysters should not cook for more than 2 or 3 minutes.

4. Put the oysters in the loaf as you finish them. Pour over them any remaining butter and put the lid on. Serve with lemon wedges and a shaker of salt. Guests can pick out oysters with fingers or forks.

*Good for a first course as well as a midnight supper. Because the oysters are a type of finger food, you might follow with more finger flexers like broiled spareribs or fried chicken (page 222). If used as a supper dish, the loaf would go well with Chinese Coleslaw (page 155) or any of the composed salads (pages 158–162).*

# SAUTÉED WHOLE FLOUNDER

Few have taught us more than Child has about different kinds of sole and flounder and different ways to cook them. Kinds are a problem because sole is a class name, where flounder is plebian. The fact that the European sole, called "Dover" in England and "sole" in France, is superior in quality to any of our flounders, flukes, and dabs, which we often call "sole," only compounds the problem. European sole is not grown here, but flown here and, therefore, costs more than native breeds under any name. The best of our own breeds are the West Coast's Petrale sole and the East Coast's winter flounder, often called "lemon sole." The mark of quality is a close-grained firm white flesh of delicate flavor.

Because the fish is flat, it is easily skinned and boned and, therefore, the fish most commonly cooked as fillets in France or America. The classical French method of cooking fillets, as Child instructed us, was to poach them simply in wine or stock and to sauce them with various degrees of elaboration. The standard French work called *Le Répertoire de la Cuisine* lists some 340 ways to sauce them. Child's method of poaching was to bring the liquid to a simmer on top of the stove and then to bake the fish briefly in a moderate oven. One had then to keep the fish warm while preparing the sauce, which usually called for some of the poaching liquid. For dinner parties, the method was awkward because of the last-minute sauce making.

Because sole fillets are usually very thin, ¼ to ¾ inch at the thickest part, they cook very quickly and break apart very quickly. A fillet ½ inch thick will be done in 2 to 3 minutes, whether poached, broiled, or fried. Thin fillets are easiest to handle by poaching, because you need lift them only once from the pan and because broiling tends to dry them out.

The whole fish, however, is another matter and it is the whole fish that renders the flesh the most flavorful when cooked on the bone. In America, Sole Meunière usually means flounder fillets, dipped in flour and sautéed in butter. In Europe, it more often refers to the whole fish which the diner himself bones on the plate. While Americans are impatient with, or fearful of, bones, the whole fish on the plate is a joy to see and to dissect and turns out to be much simpler than you may have feared. A whole browned sole on the plate was Child's first meal in France, in 1948, in Rouen. "I was quite overwhelmed," she remembers.

## Proportions

1 small flounder for each person or 1 large for 2 persons

| | |
|---|---|
| **1  1- to 2-pound flounder or sole** | **4  to 6 tablespoons butter** |
| **4  tablespoons flour** | **2  tablespoons minced parsley** |
| **Salt and freshly ground black pepper to taste** | **Lemon wedges** |

1.  Rinse the flounder in cold water and dredge well with flour. Sprinkle each side with a little salt and pepper.

2.  Melt the butter in a skillet until it is bubbly. Sauté the fish on both sides quickly, until golden brown. A fish less than 1 inch thick may take no more than 2 or 3 minutes on each side. Test for doneness with a fork in the thickest part along the center bone. The flesh should be just tender but not break apart.

3. Lift the fish onto a platter with a spatula and pour the browned butter over it. Sprinkle lightly with parsley and garnish with lemon wedges.

4. To bone, run a knife down the center of the flat fish and slip off the fillet on each side, releasing the flesh from the small line of bones along each side. Slit the underside near the tail and, by means of the tail, pick up the entire skeleton and put aside. Detach the two remaining fillets from any side bones.

*Because the fish is light, it can take a soup before and a complementary vegetable with, such as green peas, grated zucchini, or boiled new potatoes.*

# DEEP-FRIED SMELTS

Smelts are a fish so abundant in American waters, fresh and salt, that we have forgotten how to savor them. Beard speaks of the smelt runs of his youth when entire towns would disgorge their populaces along the Columbia River to pan the quivering silver with gunnysacks, bird cages, "and even old dresses knotted together." The Coastal Indians didn't even bother to eat them, but dried them and burned them for lamps, calling them candlefish.

Their oiliness makes them appropriate for deep-frying, like the Mediterranean sardine. But as a distant cousin to the salmon, the smelt's flavor and texture is more delicate than the pilchards or herrings we call sardines. If the smelt is small enough and the frying crisp enough, you can eat the fish bones and all, as you might a small sardine. Or you can bone them rather easily by removing head and backbone in one piece. They will always look better with the head on, however, and one way to serve them up attractively is to thread 3 or 4 small ones through the eyes with a skewer, which makes them both easy to fry and to serve.

Of course you can use a flour and water and egg batter for the fish, but I prefer Beard's suggestion to simply crumb them. As with catfish, the smelt is a fish that thrives in the hot oil bath that kills the flavor of daintier creatures, but that enlivens even the traditional garnish of smelt. "Always," Beard commands, "serve fried parsley with smelt."

## Proportions

for 2 to 4 servings, 12 smelts, 2 cups bread crumbs

**12 smelts, cleaned, with head
  and tail
  Salt and freshly ground
  black pepper to taste
2 cups fresh bread crumbs**

**2 eggs, beaten
  Vegetable oil for deep-frying
  Lemon wedges
  Fried Parsley (see below)**

1. Rinse the smelts, sprinkle them with salt and pepper, and dip into bread crumbs (made in a processor or rubbed by hand). Dip the crumbed fish into the beaten eggs, and dip again into the crumbs, pressing them into the fish.

2. Heat the oil to 370 degrees in a deep-fat fryer. Drop the fish into the oil a few at a time. Don't overcrowd. Fry for about 3 to 5 minutes, turning the fish once with long-handled tongs. Drain on paper towels and serve at once with lemon wedges and fried parsley.

FRIED PARSLEY: Dip a large bunch of parsley into hot fat and fry until crisp, about 2 minutes.

*Little fried fish, like smelts, are a classic first course or a luncheon main course. You can follow them with a contrasting meat like a Butterflied Pork Loin Roast (page 246) or a Butterflied Leg of Lamb (page 256), or simply accompany them with a good green salad.*

# TEMPURA SHRIMP

Claiborne was the first to emphasize the Japanese way of deep-frying food coated with batter that we know as *tempura.* Our increasing sophistication in Japanese methods is revealed in the difference between Claiborne's initial tempura recipes and his recent ones in *The New New York Times Cookbook.* Following the authority of Shizuo Tsuji, the master culinary artist of Japan known here through *Japanese Cooking: A Simple Art,* Claiborne now suggests a lighter batter and a more genuine sauce based on ingredients, available now in Japanese specialty stores, that had to be improvised way back in 1961.

The tempura that seems magically produced out of air and chopsticks in Japanese restaurants is surprisingly easy to make at home, provided you follow Tsuji's number one rule: Tempura batter must be LUMPY. The way to get lumpy batter is to barely mix the flour into egg and water and to make the batter in small batches. The aim is to produce a lacy coating that explodes somewhat on contact with the hot oil so that the lumps of dry flour act as pockets of air to make the lace. Shrimp is the one essential fish in a Japanese tempura, but the batter works beautifully with squid, scallops, flounder fillets, or small whole fish like boned smelts.

A genuine tempura sauce calls for the fish stock, with kelp and dried bonito shavings, that the Japanese call *dashi.* To the stock is added the sweetened wine called *mirin,* light soy sauce, grated white radish *(daikon),* and grated fresh ginger. Some substitutes are better than others. While powdered or instant *dashi* is available in Japanese food stores and is excellent, according to Tsuji, a fat-free chicken stock is a good alternative for a tempura dip. In the same way, a little sugar can substitute for the sweetened wine.

Getting authentic ingredients is fun but can easily decline into pedantry. The Japanese got tempura from the West, from Spanish and Portuguese missionaries in the sixteenth century, who imported egg batters along with cassock and crucifix. The Japanese refined the batter and added a sweet-salt sauce. But in fact any flavored soy is good for dipping, whether flavored with a little fresh ginger and horseradish or mustard or even hot pepper flakes.

## Proportions

for 4 to 6 servings, 24 medium shrimp, 2 eggs, 2½ cups flour

| | |
|---|---|
| **24 medium shrimp** | **2 egg yolks** |
| **Oil for deep fat frying** | **2 cups ice water** |
| **2½ cups flour** | |

### Dipping Sauce

| | |
|---|---|
| **¾ cup chicken broth** | **2 teaspoons grated gingerroot** |
| **¼ cup dark soy sauce** | **½ cup grated white radish (or** |
| **1 teaspoon sugar** | **horseradish)** |

1.   Shell and devein the shrimp, leaving the tails intact. If you don't want the shrimp to curl, cut 3 or 4 slashes along the belly of each.

2.   Preheat the oil in a deep-fat fryer in which the oil is 2 inches deep. The oil should be hot but not smoking (about 340 degrees).

3.   Prepare the batter in 2 batches at the last minute. Put ½ cup flour in a separate dish for dredging the fish before dipping it in batter so that batter will stick well. In a separate bowl, beat 1 egg yolk lightly, add 1 cup ice water all at once, stir quickly, and add 1 cup flour all at once. Stir lightly with a fork or chopsticks. Mixture should be VERY LUMPY. Make a second batch of batter when the first is used up.

4.   Hold each shrimp by the tail and dip first into flour and then into the batter and drop into the hot oil. Cook for about 3 minutes, or until golden. Remove with a slotted spoon, drain on paper towels, and serve as quickly as possible.

*Excellent as finger food with drinks (despite the sloppy dipping) or as a showy first course, to be followed by a simple roast duck or grilled Gin-Marinated Rock Cornish Hens (page 236) or a fat steamed bass.*

# BAKED COD IN GARLIC MAYONNAISE

In Beard's first book of *Fish Cookery,* baked fish was usually stuffed. We have moved away from stuffings of bread crumbs and chopped vegetables as we have moved toward sauces. We want our fish simple and our sauce either dramatic or refined.

One of the most dramatic of sauces, the hot garlic mayonnaise that the French in Provence call *bourride,* gives a fine flourish to the simple, straightforward New England cod. When the garlic mayonnaise on which the sauce is based was made old-style in a mortar, timing was tricky if not outright hazardous. Once again the processor comes to our aid to make this dish peculiarly satisfying because of cod's affinity to garlic.

Child's recipe for *bourride* in *Mastering II* is for a stew of assorted white fish, as it is often served in Nice and Marseilles, to make it a rival of *bouillabaisse.* It is much simpler for the eater, however, to eat fillets, and the cod's thick firm flesh makes it ideal for the heartiness of the sauce. Beard, in a recipe for *bourride* in *The New James Beard,* suggests poaching other fish: bass, sole, flounder, haddock. None, however, can rival cod.

In the recipe below, instead of poaching the fish in a court bouillon, I suggest poaching or baking the cod in seasoned milk. The milk will seem to be curdled by the fish juice after baking but will smooth out when strained and added to the mayonnaise.

## Proportions

for 6 servings, 3 pounds cod fillets, 6 egg yolks, 1½ cups of olive oil, 2 cups of milk

| | |
|---|---|
| 3 pounds cod fillets, about 1½ inches thick | 2 cups milk, or to cover |
| ½ teaspoon salt | 3 large cloves garlic |
| ½ teaspoon freshly ground black pepper | 1 bay leaf |
| ¼ teaspoon thyme | 1 small dried red pepper |
| | 4 sprigs parsley |

### For the Mayonnaise

| | |
|---|---|
| 6 egg yolks | 1½ cups olive oil |
| 1 tablespoon white wine vinegar or lemon juice | |

1. Season the fillets on both sides with salt, pepper, and thyme 3 or 4 hours before cooking, if possible.

2.  Heat the milk with the crushed garlic cloves, bay leaf, red pepper, and parsley.

3.  Put the cod in a baking dish that will hold the fillets in one layer. When the milk simmers, pour it over the cod and cover the dish with a tight lid or double layers of foil. Bake for 10 minutes to the inch in a 350-degree oven.

4.  Remove the cod to a platter and keep warm. Strain the milk and set the garlic cloves aside. Reduce the milk and cod broth so that it is no more than 2 cups.

5.  Put the garlic in a processor with 3 egg yolks and vinegar and process until blended. Add the olive oil in a slow steady trickle with the machine running until the mixture starts to thicken, as in plain mayonnaise.

6.  Add the remaining egg yolks to the mayonnaise and gradually pour in 1 cup of the strained milk, which will thin the mixture. Pour into the pan and add the remaining cup of milk, whisking the mixture steadily over low heat until it thickens and becomes creamy.

7.  Drain the cod fillets on the platter (as they will have exuded more juice). Pour the sauce over and serve at once.

*The dish is exceedingly rich and filling and needs a tart salad for contrast, such as Spiced Orange and Onion (page 156), or Wilted Cold Greens (page 162), or Jerusalem Artichoke and Spinach Salad (page 153).*

# BAKED SHAD WITH ROE AND SORREL

The story of shad is emblematic of the success story of fish in general in the last decade or two. The shad is one of the boniest of fish as well as one of the richest in taste. The difficulty of boning it is such that old recipes called for baking it long hours at low temperatures until the bones dissolved. I have never produced an edible fish by this method, but Claiborne, in *The New New York Times Cookbook,* claims that the secret is to "steam" a 4-pound fish in a tightly sealed pan for a full 5 hours at 300 degrees. The backbone will be soft, he says, and the splinter bones dissolved.

Because Claiborne has probably devoted more space to the shad than to any other single fish, numbering eleven recipes in his first book alone, his claims for the steamed shad carry weight. More to the point, however, is the fact that boned shad, which was once an expensive delicacy at the fish market, is now commonplace. Claiborne remarks in 1961 that there were probably no more than a dozen professional shad boners in all of New York. Demand for filleted fish of all kinds has benefited shad lovers everywhere and anyone who has tried through arrogance or ignorance to bone a shad himself will not begrudge a penny of the cost.

Over the years one of Claiborne's favorite recipes has been a whole shad, boned into two fillets, and stuffed with the roe to make a shad sandwich. Because the roe is so distinctive in flavor and yet so easily dried out when cooked alone, putting the eggs back in the fish does a double service. The simplest method is to sauté the roe very lightly in butter and seasonings in order to half cook it before spreading it between the fillets. The roe benefits from having the taste and liquid of the butter. Another method is to make a mousse of the roe, which incorporates the eggs evenly into a light airy filling.

Adding roe to shad is like adding butter to cream, so a sauce that cuts the richness is preferable to the cream sauces often recommended. The French method of combining sorrel with shad is ideal for clearing the palate with the acidic taste of a green sauce. A purée of watercress or arugula gives a similar effect if sorrel is not available.

## Proportions

for 8 servings, 2 shad fillets and 1 pair shad roe, plus 1 pound flounder to 1½ cups of heavy cream

| | |
|---|---|
| 1  **shad, boned into 2 fillets** | 1  **pair shad roe** |
| 1  **pound flounder fillets** | **Sorrel Sauce (see page 135)** |
| 1  **egg** | |
| 1½  **cups heavy cream** | |
| **Salt, freshly ground black** | |
| **pepper, and cayenne** | |
| **pepper to taste** | |

1. Sprinkle the shad fillets with salt and pepper. Cut the flounder in pieces and put in a processor with the egg. Purée the flounder for 30 seconds, add the cream and seasonings, and purée until smooth. Remove the outer membranes from the shad roe and add the roe to the mixture. Process until mixed. Taste for seasoning.

2. Open up the center flaps of each fillet and stuff with mousse. Put the two fillets together, with the skin on the outside and the mousse on the inside. Tie the fillets at 2-inch intervals with string to hold the fish in shape.

3. Lightly oil or butter a baking dish and bake the fish at 400 degrees for 30 minutes, if the fish and roe are at room temperature. Cover the dish with foil before baking to keep the fish from drying out.

4. When done, slip the fish onto a serving platter, cut and remove the strings. Pour the sorrel sauce around the fish and decorate the top with any small sorrel leaves you may have saved out from the sauce. Cut the serving pieces straight down through the full "sandwich."

*The cream sauce and rich fish demand light surroundings, like a side dish of cucumbers and snow peas or a zucchini sauté or a simple green salad.*

# SALMON IN A CRUST

Almost any kind of boned fish can be baked in almost any kind of crust with mutual benefit to both crust and fish. A baked crust is the best fish wrap of all because the fish flavors the crust while the crust protects the fish from that ever-present curse of drying out. The Russian coulibiac of salmon is one of the most elaborate of fish wraps designed to stun your guests into humility; but unless you are keen on ethnic authenticities like hunting out the chopped sturgeon marrow called "vesiga" to add to the stuffing, you can impress your guests and please yourself by far simpler methods.

In their fascinating and quite different recipes for coulibiac, Child, Claiborne, and Beard wrap their salmon in varying materials, including crêpes, *pâte à choux* or cream-puff paste, mock puff pastry, and *brioche* dough. *Brioche* dough is the most favored because it is the easiest to handle and because it best absorbs the fish juices exuded in the cooking.

A theatrical, yet simpler dish to serve is a whole fish stripped down to two fillets, stuffed with a fish mousse, and wrapped in a *brioche* made to look like a fish, with scales, fins, eyes, mouth, and tail. You can use other kinds of fish than salmon, such as bass, shad, trout, salmon trout, red snapper, etc., but the salmon's pink flesh makes a good wrapping for the inner layer of white mousse. I first ate the dish at Paul Bocuse's auberge outside Lyons, just after he'd received his third star from the prestigious *Michelin Guide*. His fish was wrapped in puff paste and when I remarked on its quality, he told me that puff paste was so easy he could teach me in a day if I would join his kitchen. I've learned that puff paste is easier than I thought, but *brioche* is easier still and far more foolproof.

## Proportions

for 8 servings, 2 salmon fillets totaling around 3 pounds, 1 pound fillet of flounder or sole, 1 cup of heavy cream, 8 cups of *brioche* dough

## For the *Brioche*

2 packages dry yeast
½ cup warm water (110 to 115 degrees)
½ pound (2 sticks) butter
8 eggs

½ cup milk
7 cups flour
1 tablespoon salt
1 tablespoon sugar

## For the Mousse

1 pound flounder or sole fillets
1 egg
1 cup heavy cream
1 tablespoon lemon juice
Salt and freshly ground black pepper to taste

Pinch of cayenne pepper
2 salmon fillets (about 3 pounds)

1.   Prepare the *brioche* dough a day ahead so that it can rise once at room temperature and a second time overnight under refrigeration. Then the dough will be chilled when you're working with it. To make the dough in a processor, lay out the ingredients and divide in 2 portions to make 1 batch at a time. Dissolve the yeast in the warm water to proof it. Cut each stick of butter into 8 pieces. Beat the eggs with the milk in a bowl and warm briefly over hot water to remove chill.

2.   Put half the butter, flour, salt, sugar, and yeast in the processor and blend until the butter is completely broken into the flour. Add half the eggs and milk and process by turning the machine on and off in spurts until the dough masses in the middle. Remove and make the second batch.

3.   Let the dough rest for 5 minutes, then knead by hand on a floured surface until the dough is smooth and shiny. Put the dough into a buttered bowl with high sides and turn it so the surface is butter-coated. Cover tightly with plastic wrap and a kitchen towel and put in a warm place to rise until tripled in bulk (about 3 hours in an oven warmed with a pan of hot water).

4.   Punch the dough down with your fist, knead it a few times, and return it to the bowl. Cover with plastic wrap and a heavy plate, and refrigerate overnight. The plate will prevent the dough from rising and spilling out of the bowl. Leave in the refrigerator until ready to use.

5.   Prepare the filling in a processor by cutting the flounder or sole fillets into 2-inch pieces and processing first with the egg and then with the cream, lemon juice, and seasonings. Taste carefully for seasoning.

6.   Sprinkle the flesh side of the salmon fillets with ½ teaspoon salt and ¼ teaspoon pepper and spread the mousse between the two fillets.

7.  Cut the dough in half and roll out in a rectangle about ⅛ inch thick. Lay on a buttered jelly roll pan and place the fish on top. Cut around the outline of the fish, leaving an inch of dough all around and enough dough at the head end of the fillets to shape a fish head.

8.  Quickly roll out the remaining dough, cut in roughly the same shape but 2 inches larger in order to cover the fillets. Press the dough together all around to seal the fish tight. With the remaining scraps of dough cut out fish "parts" with a sharp knife: a circle for an eye, a strip to shape into a mouth, 4 strips for a gill and pectoral fin, 3 strips for a dorsal fin, 3 for a pelvic fin, and 5 or 6 strips for a tail.

9.  Make an egg glaze of 1 egg beaten with 1 teaspoon water. Paint the dough with glaze all over and apply the fish parts by pressing them into the glaze. Paint over the parts with the glaze. Cut snips of dough with scissors or the sharp edge of a small biscuit cutter or metal pastry tube to simulate scales.

10.  Bake immediately, about 45 minutes at 400 degrees (the internal temperature of the fish should read 160 degrees), if the fish and filling are at room temperature. The crust will be brown and only slightly puffed. Serve with any good fish sauce like sorrel or white butter.

*This is obviously a theatrical dish of sufficient grandeur to require little else but a salad and perhaps a classic Floating Islands pudding (page 388), or a Crème Brûlée.*

# SCALLOP-SHRIMP MOUSSELINE

Say "fish dumplings" to your dinner guests and watch their eyes glaze. Say *quenelles* and watch them snap to attention. The word *quenelles* evokes feather-light poufs of fish mousse, shaped into ovals by a large spoon, and set afloat in fish stock to poach delicately until just firm enough to be netted ashore. Anyone who had eaten such *quenelles* in France, preferably at the hand of the once famed Mère Brazier in her hilltop retreat outside Lyons, could only be grateful for Child's introduction of the French *quenelle* to American cooking in a complete section in her first book. Of course *quenelles* can be as rubbery as the fish dumplings of the Depression, or as canned gefilte fish today, but of such we do not speak.

When Child first introduced the *quenelle,* she did so in the form of the flour-water-egg paste called *panade* that is the basis of cream puffs. The function of the *panade* was to stick together fish that had been finely ground, pounded in a mortar, sieved through the fine mesh of a drum sieve, and worked into a paste with chilled heavy cream. The paste was then shaped with a pair of wet dessert spoons, slipped into stock or water never allowed "to come beyond the barest suggestion of a simmer," and drained to be richly sauced by a Sauce Nantua or a Mousseline Sabayon or any other classic shellfish cream sauce. So fraught with hazard was every move that Child provided a recipe for turning the paste into a simple Fish Mousse in Case of Disaster.

As *quenelles* became fashionable, despite or because of their riskiness, Claiborne experimented with Blender Quenelles, made with sole instead of the traditional pike (or *quenelles de brochet*). The blender was much simpler than meat grinder or mortar but clogged dreadfully with a paste made of fish, egg whites, and cream. The advent of the processor heralded a new age for *quenelles* and simultaneously ended their initial vogue. Making a mousse became so simple and so open to new combinations of fish and shellfish that few wanted to bother with shaping by spoons. Why not poach, steam, or bake the mousse in various molds, or use it as a stuffing for fish fillets or turn it into terrines and pâtés? The processor, in fact, heralded a new age for fish purée of all kinds.

The proportions for any fish or shellfish mousse vary so widely, even among our four masters, that mousse-making should encourage the novice and compulsive experimenter to new daring. The most common disaster with a processed mousse is not a purée that won't hold together but a purée that has been overcooked to the point of being dry and dull. The ideal processed mousse is light, moist, and sweet with its own flavor.

One of the lightest, moistest, and sweetest ingredients for a mousse is scallops, either plain or mixed with flounder, or with shrimp for flavor and a tinge of rose. Any raw boneless fish can be used for a mousse, from flounder and sole to halibut, cod, hake, salmon, trout, shrimp, crab, oyster, lobster. And the mousse can be formed into myriad shapes from oval dumplings to muffin tins, ring molds, soufflé molds, or loaf pans. You merely adjust cooking times.

And, of course, if you can get sausage casing from your fantasized local butcher, you can make seafood sausages with a purée studded with various additions like minced parsley and mushrooms. *The New James Beard* has a good recipe for seafood-sausage-making.

One relatively standard formula for processor mousse is 1¼ to 1½ pounds of fish or seafood to 1½ cups heavy cream and either 3 egg whites or 2 whole eggs. Whole eggs will produce a richer mousse and egg whites a lighter one. I prefer to use whites for the mousse and yolks for the sauce. The recipe below uses butter to enrich and anchovy to deepen the flavor, but they are not essential.

----

# Proportions

for 6 servings 1¼ pounds of mixed seafood, 3 egg whites, 1½ cups of heavy cream

----

½ pound shrimp
2 anchovy fillets
4 tablespoons butter
¾ pound scallops
3 egg whites
1½ cups heavy cream

¼ teaspoon white pepper
¼ teaspoon nutmeg
Dash of Tabasco sauce, or
a pinch of cayenne pepper
Salt to taste

## Shrimp-Butter Sauce

12 shrimp in shells
6 tablespoons butter
1 cup fish stock or clam juice
1 cup dry white wine
1 onion, chopped
1 celery stalk, chopped
6 sprigs parsley
1 anchovy fillet

1 bay leaf
¼ teaspoon thyme
1 teaspoon tomato paste
Freshly ground black pepper
to taste
1 cup heavy cream
1 egg yolk

1.   Shell and devein the ½ pound shrimp (but save the shells) and chop the shrimp and the anchovies in a processor. Add the butter and process, then the scallops and process, then the egg whites and process. With the machine running, add the cream through the opening in the lid until the purée is smooth. Add seasonings and taste carefully. Add salt or lemon juice if the purée seems to lack flavor.

2.   For individual mousselines, butter 12 *brioche* molds or large muffin tins. Or butter a ring mold. Pack the purée in the molds and put in a baking pan. Set in the oven and pour boiling water in the pan to come halfway up the molds so that the mousse will cook evenly. Cover the tops of the molds with buttered wax paper or parchment paper to prevent the tops from browning. For individual molds, bake for 12 to 15 minutes in a 325-degree oven. For a large ring mold, bake for 25 to 30 minutes. Test by inserting a cake tester or long needle to see if it comes out clean. Remember that the mousse will continue to cook slightly from its own heat once it is removed from the oven. Therefore, remove the molds from the hot water if you are not serving immediately. Invert the molds over serving plates and pour sauce over all.

3.   To make the sauce, sauté the 12 shrimp in their shells in butter until they turn pink (3 to 4 minutes). Remove the shells, devein the shrimp, and put them aside for garnish. Return the shells to the pan and add the shells saved from the ½ pound shrimp used in the purée. Pour in the fish stock and wine, add the chopped vegetables and seasonings, and simmer for 20 to 30 minutes.

4.   Strain into a clean pan and add the cream. Reduce rapidly until the cream has thickened slightly and the sauce has reduced to about 1½ cups. Beat a little sauce into the egg yolk, which has been beaten with a fork, and add the yolk to the sauce to thicken it. Beat the sauce with a wire whisk below simmer so that the yolk won't curdle. Taste carefully for seasoning and add salt or lemon juice if wanted. Pour over the mousse-lines and garnish each individual mold with 2 of the reserved shrimp, or place the shrimp in the center of the ring mold.

*This mousse makes a fancy luncheon dish or an elegant first course for a formal dinner focused on a beef fillet or grilled or roasted game.*

# BIRDS

### Roasted

Buttery Roast Chicken · 215
Quick-Roast Turkey · 217
Corn Bread and Sausage Stuffing · 220
Roast Duck with Cracklings · 221

### Fried

Southern Fried Chicken · 222
Stir-Fried Chicken with Cashews · 224

### Sautéed

Chicken Bouillabaisse · 225
Lemon Sesame Chicken Breasts · 226

### Stewed

Old-Fashioned Chicken Fricassee · 228

### Poached

Chicken with Oysters · 229
Chicken Morocco with Lemons and Olives · 231

### Baked

Chicken Pot Pie · 233
Forty-Garlic Chicken · 235

### Grilled

Gin-Marinated Rock Cornish Hens · 236
Mustard-Grilled Quail · 237

To eat *[small birds]* à la Brillat-Savarin.—*Take hold of the bird by the bill; open your mouth wide enough to introduce the whole bird into it easily; then shut it, at the same time biting off the bill just at its base; chew properly and swallow.*

—*Pierre Blot*
Hand-book of Practical Cookery
*(1867)*

When America was less citified, birds were of two kinds—domesticated and wild, but all were fair game for the eater. In America, as in other parts of the world, the smallest of birds were spitted on a stick, 4 or 5 in a row, to be roasted over a fire and eaten whole as small sardines might be, in which you hold the fish by the tail instead of the bird by the bill.

In these latter days, when we have trashed our wilderness and made wild our cities, domesticated birds are largely factory products and wild birds almost never make their way to market unless they have been bred for the purpose. To eat really small birds à la Brillat-Savarin is next to impossible in a country where miniaturization breeds sentiment and brings in the SPCA.

When the majority of the populace had a few odd hens and a rooster in the backyard for breakfast eggs and Sunday fricassee, we were more intimate with the ways of birds both tamed and wild. When we killed the eldest hen for supper, we respected her place at the table and called her by her pet name even as we dined on her flesh. She was personally involved in our welfare. We were grateful to her.

Consider today the factory product in its plastic wrap, headless, footless, gutted, de-feathered, characterless, impersonal. The poultry counters of our supermarkets are as clean as sanatoria. We can easily count our blessings in convenience, but we have lost our living relation to birds by turning them into computer-fed, computer-bred, computer-dead abstractions. Within these sizable limits, we do well by our factory birds divided generically into chicken, duck, turkey, goose, and "game," and count ourselves lucky when we find one freshly dead and not frozen. Of the varying tastes and textures of different species we know little unless we travel outside our borders. Of the varying tastes of free-range birds within a single species we also know little unless we are country dwellers who still keep a few hens and a rooster for eggs and flesh.

Our master chefs, all of them intimate with pre-factory days and less computerized countries, have resisted complaint, however, and gotten on with the job, which is how best to cook the bird at hand. Ironically, our methods of cooking have increased in sophistication and variety as rapidly as our varieties of wild and tame birds have diminished. Often our recipes are designed to reinject flavor into flavorless flesh, much as our "butterball" turkeys are injected with water, oil, and other additives to make up for the loss of natural fat and moisture acquired by unforced feeding and breeding. Many who consider the eating of small birds, à la Brillat-Savarin, an act of barbarism are indifferent to the "barbaric" treatment of living birds as mechanical components in the machinery of industry.

Possibly the gross national productivity of our bird factories has diminished the value of their products, as we take their plumpness, blandness, cleanliness, and abundance for granted. In the midst of our elegant engineering and corporate efficiency, however, perhaps it is not yet too late to make a plea for taste. For centuries the taste of birds large and small, tame and wild, meant the taste of natural, simple roasted or grilled flesh, sizzling on a spit or in an oven. Fisher once made a plea for the simple roasted bird, so often now ignored or forgotten, with her customary vigor. "There is good advice on all sides: Escoffier, Child, Rombauer," she exhorted us in *With Bold Knife & Fork*. "Unite, slaves of the steam kettle and the shakers of meat tenderizer and MSG! Read, and be rewarded! Eat two bites of a properly roasted chicken, and L*A*F*F* (at all the rest)!"

# BUTTERY ROAST CHICKEN

A roast chicken is a beautiful thing but hardly anyone agrees on temperature or time, so that the "best" method of roasting is the one you devise yourself, with your own oven, in pursuit of the ideal bird with a crisp skin and a moist juicy interior.

Our masters agree in principle but disagree in detail on how to achieve a perfect roast chicken. They agree that the bird should be trussed; that the bird should be cooked first on one side, then on the other, and finally breast side up for even browning; and that the bird should be basted copiously.

They disagree on precise oven temperatures and time, but in a way that should bolster a healthy skepticism about hard-and-fast rules of any kind. The relative rule is that it will take about an hour to roast a 4-pound bird in an oven of 400 or 425 degrees. Beard suggests 425 degrees, Claiborne

400 degrees, and Child suggests an initial 425 degrees (for 15 minutes), followed by 350 degrees. Child's rule of thumb for birds of different weights is to count on a minimum of 45 minutes, and thereafter to add 7 minutes per pound.

What the home cook often forgets is that the bird should be at room temperature to begin with to shorten the roasting time. What the home cook often wants to forget is the trussing of the bird, which makes for a tidy shape but why bother? It was Child who first taught many of us how to make a roaster look professional by trussing it. We bought poultry needles, threaded them, and, studying the diagrams of *Mastering I*, pierced thighs in one direction and wings in another, struggling to keep the thread taut and the knots tight. It was a job, but we were determined to out-French the French. Child made the job look easy in illustrative photographs in *From Julia Child's Kitchen*. Beard made the job even easier in the explanatory drawings of *Theory & Practice*.

Despite such instruction, however, I seldom truss a plain unstuffed bird, for the simple reason that the thigh meat will cook more quickly untrussed. Trussing compounds the basic bird problem of how to cook dark meat without overcooking and drying out the white. One approach to the problem is to roast the chicken breast side down, after an initial searing, so that the internal juices will baste the bird from the inside and keep the breast meat moist.

Another approach is to create a self-basting bird by spreading an herb-flavored butter under the skin over the breast. This is a variant on the classical French method of slipping truffle slices under the skin to produce the dish wittily called from its half-white, half-black appearance, A Bird in Half-Mourning. A butter flavored with chervil or thyme or tarragon, or even a bit of *pesto* sauce, does better than truffles in providing moisture as well as flavor.

You loosen the skin over the breast, and thighs if you wish, by working your fingers gently under the skin from the vent to the wishbone, being careful not to tear the skin closest to the vent. If you do, you can sew or skewer it, to keep the butter in. You can also put a bit of flavored butter in the cavity, which will help perfume the entire bird.

You can, of course, combine methods, as I've done here. I've worked butter under the skin to moisten and flavor the breast meat and I've adopted the searing method of turning the bird breast side up, down, and up again in order to get a really crisp skin. If you have fresh tarragon, so much the better, but dried works well.

## Proportions

for 3 to 4 servings, a 3- to 4-pound roaster

| 1 3- to 4-pound roasting<br>chicken | Salt and freshly ground<br>black pepper to taste |
|---|---|
| ¼ pound (1 stick) butter | |
| 3 tablespoons chopped fresh<br>tarragon, or 1½ tablespoons<br>dried | |

1. If the bird has been refrigerated, let it come to room temperature. Soften half the butter, mix it with the tarragon, and work two thirds of the herbed butter under the skin. Put the remaining herbed butter in the cavity of the bird.

2. Make sure the skin is completely dry, then spread it with the remaining softened butter. Sear the bird breast side up on a V-shaped rack in a 500-degree oven for 15 minutes. Reduce the oven temperature to 375 degrees. Baste the bird well, turn it breast side down, and roast for 30 minutes. Baste again, sprinkle the back with salt and pepper, turn the bird breast side up again, baste and sprinkle with salt and pepper. Roast for another 15 minutes, or until the thickest part of the thigh registers 165 to 170 degrees. (If the skin is not brown enough, turn the oven temperature up again for the final 15 minutes.) Serve the bird in its own juices and butter.

*Chicken is so adaptable that it marries happily with rice or potatoes, green or yellow vegetables, salads, and soups of all kinds. Because roast chicken is simple, now is the time to dress up its surroundings with a soup such as Green Sorrel (page 110), Hot Vichyssoise (page 111), or Red Pepper and Tomato (page 108). Chicken is one of the best main dishes to follow with a toothsome rich dessert such as a Chocolate Mousse Cake (page 396) or an Apple Bread-and-Butter Pudding (page 387).*

# QUICK-ROAST TURKEY

A freshly killed and plucked turkey is increasingly a luxury available only at Thanksgiving and Christmas. The frozen factory product available year round benefits only the producer, not the consumer, no matter how much oil and water has been injected for "self-basting" nor how many parts have been repackaged and reconstituted. An unfrozen fresh bird cooks best, tastes best, so buy one when you can.

The problem in cooking turkey is how to provide equal opportunity for its two separate parts, white and dark. To make the dark tender is to dry out the white. If you don't have to display the whole bird, you can cut off the breast from either side while it is still faintly rare and continue to cook the legs and thighs, as you might do with a duck. Usually, however, the display is the point for holiday and buffet tables, so compromise is in order. The larger the bird the better, to equalize the time needed to cook both breast and thigh.

A 25-pound bird is best of all and, contrary to expectation, does not take a full half day to cook. With the high-temperature method suggested below, most commonly used professionally, a 25-pounder at room temperature, *not chilled*, will be done in 2½ to 3 hours. A 15-pounder may be done in 1½. The point is not to measure pounds by minutes mechanically, since the temperature of the bird before it goes into the oven is more crucial than its weight. The best measure is a thermometer that should register 160 degrees inserted into the thickest part of the breast and 170 to 175 degrees inserted into the thickest part of the thigh, being careful not to touch bone. "Should" is variable. We are eating turkey rarer today than yesterday. Only a few years ago 180 degrees was considered rare and 185 degrees medium. Today, Claiborne recommends 160 degrees for the whole bird, based on that temperature for the stuffing. Whatever temperature you prefer, you must let the turkey rest a good 30 minutes before carving to avoid losing juice.

The purpose of the high-temperature method is to seal the skin and crisp it, before turning the heat down to cook the interior. If the turkey is small, you may want to turn it on one side and then the other, before turning it breast up, in order to brown the skin evenly. If the skin browns too fast, cover it loosely with foil. If the skin is not brown enough after the initial high temperature, keep the temperature high or turn it high again at the end.

The skin will taste best if you baste it every 30 minutes or less with butter and pan drippings as they come. If frequent basting is difficult, the best substitute is to soak several layers of cheesecloth in butter and chicken or duck fat, which tends to cling, and to cover the breast and thighs after the initial searing. Salting the skin at the end of cooking, instead of at the beginning, helps to keep the meat from losing juice.

The major disadvantage of the high-temperature method is smoke. Butter spattering on a large bird in a small oven may generate more smoke than you like, but you can delay it somewhat by searing first in oil, then in butter.

The bird will cook faster and be easier to serve if you bake the stuffing separately, in a casserole. The stuffing will stay crisp instead of soggy and there will be more pan juices for the sauce. You can even bake the stuffing a day ahead and reheat it, moistening it as much as you choose with turkey fat, juice, or butter. The stuffing suggested below of corn bread and sausage combines two of the best traditional American stuffings to make an American trinity of corn, pork, and our most famous native bird.

# High-Temperature Roasting Chart

Under 12 pounds:  1 to 1½ hours
12 to 15 pounds:  1½ to 2 hours
15 to 20 pounds:  2 to 2½ hours
20 to 25 pounds:  2½ to 3 hours

# Proportions

for 12 servings, a 15-pound turkey with 12 cups of stuffing

1 **15-pound turkey**
2 **to 3 tablespoons olive oil**
**Salt and freshly ground
black pepper**

¼ **pound (1 stick) butter**

## For the Pan Gravy

**Turkey neck and giblets,
including liver**
1 **onion, sliced**
1 **celery stalk with leaves,
chopped**

1 **carrot, sliced**
1 **bay leaf**
1 **teaspoon thyme**
**Salt and freshly ground black
pepper**

1. Leave the turkey at room temperature for 4 or 5 hours if it comes from the refrigerator. The colder the turkey the longer the cooking time and the more chance the meat has to dry out. Rub the turkey all over with the oil before putting it on a rack in a roasting pan.

2. Put the turkey breast side up in a 450-degree oven for 15 minutes. Baste with melted butter and roast for another 30 minutes. Turn the oven down to 375 degrees and continue to roast, basting every 20 to 30 minutes. If the turkey starts to get too brown, cover the top lightly with foil. Or turn the oven to 350 degrees. After 1½ hours, test the temperature of the breast with a thermometer. The breast will be done at 160 degrees, the thighs at 170 degrees.

3. While the bird roasts, prepare the stock of giblets, neck, vegetables, and seasonings in water or broth to cover. Bring gently to a boil, remove the foam, and simmer until the toughest giblet, the gizzard, is tender. Remove the turkey liver as soon as it is tender (about 10 minutes) and set it aside. When the other giblets are done, strain, save the heart and gizzard, and reduce the stock to about 1 cup. Dice the giblets fine and add to the stock.

4. When the turkey registers between 160 and 170 degrees, remove it from the oven and let it rest before carving. Sprinkle the skin with salt and pepper. Tip the roasting pan so that you can spoon off some of

the butter and fat to get at the pan juices beneath. Add the degreased juices to the stock and enough of the butter to make a rich but not oily sauce.

5.   To carve the turkey, cut off the wings and the legs at the joint to get at the breast. Cut the breast in thin slices, beginning at the wing corner and cutting parallel to the breast bone. Slice the dark meat from the thighs and legs and arrange on a platter. Serve the pan gravy separately.

# CORN BREAD AND SAUSAGE STUFFING

## Proportions

allow 1 cup per serving, or about 12 cups for a 15-pound turkey

4 cups corn bread (page 338)
3 cups cubed and trimmed white bread
1 pound sausage meat
2 medium-size onions, chopped
4 celery stalks with leaves, chopped

½ cup finely chopped parsley
1½ teaspoons salt
1 teaspoon thyme
1 teaspoon freshly ground black pepper
½ teaspoon rosemary
¼ teaspoon sage
2 hard-boiled eggs, chopped

1.   Make the corn bread a day ahead, cut in cubes, and toast in a 350-degree oven, along with the white bread cubes. (Trim the crusts from the slices of white bread and cut the slices a few at a time lengthwise and crosswise into ½-inch cubes.)

2.   Sauté the sausage meat lightly to render some of the fat and set aside before the meat is fully cooked. Sauté the chopped onions and celery to soften them only slightly. If the sausage has not rendered enough fat, add butter to the pan.

3.   Mix all the ingredients with the seasonings and the chopped eggs in a casserole. Taste some bread cubes for seasoning and adjust. If the crumbs are too dry, add a little turkey stock or melted butter or both. Cover and bake in a 350-degree oven for 30 minutes. For a crusty top, remove the cover for the last 10 minutes or so.

*Traditional Thanksgiving accompaniments are braised chestnuts, creamed onions, puréed sweet potatoes, brussels sprouts, or green beans, along with cranberry sauce and pumpkin and mince pies. But turkey is like chicken in its adaptability and travels well with more adventuresome companions.*

# ROAST DUCK WITH CRACKLINGS

The problem with duck is like the problem with turkey only more so: how to get a crisp skin, a rare breast, and cooked thighs all at once. The problem is compounded by the American duck, which is usually a factory product bred for uniformity and a thick layer of fat. Instead of the *nantais,* the *rouennais,* the *canard de barbarie* of France, we have the White Pekin, frozen and thawed. With frozen birds it is more important than ever not to overcook the flesh which inevitably loses juice in the thawing. But how can you crisp the skin and get rid of that thick subcutaneous blanket of fat?

One solution is to make cracklings of the skin. Child suggests, in *Julia Child & More Company,* that you skin the bird after an initial bake sufficient for the breast but not the thighs. You can then crumb the skinned thighs and cook them further, while you crisp the cut-up strips of skin. Beard suggests other solutions. One is to crisp the skin at the end, baking the duck at 350 degrees for 1 hour for rare, then raising the oven to 500 degrees for a final 15 minutes. (Be sure to pour out the fat first.) Another is to make cracklings of the skin by deep frying them rather than baking them.

I have followed Child's method below, because this French way of handling duck gives the cook maximum control over skin, breast, and thigh and makes the bird easiest to serve at the table because the carving is already done. The sauce suggested here is essentially pan gravy, which heats and enhances the thin slices of breast. Since the familiar orange sauce has become as subject to restaurant abuse as simultaneously fatty and stringy ducks, it's better to go for a lemon sauce to give tartness or a classical sauce of whole green olives.

## Proportions

for 2 large or 4 small servings, 1 duck of 4 to 5 pounds

**1  4- to 5-pound duckling**

### For the Sauce

|  |  |
|---|---|
| **Duck neck and giblets** | **½  teaspoon thyme** |
| **1  carrot, chopped** | **3  sprigs parsley** |
| **1  onion, chopped** | **Salt and freshly ground** |
| **¼  cup dry white wine** | **black pepper to taste** |
| **1  bay leaf** | **2  tablespoons Madeira** |

## For the Duck Legs

⅓ cup Dijon mustard      2 teaspoons honey
1 tablespoon lemon juice      1 cup fresh bread crumbs

    1. Dry the duck well with paper towels after thawing. Prick the skin all over with a fork, especially in the fatty areas around the thighs. Bake in a 350-degree oven for 30 minutes.

    2. Cut all the skin from the bird, removing the thickest layers of fat from the back of the skin. Cut in strips ¼ inch wide and spread in a roasting pan. Raise the oven temperature to 400 degrees and begin to roast cracklings while carving the meat.

    3. Remove the breast on each side and slice thin. Put on a warm serving platter. Remove all fat from the legs and coat with a mixture of mustard, lemon juice, and honey. Dip each leg in bread crumbs (made in a processor) and put in a separate baking pan. Roast for about 30 minutes in a 400-degree oven until the flesh is tender and the crumbs are well browned. Pour the fat from the cracklings once or twice.

    4. While the duck is cooking, prepare the stock by cooking the neck and giblets in wine and water to cover, with the carrot, onion, and seasonings. Strain and save the giblets for some other purpose. Boil the liquid down to about ½ cup and add the Madeira. Add any duck juices released in the carving.

    5. To serve, pour the hot sauce over the breast slices, framed by a leg on either side, a heap of cracklings at the top of the platter, and a bunch of watercress at the bottom.

*Duck does well with an acidic Orange and Onion Salad (page 156), on the one hand, or with a creamy Parsnip Purée (page 297) or Sour Sweet Potato Purée (page 298), on the other.*

# SOUTHERN FRIED CHICKEN

No matter how sophisticated he has become in French sautés, many an American wants his chicken fried, the American way, with a crusty outside and a tender inside like the old Yank himself. There's no particular reason for pan-fried chicken to become identified with the South, except that chickens were plentiful and the cooking was good. Back in 1893, Marion Harland in Brooklyn acknowledges the tradition when she says that fried chicken, dredged in seasoned flour and browned in lard is "a standard dish in the Old Dominion, and tastes nowhere else as it does when eaten on Virginia soil." Today American fried chicken is eaten from Tokyo to Timbuktu as a product of the Kentucky soil fabricated by Colonel Sanders, and the reason for its continuing popularity is that frying makes chicken a finger food that, properly prepared with good chickens in good fat, is in truth finger-lickin' good.

In *The New New York Times Cookbook*, Claiborne gives his family recipe from Mississippi for Southern-Fried Chicken that calls for Tabasco sauce instead of cayenne pepper or some other hot pepper for seasoning. Anyone who has known an indigenous southern cook has discovered that the secret of a good-tasting fried chicken lies first in soaking the cut-up pieces for an hour or so in milk that has been seasoned with salt, black pepper, and red pepper or Tabasco sauce. And second in frying the pieces in about an inch and a half of good-tasting fat, such as a combination of lard or bacon fat or duck fat and butter. Vegetable oil is convenient, but the taste won't be as finger-lickin' good.

## Proportions

for 4 servings, 1 frying chicken of 2½ to 3 pounds, 1¼ pounds fat

| | |
|---|---|
| 1 2½- to 3-pound frying chicken | 1½ cups flour |
| 1 cup milk | ¾ to 1 pound lard, fat, or oil |
| 2 teaspoons salt | ¼ pound (1 stick) butter |
| 1 teaspoon freshly ground black pepper | |
| Pinch of cayenne pepper, or ¼ teaspoon red pepper flakes, or a dash of Tabasco sauce | |

1. Cut the chicken into 6 main pieces (2 breasts, 2 thighs, 2 legs), reserving the back and wings for stock, or frying them if you like to nibble bones. Add the seasonings to the milk and pour the mixture over the chicken, soaking the pieces for an hour at room temperature.

2. Dip the chicken pieces into the flour and pat well so that the flour sticks. Set aside while heating the fat.

3. Heat the lard or other fat and butter in a heavy cast-iron skillet until hot but not smoking. Add the chicken pieces without crowding, so that the pieces don't touch. Keep the heat high enough so that the fat bubbles but the flour coating does not burn. Keep turning the pieces with tongs or a long-handled slotted spoon to brown them evenly.

4. Test the breasts after 10 minutes by inserting a knife point at the thickest part. If the juice runs clear and not pink, remove and keep warm. The breasts will be done in 10 to 15 minutes, depending on the temperature of the fat. The dark meat will be done in 20 to 30 minutes. Drain on paper towels and serve either hot or at room temperature.

*Good with potato salad, coleslaw, or spinach salad.*

# STIR-FRIED CHICKEN WITH CASHEWS

The Chinese way of frying food quickly in a wide skillet, or wok, is ideal for cooking the white meat of chicken that so quickly overcooks. Anyone experimenting at home will come up with dozens of different combinations of ingredients, flavors, and seasonings, from mild to tongue-searing hot, all of which will complement that most complaisant of hosts, or hostesses, a well-bred chicken.

The principle is almost always the same: to cook cubed raw chicken for a minute in hot vegetable oil before adding crisp cut-up vegetables and/or other crunchers like nuts. With stir-frying, crispness is all. What once seemed exotic to Americans, the use of walnuts, peanuts, or cashews with fowl has become commonplace through the proliferation of Szechuan and now Thai and Vietnamese restaurants in American cities. Nut-lovers might argue that chicken is merely an excuse to make every dish from soup to nuts a nut-purveyor, but however addictive nuts are, their rich oiliness marries well with the virginal white breast.

## Proportions

for 4 servings, 2 whole chicken breasts to 2 cups nuts to 3 cups vegetables

2 whole chicken breasts, split, skinned, and boned
1 tablespoon cornstarch
½ cup chicken broth
½ teaspoon soy sauce
½ cup peanut oil
4 to 6 Szechuan peppercorns
1 small hot chili pepper, minced, or ½ teaspoon red pepper flakes

1 cup Jerusalem artichokes, peeled and sliced, or 1 cup fresh or canned water chestnuts
1 cup thinly sliced sweet red peppers
1 cup snow peas or sugar-snap peas
2 cups roasted cashew nuts

1. Cut the chicken breasts into 1-inch cubes. Soften the cornstarch in broth and soy sauce and set aside.

2. Heat the oil in a skillet or wok with the peppercorns and hot pepper. Add the chicken and cook, stirring, for 1 minute. Add the artichokes and peppers and cook for another minute. Then add the snow peas and nuts, and cook for a minute or two, or until the chicken is just tender.

3. Quickly add the cornstarch-broth mixture, stir well, and serve on a platter. The vegetables should be very crisp, the nuts salty and crunchy, and the chicken very hot with pepper. Reduce the amount of pepper if you don't like it hot.

*Because this is a one-dish meal with vegetables included, Steamed White Rice (page 307) is a good accompaniment and some kind of fresh fruit or fruit salad a good conclusion.*

# CHICKEN BOUILLABAISSE

Where Americans say fry, the French say sauté. Fry implies the use of fat in some quantity. Sauté implies less fat and usually a little liquid such as wine. To baptize chicken with wine was as shocking in my Bible-belt-oriented childhood as to play cards on Sunday. I remember regarding one of my teachers with grave suspicion when he recited his favorite recipe for chicken, which included not only the forbidden juice of grape but the accursed clove of garlic. In my little corner of midwestern California, he was a man ahead of his time.

Forty years later garlic and wine seem almost classically austere in the spate of ever more exotic spices and liquors. Forty years later the marriage of garlic, wine, and tomatoes, which once evoked the foreignness of Mediterranean shores, is now as common as Sunday poker. So much have we made this foreign union our own that when Child was devising new recipes for *Julia Child & Company* she labeled a chicken dish by the name of a familiar sauce for fish, to create Chicken Bouillabaisse. So much do we demand new sensations that garlic, wine, and tomatoes are not enough. Now we must add for garnish the garlic and hot-pepper sauce called, unpronounceably, *rouille.* I include an adaptation of it here not only as a cultural and linguistic curiosity, but as an easier and more practical dish than Fish Bouillabaisse. Those who choke down fish or fowl for the sake of the sauce will find contentment here.

## Proportions

for 4 servings, 1 3½-pound fryer, 2 cups of fresh tomatoes, 3 cloves garlic, 1 cup of dry vermouth

1 3½-pound fryer, cut up
4 tablespoons olive oil
2 leeks, chopped
3 cloves garlic, chopped
2 cups fresh peeled, seeded, and chopped tomatoes
½ teaspoon fennel seeds
Large pinch of saffron threads

1 bay leaf
Salt and freshly ground black pepper to taste
1 cup dry vermouth
2 tablespoons Cognac
⅓ cup chopped parsley

1.  Brown the chicken quickly in the oil, turning the pieces to brown them evenly (about 10 minutes). Add the leeks and garlic and cook over low heat for about 5 minutes. Stir in the tomatoes and seasonings, and pour on the vermouth and Cognac. Bring to simmer, cover partially, and cook for 15 to 20 minutes, turning the chicken once.

2.  Remove the chicken to a warm platter and boil the sauce down rapidly to reduce it. Taste carefully for seasoning, pour the sauce over the chicken, and sprinkle with the chopped parsley. Serve with separate sauceboat of *rouille*.

*Best with a simple green salad.*

# SAUCE *ROUILLE*

6 cloves garlic, chopped
½ teaspoon salt
2 tablespoons fresh bread crumbs

2 tablespoons tomato paste
1 dried red pepper, or 1 teaspoon red pepper flakes
4 tablespoons olive oil

Put all the ingredients in a processor or blender and mix to a smooth paste. If you need more liquid, add a tablespoon or two of the chicken sauce, or more oil as necessary. The sauce should resemble a very hot, very thick mayonnaise.

# LEMON-SESAME CHICKEN BREASTS

Time was when a boned chicken breast was the sign of carriage trade, but with a market full of inexpensive chicken meat, boned breasts are supermarket fare nowadays. It's cheaper, of course, to bone your own, with the advantage of having a few more bones to add to your stock pile. Child taught us how to bone breasts in *Mastering I* and how to cook them by sprinkling with salt and lemon juice, rolling them in butter and baking at 400 degrees for 6 minutes or until the meat is "springy to the touch."

Most breasts in my oven seem to take longer than 6 minutes and sautéing seems easier in any case. For a really speedy sauté, you can always treat the meat like veal scallops, flattening each breast with a wooden mallet to make a thin fillet.

The recipe below is a simple variation on a chicken sauté in which the breast meat is marinated in sesame-flavored oil and lemon before cooking. After cooking, the juices are swept into a cream sauce with additional lemon juice. The flavor is as delicate and lovely as the ivory beige color of the sauce.

## Proportions

for 4 servings, 2 whole breasts, 1 cup of heavy cream

2 whole breasts, split, boned, and skinned
Juice of 2 lemons, plus the zest of 1
1 tablespoon sesame paste
1 teaspoon soy sauce
1 small green or red chili pepper, minced, or ½ teaspoon red pepper flakes

Freshly ground black pepper to taste
2 tablespoons sesame or peanut oil
1 cup heavy cream

1. Trim the breasts and flatten them with the side of a knife. Marinate for 2 to 3 hours at room temperature in a mixture of the juice of 1 lemon, the sesame paste, soy sauce, and peppers.

2. Remove the zest of the second lemon and set it aside for the garnish. Sauté the breasts quickly in the hot oil for 4 to 5 minutes, or until just tender. Remove to a warm serving dish.

3. Pour the heavy cream into a pan and thicken slightly over high heat. Pour the liquid into a blender with 2 tablespoons of lemon juice and the juice exuded by the breasts on the serving platter. Blend and taste carefully for seasoning. The sauce should be very lemony, so add more juice if necessary. Pour the sauce over the chicken and garnish with the lemon zest. Because there is no butter, the chicken and sauce are as good room-temperature warm as hot.

*The Chinese connection suggests stir-fried vegetables for accompaniment, along with Steamed White Rice (page 307) to soak up the sauce.*

# OLD-FASHIONED CHICKEN FRICASSEE

To fricassee meat or fowl originally meant to mince and cook in a sauce in order to make the tough tender. Chicken Fricassee, a standard old-fashioned American dish, originally referred to a stewing hen or cock that had outlived its usefulness in the egg way and was fit only for the pot. The fowl was cut up, stewed slowly in water, broth, or milk and finished off with a white gravy. During the Depression a stewing chicken was a Sunday treat in many households, particularly if a few hard-boiled embryonic egg yolks were floating in the gravy.

Nowadays, a stewing chicken, properly 12 months old and weighing over 3 pounds, is as hard to come by as a piece of mutton, and for the same reasons. Such senior citizens are an inconvenience for the food factories geared to maximize uniformity of size, weight, age, and breed. A genuine stewing fowl—either hen or cock—is a nostalgic relic of another era, yet traditions of stewing continue even though the tenderizing function has changed.

Take Child's immensely popular recipe for Coq au Vin, introduced in *Mastering I,* in which she demonstrated how the French made an old cock tender by stewing it in a hearty Burgundy or Beaujolais, flavored with onions, mushrooms, and bacon. For a time, Coq au Vin became a must for every aspiring American bistro or home buffet, even though a rooster was nowhere in sight and the frying chicken specified by Child would be tender in half an hour. But the idea of chicken heady with garlic in a wine-dark sauce seized the imagination of eaters used to chicken blond and bland. Coq au Vin became a generic name for any chicken in a red wine sauce with vaguely French pretensions.

Actually, however, as Child pointed out, Coq au Vin is simply a fricassee in a brown sauce instead of a white sauce. Child, accordingly, also gives in *Mastering I* a good recipe for a white fricassee with the same traditional vegetables as Coq au Vin—onions and mushrooms—using white wine instead of red and finishing off with a cream sauce. It's essentially the same recipe that Pierre Blot recommended for "Ladies and Professional Cooks" in 1867, with the exception of his three suggested garnitures of chicken-combs, truffles, and a boiled crawfish "here and there." Enriched with egg yolks and cream and served on a nest of white rice, a white chicken fricassee is as classically American as a Coq au Vin is French.

## Proportions

for 4 servings, 1 3½-pound fryer, 3 cups of liquid, 20 small onions, ½ pound mushrooms

| | |
|---|---|
| 4 tablespoons butter | 2 cups boiling chicken stock |
| 1 3½-pound fryer, cut up | or broth |
| 20 small white onions, peeled | 1 cup dry white wine or |
| ½ teaspoon salt | vermouth |
| ¼ teaspoon freshly ground | ½ pound small button |
| black pepper | mushrooms |
| 3 tablespoons flour | |

### For the Sauce

| | |
|---|---|
| 2 egg yolks | Pinch of nutmeg |
| ½ cup heavy cream | ⅓ cup chopped parsley |

1. Melt the butter in an enamel-lined skillet or casserole. Add the chicken and onions and cook until both have turned lightly golden, not brown (5 to 10 minutes). Turn the pieces frequently. Add salt and pepper, sprinkle on the flour, and cook slowly for about 5 minutes.

2. Remove from the heat, add the boiling stock and wine all at once, and stir to make a smooth sauce. Bring to a simmer, add the mushrooms, cover, and cook at a very low simmer for 25 to 30 minutes, or until the chicken drumsticks are tender.

3. Remove the chicken, onions, and mushrooms with a slotted spoon to a warm serving dish. Raise the heat and reduce the sauce to about 2 cups. Beat the egg yolks into the cream, then beat a little sauce into the cream mixture, and add the mixture to the sauce, beating vigorously until the sauce comes to a boil. Add the nutmeg, taste for seasoning, and pour the sauce over the chicken and vegetables. Sprinkle with chopped parsley and serve.

*Rice is the classic accompaniment, but America has also favored corn bread. Since the sauce is rich, plain carrots or peas or green beans are appropriate.*

# POACHED CHICKEN WITH OYSTERS

One of the most famous chickens of France, the *Poularde de Bresse,* raised in Brillat-Savarin's hometown, is traditionally cooked in the most simple way—by poaching. Of course truffles are frequently slipped under the skin and the whole bird enclosed in a pig's caul to make this simple dish a culinary epiphany. But even without these luxuries, a really good chicken, or a plump capon, is most intensely itself when simmered in a chicken stock that returns to the flesh what was previously drawn from the bone.

The numerous authors of the *Kansas Home Cook-Book* of 1886 understood the virtues of cooking a fowl in its own juice when they recommended the following method for poaching:

> Take a young fowl; fill the inside with oysters or stuffing, place in a jar, and plunge into a kettle of boiling water. Boil till tender. There will be gravy in the jar from the juice of the fowl.

The idea of filling the inside of a young fowl with oysters *and* stuffing is too good to resist and makes a happy variation on the more usual stuffing, today, of pork and veal. A capon of 5 or 6 pounds is ideal because the flesh is thick, juicy, white, and tender, but a roaster of the same weight will also serve.

For the best flavor, the poaching liquid should be a chicken stock or mixed stock. But because you will need a lot of liquid, enough to cover, you may have to add wine or water. With an oyster stuffing, you can add clam juice as well. Both Beard and Child give recipes for poaching chicken in just plain cold water, with vegetables added to make a broth, but the resulting taste is weaker. It's worth making stock ahead or buying quart cans of chicken broth.

In *Julia Child & More Company,* Child demonstrates the best way to truss a chicken for poaching (or roasting if you don't want to break the skin); but you don't need to truss, particularly if you have a pot that the chicken can just fill, with space an inch or two above it for liquid to cover. You will need to close the opening of the vent tightly, however, by sewing or trussing or skewering to keep the stuffing in place. The trick in poaching is to keep the liquid at the barest possible simmer so that the flesh will become tender without breaking apart and toughening.

---

## Proportions

for 6 to 8 servings, a 5- to 6-pound capon or roaster in liquid to cover (anywhere from 3 to 6 quarts), with 1 pint oysters

### For the Oyster Stuffing

1 small onion, minced
6 tablespoons butter
1 cup fresh bread crumbs
1 pint oysters and liquor

¼ cup minced parsley
Salt and freshly ground
black pepper to taste

### For the Poached Chicken

1 5- to 6-pound capon or
   roaster
½ lemon

Boiling chicken stock (or
equivalent) to cover

---

1.  Cook the onion in the butter until it is soft. Then mix with the bread crumbs, oysters, parsley, and seasonings.

2.  Rub the interior of the chicken with ½ lemon and squeeze some of the juice into the cavity. Skewer the neck skin across the back to hold it in place. Fill the cavity with the oyster stuffing and truss the legs closed by looping string first around the tail piece and then around the end of each drumstick. Pull tight and tie a knot. Fold wings akimbo and, if you want, secure them by looping the trussing string, on each side, around each wing and tying the string tightly across the back. The wings are less important than the vent. To keep the stuffing safe and dry, it may be necessary to close the vent with a crust of bread and sew or skewer the skin closed.

3.  Put the chicken in a pot and cover with boiling liquid by at least 1 inch. Bring rapidly to a simmer, skim carefully, partially cover the pot, and maintain at the lowest possible simmer, anywhere from 1 to 2 hours, depending on the size of the pot and the kind of chicken. When cooked, the thigh should be tender at the thickest point and register 170 to 175 degrees on a thermometer.

4.  If possible, carve the chicken at the table and serve with extra lemon quarters for the oyster stuffing. You can serve with a bowl of broth at the side or serve the broth as a soup course.

*If you want to serve the chicken with vegetables, such as carrots and leeks, you can cook them whole along with the chicken for the last half hour if there is room in the pot. If not, cut them in lengthwise slivers (julienne), to cook quickly in the broth after the chicken is removed and kept warm and moist by covering in foil or plastic wrap. Follow with a light salad and a pie or cake or even an Indian Pudding (page 385) for dessert.*

# CHICKEN MOROCCO WITH LEMONS AND OLIVES

A good example of how a new recipe can become part of a shared repertory is Paula Wolfert's recipe for chicken with preserved lemons and Mediterranean olives in her book *Moroccan Cookery*. In our search for new culinary geographies, Morocco was prime territory, combining French ways with more exotic Arabic ones, and Wolfert's research was precise. Both Beard and Claiborne have adapted her recipe to American usages and the differences illuminate their characteristic methods.

Claiborne follows Wolfert's recipe closely, offering it as another adventure into the wide world of cooking. He explains how to preserve lemons whole in salt and how to use them to help marinate the chicken before cooking. Beard, on the other hand, absorbs the recipe into his own characteristic style, simplifying the pickled lemons by slicing them and covering them with oil as well as salt, and then using them as garnish rather than marinade. While no single ingredient is in the same proportion, except for ½ cup oil, the idea is the same and the results are similar. To see how our tutors adapt recipes is to see how easily we can adapt our own, to our own tastes and ways of cooking.

In the recipe below, I've followed Claiborne's lead in preserving lemons whole and using them for the marinade because it makes this dish more distinctively Moroccan. Elsewhere, I've followed Beard in using turmeric instead of fresh coriander and some chicken broth instead of water.

## Proportions

for 4 servings, 1 3-pound chicken, 1 preserved lemon, ½ cup of olives

| | |
|---|---|
| 6 **to 8 lemons** | 1 **3-pound chicken** |
| **Kosher or coarse salt** | ½ **cup olive oil** |
| 1 **preserved lemon** | 1 **large onion, minced** |
| 3 **cloves garlic, chopped** | ½ **teaspoon salt or to taste** |
| 1 **teaspoon ginger** | 1 **cup chicken broth** |
| ½ **teaspoon turmeric** | ½ **cup black Mediterranean** |
| **Pinch of saffron threads** | **olives (oil-cured or Greek** |
| ½ **teaspoon freshly ground** | **kalamatas)** |
| **black pepper** | |

1. To preserve lemons, cut each lemon from the top, in four segments, without cutting all the way through the base. Put ¼ inch of kosher salt in the bottom of a sterilized Mason jar. Pack the inside of each lemon with salt and push down into the jar to make alternate layers of lemon and salt. Press down hard to release enough lemon juice to cover the lemons. Seal the jar and let stand in a cool place for about 2 weeks. Rinse the lemons before using.

2. When ready to use with the chicken, rinse 1 lemon and separate the pulp from the skin. Reserve the skin and process the pulp in a food processor or blender with the garlic and spices and oil. Rub the whole chicken inside and out with the mixture, cover with plastic wrap, and marinate overnight.

3. Put the chicken in a pot just large enough to hold it, add the onion, salt, chicken broth, and barely enough water to cover. Bring to a simmer, cover the pot for 15 minutes to ensure the top of the breast is cooked. Then remove the lid partially and simmer for 30 to 40 minutes longer.

4. When the chicken is tender, remove to a baking dish. Add the reserved lemon peel, slivered, to the chicken stock, along with the olives, and reduce the liquid slightly. Pour over the chicken and bake in a 500-degree oven to brown the top of the chicken. Serve with an additional rinsed and quartered lemon as garnish, if you wish.

*Since the main dish is exotic, it's good to begin with a familiar but congruent appetizer, such as artichokes, and to end with a fresh fruit, such as oranges or pears, spiced perhaps with cinnamon or cumin and sweetened with honey.*

# CHICKEN POT PIE

One of the best ways of using leftover chicken (or turkey) is to cube the meat in large chunks, add lightly cooked vegetables, put them in a creamy sauce, and cover them with crust to make a pie. Miss Eliza Leslie long ago explained the appeal of a pie made from "a pair of large fine fowls," when she advised: "Let there be plenty of paste, as it is always much liked by the eaters of pot pie."

She suggests an English suet paste based on the proportions of twice as much flour as minced suet (3 pounds flour to 1½ pounds minced suet), but the familiar short paste will please eaters of pot pie. Americans have traditionally been fond of a biscuit topping instead of a crust, but our current palate that eschews flour dumplings eschews biscuit dough cooked in liquid as being too heavy. A crisp crust is more to our taste and better seals the liquid within.

The recipe below combines Claiborne's instructions for an English Chicken Pot Pie and Beard's for an Old-Fashioned Chicken Pie. We might conclude, rightly, that old-fashioned ways of cooking in America were largely English. Eliza Leslie suggests "the addition of a quarter of a hundred oysters" to such a pie, but if oysters are too costly there are the humbler carrot, onion, and mushroom.

## Proportions

for 6 to 8 servings, meat from a 4- to 5-pound chicken, 6 cups of vegetables, 4 cups of sauce

### Short Paste

2 cups flour
8 tablespoons butter
4 tablespoons lard

½ teaspoon salt
2 to 3 tablespoons ice water

## Pie Filling

12 to 16 small white onions, peeled
2 medium carrots, peeled and chopped
3 celery stalks, chopped
4 cups chicken stock
½ pound small button mushrooms
1 4- to 5-pound chicken, cooked, skinned, boned, and cubed
5 tablespoons butter
4 tablespoons flour
1 cup heavy cream
Salt and freshly ground black pepper to taste
Pinch of nutmeg or mace

1.   Make the pastry in a processor (see Butter Crust, page 348) and refrigerate while assembling and preparing the ingredients for the pie.

2.   Poach the onions, carrots, and celery in the chicken stock, in a covered pot, until just tender. (The onions will take longest, about 20 to 30 minutes, and a cross cut in their root end will help keep them from bursting.) Add the whole mushrooms and simmer for 3 or 4 minutes only. Drain the vegetables and reserve the stock for the sauce.

3.   Remove the chicken from the bones, cut it in 1- to 2-inch cubes, and add it to the vegetables.

4.   Melt the butter in a saucepan, add the flour, and stir together for 2 or 3 minutes. Add 2 cups of the hot stock all at once and beat until smooth. Add the heavy cream and simmer until the sauce is thick. Add more stock to get the thickness or thinness wanted. Add salt, pepper, and nutmeg and taste carefully for seasoning.

5.   Arrange the chicken and vegetables in a baking dish and pour the sauce over all. Quickly roll out the pastry about ¼ inch thick to cover the top of the dish. Place an oven-proof eggcup in the center of the dish to help hold up the crust. Lay the pastry on top and crimp the dough around the edges to seal the dough to the dish. Make a few decorative slashes in the pastry to release steam.

6.   Bake at 450 degrees for 10 minutes to set the pastry, then lower the oven temperature to 375 degrees for about 25 to 30 minutes to finish baking the crust.

*Fresh berries or similar fruits, plain or in the form of sherbets, would make a sensible finale to this all-inclusive pie, but the pie also suggests something as unsensible as vanilla ice cream (page 394).*

# FORTY-GARLIC CHICKEN

I first came on Beard's recipe for chicken with forty cloves of garlic printed in *The New York Times* some thirty years ago. The dish became a staple of his cooking classes because, he says, the transformation under slow heat of all that garlic never failed to astonish his students. In the 1950s, to embark on any dish calling for forty cloves of garlic was tantamount to joining the Communist Party. It simply wasn't done—in public, anyway. But with garlic, subversion by a foreign power proved illusory and fear of its strength groundless. In a sealed pot with a little Cognac, the garlic was forced to accommodate itself to the blander beneficent chicken, to the mutual advantage of each.

Today, when the exchange of flavors between garlic and chicken is as commonplace as the exchange of students between foreign powers and the states, astonishment yields to certainty. It is one of the most reliable of chicken dishes and one of the most pleasurable: reliable because you cook it for an hour and a half without touching it; pleasurable because of the delicate intermingling of flavors.

Originally Beard called for a whole chicken cut in quarters, but, in *The New James Beard,* he sensibly substitutes all dark meat since the cooking time is too long for white. He also substitutes vermouth for Cognac, but if you can afford the Cognac it makes a richer brew. I have often substituted other herbs for tarragon and other vegetables, such as fennel or endive, for celery with the same pleasurable results; but because his recipe is a "classic Beard," I've combined the ingredients of his original and most recent version.

## Proportions

for 8 servings, 8 whole chicken legs, 2 cups of vegetables, 40 unpeeled cloves of garlic

⅔ cup olive oil
8 whole chicken legs (drumsticks and thighs, attached)
4 celery stalks, cut in strips
2 medium onions, chopped
40 cloves garlic, unpeeled
¼ cup chopped parsley
1 tablespoon fresh tarragon, chervil, or basil, or 1 teaspoon dried

2 teaspoons salt
½ teaspoon freshly ground black pepper
¼ teaspoon nutmeg or mace
⅓ cup Cognac, or ½ cup dry vermouth

1. Put the oil in a heavy casserole and turn each piece of chicken in it so that oil coats the pieces evenly. Add the vegetables and garlic (separated but left unpeeled), herbs and seasonings, and pour the Cognac on top. Mix well.

2. Cover the casserole with foil before putting on the lid to seal the pot. Bake in a 375-degree oven for 1½ hours. Serve directly from the casserole with slices of hot French bread or toast for the garlic. Squeeze the garlic from the husks and spread it on bread, to eat with the chicken. (Because there is no butter to solidify, the dish is also good "cold," meaning room temperature. You can turn the oil into a dressing by adding a little lemon or vinegar.)

*A crisp vegetable or salad is appropriate here.*

# GIN-MARINATED ROCK CORNISH HENS

The Rock Cornish Game Hen is badly misnamed because it has nothing to do with game. It is simply a mini-chicken, from a cross breeding of cocks from Cornwall and hens from Plymouth Rock as long ago as the eighteenth century. The witty pianist Victor Borge revived their use in our time when he marketed them commercially, but the rock-hard frozen capsule seldom lived up even to its misnomer. Fresh Cornish Hens are another matter and can be made to taste as good as any chicken.

A good way to enliven their mild flavor is to marinate them before grilling or roasting. I tried the following marinade in the summer when I had a bed of fresh mint outside and gin for gin-and-tonics inside. To heighten the flavor of gin, I added juniper. Because mint evokes a whole range of Middle Eastern spices, I threw in a dash of cardamom. The best way to test an improvised marinade is to taste it and to keep on tasting if it seems lacking in character. This one gave character to a fowl that is too often dull and insipid.

## Proportions

for 4 servings, 4 hens, ¾ cup of gin, ½ cup of olive oil

| | |
|---|---|
| **4 fresh Rock Cornish hens** | **½ teaspoon freshly ground** |
| **¾ cup gin** | **white or black pepper** |
| **½ cup olive oil** | **¾ teaspoon salt** |
| **16 juniper berries** | **1 teaspoon cardamom** |
| **1 cup chopped fresh mint** | **Fresh mint for garnish** |

1. Put the birds in a plastic bag or bags and marinate overnight with the mixture of gin, oil, herbs, and spices.

2.   When ready to cook, split each hen alongside the back bone and butterfly them flat to cook evenly. Remove the backbones and use for stock. Heat a charcoal grill and start the birds bone side down. It will take 8 to 10 minutes a side to cook them. (You can cook them the same way in the broiler, where they may take slightly less time—5 to 8 minutes.) Serve with a sprig or two of fresh mint for garnish.

*With a simple grilled bird like this, the vegetable can be more complicated: a Ratatouille (page 293) or a Grated Potato Pancake (page 295). Desserts, too, can be fancy, as in a Soufflé Grand Marnier (page 390) or a Pistachio-Nut Cheesecake (page 380).*

# MUSTARD-GRILLED QUAIL

At last, a few game birds, such as quail, are being raised and marketed for specialty stores as well as restaurants, so that we no longer have to rely on the kindness of friends. There are several species of American quail, as Waverley Root informs us in *Food*, but they all have in common a firm flesh and a size small enough to turn them into ideal finger food. Apart from taste, they are the quickest and easiest of domestic game birds to cook and certainly the easiest to eat.

Fortunately, Beard's original *Fowl and Game Cookery* of 1944 has been revised and reissued in 1979, and it is a handy reference not only for the relatively familiar quail, squab, and pheasant, but also for the more outré snipe and woodcock. The recipe below is so simple that quail, if it were only cheaper, might supplant barbecued spareribs as our primary grilled finger food.

## Proportions

for 4 servings, 4 quail for a first course (double the amount for a main dish because quail *are* small)

| | |
|---|---|
| **4 quail** | **4 slices thick bacon** |
| **⅓ cup Dijon mustard** | |

Split the quail down the back with a sharp knife and flatten each bird with the palm of your hand. Brush the skin side of the breasts and legs with the Dijon mustard and lay 1 slice of bacon over each quail. Place on a rack under a broiler and broil for 5 to 10 minutes, or until the bacon is crisp. Remove the bacon to avoid burning it, and broil the birds 5 to 10 minutes longer, or until well browned. To eat, tear apart with the fingers and nibble the bones.

*For a first course, serve quail before some classic roast of beef, veal, or lamb. For a main course, quail enjoys the company of a rich vegetable dish, such as Scalloped Potatoes with Cheese (page 289).*

# MEATS

*VEAL—If the vein in the shoulder look blue or bright red, it is newly killed; but if black, green, or yellow, it is stale. The leg is known to be new by the stiffness of the joint. The head of a calf or a lamb is known by the eyes; if sunk or wrinkled, it is stale; if plump and lively, it is fresh.*

—Lydia Maria Child
The American Frugal Housewife
*(1833)*

Imagine encountering in the aseptic white counters of your supermarket the head of a calf or a lamb. Imagine buying meat like fish by the plumpness and liveliness of its eyes. Americans who have not traveled abroad may never in their lives encounter a blue or yellow-veined shoulder or a fresh or wrinkled eye of a calf or lamb, its carcass stripped to display its inward parts, which festoon the theater of the butcher at his work. Americans at home may never encounter a butcher at his work. The frequent advice of our master chefs to "get to know your local butcher" is almost as anachronistic as advising us to get to know your local baker or candlestick-maker. The local butcher has all but disappeared, the last element to go in a long chain that begins with the disappearance of the buffalo.

Until the Civil War, the Great Plains of America were salt pork and buffalo and Indian country. To get rid of the buffalo was one way to get rid of the Indians. Where wild Longhorns replaced the one, cowboys replaced the other. For the first time fresh beef replaced salt pork. Beef quickly replaced almost everything else as well. A hundred years ago, the most common American meal for man, woman, and child at breakfast, lunch, and dinner was beefsteak. While ecologists and dietitians scold Americans for eating too much meat today, we eat less than our ancestors of a century or so ago. In 1840, Americans ate annually about 178 pounds of meat per person. In 1976, we ate annually about 165 pounds per person, or about 3 pounds a week. Today Americans are not even the greatest steak-eaters. That honor goes to the French in Europe and in the rest of the world to the Argentines and Australians.

Nevertheless, Americans have been beef-eaters ever since the era of cheap beef began with the replacement of the cowboy by the railroad cattle car. When the Grand Trunk Railway reluctantly gambled in 1882 on the refrigerator car of Gustavus Franklin Swift, the centralized slaughterhouse began and with it a parcel of trouble. The housewife could not determine the freshness of a calf slaughtered 1,000 miles away. The housewife could not determine what preservatives and additives might have been added to disguise rotten meat or "embalmed beef," as Upton Sinclair called it in *The Jungle* in 1906. His exposure of the abuses of the Chicago meat-killing and meat-packing factories set the industry back for two decades and produced the first wave of American vegetarians. In 1927, the first federal inspectors finally set standards of "wholesomeness" and "quality" for beef, but they soon lost their relevance with the fall of the stock market, when "sludge" replaced meat. "Sludge," as described by Fisher, was "strictly for hunger."

During the Depression, hunger whetted our appetites for beef as scarcity whetted our appetites for beef during the Second World War. The meat that at first we couldn't afford we then couldn't buy at any price— short of a black marketeer's. Families surviving on sludge and spaghetti were urged by Fisher and others to explore thriftier or more available parts of the animal than thigh or rib and "to savor to the fullest the beasts we have killed" by enjoying a head, a tongue, an ear, a heart.

Wartime editions like the 1943 *Joy of Cooking* included special sections on Meat Stretching and Meat Substitutes; a mere 50 pages encompassed Meats relative to 200 pages for Desserts. Books like the *Victory Vitamin Cook Book* urged meat extenders like Tamale Pie and ventured the notion that families might even grow fond of meatless dishes. Wisely, its authors added, "but we're still betting on the popularity of steaks, chops, and roasts after our boys are back home, after the starving nations have been fed, and after peace is once more back upon this troubled world."

It was a safe prediction. Our boys got the taste of Spam out of their mouths, and our civilians the taste of tamale pie, by a general rush to steaks, chops, and roasts. Reflecting peacetime euphoria, and postwar affluence, the meat sections in the cookbooks of our four masters became the largest and most detailed, while explanatory charts of cuts of meat and methods of cooking them became the most lovingly exhaustive. For the first time since the mid nineteenth century, the crunch of flesh and bone began to replace America's sweet tooth.

Once again beef was king. By 1976, beef was 50 percent more popular than pork and 100 percent more popular than lamb. Lamb fell to an astonishingly low 1.7 pounds per person and the higher rate of pork depended largely on the popularity of bacon and ham. But once again more means less: less variety and less quality, the more beef captures the mass meat market. Beef is increasingly grass-fed instead of grain-fed to produce leaner, chewier, tougher meat that is rapidly fattened for total weight, not marbling, and that is rapidly "aged" for two to three weeks, rather than two months. And the beef industry has now changed the grading of meat to upgrade the second-rate Choice to Prime. "It's really pretty bad," Beard laments in *The New James Beard*.

Beard's solution is to push pork, always his favorite meat for its edibility from pig snout to pig tail, but now more desirable than ever because its quality is higher than the current quality of beef. Child's solution is to teach us more about the anatomy of the animals we eat so that we can do more of our own butchering at home and thus get the variety of cuts we can't get at the supermarket. Claiborne's solution is to move away from meat toward fish. In *The New New York Times Cookbook,* for the first time the Fish section is as large as the Meat section.

As for Fisher, she confesses that she and her friends scarcely eat meat anymore at all, as a matter not of morals but of taste. Were she writing a cookbook today, she would not include the recipe she gave us in *How to Cook a Wolf* called Aunt Gwen's Cold Shape, as a euphemism for the headcheese made from a calf's head. Nor would she need to describe her own timidity on first encountering a *tête de veau* in France. Today, the problem would be to find a head to be intimidated by, although her description is as quaintly precise as Lydia Maria Child's in 1833, and I quote Fisher's for the historical interest of a generation weaned principally on prebutchered, plastic-wrapped steaks, roasts, and chops.

The main trouble, perhaps, was that it was not a veal's head at all but half a veal's head. There was the half-tongue, lolling stiffly from the neat half-mouth. There was the one eye, closed on a savory wink. There was the lone ear, lopped loose and faintly pink over the odd wrinkles of the demi-forehead. And there, by the single pallid nostril, were three stiff white hairs.

# STEAK TARTARE

A good indicator of the shift in taste from cooked to raw in the last decade is the current popularity of steak tartare, wherein we have rediscovered a dish introduced to America at the end of the last century. An American cookbook of the nineties, *The Epicurean* by Charles Ranhofer of Delmonico's, calls it "bifteck de Hambourg à la Tartare," suggesting that hamburger raw and cooked came from the same German source. So thoroughly did America make even raw hamburger its own that *Larousse Gastronomique,* that French bible of gastronomy, calls steak tartare "bifteck à l'Américaine."

Traditionally, it was made of the best beef—finely ground tenderloin or sirloin—and was flavored with finely minced onions, as were most of the minced beef cakes from Hamburg. An egg was essential, one equally raw and "very fresh egg," as Ranhofer said, "or else the yolk only." Traditionally, the meat was molded into a nest to contain the whole egg or the yolk only, nestled in its broken shell. The focus on a raw egg suggests that the dish may have been considered a remedy like the "prairie oyster" for a morning after, when a double shot of raw protein might reinvigorate the flagging virility of even a Tartar.

The dish pretty much disappeared from cookbooks during the years of austerity after 1900, but Beard recaptured it in his *Fireside Cookbook* of 1949. By the 1970s, Child suggests serving it as an alternative to raw oysters for a large buffet (in *Julia Child & Company*), and Claiborne treats it in his *New New York Times Cookbook* as an elegant appetizer, spiked with Cognac. Because the fun of the dish is in mixing your own gloppy egg with a variety of garnishes into the meat, and because you must have a substantial portion to do that, I find it a good one-dish meal for lunch or supper. It is also a quick one.

## Proportions

for 4 servings, 1 pound ground beef, 4 egg yolks, 1 cup chopped garnishes

| | |
|---|---|
| 1 **pound tenderloin, sirloin, or top round** | ¼ **cup minced parsley** |
| 4 **egg yolks with shells** | **Worcestershire sauce** |
| ½ **cup minced onion** | **Dijon mustard** |
| 8 **anchovies, drained** | **Cognac** |
| ¼ **cup capers, drained** | **Salt and freshly ground black pepper to taste** |

1. Grind the meat fine (have a butcher grind it twice or chop it in a food processor after cutting the meat into 1-inch cubes and freezing them briefly so that the processor won't mush them).

2. Divide the meat into 4 portions, shape into nests with a well in the center of each, and set upright in each an egg yolk in half an eggshell.

3. Surround the meat with small portions of each garnish or serve the garnishes separately. Arrange the Worcestershire sauce, mustard, and Cognac with salt and pepper grinder so that each person may season his own. Serve with buttered toast or grilled slices of French bread.

*For a one-dish meal, it is good with a green salad or potato salad or a vegetable, such as Broccoli Sautéed with Garlic (page 290).*

# BEEF RIB ROAST: HIGH/MEDIUM/LOW

"Roasting proper is almost unknown in these days of stoves and ranges," says one of the authors of *The Buckeye Cookbook* in 1883, "baking, a much inferior process, having taken its place." Roasting proper is even less known in 1983 in these days of electric grills and microwave ovens. "First build your fireplace" would be the first step in roasting proper nowadays and the second would be, "Next catch your slavey to tend it." Only third would be the directive to "Catch your hare or ox or pig" to butcher, dress, and impale on a spit before a crackling fire with a pan below to catch the drippings.

Most of us know only about roasting improper—that is, baking meat to get the effect of a roast. If we know that baking, when it comes to meat, is a process inferior to roasting, we may make better sense of the widely differing and often opposing directions for achieving a good proper beef roast. What that means is a crisply seared crust and a juicy pink interior. There are several ways to achieve it, even with the modern bake oven. The method we choose will depend in part on how much time we have and how much meat we have, but the better we understand the principles of "roasting," the more flexible we can be in adjusting temperature and time to occasion.

Child's directions in Dinner for the Boss, in *Julia Child & Company*, includes a photographically clear discussion of How to Buy and Trim a Rib Roast of Beef and how to roast it by the even temperature method. The first point in buying a rib roast is to go all out, because it's a luxury item to begin with. Get the best Prime possible, aged and well marbled. Get a fairly large roast rather than a small one: that is, 3 to 5 ribs, or about 8 to 14 pounds if you estimate 2½ pounds per rib. Get ribs cut from the loin or "small end" rather than ribs cut from the shoulder or large end. You'll get the best value per pound and the juiciest beef with a sizable roast that you can serve hot for the boss and cold for the rest of the week —or hashed, or cubed for a steak and kidney pie. You'll get the best flavor by roasting the meat with the bone in, rather than having it boned and rolled to make carving easier. For carving, cut off the ribs in a single horizontal slice after roasting; the meat will lie flat for easy slicing, and you can serve the bones along with the sliced meat.

As for temperatures, there are no foolproof formulae because there are too many variables, including the temperature of the meat before it goes into the oven and the emotional temperature of the cook, who may be hotly impatient or coldly anxious. There are only guidelines and the best one is to think of baking meat like baking bread: Don't hurry it, give it plenty of time. Once roasted, the meat will keep warm in a very low oven (115 degrees) for at least an hour and a half, which also gives plenty of time for the juices to settle.

The biggest variable is how rare the cook wants his beef and that is as subject as other things to temperament and fashion and history. Twenty years ago, Claiborne in his *Menu Cookbook* called beef rare at 140 degrees. Today, only the National Livestock and Meat Board and cookbooks similarly concerned with microbes rather than taste would call 140 degrees rare rather than medium. Today, rare for beef is 120 degrees, medium is 140 degrees, and well-done is anything over 160 degrees. The most accurate tester is the pocket "instant" thermometer originally developed for microwave ovens, but always make sure that the thermometer does not touch bone when you insert it. Remember, too, that the roast removed from the oven will continue to cook internally, depending on its size, so that 120 degrees may climb up to 125 degrees or more. And, most important of all, remember that guidelines for timing apply only if the meat is at room temperature before roasting.

There are two basic methods: One is to roast at even heat all the way, and the other is to sear first at a high temperature, then to roast at a lower one. Child favors an even heat at medium temperature: about 13 minutes a pound at 325 degrees for rare beef (of 120 degrees internal temperature). A 10-pound roast, then, would take a little over 2 hours. Through the works of Adelle Davis, many have favored a much lower temperature of 250 degrees, which softens the meat and prevents any juice loss. A 10-pound roast at this temperature might take 4 to 5 hours, but Davis thought slow steady heat more "natural" than other kinds. "If you want delightfully roasted meat," she said, "let it alone and honor its privacy."

The searing method is the one usually favored by restaurant chefs, but there is little agreement about details of timing. In *The New New York Times Cookbook,* Claiborne suggests a complicated schedule of temperature lowering from 500 degrees to 400 degrees to 350 degrees. But he also cites a popular method, devised by Anne Seranne, of an initial searing of 5 minutes a pound in a 500-degree oven, after which you turn the oven off and let the meat cook for 2 or 3 hours as the oven cools. A 10-pound roast takes at least 3 hours, during which time you must remember NOT to open the oven door AT ANY TIME. The method is good for the cook who wants to throw the roast in and forget about it until it is ready to slice and serve.

The searing method I prefer, however, is the one advocated by Beard *(Theory & Practice of Good Cooking)* for roasting birds as well as beef, in which you sear high, then lower the oven to medium. For beef, he estimates 12 minutes a pound at 500 degrees, lowered to 325 degrees. A 10-pound roast would take about 2 hours, or approximately the same time as a 10-pound roast in Child's even-temperature method. The point of searing is to seal in the juices and to produce a crustier skin and fat. If you believe with Beard, as I do, that "the true flavor of the meat lurks in the fine crisp fat," then this is the best method for old-fashioned "roasting proper."

## ROASTING CHART: 2 methods

*Even-Temperature Method:* 325-degree oven, 13 minutes a pound.
*Searing Method:* 500-degree oven for first quarter, 325 degrees for remaining time. Estimate 12 minutes a pound for total.

## Proportions

for 8 to 12 servings, 3 to 5 ribs or 8 to 12 pounds (trimmed of short ribs and back bone)

| | |
|---|---|
| 1 **3- to 5-rib roast (8 to 12 pounds)** | 2 **tablespoons melted butter** |
| **Freshly ground black pepper to taste** | 2 **cups beef stock or broth** |
| | **Salt** |

1.   Make sure the beef is at room temperature or the meat will take longer to cook. Rub the roast with ground pepper, but NOT salt, and place it fat side up on a rack in a roasting pan.

2.   Sear in a 500-degree oven for 35 to 40 minutes, basting the cut ends once or twice with melted butter and fat as it accumulates. Reduce the oven temperature to 325 degrees and cook for 1 hour, basting once or twice. Insert a thermometer into the thickest part of the roast: When the temperature is over 100 degrees, check frequently (every 10 or 15 minutes) because the temperature will rise faster at the end of the cooking time than at the beginning.

3.   Remove the roast when the thermometer registers 120 degrees and let the meat rest in a warm place for 15 to 30 minutes. Resting is essential for the juices to retract. If you are making Yorkshire Pudding, have the batter ready and raise the oven temperature to 425 degrees. Salt the meat lightly just before carving.

4.   Pour off the fat from the roasting pan, saving ½ cup to make Yorkshire pudding, and stir the beef broth into the remaining drippings to make pan juice for gravy. Reduce until the broth is intensely flavorful.

*Roast beef is so simply itself that it can take a rich soup before, like Hot Vichyssoise (page 111), Cream of Mussel (page 113), or Lobster Bisque (page 114). Or a rich salad like Caesar's (page 158). For the same reason, it lends itself to a fulsome dessert like the Praline Torte (page 382).*

# YORKSHIRE PUDDING, PANCAKE STYLE

The traditional Yorkshire pudding is halfway between a popover and a pancake, containing the same ingredients of milk, flour, and egg, and puffed at high heat. But what makes Yorkshire pudding delectable is its brown crust flavored with beef when the batter hits the hot fat. To maximize these delights, I have taken to making Yorkshire Pudding in a 12-inch cast-iron skillet, according to a recipe that Claiborne calls David Eyre's Pancake and Beard calls Manka's Babies. The names are far more idiosyncratic than the product, which is simply an egg batter spread thin in a skillet with hot butter or fat and puffed in a hot oven. The result is a brown crusty round that you can cut like a pizza, with the advantage that everybody gets an outside—that is, crusty—piece.

## Proportions

for 8 servings, 4 eggs to 1 cup each of milk and flour

½  cup beef fat
4  eggs
1  cup milk
1  cup flour

½  teaspoon salt
¼  teaspoon freshly ground
    black pepper

1.  Heat the fat in a 10- to 12-inch iron skillet (or skillet with oven-proof handle) until sizzling.
2.  Put the eggs, milk, flour, and seasonings into a blender or processor, or beat together quickly by hand, and mix until just smooth. Pour the batter immediately into the hot skillet and put into a 425-degree oven.
3.  Bake for 10 to 20 minutes, or until brown and puffy.

# BUTTERFLIED PORK LOIN ROAST

With pork, the roast that is equivalent in quality to a rib roast of beef is not the ribs but the loin. Technically a pork loin runs from shoulder to hip, but in practice a "center cut" loin includes only the two last ribs, the sirloin and tenderloin: in other words, the choicest, tenderest meat.

Because pork fat is the most useful and most widely used animal fat, pork meat has suffered from guilt by association, and therefore has declined in popular favor. Visions of cholesterol terrify the nutritionists as ethnic associations repulse the snobbish. Both Child and Beard have had to come to the defense of "poor piggy," as Child calls him, and as Beard reiterates, "my favorite meat . . . from the fancy loin to the humble hock." Ironically, the problem with cooking a pork loin is that the meat is *not* marbled with fat as good beef is. The fat is on the outside and the fat-free meat within tends to dry out quickly and become tough and stringy by overcooking.

With pork as with beef, rare today means 20 degrees rarer than yesterday. Twenty years ago, Claiborne cited 185 degrees as the proper interior temperature for pork. Today, the tastemakers agree that 160 degrees is the ideal temperature for a pork that is safely cooked but still tender and juicy. Myths persist and the fear of trichinosis, despite both the rarity of the disease and the fact that no trichinae if existent can survive beyond

137 degrees Fahrenheit, prevents many still from ever savoring properly the joys of roast pig.

Because pork is almost as versatile as chicken in absorbing and complementing other flavors, pork takes well to dry and wet marinades. In *Mastering I*, Child suggested a favorite salt marinade of 1 teaspoon per pound of meat, mixed with pepper, thyme, bay leaf, allspice, and garlic. Today, we're apt to cut down the salt and up the garlic, but the principle is the same of conferring flavor from the outside before the roasting begins.

Suggested temperatures vary less than beef, hovering within a 50-degree spread between 375 and 425 degrees. Again, an "instant" thermometer is the best guide for doneness, but you can estimate around 25 minutes a pound, or around 2 hours for a 5-pound roast with bone in.

Bone out is another matter, taking half the time if the loin is not rolled but, as Child suggests in *More Company*, butterflied, as you might do with a leg of lamb. If you want the flavor of the bones, you can roast them along with the pork. There are three advantages to a butterflied roast: The shorter cooking time avoids drying out the meat; more surface is exposed to seasoning; and the roast is easier to carve. Below, I've adapted Child's recipe to make a roast so easy that any child old enough to turn on an oven and read a thermometer can make a nearly perfect roast.

## Proportions

for 6 servings, a 5-pound center cut, boned to make about 3 pounds

| | |
|---|---|
| 1 **5-pound pork loin, boned to 3 pounds** | ¼ **teaspoon freshly ground black pepper** |
| 1½ **teaspoons salt** | 2 **tablespoons olive oil** |
| 3 **cloves garlic** | **Chicken or beef stock or** |
| 1 **tablespoon dried rosemary** | **wine** |

1.   If you can't get a butcher to remove the backbone, it is easy to remove it yourself by cutting lengthwise along either side of the bone.

2.   Grind the spices and garlic together with the oil in a blender, processor, or mortar and pestle, and rub into the meat on both sides. Wrap the meat in a plastic bag and refrigerate overnight, if you have time. Otherwise, leave the meat at room temperature for a few hours.

3.   Put the meat fat side up on the pork bones (or on a rack) in a roasting pan and bake at 425 degrees for a little less than an hour, basting once or twice with pan juices, or until the thermometer reads 160 degrees. The flatter the roast the quicker it will cook. Baste once or twice with the pan juices during roasting. If the fat is not crusty enough, run it under a hot broiler for a few minutes. Let the meat rest for 15 minutes or so before slicing.

4.   To make pan gravy from the bones, pour off the excess fat from the roasting pan and add chicken stock or a little boiling water and wine to the pan to deglaze the juices.

*Pork has an affinity with a full range of fruits and vegetables, including Scalloped Potatoes with Cheese (page 289), Spaghetti Squash in Garlic Butter (page 287), Carrots Glazed with Orange (page 286), and especially a Parsnip Purée (page 297). Pork is also good with apples, peaches, or pears, sautéed quickly in butter.*

# ROAST SPARERIBS

The culinary equivalent of short ribs of beef are the "long" ribs of pork we call spareribs. No country in the world cooks and eats spareribs with the variety and gusto that we do. Barbecued ribs are as traditional as ketchup, but even more venerable historically are just plain roasted ribs. Ketchup did not make significant incursions until the 1890s, when the bottle began to sneak onto the table and then into the sauce, as witness Marion Harland's note on roasted ribs in her 1893 *Common Sense in the Household:* "Send tomato catsup around with it, or if you prefer, put a liberal spoonful in the gravy, after it is strained."

Since the ribs are what are left after the loin is removed from the top and after the layer of fat and lean that will become bacon is removed from the sides, how meaty or fatty or "spare" the ribs are will vary widely. Barbecue sauce became popular with ribs because the sides were thought of as lean and dry. If the sides you buy seem excessively fat, you can always parboil them for a couple of minutes, as Irma Rombauer favored, or roast them at higher than usual temperatures to make the fat crisp. Or you can do an old southern trick of rubbing them well with vinegar.

So ubiquitous is some kind of sweet-and-sour barbecue sauce on ribs, from Kansas to Peking, that it comes as a relief to let the ribs speak for themselves once in a while. Seasoned well with mixed dried herbs and garlic and more garlic, they are much easier to eat than when they are dripping with sauce, and they are more eloquent of the quintessential pig.

------

## Proportions

for 6 servings, 2 sides (about 4 pounds) spareribs

| | |
|---|---|
| **2 sides (4 pounds) spareribs** | **½ teaspoon each rosemary,** |
| **6 cloves garlic, chopped fine** | **sage, and thyme** |
| **1 tablespoon coarse salt** | |
| **1 teaspoon freshly ground** | |
| **black pepper** | |

1.  Rub the ribs top and bottom with the garlic and mixed seasonings and let stand, if possible, an hour or two.
2.  Roast fat side up in a 350-degree oven for 30 minutes, then turn and roast on the other side. If you want the fat very crisp, roast for another 10 minutes or so. Cut the ribs into smaller sections, depending on the size of the ribs. These are as good cold as hot.

*Ribs are good with folksy dishes like greens or beans or potato salads and coleslaws. Or they can be dressed up with fancier company like a Sweet Potato Purée (page 298), or Ratatouille (page 293). An Indian Pudding (page 385) makes a good dessert.*

# ROAST SUCKLING PIG

Nineteenth-century cookbooks usually began their pork instructions with advice on how to dress a pig newly killed ("that morning if possible," Miss Leslie advises). While Mrs. Harland allows that no lady-housekeeper will be called upon to slaughter a full-grown shoat with hatchet or cleaver, "it is well that she should know how to clean and dress the baby pig, which is not larger than a Thanksgiving turkey." What she was then called upon to do, in the way of removing hair by scalding water and whisk broom and of cleaning entrails and sweetening the interior with soda and salt to make the pig "fair and white" for stuffing and roasting, would cause many a present lady housekeeper to forgo even the babiest of pigs.

Fortunately, fair and white baby pigs are more common now at specialty butcher shops than a decade ago, when they had all but disappeared. But it is still a problem to find one not larger, or at least no longer, than a Thanksgiving turkey, so that one can roast it in the oven instead of on a spit or pit outdoors. The best pig I ever had was wrapped in maguey leaves and pit-buried for eighteen hours at the foot of a garden in Chiapas, Mexico, before it was devoured tail, ear, and bone by the villagers, leaving not a whisker behind. But that's a different kind of roasting place.

Recipes for oven-roasting are increasing with the return of baby pigs. Both Claiborne and Beard offer one in their newest books. The principle is simple enough if the oven is bigger than the pig and the cook unfazed by sewing, skewering, or clamping the pork belly together to keep the stuffing inside the pig.

Keep the stuffing simple, as Beard suggests, because the pig is rich and succulent in itself. The skin needs to be basted often, because the skin is really the best part. You can baste with olive or some other vegetable oil, or with the marinade suggested below, which echoes faintly what the villagers of Chiapas taught me at the foot of a garden.

# Proportions

for 12 to 14 servings, a 12- to 14-pound suckling pig with 2 cups of marinade and about 6 cups of stuffing

**1  12- to 14-pound suckling pig**

## Marinade

2  tablespoons salt
3  cloves garlic, mashed
1  tablespoon oregano
¼  teaspoon cumin
1  teaspoon freshly ground
   black pepper

Pinch of cayenne or other
   hot pepper
2  cups orange juice
¼  cup olive oil

## Stuffing

½  cup chopped onion
4  tablespoons butter
   Pig innards (liver, heart,
   kidneys), finely chopped
5  cups cooked rice
¼  cup chopped parsley, or 1
   tablespoon chopped fresh
   cilantro

1  teaspoon thyme
½  cup toasted pumpkin seeds
   or pine nuts
   Salt and freshly ground
   black pepper to taste
   Coriander or parsley sprigs
   for garnish

1.   Score the skin of the pig across the back and sides and marinate with the mixture of juice, oil, and spices for 24 hours, or overnight, in the refrigerator. The best container is a large plastic bag, such as a trash bag.

2.   Prepare the stuffing by sautéing the onions in butter, together with the finely chopped pig innards, until lightly cooked. Add to the cooked white rice, together with the other seasonings. Stuff the cavity of the pig lightly and sew or skewer closed.

3.   Place the pig in a roasting pan feet side down and bake at 350 degrees for 2½ to 3½ hours, or to an internal temperature of 160 degrees in the thickest part of the thigh not touching bone. Baste every 15 minutes or so, if possible, with the marinade.

4.   Place the pig on a carving board and garnish with a bunch of fresh parsley or fresh coriander in its mouth. It's easier to first present the pig to your guests, then remove it to carve, because the carving can be messy. First remove the hams, then cut the length of the backbone and remove the head. Cut through the rib and loin sections on each side. Each

serving should consist of a piece of meat, some stuffing, and a sprig of coriander or parsley.

*Whole cut pineapples, fresh melons, mangos, or papayas are the sort of thing to serve for dessert. If the season is wrong for these fruits, try a tray of baked apples spiked with Calvados or baked oranges with Grand Marnier.*

# LAMB CROWN ROAST

The cut of lamb that corresponds to beef ribs is a rack of lamb that comprises the 7 rib chops between shoulder and loin. Properly trimmed, the cut is expensive because you remove about two thirds of its original weight in bone, fat, and meat scraps to leave only the eye of the meat, protected by a very thin layer of fat attached to the row of slender bones. In effect, the rack is a row of rib chops that have been "frenched," and for a long time only luxury French restaurants in this country served them, usually with the little paper crowns that look like shredded chef's hats on the rib ends.

As with beef, the problem with the best lamb is how to get it, since restaurants buy up the finest Prime, leaving secondary grades for the supermarkets. Child's advice "to find a good meat market and make friends with the head butcher" assumes a world in which there are still local meat markets. But if you can find a butcher who'll sell you a good Prime rack to begin with, you can also find one who will trim it by removing the backbone, the layer of fat and meat called the "cap," and the fat and meat around the individual ribs. (See the photographs in *Julia Child & More Company* if you want to do it yourself.) The same butcher will sew two or three racks together, in a circle, to make the Edwardianly grand creation called a crown roast.

A plain rack is so simple to cook that you can either roast it in a hot oven or brown it in a skillet on top of the stove as you would individual chops. A crown roast is complicated only by the need to have some kind of stuffing to fill that hollow crown. Beard suggests a number of vegetable fillings, such as green peas with pearl onions, or sautéed mushrooms, or puréed chestnuts. More traditionally, the roast is filled with a ground meat stuffing, partly to incorporate the lamb meat trimmed from the bone. Beard objects that a stuffing of ground meat easily dries out, but a stuffing that mixes vegetables and meats seems a good compromise and evokes the traditions of princely tables. In his *New New York Times Cookbook*, Claiborne suggests a stuffing using eggplant and ground meats and I have made a variant of that below.

# Proportions

for 6 to 8 servings, 2 racks sewn together to make a crown roast (around 3 to 4 pounds dressed weight), plus 1 pound meat for stuffing

**1 crown roast of 2 racks**　　　　　**Salt and freshly ground black pepper to taste**

## Stuffing

2 tablespoons olive oil
1 medium onion, finely chopped
1 medium eggplant, peeled and diced
1 clove garlic, minced
¾ pound ground lamb

¼ pound ground sausage
½ cup fresh bread crumbs
¼ cup minced parsley
1 egg
Salt and freshly ground black pepper to taste

1. Sprinkle the roast inside and out with salt and pepper and put it in a shallow roasting pan.

2. Prepare the stuffing by cooking the onion in the oil until it is soft. Add the eggplant, garlic, ground lamb, and sausage and cook briefly, just enough to loosen up the meat. Remove from the heat and add the bread crumbs and parsley. Blend in egg and seasonings.

3. Pile stuffing lightly in the center of the roast. Brush the outside of the roast with a little olive oil and sprinkle a little oil on top of the stuffing.

4. Roast in a 450-degree oven for 25 to 30 minutes, or until an "instant" thermometer (inserted in meat not touching bone) registers 125 degrees. The meat should be very pink and juicy, as pink as rare roast beef. Carve at the table, cutting two chops at a time per serving, and adding a slice of stuffing.

*Good with classic vegetables like green peas or green beans, carrots, or potatoes. Or with a green salad followed by a fairly grand dessert such as a Praline Torte (page 382) or Lemon Meringue Pie (page 374).*

# STEAK AU POIVRE

Originally, broiling referred to a method of cooking by scorching heat, and grilling referred to a utensil, the gridiron or grill used in broiling. Today, we use the terms interchangeably, but where grilling suggests a fire of hot coals outdoors, broiling suggests the indoor stove or range.

The location of the heat matters far less, of course, than the nature of its source. Gas or electricity cannot impart flavor, only intensity. The standardized charcoal sold for outdoor grills does not impart flavor either, although the smoke of burning fat does. Originally, the nature of the wood was one of the essential flavors of broiled meats and only recently have we begun to rediscover the different flavors of apple, hickory, fir, spruce, and mesquite.

Apart from the flavor of special woods, the function of grill or broiler is merely to give an intense localized heat. The point of broiling is to seal the juices within a piece of meat by scorching the exterior, so meat that is flat and thin, rather than thick and round, does best. To adjust temperatures, we usually change the position of the meat to move it toward or away from the flame, rather than trying to alter the flame. Therefore, we need to estimate, in broiling, not only how long but how *close*. For very thick pieces of meat, you can always combine grilling or broiling with roasting or baking.

The outdoor barbecue with its variously elaborate equipment, including fork and tong and mitt holders and aprons labeled "Dad," did not come in big until after the war when people could afford a "second" broiler and the meat to put on it. The popularity of the barbecue may, in fact, have been an extension of the war with the red-blooded hunter home from the hill, bearing a symbolic steak as trophy of other killings. By the sixties, when Beard wrote *Delights and Prejudices* and devoted a chapter to outdoor grilling, the *barbe à la queue*, practiced first by the Louisiana French, had become a national pastime. And in France, the American barbecue was catching on like American jeans. But when Beard wrote his first book on the subject in 1941, and called it *Cook It Outdoors*, the idea was still a novelty except to hunters and fishers, Boy and Girl Scout campers, and scattered Indian tribes.

"I consider myself a pioneer in outdoor cooking," Beard wrote in his autobiography. Nobody has covered more extensively the methods and results of grilling and broiling, outdoors or in. When he wrote *Delights and Prejudices*, the quality of American beefsteak was at its peak and, therefore, ideal for grilling since it was fatty, tender, and flavorful. Now, as the flavor has gone out with the fat, steaks are drier and chewier, more like the European steak that is better sautéed than grilled. To reduce fat, American beef cattle now are increasingly grass-fed rather than grain-fed, so a grilled steak today is not what it was yesterday and may need help with both flavor and texture if it is cooked in the simplest of all methods by direct exposure to dry heat—the method of the campfire.

Steak au poivre, one of Beard's all-time favorites for grilling, is also (as the name suggests) an all-time French favorite for pan-broiling, where the skillet becomes a stove-top grill. It was also the most popular of the steak recipes Child used in *Mastering I*. The dish is one of those many junctures where an American method of Beard crosses a French method of Child to produce a thoroughly Americanized product. Today, steak au poivre is a particularly good way to load the meat with flavor and still cook it simply by broiler or grill. Significantly, Beard's only steak recipes in *The New James Beard* are not for grilling at all, but for sautéing. And Claiborne's recipe for steak au poivre in *The New New York Times Cookbook* suggests grill and skillet as equal alternatives.

## Proportions

for 6 servings, 3 pounds boneless meat from the top loin, whether bone is in or out of the cut (called variously strip, shell, club, top loin, sirloin strip)

| | |
|---|---|
| **2 tablespoons black peppercorns or mixture of white, black, and Szechuan peppercorns** | **Steaks to total 3 pounds, cut 1½ inches thick**<br>**2 tablespoons olive oil** |

1.   Crush the peppercorns either by grinding coarsely in a blender or spice mill or by flattening in a plastic bag with the bottom of a heavy skillet. Push the pepper into both sides of the steak. Rub both sides with olive oil and let stand for 2 or 3 hours if possible.

2.   If using an indoor broiler, place the steak 3 inches from the flame and cook for 4 to 6 minutes per side. If the steak is thinner, move it closer to the flame so that the meat will cook faster. If charcoal broiling, the heat will be more intense, so you will need to sear the meat quickly on both sides, then move the grill farther from the coals to cook the interior.

3.   When cooked, let the steaks rest for 5 minutes before slicing vertically into bias strips. For the best flavor pour a little melted butter over them. The large amount of pepper eliminates the need for salt.

*If the season is right, serve with corn in the husk or sliced tomatoes sprinkled with basil and follow with fresh peach or vanilla ice cream.*

# TURKISH SPICED KEBABS

The simplest way to grill, as any child knows who has ever impaled a hot dog on a stick and held it over a fire, is to thread more or less bite-sized pieces of meat on a skewer that will not burn up before the meat does. Wherever nomads roam or wherever the daily hearth is improvised, whether on the sidewalks of Istanbul or the deserts of the Sahara or the plains of Wyoming, meat-on-a-stick is a way of life.

Meat specifically prepared for a stick Americans know by way of the Greeks, Turks, and Russians nomadic enough to have crossed the Atlantic during the last century or so and to have brought with them their shashliks and kebabs. Sis, meaning stick, and kebab, meaning lamb, spells "shish kebab" and has become a generic term for a number of meats ground or cubed and skewered. In the last few years, kebab-sellers have invaded even the sidewalks of New York, the vertically skewered *gyro* or *donner kebab* competing hot and heavy with Nathan's hot dogs.

We can make individual *donner kebabs* at home by molding cigar-shaped patties on long skewers, as the Turks do, serving them with yogurt. Ground meat, interestingly spiced, has an advantage over cubed meat for kebabs in that it requires no marinade. You can also use a cheaper cut of meat, provided you get rid of gristle and fat. Or you can use an expensive cut and grill the patties as rare as the finest beef.

Beard traces the origins of the "cult of the shish kebab" in America to immigrants before and immediately after the First World War, particularly when Russian émigrés settled the coasts. Claiborne notes that after the Second World War, the shish kebab craze was second only to the national rage for pizza. It's no accident that both kebabs and pizza suggest a world in which eating on the run is more common than eating at the table. For finger food, the kebab has it all over the pizza, and perhaps as our cities become increasingly preserves for urban nomads the kebab spit will eventually replace the pizza parlor.

## Proportions

for 4 to 8 servings, 2 pounds ground lamb, 1 onion, 2 eggs, 2 cloves garlic

| | |
|---|---|
| 2 **pounds ground lamb** | ¼ **teaspoon red pepper flakes** |
| 1 **small onion, minced (¼ cup)** | ½ **cup minced parsley** |
| 2 **cloves garlic, minced** | ½ **teaspoon salt or to taste** |
| 2 **eggs** | ⅓ **cup olive oil** |
| 1 **teaspoon dried dill, or 1½** | ½ **pint plain yogurt** |
| **tablespoons fresh dill** | **Paprika** |
| ½ **teaspoon thyme** | |

1. Mix the ground lamb together with onion, garlic, eggs, and spices and taste for seasoning (raw lamb is as palatable as raw beef). Shape the meat into 8 thick cigars around 8 skewers.

2. Roll each meat cylinder in olive oil and put onto a hot grill or under a hot broiler, turning as necessary to brown them evenly. They will cook very quickly because of the metal running through the center.

3. Slip out the skewer to serve and put one or two meat cylinders on each plate with a large dollop of yogurt sprinkled with paprika.

*Rice or kasha is a good accompaniment to kebabs, or a vegetable mix, such as Ratatouille (page 293) or Eggplant Caviar (page 83).*

# BUTTERFLIED LEG OF LAMB

A slab of lamb shaped roughly like a thick steak and charcoal grilled gives quick evidence of how much associations alter taste. When I have served leg of lamb in this way at my outdoor table, any number of diners over the years have praised the beef and felt tricked to learn it was sheep. You can avoid this by announcing that you have butterflied, or boned, a leg of lamb to make a single large piece suitable for grilling. Better that your guests find you pompous than treacherous.

The popularity of the barbecue has created new uses for it and butterflied lamb is one of the best, I think, because it's a welcome variant on the eternal beefsteak. It's as easy to carve as a steak, and it allows an herb marinade to penetrate more surfaces than if the leg were left with the bone in and roasted.

Occasionally, a butcher will consent to butterfly the leg for you, but the job is not hard if you know where the bones are and cut around them ruthlessly. You will waste no meat because you can use the bones for soup and you will have to make further cuts in the boned side anyway so that the meat will cook evenly. Child, in *Child & Company,* gives complete directions, with photographs, for cutting out the bones of a whole leg, including hipbone, leg bone, and shank. The hipbone-tail assembly is a bit tricky, she admits, but otherwise a short sharp knife to scrape flesh from bone and a longer sharp knife to cut off the tough skin and thick layer of fat covering the outside turns a lamb leg into a butterfly.

You will want to make two or three long gashes in the "lobes," or thickest hunks, or the thinner hunks will overcook. The boned meat will look rather a mess, but the meat will contract in the cooking. If you want it tidier, you can push the meat together with skewers. The gashes will also bring more surface in contact with the marinade, which is the major excuse for the dish to begin with.

An oil, lemon, and herb marinade is more or less traditional here, evoking the grilled meats of Provence or Greece. But Claiborne in *The New New York Times Cookbook* suggests grilling a boneless leg Indian style, with a full range of Eastern spices like turmeric, mace, ginger, coriander, cumin, and the aromatic mixture called garam masala.

The marinade I've used below can be varied infinitely, but the constants are some kind of salt (soy rather than anchovy, if you prefer), acid, and oil, and some kind of heady seasonings from either the herb garden or spice chest.

## Proportions

for 10 to 12 servings, a 7- to 9-pound whole leg and about 1 cup of marinade

| 1 7- to 9-pound whole leg of lamb, butterflied and trimmed | 2 to 3 tablespoons mixed dried herbs (thyme, rosemary, bay leaf) |
|---|---|

### Marinade

| ½ cup olive oil | 3 to 4 cloves garlic, chopped |
|---|---|
| Juice of ½ lemon | 10 black peppercorns, crushed |
| 6 to 8 anchovy fillets | ½ cup parsley |

1. Make certain that the meat is trimmed of all fat, gristle, cartilage, and skin. Rub the dried herbs into the meat well on both sides. Make a marinade by putting the remaining ingredients into a blender and processing only until the parsley is chopped but not liquefied. Put the meat into a plastic bag and pour the marinade over the meat, making sure both sides are covered. Refrigerate overnight or let stand at room temperature for at least a few hours.

2. Prepare the coals for the barbecue grill. When the coals are ashen and hot, put the lamb directly on the grill, as you would a beefsteak, or between an oiled and hinged rack to make turning easier. Sear both sides well, then raise or lower the meat to cook the interior to 125 degrees. (Timing depends on the kind and size and heat of the grill, but you can estimate 40 minutes to 1 hour.) Let the cooked meat rest briefly before carving, then cut into thin diagonal slices. Use the remaining marinade as a sauce.

*Good with any kind of salad greens or with bean or rice salads. Eggplant dishes and lentil dishes are also good with lamb.*

# HAMBURGER FOUR DIFFERENT WAYS

Because hamburgers symbolize in a mouthful the essence of American cooking, how to cook them is a matter of loving dispute based on minute distinctions. Once upon a time the hamburger was either grilled, pan-broiled, or fried. To pan-broil, according to Mrs. Lincoln in her *Boston School Kitchen Text-Book,* was to cook in a "dry, hissing-hot frying pan," with no fat or grease and in a pan so hot it was blue. "This is not frying," she insisted, but "broiling on hot iron." Frying was to cook in fat. Sautéing was not mentioned by Mrs. Lincoln, or by scarcely any American cookbook writers, until after the Second World War.

When it was mentioned, it was scorned as a French barbarism, as in the 1883 *Buckeye Cookbook:* "The process of cooking in just enough fat to prevent sticking has not yet been named in English, and is *sautéing,* but is popularly known as frying, and ought to be banished from all civilized kitchens."

Today the process of cooking in minimal fat still has no English name and has succumbed entirely to the French, at what cost to civilized kitchens is yet to be seen. Today, even the hamburger, the essence of American Fried, is not fried but sautéed. Sautéed has come to mean not something that has leaped in a pan shaken by a cook's hand to keep the food from sticking, but anything fried with dignity in less than a full bath of hot oil. The Frenchification of American cooking after the war is amply evident in our four chefs' treatment of the hamburger, to which each devotes a definitive passage and usually more than one. A brief excursus may show how American Fried became American Sautéed.

Fisher's hamburger in 1949 in *An Alphabet for Gourmets* is the most candidly personal as it is the most outrageously French. Gagging over memories of the "Rite-Spot Specials" consumed in her youth, she opts for a hamburger of best sirloin, "à la Mode de Moi-même," seared (avoiding either fried or sautéed) in a very hot skillet and sauced in red wine, butter, chopped fresh herbs, and oyster sauce, along with the pan juices "Brillat-Savarin would have called the 'osmazome.'"

Child, in *The French Chef Cookbook* in 1968, based on her first television series, serves up Hamburgers à la Française, in which the hamburgers are more like meatballs moistened with suet or marrow, seasoned with minced onions and herbs, held together by egg, and sautéed in butter and oil. She then sauces them with the red wine, beef stock, and beef marrow sauce called Bordelaise.

Ever the internationalist, Claiborne in his first *Times* cookbook gives us Hamburgers au Poivre and Hamburgers with Dill, both seared in a skillet and finished off with butter, Tabasco sauce, Worcestershire sauce, and lemon juice. In his latest cookbook, the finishing sauce continues but the names change, and it's now Hamburger Deluxe, followed by Pizza Burgers with marinara sauce, Mexican Burgers with chili sauce, and Hamburgers à la Holstein with eggs and anchovies. Claiborne now favors the charcoal grill over the skillet and avoids the fry/sauté dilemma by referring to "skillet cookery."

In his *Theory & Practice of Good Cooking*, Beard comes right out with Sautéed Hamburgers, preferring them "pan-fried or sautéed" to broiled because they stay juicier and are easier to control. He sticks to top round or chuck with 20 to 25 percent fat, rather than the sirloin favored elsewhere, and sautés the patties in peanut oil or a mixture of butter and oil. As for sauces, he runs through a dozen ways to vary the pan juices, with red wine or white, vermouth or Cognac, and to vary the meat by incorporating onions or cheese, pine nuts or pepper. In truth, though, all of the variants pale beside the hamburgers his mother cooked on a griddle over the open fire at their beach picnics on the Oregon shore. These she shaped into thickish cakes seasoned with onion, herbs, garlic, salt, and pepper, and served "as a novelty," along with the serious dishes of pickled salmon or cold ham or baked beans and spicy sausages.

What they all agree on is that the meat should be of good quality, the skillet should be very hot, and the flavor of the raw meat should be enhanced by a little something extra. All of them aim for a patty that is well-seared and crusty on the outside, juicy and pink within, the opposite of the thin, flaccid, uniformly gray, microwaved product we are now exporting from Moscow to Peking as American Fried.

My only variation on the American Sautéed is to suggest a way in which you can guarantee the patty will be juicy and flavorful from the inside out by mixing in some softened herb butter. Whatever butter leaks from the patty you then use as pan-juice sauce.

## Proportions

for 4 servings, 2 pounds ground round, sirloin, or chuck

| | |
|---|---|
| 4 anchovies | 4 tablespoons butter, softened |
| 1 teaspoon dried tarragon, or 2 tablespoons fresh | 2 pounds ground beef |
| | 2 tablespoons olive oil |
| ½ teaspoon chervil | |
| ½ teaspoon freshly ground black pepper | |

1. Beat the anchovies, dried herbs, and pepper into the softened butter. Mix the butter into the meat with your fingers, so that the meat stays light rather than packed.

2. Shape the meat gently into 4 large oblongs about 2 inches high. Heat the oil in a heavy cast-iron skillet until hot but not smoking. Sear the patties quickly about 4 to 5 minutes on each side. Press the meat with your finger to test doneness by the amount of firmness or cut into the patty with a knife tip to judge pinkness.

*Serve with homemade french fries or potato pancakes or baked potatoes seasoned with garlic and butter. Or with polenta with cheese and chilies. Finish off with pie, cake, or ice cream.*

# VEAL SCALLOPS WITH LEMON

Sautéing properly refers to a dish like veal scallops, where bite-sized slices of meat are so tender and thin that the cook need only shake them a minute or two in sizzling butter and they are done. That we think of such veal dishes as Italian and give them Italo-American names such as Veal Scaloppini or Veal Piccata or à la Marsala says more about turn-of-the-century immigration than about cooking sources. In American cooking, veal scallops are actually as old and as English as the thirteen colonies.

*Martha Washington's Booke of Cookery* told colonial housewives how to scotch their collops: that is, how to beat slices of mutton, veal, or beef paper-thin to tenderize them. The slices were called collops, perhaps, because a bite-sized round of meat, particularly from a baby white veal, resembled the round white seafood scallop removed from its fluted shell. Martha's *Booke* also told housewives how to fry collops crisp in fresh butter and how to sauce them with bread crumbs, anchovies, capers, or oysters—"& leamon minced." The perfect harmony of lemon and veal has been sung for several centuries.

In the latter part of this century, collops, or scallops, are the most popular cut of veal because they make a two-minute meal of quality and taste, coming close to fulfilling the working guy's and gal's ideal of "instant gourmet." Scallops that take longer than one minute per side aren't scallops at all. When Child explained the Escalopes de Veau of the French in *Mastering I,* she designated scallops ¼ inch thick to be cooked 8 to 10 minutes. That seems a long toughening time and quite unlike the scallops we cook today. In *The New James Beard,* Beard calls for the more likely 1 minute a side, provided the scallops are thin like paper, instead of thick like cardboard.

Scallops are usually cut from the leg and if the butcher hasn't flattened the pieces thin enough, it is an easy matter to flatten them more. Put them between pieces of wax paper and pound them with the bottom of a skillet or the flat side of a mallet or the round of a rolling pin. It is also important to remove any traces of filament or fat. If the pieces are large, you can then cut them into strips about 3 by 3 inches, or whatever uniform shape your meat slices will best form. The scallops will shrink and firm up in the cooking.

Beard and Claiborne both recommend flouring the scallops lightly because it helps them to brown. As for seasoning, you can mix salt and pepper with the flour, you can season them after cooking or, as I prefer, season them on both sides before flouring to guarantee each scallop is seasoned well.

## Proportions

for 4 servings, 1½ pounds veal scallops, or about 8 large pieces

| | |
|---|---|
| 1½  **pounds veal scallops, pounded thin** | 6  **tablespoons butter** |
| **Salt and freshly ground black pepper** | 3  **tablespoons olive oil** |
| | ¼  **cup lemon juice** |
| ½  **cup flour for dredging** | 8  **thin lemon slices** |
| | 2  **tablespoons minced parsley** |

1. Season the scallops on both sides with salt and pepper. Cut them into strips about 3 by 3 inches if the scallops are large. Flour lightly on both sides.

2. Heat the butter and oil in a large heavy skillet (cast iron if you have it) until hot but not smoking. Add the meat a few strips at a time so that they don't touch. Cook for 1 minute on each side and lift onto a serving platter.

3. Add the lemon juice to the skillet, scrape up the pan juices, and pour over the scallops. Arrange a row of lemon slices the length of the platter on top of the scallops. Sprinkle parsley over the lemons.

*This is a simple dish that might be preceded by Artichokes Bagna Cauda (page 278), or Asparagus Maltaise (page 279), and followed by a green salad, cheese, and fruit.*

# LIVER WITH MUSTARD CREAM

The same sauté principle applies to veal liver as to veal scallops, and it's a pity that most American restaurants do liver so badly that it is not one of the glories of sauté cooking as in France, but one of the shames of American fast-fry cookery. The problem begins in the butcher shop. What is sold as a calf's liver in America is often from a fairly old calf, more in fact like a middling young beef. Maybe if we demanded and got "veal" liver, the status of liver might rise to the French Foie de Veau, which often approaches the taste and buttery texture of a fresh *foie gras*.

The second problem is that often the liver is not trimmed but retains the tough outer skin and rubbery inner veining. It's essential to remove everything that is not pure meat and you can, of course, cut larger pieces of liver into small strips as you do with veal scallops. Ideally, liver is cut about ½ inch thick so that it is thin enough to sauté quickly, yet just thick enough to stay pink and juicy inside.

The third problem is that restaurant liver is almost always overcooked, which means gray, tough, and as rubbery as overcooked squid. It's a crying shame. If we treated a calf's liver as tenderly as we would our own, we would not slap it into a smoking fry pan to shrivel and curl. Rather, we would cook it but 2 quick minutes a side, only slightly longer than calf scallops, and sauce it similarly with a little lemon butter or, as here, a little mustard cream.

Child gives a rather complicated way of sautéing liver quickly, then coating it with Dijon mustard and bread crumbs and browning it in a broiler. But you can get the same classic flavor of liver and mustard by the far simpler means of deglazing the skillet with mustard and cream, or even a little yogurt, as Beard suggests.

for 4 servings, 1½ pounds calf's liver, ⅓ cup butter/oil

| | |
|---|---|
| 1½ **pounds well-trimmed calf's liver, cut ½ inch thick** | 3 **tablespoons olive oil** |
| **Salt and freshly ground black pepper to taste** | ¼ **cup dry white wine or beef stock** |
| ½ **cup flour for dredging** | 2 **tablespoons Dijon mustard** |
| 3 **tablespoons butter** | ½ **cup heavy cream** |

1.  Season the liver slices on both sides with salt and pepper and flour them lightly. Heat the butter and oil in a large heavy skillet until hot but not smoking.

2.  Sauté the liver a few pieces at a time, so that the pieces don't touch each other, about 2 minutes a side. Remove the pieces as soon as they are done and arrange them on a serving platter.

3.  Quickly deglaze the pan with the wine or stock. Stir in the mustard and heavy cream and pour over the liver.

*The cream sauce makes the meat fairly rich, so a crisp vegetable or salad is in order.*

# FRANCO-YANKEE POT ROAST

What the difference is between a French pot roast and a Yankee pot roast would be hard to say, since American cookbooks as early as Mrs. Child's *Frugal Housewife* and Miss Leslie's *Directions for Cookery* named their braised pot roasts "A-La-Mode Beef." In the early nineteenth century, that seemed to mean a round of beef with a bread stuffing inserted when the leg bone was removed. The stuffing was highly scented with nutmeg and cloves or marjoram and basil. The beef was tied to keep it in shape, then boiled or baked slowly in water, flavored with bacon, vegetables, and a pair of calves' feet. And finally the broth was finished off with a pint of claret or "a teacupfull of port wine and the same quantity of pickled mushrooms."

Because we cut our round roasts into top and bottom, there's no place to put stuffing anymore, but the principle of making less tender cuts of meat more tender by slow cooking in liquid will endure as long as there is meat to cook. Strictly speaking, to braise means first to brown in fat and then to simmer in liquid. The browning is what distinguishes the method from stewing, since braising, like *brazier*, comes from a French word for live coals. In effect, then, braising simply takes roasting or grilling or sautéing a second step and turns dry heat to wet inside a pot.

The advantage of braising is that the liquid becomes a splendid medium for imparting flavor to meat that may have little of its own, particularly a piece like the round that is all muscle and no fat. The flavor permeates the meat so well that many prefer a pot roast the second or third day and like it cold almost better than hot. It is one of the reasons pot roast thinly sliced under a layer of clear beef jelly makes such a good dish for a hot summer's day.

A braised pot roast of beef is so basic that under whatever name—daube de boeuf, boeuf à la mode, boeuf braisé au vin rouge, or just plain Yankee pot roast—the essentials are the same: meat, vegetables, and liquid. The liquid can be beef broth, beef stock, red wine, tomato juice, or any combination of these. The vegetables are usually onions, carrots, celery, and garlic. The herbs are those of a bouquet garni: parsley, thyme, bay leaf, and allspice or cloves. The meat is usually top or bottom round, boneless chuck, or brisket. Vegetables added to make a one-dish meal are usually small white onions, carrots, small potatoes, and sometimes leeks and whole mushrooms and small turnips, or other roots that take your fancy. A former essential for a rich beef broth—a pig's foot or calf's foot —can be approximated today by a piece of pork rind or chicken gizzards.

In their many books, our chefs have repeated recipes so many times for à la mode beef that it is almost as formulaic as baseball. I have tried to make the synthesis below as simple as possible, reducing the process to its elements.

## Proportions

for 6 to 8 servings, a 4- to 6-pound beef roast of bottom round to 4 cups of liquid and 3 cups of flavoring vegetables

| | |
|---|---|
| 1 4- to 6-pound beef roast | 2 cups beef stock |
| Salt and freshly ground | 2 cups dry red wine |
| black pepper to taste | 1 small piece pork rind or ¼ |
| ¼ cup flour | pound chicken gizzards |
| ¼ cup rendered beef or pork | 6 springs parsley |
| fat, or vegetable oil | 2 bay leaves |
| 1 large onion, carrot, and | ½ teaspoon thyme |
| celery stalk, chopped | 6 whole cloves or Szechuan |
| 2 cloves garlic, mashed | peppercorns |

### Vegetable Garnish

| | |
|---|---|
| 12 small white onions | 3 white turnips |
| 6 leeks | 12 small new potatoes |
| 3 carrots | |

1.   Sprinkle the meat on all sides with salt and pepper and dredge with flour. Heat the fat or oil in a heavy skillet or Dutch oven until hot but not smoking. Brown the meat briskly on all sides. Add the vegetables and brown them a few minutes with the meat.

2.   Transfer the meat and vegetables to a deep lidded casserole, if you've used a skillet, and pour hot stock into the browning pan to dissolve the meat juices. Pour over the meat and add the wine, pork rind, and seasonings.

3.   Bring the liquid barely to a simmer on top of the stove, cover, and transfer to a 300-degree oven for about 2 hours. Turn the beef once while it is cooking. The liquid should stay at a slow simmer. The beef is tender when a sharp fork can pierce it with ease.

4.   Remove the meat to a carving platter. Strain the liquid and return it to the casserole. If too much fat has been rendered, degrease the liquid by skimming the fat from the top.

5.   Add the prepared vegetables (peeled and quartered where needed with carrots and turnips) to the liquid, cover, and simmer until tender (about 15 minutes).

6.   Carve the meat in thin slices and either return to the casserole to serve or lay on a serving platter with the vegetables on either side. Serve the sauce separately. A sprinkling of minced parsley will dress up the serving platter.

*A fruit pie or tart or a Floating Islands pudding (page 388) makes a good conclusion.*

# STUFFED VEAL BREAST

Until fairly recently in America, veal was not always a prestigious meat but was often treated as a cheap substitute for chicken or as a hopelessly pallid chop. One had to go to Italy or France to discover a world of vealery unknown to the beef-eating West. Many of us were introduced to veal through Child's elaborate recipe for Veal Orloff or Claiborne's for Vitello Tonnato or Beard's for Veal Birds. A simple veal roast was not thought of. But as the price of veal rose, so did our demand and expertise in distinguishing between factory veal and hand-fed veal. The price of both is high, but only the pure white meat produced by special feeding and labeled sometimes "plume de veau" or "Dutch-process" veal is suitable for a simple roast or chop or scallop.

There are, however, good ways of using cheaper cuts of top-quality veal or even of factory veal, where flavor comes from the gelatinous bone rather than flesh. The Italian *ossobuco,* for instance, is a thrifty and delicious peasant dish made by braising the marrowed shank in a tomato sauce garnished with garlic and lemon. Another thrifty dish is made from the thin bony strip of veal breast that can serve to wrap a stuffing. It is doubly thrifty because the mingling of flavors improves with age when the breast is reheated in its sauce or served cold. The Italians stuff the breast with a hard-boiled egg surrounded by greens to make a visual masterpiece called *cima alla genovese* to serve at a cold buffet. But it's hard to go wrong with simpler stuffings of almost any kind. Spinach is traditional because the color is striking and its acidity complements the blandness of veal, but other greens work toward the same end, such as chard, mustard, sorrel, and even arugula.

Beard, by the way, suggests roasting a veal breast straight, without stuffing, treating it as if it were a flank steak. He seasons it with a little garlic, browns it under the broiler, and roasts it in the oven. Total time is less than an hour. Braising is the best method for a stuffed breast, however, to bring its many flavors together.

# Proportions

for 6 servings, a 4- to 6-pound breast of veal, to 2 cups of stuffing

1 4- to 6-pound veal breast, with pocket for stuffing
Salt and freshly ground black pepper to taste

2 tablespoons olive oil

## Stuffing

2 cups packed spinach leaves
3 cloves garlic, minced
1 teaspoon anchovy paste, or 2 anchovy fillets
½ cup minced prosciutto or ham

1 cup fresh bread crumbs, or 1 cup cooked rice
1 egg, beaten
3 bay leaves, crumbled
½ small hot red pepper, minced, or ¼ teaspoon red pepper flakes

## Sauce

1 medium onion, chopped
2 carrots, chopped
1 cup dry white wine
2 tomatoes, peeled and chopped

3 sprigs parsley
2 cups beef or chicken stock

1. Sprinkle the veal lightly with salt and pepper on all sides. Prepare the stuffing by first wilting the spinach leaves in a little extra oil in a covered skillet. Drain the leaves well and chop fine. Mix together with

the remaining stuffing ingredients. Pack the stuffing into a pocket cut into the thickest part of the veal breast. Fasten the edges together by sewing with a needle and strong thread or by skewering.

2. Heat the olive oil in a heavy skillet or Dutch oven and brown the breast on both sides, together with onions and carrots. Transfer the meat and vegetables to a deep casserole, if necessary, and deglaze the skillet with the wine. Add the tomatoes, parsley, and stock and bake, covered, at 350 degrees for 1½ to 2 hours, or until tender.

3. Lift the meat from the sauce. Skim the excess fat from the sauce. Put the liquid and vegetables in a blender and liquefy. If the sauce is too thin, return it to the pot and reduce by rapid boiling. Remove the thread or skewers from the roast and carve in thin vertical slices. The meat will carve much better cold than hot.

*Despite its appearance, this is a filling dish and goes best with a green salad or a vegetable simply prepared. A lemon or orange ice is a good dessert.*

# COUNTRY HAM WITH CIDER

Before the industrialization of America, all hams were country hams, cured and smoked in as many different ways as there were farms to preserve the pigs they had slaughtered. Refrigeration has removed the need to preserve by curing, but reason not the need. We continue to cure pork rumps because we like the taste of salted meat—but evidently not quite as salty as our ancestors did who sawed their ham slices thick and fried them up in pan juice and coffee to make Red-eye Gravy.

Today the majority of American ham is precooked but barely cured and most often by injecting a salt solution into the meat to give an instant "ham flavor." The old country way is too slow and too expensive. The best taste, however, comes from a dry cure of salt and spices, followed by slow smoking over hickory wood or beech and finished by long aging, up to a year or more, while the flavor grows. Mail-order smokehouses still furnish us with such hams, the most famous of which are the Smithfield hams of Virginia.

But many non-southerners are reluctant to order them because the investment is high and the cooking is puzzling to those accustomed to the paler supermarket variety. A country ham requires longer preparation in order to de-salt it, but the difference in flavor is worth every penny and every minute. Soaking in cold water gets rid of excess salt and loosens any mold (harmless) on the rind. Simmering in a liquid like cider, instead of water, lends a faintly sweet aroma and further counters the salt. A final mustard glaze makes a handsome and traditional finish, but the trick in serving is to cut slices, whether hot or cold, very, very thin. It's best to think of an American country ham, in fact, as much closer to a raw ham from Parma or Westphalia than to a precooked ham from Chicago.

## Proportions

A whole ham may be anywhere from 10 to 20 pounds. Allow ¼ to ⅓ pound per serving. Since the flavor is intense, a little goes a long way.

1 **country ham, about 15 pounds**
1 **gallon fresh cider**
1 **cup dark brown sugar**
3 **tablespoons Dijon mustard**
24 **whole cloves**

1. Soak the ham for two to three days in cold water to cover, changing the water every day. Drain, scrub the rind well, and cut off any bits of mold. Put in a covered pot and simmer on the stove top, or in the oven, in the cider. Cook for about 20 minutes per pound or until the internal temperature reaches 160 degrees. Turn the ham at least once during the cooking to immerse both sides in the liquid. Let the meat cool in the cider until cool enough to handle.

2. Remove the outer rind and all fat but a thin even layer. (You can save the fat for other uses.) Score the fat into diamonds and cover with a glaze of sugar and mustard mixed together. Stud the scored fat with cloves and bake in a 350-degree oven for about an hour, or long enough to brown the glaze richly and to reheat the meat. If the cut end appears to be drying out, baste it with some of the cider.

*Potatoes or a puréed, mildly spiced vegetable complement the ham's saltiness. Ham is especially good with puréed sweet potatoes. For dessert, a Pumpkin Chip Pie (page 372) or Apple-Pecan Pie (page 370).*

# HOME-CORNED BEEF

To corn is to preserve by curing in grains—i.e., "corns"—of salt. While we call corned pork "ham," we retain the word "corned" for beef. Brisket is the cut that is traditionally corned because its outer and inner layer of fat helps both to preserve and flavor the meat during its slow curing and cooking. Home-cured beef was once a staple of the American kitchen, which produced such hearty winter meals as Corned Beef and Cabbage and the New England Boiled Dinner. But its very popularity helped to kill it, as aspiring immigrants like Maggie scorned the commoner tastes of her Jiggs.

Today we may scorn the corned beef in the markets for different reasons: The quality of the meat is often as poor as the quality of the brine and it's almost certain to be bright red from the nitrate called saltpeter.

By curing at home, you can buy the meat you want, prepare the flavored brine you want, and eliminate nitrates altogether. The result is a reminder of what made corned beef a class dish for high and low before the Maggies became a culinary majority.

The process is simple enough if you cure the beef in your refrigerator. The traditional method was to immerse the meat in an earthenware crock reserved for pickling and to keep the meat under the brine by a weighted board. In his *American Cookery,* Beard outlines in detail the traditional way. But Child, in *Child & Company,* gets rid of the crock and the brine by using a plastic bag and a dry cure of salt and spices. Because Child's method is easier and saves space, I've made a variant of her recipe below. The disadvantage of the dry cure is that it takes longer, a minimum of 2 weeks, for the flavor to penetrate. The brine, on the other hand, will do its work in a week to 10 days. With either cure, the meat becomes saltier the longer it's pickled.

## Proportions

for a 9- to 10-pound brisket, 1 cup each of salt and sugar, plus spices

| | |
|---|---|
| 1  9- to 10-pound beef brisket | 3  bay leaves, crumbled |
| 1  cup coarse or kosher salt | 6  to 8 juniper berries, crushed |
| 1  cup dark brown sugar | 12  black peppercorns, bruised |
| 4  cloves garlic, unpeeled | 4  to 5 whole cloves |

1.  Trim the meat if the fat seems excessive. Mix the seasonings together and rub them into the surface of the meat. Put the meat in a plastic bag, squeeze it to remove air, and close tightly.

2.  Place the bag in a bowl or on a plate and weight the meat by putting a heavy can or its equivalent on a plate or a pan on top of the meat. Refrigerate at 37 degrees for 2 weeks, turning the bag daily, so that the salt and sugar will penetrate the meat evenly as they liquefy.

3.  When ready to cook, wash the meat in cold water and soak overnight to remove any excess salty taste. Put in a deep pot, add enough stock to cover, bring to simmer, partially cover the pot, and cook very slowly for 3 to 4 hours, or until the meat is fork tender.

*Steamed carrots, cabbage, potatoes, onions, leeks are all traditional accompaniments, but baked or puréed squash is also good.*

# STEAK, KIDNEY, AND OYSTER PIE

When our cooking was more English than French, a beefsteak pie covered with a pastry of "one pound of butter to two pounds of sifted flour," as Miss Eliza Leslie directs, was a common dish for dressing up the table. Skilled pastry makers covered their pies with puff paste, and now that more cooks are turning their hand to pastry, the dish is a good one to revive. The richness of kidneys, combined with mushrooms or oysters, as Miss Leslie and others were wont to do, is peculiarly satisfying and the dish is certainly showy when an earthenware baking dish is topped by a round puffed cap of golden brown.

I find that the best way to avoid overcooking the oysters or kidneys is to precook the beef or to use leftover beef when I have it. Beard in *American Cookery* calls for a long baking time of 2 hours, because he merely browns the meat before putting it in the pie. Such a lengthy time, however, makes it hard not to overbrown the crust as well as to overcook the oysters.

Claiborne's solution in *The New New York Times Cookbook* is to precook both kidneys and beef, using a tender cut, such as fillet in any case, so that it will cook quickly. His recipe calls for mushrooms and hard-boiled eggs, instead of oysters, but whatever is baked with the beef will flavor it deliciously in the "steam" pot created by the crust.

## Proportions

for 8 to 10 servings, 2 pounds beef, 2 veal kidneys, 1 dozen oysters, enough pastry for a 2-crust pie

| | |
|---|---|
| 2 pounds fillet, top sirloin, chuck, or round steak, cubed | 4 tablespoons flour |
| | 3 cups hot beef stock or broth |
| 2 veal kidneys (or small beef kidneys) | 2 tablespoons tomato paste |
| | 1 teaspoon thyme |
| 4 tablespoons butter or beef fat | Salt and freshly ground black pepper to taste |
| 2 tablespoons olive oil | 1 dozen oysters |
| 12 large mushrooms caps | 1 egg yolk |
| 1 cup chopped onion | Short Pastry (page 348) or Puff Pastry (page 351) |

1. Cut the beef into 1- to 2-inch cubes or strips. Cut the kidneys into ½-inch rounds. Heat the butter and oil in a heavy skillet and brown the beef steak on all sides over a high flame. Remove the beef and brown the kidneys quickly on both sides. Remove the kidneys and set aside.

2. Brown the mushroom caps quickly and remove. Add the onions and cook for about 2 minutes. Stir in the flour and brown for a minute or two before adding the hot beef stock all at once. Stir in tomato paste and seasonings.

3. If the beef needs more cooking, return it to the sauce and simmer it gently until just tender. The length of time depends on the cut of meat. Remove from the heat. Add the kidneys and their juices, and the

mushrooms, and put in a baking dish that the mixture does not quite fill so that it will not bubble over when the crust seals it. Add the oysters and push them gently under the liquid.

4.   Mix an egg yolk with a little water and paint the outside of the baking dish just below the rim so that the dough will stick to the dish and form a lid.

5.   Roll out the pastry to fit the top of the dish, allowing about a 1½-inch margin for sealing. Set the pastry over the dish and crimp the edges all around. Cut a small vent in the center and insert a small paper cone (or a metal cone used for pastry decorating) to allow steam to escape. Cut pastry leaves with a sharp knife for decoration and stick them to the top of the pastry with the egg yolk mixture. Brush the crust all over with the mixture to help the crust brown.

6.   Bake in a 350-degree oven for about 30 to 45 minutes, or long enough to make sure that the crust is cooked through. For serving, section the crust as you go and lift each section with a spatula or large serving spoon onto a plate. Serve the meat in its sauce at the side.

*A salad of greens or fresh crisp vegetables will cut the richness of the pie. Fruit and cheese make a classic ending.*

# SWEETBREADS CREAMED WITH MUSHROOMS

Often dishes we think of as typically American, such as the chili con carne of Tex-Mex fame, have a far shorter history in this country than dishes we may think of as typically European, like sweetbreads. But when slaughtering and butchering were done in the backyard, innards of all kinds belonged to the American table as much as steaks and chops. Eliza Leslie invokes that world in a paragraph as she describes how to roast sweetbreads by glazing them with egg and bread crumbs, dipping them in butter melted over hot coals, and skewering them on a spit to roast "before a clear fire, at least a quarter of an hour."

As the slaughtering and packaging of meat became increasingly remote from the home fires and table, innards such as sweetbreads became increasingly limited to restaurants, and to French restaurants at that. Sweetbreads became *Ris de Veau.* I first learned about sweetbreads from Child's *Mastering I,* and when I first served them as Ris de Veau à la Crème et aux Champignons, I found my guests discretely concealing uneaten portions beneath the parsley garnish.

Today, fresh unfrozen sweetbreads are more easily available than twenty years ago, at least at fancy food markets, although the high price of sweetbreads reflects the high cost of the calf that has furnished the thymus gland of his adolescence for our adult pleasure. The pleasure is worth cultivating because the delicate taste and texture are like nothing else except the calf's brains, which are chancier to serve to dinner guests than his thymus.

Child's directions for preparing sweetbreads were sufficiently time-consuming to deter any but hard-core experimenters or sweetbread lovers. She called for a four-hour soaking in cold water before trimming, blanching, or braising the lobes. Beard's system in *The New James Beard* seems to produce the same results of softening and whitening the lobes and their filaments in much less time by soaking in ice water. Cream sauce flavored with mushrooms is such a classic combination for sweetbreads that it is pleasant to find recipes for it not only in Child and Beard but in Mrs. Sarah Rorer and Marion Harland and even in the compilers of *The Buckeye Cookbook*.

## Proportions

for 4 to 6 servings, 2 whole sweetbreads (which means 2 pairs or about 2 pounds) to 1 pound of mushrooms to 2 cups of cream sauce

**2 whole sweetbreads (2 pounds)**    **1 pound mushrooms, whole**
**6 tablespoons butter**    **buttons or large, sliced**

### Cream Sauce

**3 tablespoons butter**    **2 egg yolks**
**2 tablespoons flour**    **Salt and freshly ground black**
**1 cup hot strong chicken stock**    **pepper to taste**
**1 cup heavy cream**
**2 to 3 tablespoons sherry or**
**Madeira**

1.    Soak the sweetbreads in ice water for half an hour. Put them in a pan with enough cold water to cover, with 1 teaspoon salt and 1 table-spoon lemon juice for blanching. Bring to a boil, immediately reduce the heat, and simmer for 10 minutes. Drain and plunge the sweetbreads into ice water to stop the cooking process. Remove the covering membrane and connecting tubes and any fat. Cut the sweetbreads into ½-inch slices.

2.    Sauté the sweetbreads and whole mushrooms, if possible, in 6 tablespoons of butter in a hot skillet for 4 to 5 minutes. Remove from the heat.

3.    Make a cream sauce by cooking the butter and flour together for a minute or two before adding the hot stock all at once and stirring rapidly. Thin with ½ cup heavy cream and mix the remaining cream with the sherry and the 2 egg yolks. Add a little of the hot liquid to the egg mixture and then stir it slowly into the sauce. Pour in the juices from the

sweetbreads and mushrooms. Add salt and pepper to taste. When the sauce is the right consistency (thicken by reducing or thin with more stock or cream), add the sweetbreads and mushrooms. Serve in patty shells or with buttered toast and garnish with a sprig of parsley.

*With all that cream, fresh greens should accompany and fresh fruit, or a fruit ice like Strawberry-Cassis (page 394), should follow.*

# TRIPES NIÇOISE

"The main trouble with tripe," as Fisher says, "is that in my present dwelling place . . . I could count on one hand the people who would eat it with me." In the America of 100 years ago, she would not have had that trouble. A hundred years ago so large was the demand for tripe that it could be bought already cleaned and prepared for final cooking just as it is today. Fisher recalls her macabre interest in the way their cook whacked "the slippery ivory-white rubber" with scrub brushes and soaked it in baking soda until it foamed "in an evil way." But cooks who wanted to spare themselves the trouble of turning the lining of the cow's second stomach, the reticulum, into honeycomb tripe ready to cook could run to the butcher's and find it there, fresh or pickled.

Because the French have done more than anybody else with cow's stomachs, and more with all four of them—not just the lining of the second one—the most commonly known tripe dishes have French names and French associations. In this country, Tripes à la Mode de Caen is almost synonymous with tripe, except for the few who know the Philadelphia way of fixing tripe in a Pepper Pot Soup. The Caen way of fixing tripe is to stew it very slowly in a special sealed tripe pot with onions and herbs and a pig's foot for jelly and some Calvados if you're lucky.

The distinctive flavor lies in the slow simmering of tripe and onions, and other French cities claim honors for that: Lyons for Tripes Lyonnaise or Nice for Tripes Niçoise. Each of our four American cooks provides remarkably similar recipes for tripe stewed with onions and other vegetables, usually in wine, as quicker alternatives to the Caen way of eight hours in a special *tripier* pot. The way of Nice is to add the Provençal flavors of tomatoes and garlic, which Beard enforces by suggesting the use of a Provençal rosé for the cooking wine.

---

## Proportions

for 4 to 6 servings, 2 pounds honeycomb tripe to 4 cups of onions, 2 cups of tomatoes, and 2 cups of wine

| | |
|---|---|
| **4 cups sliced onions** | **2 cups (1 pound) tomatoes,** |
| **¼ cup olive oil** | **peeled, seeded, and chopped** |

---

| | |
|---|---|
| 4 cloves garlic, mashed | 1 teaspoon thyme |
| 1 8-inch-square pork rind, or 1 pig's foot | 1 bay leaf |
| 2 cups dry rosé or dry white wine | 1 teaspoon fennel seeds<br>Salt and freshly ground black pepper to taste |
| 2 pounds honeycomb tripe, cut in strips | ¼ cup grated Parmesan cheese (optional) |

1. In a deep casserole, cook the onions in the olive oil until they are limp. Add the tomatoes, garlic, pork rind, and wine. Cut the tripe in strips about 1 by 3 inches and add to the casserole. Add the seasonings, cover the casserole with foil and then with the lid to keep in the steam.

2. Bake in a low oven (325 degrees) for about 3 hours. Test a piece of tripe. It should be fork-tender but still slightly chewy. Serve, if you like, with grated Parmesan cheese.

*Crusty French bread will soak up the sauce, while a green salad will complement it. For dessert, try apple slices sprinkled with sugar and sautéed in butter.*

# VEGETABLES

## Boiled/Steamed

Artichokes *Bagna Cauda* · 278
Asparagus Maltaise · 279
Corn in the Husk · 281
Green Beans with Walnuts · 283

## Braised/Baked

Green Peas, French Style · 285
Carrots Glazed with Orange · 286
Spaghetti Squash in Garlic Butter · 287
Scalloped Potatoes with Cheese · 289

## Stir-Fried/Sautéed

Broccoli Sautéed with Garlic · 290
Grated Zucchini Sauté · 291
*Ratatouille* · 293
Cucumbers with Snow Peas · 294
Grated Potato Pancake · 295

## Puréed

Parsnip Purée · 297
Sour Sweet Potato Purée · 298

*TO PLANT SPARRAGUS: To plant the rootes or seeds of sparragus, make ye bed as bigg as you will have it, & digg ye earth out a yerd deepe, & fill up ye place again with old cows dung or horse dung well rotted. & If you have any rams horns, or shaveings of horne, it will make it much ye better.*

—Martha Washington's Booke of Cookery *(1749)*

Most of the instructions in early cookbooks for vegetables have not to do with cooking, but with growing, harvesting, and preserving. Vegetables were "put down" or "put up." They were put down in the cellar, sometimes by burying in earth or sand, or they were put up by pickling or home "canning." Naturally, in a land of pioneer farming, only vegetables that kept well were worth bothering with: squashes, cabbages, potatoes, parsnips, beets—all the earthy roots and stalks and tubers that for centuries European peasants had learned to save and savor. In the new land, farmers learned from its natives how to "put up" by drying the white seeds of maize and the green seeds of beans to savor them in winter months as *m'sick-quotash, sukquttahash,* or, as it became Anglicized, *succotash.* In the beginning, little time or labor could be wasted on seeds or plants that could not be buried, pickled, or dried.

Considering the hardships of farming in these intemperate climes, it's surprising how many exceptions there were to this rule. Green vegetables, such as asparagus, broccoli, artichokes, and spinach, were common in early nineteenth-century gardening and cooking manuals. But vegetables more than any other food, except their natural kin fruit, were subject to extremes of controversy because they were associated, for good and bad, with health. The "tomata," as it was often spelled, was thought to be not only a poison but also a source of cancer. Fresh produce of every kind was blamed for a major cholera epidemic in 1832, when the prejudice of thrifty farmers against leafy vegetables was strengthened by doctors. Even root vegetables suffered from home dietitians like Catherine Beecher, who warned against peas, beans, onions, cabbages, and turnips for folk with weak digestion.

The horrific cooking times for vegetables that amuse us today were aimed at health. "Every sort of vegetable should be cooked till tender," Miss Eliza Leslie stated, "as if the least hard or under-done, they are both unpalatable and unwholesome." To specify what she meant by tender, she advised 1½ hours for green beans, 2 hours for limas, 1 hour for asparagus (if old, 1¼ hours), and 2 to 3 hours for artichokes. In addition, vegetables of all kinds should lie in cold water awhile before cooking, presumably to purify them of insects as well as of dirt and to keep them crisp until put in the boiler for softening. That the vegetables themselves, under such hydrotherapy, turned to water Miss Leslie herself seems to recognize in her final warning: "When done, they should be carefully drained before they go to table, or they will be washy all through, and leave puddles of discoloured water in the bottoms of the dishes, to the disgust of the company and the discredit of the cook."

At the opposite extreme were the preachments of contemporary food evangelists, prophets like the Reverend Sylvester Graham or the later Ellen A. White and Jethro Kloss. Fresh vegetables and fruits were the pathway to heaven and were best eaten as God grew them—raw. To the evangelists, water was as necessary as the vegetable, both to be ingested in their pure state, so that together they might cleanse body and soul of the impurities civilization was heir to.

The moral minority in the 1840s, in the heartland of beef-eating America, were those who preached that the vegetable was the *only* natural food of man. The vegetarian and the organic gardener cultivated such food in the name of theology. But science also was beginning to sanctify the "unwholesome" vegetable in the name of life-giving chemicals. The status of vegetables in their natural state zoomed when, in 1911, Casimir Funk added a prefix to the compounds called "amines" and labeled them "vita." To such unlikely sources as teetotaler Graham and chemist Funk do we owe the raw carrot sticks that we nibble not only in our youth but at the fashionable cocktail parties of our middle age.

When our cooking traditions were largely English rather than French, the vegetable raw needed all the help it could get. While the Reverend Graham might think the French no better than Satan in corrupting God's nature, the worldly knew different. The Frenchman Pierre Blot, in his *Hand-Book of Practical Cookery* of 1867, begins not with roots or tubers or stalks but "Green vegetables." They "must look fresh," he says, "and have nothing rotten about them." He proceeds to treat each vegetable in several different ways beyond boiling in water and suggests that some, such as cucumbers and artichokes, are good raw. Asparagus, he advises, is better when "rather underdone"—firm and still crisp. As for exact cooking times, he throws up his hands. You should boil carrots until tender, but "It is impossible to tell how long it takes, as it depends how young and tender they are."

Most Americans, however, followed the English tradition rather than the French until after the Second World War. While the discovery of vitamins reversed the waterbath principle and urged the use of steamers instead of boilers, the formula was still Mrs. Lincoln's of 1887. Her command for all fresh green vegetables was, "Cook rapidly until soft." In the name of progress and health, new cookware was introduced like the "waterless cookers" and pressure cookers of the thirties and forties, but the aim was the same. Asparagus that took 20 to 25 minutes in a boiling pot took only 2½ minutes in a pressure cooker to be rendered soft.

Americans were accustomed to soft because they were accustomed to canned and then frozen, with cooking directions that could only render the steamed or blanched soft and softer. But the Victory Gardens of the war reintroduced, as a side effect, the possibilities of fresh, crisp, and raw. For the first time, many experienced the pleasure of eating on the stalk what he had grown with his own hands, with or without the benefit of cow dung or horse dung or ram's horns or shavings. We were ready for a new vegetable love, as Fisher expressed it almost forty years ago in her recipe for Petits Pois à la Française, in *How to Cook a Wolf.* Or as Beard expressed it in his first *James Beard Cookbook* in a recipe for Boiled Asparagus, which he urges us to cook until only the tips are tender. "The stalks will still be bitey," he admits, "but this crunchy texture is very good." We had to be told.

We were ready then for the Frenchification of our new vegetable love through Claiborne and Child. We were ready for Claiborne's Asparagus Polonaise and almost ready for Child's Timbale d'Asperges—almost but not quite. Child shocked us by her French way of cooking green vegetables in "a very large kettle of rapidly boiling salted water," we who had learned finally about vitamins and waterless cookers. This was heresy and worse, for the purpose of blanching had nothing to do with health. Its sole aim was color, texture, and flavor. The French way was dedicated not to purity but pleasure. Child was, by God, a hedonist.

In the sixties and seventies, food hedonists multiplied almost as fast as food evangelists, and instead of fighting it out at the barricades they united in vegetable love. The new-wave cooking of France made the color, texture, and flavor of the vegetable central to its minimalist art. The new-wave morality of America made the varying colors, textures, and flavors of the all-vegetable plate central to its salvation. Vegetables were no longer humble creatures of the earth to "put down" or "put up," but a world complete unto themselves, revealing the hand of God and Mammon. Today this strange alliance of pleasure and purity has resulted in cookbooks like *The Vegetarian Epicure,* in restaurants like the stylish Green's run by the Tassajara Zens in California, in vogues like the wok and Oriental stir-fry. A stir-fried snow pea is as far from 1¼-hour boiled asparagus as the Mississippi from the Yangtze, or the Humber from the Ganges. The best food prophet of all turns out to be a seventeenth-century English poet who knew that, given world enough and time, our vegetable love would grow vaster than empires.

# ARTICHOKES *BAGNA CAUDA*

Artichokes were not native to America but they were imported early enough "To Make an Hartichoak Pie," according to the receipt in *Martha Washington's Booke of Cookery*. This one called for "hartychoak" bottoms put in "a coffin of paste" with butter, sugar, marrow, cinnamon, ginger, and the vinegary verjuice. The French had brought artichokes early to our eastern coast and the Italians later to the West, to make Castroville, California, the present artichoke capital of the world.

Although England knew the wild artichoke as an herb, the root of which was a specific "against the ranke smell of the arme-holes," the garden artichoke was French. English and American cookbooks called it the globe or French artichoke to distinguish it from an unrelated ubiquitous tuber, the Jerusalem artichoke. And French it has remained in association, probably because the French use so many varieties of it from raw to cooked as a classic appetizer.

Until after the Second World War, many Americans regarded the artichoke with suspicion because it seemed to be an inedible thistle. Fisher recalls the vegetable snobbism of her midwestern grandmother, who would say of an *arriviste* that she's "the kind of woman who serves artichokes!" I know an instance of such snobbism in reverse when a friend lost a job because he did not know how to eat an artichoke. Confronted with the thistle at a dinner interview, he panicked and, instead of observing his host, plunged in recklessly with knife and fork to consume every choking morsel.

Cooking an artichoke is simple enough. You either boil it or steam it for 30 or 40 minutes, or until a leaf will pull out easily. But to make an artichoke a work of art requires further manicuring by trimming the base and outer leaves, clipping the end of each pointed leaf, cooking the globe in a non-aluminum pot, and tying a lemon slice to each bottom. To such refinements Fisher cries, *"Mercy!* . . . I like runty artichokes, the kind most greengrocers do not sell, and I have used a large aluminum soup kettle for some thirty years to cook them in, and I would feel silly tying bandages of lemon onto them."

Limited to the large globes of the supermarket, I do like the look of the clipped and trimmed thistle, especially because I like the choke removed and the hollow filled with a pool of spiced oil or creamy hollandaise or freshly whipped mayonnaise. Our current masters provide dozens of recipes for solider stuffings, for those who like their thistles stuffed with shellfish or mushroom or sausage or even sweetbreads. But I find that such stuffings distract from the sexiness of stripping the globe leaf by leaf to reveal, at last, its delectable bottom.

To vary a French vinaigrette, I have used the Italian hot oil bath of anchovy and garlic called *bagna cauda*. Artichokes taste best, I find, at room temperature, so that a sauce can be either hot or cold, but a hot oil sauce is just unexpected enough to renew our surprise that one can eat a thistle at all.

## Proportions

for 4 servings, 4 artichokes to 1⅓ cups of sauce

**4 large artichokes**            **Salt**
**½ lemon**

### *Bagna Cauda* Sauce

**⅓ cup (¾ stick) butter**         **6 to 8 anchovy fillets**
**⅔ cup fruity olive oil**          **10 cloves garlic, mashed**

1.  Wash the artichokes well under running water. Cut off the stem at the base and pull off the small or withered leaves around the base. Cut off the top of the center cone with a sharp knife and trim off the point of each leaf with scissors.
2.  Rub the cut portions of the leaf and base with the lemon to prevent discoloring. Drop the artichokes in a large kettle of boiling water, salted about 1 teaspoon per quart. Boil slowly, uncovered, for 30 to 40 minutes, or until an inside leaf pulls out easily. Stir the globes occasionally to keep them cooking evenly when they bob to the surface, or else weight them down with a plate.
3.  Remove them when done with a slotted spoon and drain upside down in a colander. When they are cool enough to handle, remove the inner cone of leaves to get at the choke. With a teaspoon, scoop out the hairy growth covering the top of the artichoke heart.
4.  To prepare the sauce, heat the butter and oil. Add the anchovies and garlic and simmer over low heat for about 30 minutes. Pour into a blender and liquefy. Pour about ⅓ cup of the sauce into the center of each artichoke set upright on its serving plate.

*No matter how common they are, artichokes make a dressy beginning for any meal and set the rhythm leaf by leaf of what's to come. They can be followed by something as simple as an omelet or as special as a crown roast of lamb.*

# ASPARAGUS MALTAISE

We assume that Martha Washington must have had her gardeners plant sparragus because there is one species named after her today and another after George. Colonists once cultivated the white asparagus, so loved by

Europeans, which we now get mostly in cans. Today, Americans cultivate green varieties almost exclusively and one kind or another is available most of the year. What varies is not color but size, depending largely on the harvester and the season. The narrow thin stalks that take but a minute to cook and must be eaten whole are harbingers of spring, but otherwise asparagus is so widely grown and marketed that it is no longer for us the seasonal crop still celebrated rapturously by North Europeans in *Spargelfesten*.

Child explains that "the French method of cooking asparagus" is to peel it, tie it in bundles, and boil it in large quantities of water. That may be, but it has also been the American method since Martha Washington's time. The problem with asparagus is the difference in cooking time between stalk and tip. The solution is to peel enough of the skin from the stalk to moderate the difference. Peeled skins need not go to waste because you can throw them in a freezer bag and use them later for soup.

A more cumbersome solution is to use a double boiler, with the upper part inverted and the bundled stalks set upright, in order to boil the stalks while steaming the tops. But I find the device of making the stalk fit the pot chancy. For the same reason, asparagus steamers seem an awkward piece of equipment, sanctioned more by nostalgia for the way mother did things than by practical use. Beard's way seems simplest and best and even Child has come round to it in *Child & More Company*. Peel yes, but bundle no. Just lay the asparagus spears flat in a skillet deep enough to hold them as layered as the skillet requires. Beard covers the spears with cold water, brings it to a boil, and boils for 6 to 8 minutes. Child adds boiling water and removes the spears 4 to 5 minutes after the water returns to a boil. Either way, you must boil the spears uncovered to retain their bright green color.

In 1848, Miss Leslie remarked, "To serve up asparagus with long stalks is now becoming obsolete," and she recommended cutting the stalks short and serving with melted butter on toast. Toast or biscuit remained a favorite accompaniment and reached its pinnacle in a popular dish called Asparagus in Ambush, which consisted of asparagus tips baked in a custard of milk and egg and used to fill hollowed-out biscuits or rolls. It sounds like a prairie quiche.

France of course gave us hollandaise to replace the simpler sauce of melted butter and chopped hard-boiled egg. But the variant of hollandaise made with orange juice as well as lemon and called *maltaise* seems to have a peculiar affinity to asparagus and makes a happy variation on a classic theme.

## Proportions

for 4 to 6 servings, 2 pounds asparagus to 1 cup of sauce

**2 pounds asparagus**                    **Salt**

### Maltaise Sauce

**3 egg yolks**                    **3 tablespoons orange juice**
**1 tablespoon lemon juice**       **¼ pound (1 stick) butter**
**¼ teaspoon salt**               **Grated rind of 1 orange**

1.  If the stalks are large and thick, snap off the bottoms where they break easily. Peel the skins with a vegetable peeler or paring knife from the bottom of the tips to the end and trim the ends. (Child recommends using the entire stalk and paring the butt end more deeply. It depends on the asparagus.)

2.  Lay the asparagus flat in a large skillet. Bring 2 to 3 quarts of water to a boil in a separate pan and, when boiling, pour over the asparagus to cover. Add salt to taste. Bring the asparagus to a boil rapidly and boil, uncovered, slowly, for 4 to 5 minutes. The spears are tender when they just begin to bend or when their tips bob when shaken.

3.  Drain immediately by pouring into a colander or, if you are expert, by using the skillet's lid. Lift the spears onto paper towels to dry more quickly and evenly.

4.  To prepare the sauce, put the yolks, lemon juice, salt, and 1 tablespoon of the orange juice in a processor or blender and process for 10 seconds. Melt the butter and add it, while it is still bubbling, in a slow steady stream. Add the grated orange rind and remaining orange juice according to thickness or thinness wanted.

5.  Serve the asparagus by lining the points in the same direction. Serve the sauce separately. The best way to eat asparagus is with the fingers, dipping the points in the sauce and nibbling down to the end.

*Taking a tip from Europe, Americans are now more apt to serve asparagus as a first course than as an accompanying vegetable. With a rich sauce such as hollandaise or maltaise, asparagus needs to stand on its own, either before or after a main dish—or, for luncheon, all by itself.*

# CORN IN THE HUSK

Until 1902, when Golden Bantam was introduced, almost all sweet eating corn was white. This was the corn that the Indians had for centuries dried for hominy or ground for meal, as the yellow varieties of maize were considered fit for beast but not man. Not until the middle of the nineteenth century, however, was a variety of sweet white corn developed specifically to be eaten as a fresh vegetable, a variety called sugar-corn or *Zea Mays,* according to Mrs. Rorer. Before that, fresh corn was eaten when it was still "green," or barely ripe, because the ears were sweetest when youngest. To test their youth, Mrs. Harland suggested the fingernail test: "When the grain is pierced, the milk should escape in a jet, and not be thick."

The cooking method favored by Mrs. Rorer and Mrs. Harland was to boil the corn with the husks on, since they thought the husks helped keep the sweetness in. They had Indian tradition behind them; the Indians steamed corn in pits or roasted it in ashes within the protective husk. The later, more urban way was to remove the roughest layer of outer husk and "every particle of the silk" within, but to retain the thin green layers of husk and, if necessary, to tie them at the top with a bit of thread.

Even with the sweetness in, corn was distrusted for its indigestibility. Mrs. Rorer suggested to the delicate that they score each row of grains on the cooked cob, "and with the teeth press out the centre of the grains, leaving the hulls on the cob."

Her method might suit those for whom corn presents a different kind of problem, one of dentistry rather than digestion. Fisher confesses that she does not bite into corn on the cob "because when I was not quite ten I had a few teeth knocked out by two fat boys sparking downhill on one bicycle . . ." Consequently, she learned to shave raw milky kernels from the cob into a little hot butter in a skillet. For "shaved corn," Child suggests a wooden corn scraper, of the type still carried by some mail-order country stores, to save labor when making cream-style corn for puddings or corn oysters or dodgers, or for those whose teeth are not their own.

As for simple boiled corn, each has his own method. Beard prefers to lay shucked ears flat in cold water in a skillet. He brings the water to a boil over high heat; when it reaches a full boil, he removes the corn at once. Claiborne's method is the opposite. He begins by boiling water in a kettle to which he adds the shucked ears and covers them. When the water returns to the boil, he removes the kettle from the heat and leaves the corn immersed for 5 minutes.

I propose yet another method by returning to the older ways of boiling corn in their husks. I can't guarantee that the husks retain sweetness but they do retain heat and keep the ears warmer 'twixt stove and table. There is also the eater's pleasure in stripping the green to reveal rows of milky pearls within, a pleasure well known to erotic eaters of such striptease foods as corn and peas and bananas.

## Proportions

1 or 2 ears per person

| | |
|---|---|
| 6 ears fresh white corn, husks on | Salt and freshly ground black pepper |
| 1 tablespoon sugar | |
| ¼ pound (1 stick) butter, melted | |

1. Take off the roughest outer leaves of the corn. Pull back the inner green leaves and remove all the silk. Tie the inner leaves together at the top of the ears with wire twists (used for plastic bags) or small rubber bands.

2. In a large kettle, bring to the boil enough water to cover the corn. Do not add salt but add *instead* 1 tablespoon of sugar. Drop the ears into the water and return to a boil, partly covered, over high heat. Boil for 3 to 4 minutes, *no more.* Longer cooking makes for tougher corn, as the corn's natural sugar turns to starch.

3. Put the melted butter in a small pot. To serve, pour a little butter on each plate which the guests can salt and pepper to taste. Let each guest husk his own corn and dip it in the seasoned butter.

*Corn is a summer food, however cooked, and an outdoor food whenever possible. It's a natural for grilled fish, boiled lobsters, grilled steaks or chickens. And it's wise to serve it as a first course to avoid any interruption of hand and mouth coordination.*

# GREEN BEANS WITH WALNUTS

Green, French, snap, or string beans, being one and the same, used always to come equipped with "troublesome *attachés,* " as Mrs. Harland calls them in her *Common Sense in the Household,* which must be removed before cooking. Few remove the strings as deftly as they should, she warns, for "It is a tedious and disagreeable business, this pulling bits of woody thread out of one's mouth when he wants to enjoy his dinner."

While the name remains, the "string" fortunately has been bred out of our current bean. All the cook need do is slice off the ends, straight, or on the dressier diagonal. Cutting further does not improve the taste and fragments the beauty of a long bean. Occasionally, today, the most beautiful of green beans, the tiny French *haricot vert,* appears in the American market at a high price and is worth it. At least in the bean market, the cost of the young and the beautiful and the slim is immediate and relatively painless, for only pleasure can come of it.

The French often stew larger green beans in the cooking juices of a piece of braised meat so that the beans absorb the flavor of the roast. Or they cook them up with salt pork as many Americans still do in the South, according to a basic recipe Claiborne (in *The New New York Times Cookbook*) calls both Haricots Verts à la Paysanne Landaise and Green Beans Peasant-style.

Claiborne prefers to steam beans, but Child and Beard opt for blanching them, uncovered, to retain their bright green color. The main trick is to keep the water boiling by dropping in the beans a handful at a time. For this purpose, Child has been known, occasionally, to insert into the water a fiery hot "buffalo iron," according to Beard, who says slyly that he thinks he can get along without one. The cooking of green beans provokes controversy because the degrees between mushy and raw are so many. A 2- to 3-minute blanch is good for beans to be eaten "raw" as finger food on an appetizer tray. A slightly longer time of 6 to 8 minutes will still keep the crunch. Child and Beard both prefer 10 to 15 minutes for a "bitey-crisp" bean, but for me that's over the hill unless the beans are too thick to begin with. The point is to test by tasting and to drain quickly the moment the beans reach the desired crunch.

A trick many of us learned first from Child was to slightly undercook the beans well ahead of time and run them under cold water to stop their cooking. The beans were then ready for a last-minute heating in butter or other sauce. By this route many of us learned how delicious still crisp beans were at room temperature, plain in their colander, or dipped into a little walnut oil and balsamic vinegar. By this route beans sometimes never made it to the table at all.

## Proportions

for 4 servings, 2 pounds beans to ½ cup of walnuts

**2 pounds green beans,** *haricots verts* **when possible**
**¼ cup walnut oil**

**1 teaspoon balsamic vinegar or white wine vinegar**
**½ cup finely chopped walnuts**

1. Rinse the beans and trim the ends on the diagonal. Drop by handfuls into a large kettle of salted boiling water. Boil for 3 to 8 minutes, depending on the size of the beans, but test throughout.
2. Drain the beans immediately and run cold water over them to stop cooking, as you are going to serve these beans at room temperature.
3. Combine the oil and vinegar together as a dressing and mix with beans. Transfer the beans to a serving dish and sprinkle with the chopped walnuts.

*Serve as a first course or as a salad.*

# GREEN PEAS, FRENCH STYLE

Fisher has evoked peas, perfect peas, in a number of memorable passages, summed briefly thus: "The best way to eat fresh ones is to be alive on the right day, with the men picking and the women shelling, and everybody capering in the sweet early summer weather, and the big pot of water boiling, and the table set with little cool roasted chickens and pitchers of white wine." And as we begin to slaver, she adds, with malice, "So . . . how often does this happen?"

Now that peas are no longer a harbinger of early summer but rather of the refrigerator car and frozen food counter, this happens less and less. In the market, peas too often conceal within a pretty pod their dull and starchy age. Too often the frozen product is simply more reliable, so why bother with laborious shelling? No reason, unless you happen to be alive on the right day and remember the taste of a very sweet, fresh, young, and tender pea plucked straight from pod to mouth and unless you happen to have a garden, your own or somebody else's, to pick and shell and caper in. But there are alternative ways of procuring the perfectly fresh pea. Beard suggests snitching a pod or two from the market stall and opening and eating the peas on the spot to test their sweetness, but that practice is discouraged by most markets I know.

If you succeed in finding young and tender peas, you can blanch them in a lot of water or a little water or braise them in butter or cream. The English fashion with peas, said Mrs. Rorer, was to add mint, a fashion Claiborne gives a French name to in Garden Peas à la Menthe. But the French fashion was to braise peas with lettuce "until the lettuce is melted," as Mrs. Rorer says, and has yielded its water to make the peas tender. Child gives a classic recipe for Petits Pois Frais à la Française in *Mastering I* and calls it "the glory of pea cookery." The mixture of tender greens—peas, lettuce, and spring onions—steamed in sugared butter does make for perfect peas, I believe, although I have noticed un-French guests pushing aside their melted lettuce with distrust. The lettuce looks more presentable if it's quartered and tied with string to keep its shape during cooking, but this seems to me an unnecessary refinement on the old-fashioned shredding.

## Proportions

for 4 servings, 2 pounds peas in pod, 1 head Boston lettuce, 8 green onions

| 2 | pounds peas (about 2 cups shelled) | 4 | tablespoons water |
|---|---|---|---|
| 8 | green onions, chopped | | Salt and freshly ground black pepper to taste |
| 4 | tablespoons butter | 1 | head Boston lettuce, |
| 1 | teaspoon sugar | | shredded |

Shell the peas just before cooking. Chop the onions, including some of the green. In a saucepan, combine the peas, onions, butter, sugar, water, and seasonings. Put the shredded lettuce on top. Cover the pan tightly and bring to a boil. Lower the heat to simmer and simmer slowly for 10 to 15 minutes according to the size of the peas. Stir the peas a couple of times while they cook and add water if necessary. If there's too much water at the end of the cooking time, remove the vegetables with a slotted spoon and reduce the cooking liquid by boiling. Add more butter according to taste.

*Peas of this quality deserve to be served as a separate course, but they lend their sweetness well to a roast chicken or duck or veal or a cream-sauced pasta.*

# CARROTS GLAZED WITH ORANGE

How to cook carrots depends entirely on the carrot and the cook. At one time, Americans apparently sliced old and hard carrots and roasted them to use as a coffee substitute or "extract," says Mrs. Rorer. Or they roasted and boiled them to make a yellow dye for coloring butter. Sometimes, when the carrot was young and fresh, they ate them. The problem today is how to get, short of growing them oneself, carrots that are young and fresh and small—finger-length, say, instead of foot-length. While supermarkets are beginning to carry bags of topless "finger" carrots, they are often not sweet but rather bitter. There's no way to tell but to taste.

The scraped as opposed to the peeled carrot is not a post-vitamin phenomenon. Most American cookbooks used the word "scrape" long before vitamin C declared itself and before the American mania for raw carrots as a quick and crunchy vitamin fix substituted "scrubbed" for scraped. All the more shocking, then, was Child's directive in *Mastering I* to peel, actually *peel,* carrots with a vegetable peeler. She chose art over vitamins, and once the carrots were uniformly peeled she further trimmed and shaped them into long ovals like garlic or olives. This was the French way, as was braising carrots in butter instead of boiling them in water.

To children raised on a canned mixture called peas-and-carrots, carrots sliced thin, glazed in sugar and butter, and sprinkled with green parsley, were found to be surprisingly good. They also looked good. There might be some hope for cooked carrots after all. Carrots came to life on restaurant menus as Carrots Vichy, although the carrot had not been near the bottled Vichy water that gave it its name. The idea of cooking carrots in a very little liquid jibed with the idea that raw carrots were best and resulted in a whole new era for the carrot as it moved into salads, breads, and cakes.

The principle of glazing carrots is to let the liquid boil off until only a syrupy glaze remains. The liquid may be stock or cream or water or, as I suggest below, orange juice. The raw carrot and orange salad of my youth is like a double shot to the vitamin addict, but there's a taste addiction as well in the chemistry of the two. The acidic sweetness of the orange perks up the dull and gives an added kick to the familiar. Carrot and orange go together, maybe because our largest supply of each comes from the same place—California. Instead of Carrots Vichy, we have Carrots California.

---

## Proportions

for 4 servings, 1 pound carrots to ½ cup of orange juice

| | |
|---|---|
| 1 **pound carrots** | 2 **tablespoons minced fresh** |
| 1 **teaspoon sugar** | **parsley or chervil for** |
| ½ **cup fresh orange juice** | **garnish** |
| 4 **tablespoons butter, melted** | |
| **Salt and freshly ground** | |
| **black pepper to taste** | |

Trim, scrape, and slice the carrots into thin rounds, in the processor or by hand. Put them in a frying pan with the sugar, orange juice, melted butter, and salt and pepper. Cover and bring to a boil. Uncover and cook over moderately high heat, shaking the carrots to cook them evenly, until the liquid is reduced and the carrots are tender (5 to 10 minutes). Sprinkle with parsley and serve.

*The sweet-sour of the glaze suggests their appropriateness with duck or pork or any kind of game.*

# SPAGHETTI SQUASH IN GARLIC BUTTER

While the Indians and colonists feasted on a variety of native squashes, with intriguing names like White Patty-Pan, the aptly named Spaghetti Squash was not among them. Spaghetti squash is a newcomer to the squash scene. It has the odd attribute of looking like a squash and cooking like a squash but tasting like a yellow-orange pasta. Beard, in fact, suggests serving it with any delicate pasta sauce. Child suggests a heartier but no less Italianate sauce of diced eggplant, fried in garlic and oil.

Our nineteenth-century cooks took squash as they came, named for the season, winter and summer, and cooked them season in and season out by boiling until tender. "Drain, squeeze, and press it well, and mash it with a very little butter, pepper and salt," Miss Leslie advised and others followed. The recipes are so uniform, in fact, that it would suggest cooks got bored with serving squash at all. Our modern solution, then, has been not to alter the recipe but to alter the squash.

Spaghetti squash takes its name from the peculiarity of its interior. Once the web of seeds is removed, the cooked flesh shreds into spaghetti-like strands. Some say the taste of pasta in the spaghetti squash is entirely in the eye of the beholder. But like an unseasoned and unsauced strand of spaghetti, what the strand of squash has is texture—and color. The squash is a brilliant saffron yellow. Garlic butter, made with lots of parsley, does well by the color and does well by the delicate feathery strands, which you can toss with a couple of forks as you might a heap of pasta, adding Parmesan and a few vigorous sprinklings from the pepper mill to complete the charade. If you are serving squash-haters and pasta-lovers, you can go all the way and pretend you are serving Squashed Spaghetti.

## Proportions

for 4 servings, 1 spaghetti squash (about 10 inches long) to ¼ pound butter

| | |
|---|---|
| 1 spaghetti squash | Salt and freshly ground |
| ¼ pound (1 stick) butter | black pepper to taste |
| 3 cloves garlic, minced | 4 tablespoons grated |
| 4 tablespoons minced parsley | Parmesan cheese |

1. Bake, boil, or steam the whole squash. (Bake for 1½ hours in a 350-degree oven. OR, boil or steam for 20 to 30 minutes.) Split lengthwise, drain, and remove the seeds and coarse surrounding threads. Scrape the squash lengthwise with a large spoon or fork into a serving bowl.

2. Melt the butter with the garlic. Add parsley, salt, and pepper and pour over the squash. Toss with a fork and spoon or a pair of forks as you would spaghetti. Add the Parmesan cheese, if you like, or pass it in a separate bowl.

*Garnished so richly, the vegetable can be a main dish like the spaghetti it imitates, or it can be a fitting accompaniment to pork, beef, or other sturdy roasts.*

# SCALLOPED POTATOES WITH CHEESE

Baking something with cheese to make a bubbling brown crust is so typical of French cooking that we give a French name to it, *au gratin*. Baking potatoes with cheese and cream is so typical of French regional cooking that we give French regional names to it, names like *Gratin Dauphinois*. But the same dish has appeared on our own shores and in our own regions for the last hundred years under the puzzling label of Scalloped Potatoes. What, one might ask, makes a potato scalloped? Not the slicing of it into white rounds that one might think resembled scallops, but the baking of it in a casserole until crusty brown. And what has that to do with a scallop? Not a scallop but its shell.

In 1893, to scallop a potato meant to mash potatoes with milk and butter and to put the mixture in buttered scallop shells with a little grated cheese on top to brown in the oven, according to Mrs. Harland's recipe for Potato Scallops. By the time of Mrs. Rorer's 1904 cookbook (*Mrs. Rorer's New Cook Book*), the scallop shells had been abandoned in favor of a baking dish and the potatoes were chopped instead of mashed to appear under the new class name, Delmonico Potatoes.

Scalloped potatoes became a standard fixture at church suppers in the first decades of the new century because they were dressier than simple baked, mashed, or boiled potatoes. They were also richly filling. You could make them as rich as you liked by using heavy and heavier cream. While a *gratin dauphinois* adds a bit of garlic and *gratin lyonnaise* a bit of onion and *gratin savoyard* substitutes stock for milk, an American potato can be scalloped with any of these variants and still be a scalloped potato. Child's recipe for Gratin Dauphinois in *Mastering I* calls for all milk, while Claiborne's in *The New New York Times Cookbook* calls for 2 milk to 1 cream. If you use all cream you must keep the temperature below simmering or the liquid will curdle.

## Proportions

for 6 servings, 2 pounds Idaho potatoes to 1 cup of combined milk and cream to 1 cup of Swiss cheese

| | |
|---|---|
| **2 pounds Idaho potatoes, peeled and sliced** | **1 cup grated Swiss (or Gruyère) cheese** |
| **4 tablespoons butter** | **½ cup each of milk and cream** |
| **Salt and freshly ground black pepper to taste** | |

1. Peel the potatoes and slice them ⅛ inch thick either by hand or in a processor. Put the slices in cold water until they are needed.

2.   Butter a shallow baking dish (10 inches long by 2 inches deep is good) with a tablespoon of the butter. Drain the potatoes and dry them with paper towels. Layer half the slices in the bottom of the dish. Sprinkle with salt, pepper, and half the cheese. Repeat with the remaining potatoes, seasoning, and cheese.

3.   Heat the milk and cream to the simmer and pour over the potatoes. Dot the top with the remaining butter and bake in a 375-degree oven for about 1 hour, or until the potatoes are fork tender.

*Good with any plain unsauced roasted meats or birds, and especially good with a leg of lamb.*

# BROCCOLI SAUTÉED WITH GARLIC

Now that broccoli is another of our year-round frozen vegetables, it's hard to realize that it was once known as winter cauliflower. In books as early as Miss Leslie's, "brocoli" was coupled with cauliflower and prepared the same way: Split or quarter the head and tie it together again "before it goes into the pot." The name cauliflower, meaning "flower of the cabbage," comes to us from Italy, as does broccoli, which means "cabbage sprout." Somehow, it seems odd that both cauliflower and broccoli should be children of the cabbage, but so they are.

While the broccoli came to us from Italy (by way of the Orient and Moorish Spain), we have only recently begun to cook the vegetable in an Italian way. Now that the sauté pan has replaced the boiling pot and now that garlic has become socially acceptable, we have learned from the Italians how to sauté the open-sprouted heads of purple and green in garlic and oil. By the same means, we have even developed a taste for the bitter green leaves of the plant called "broccoli rabe" or "rape."

The French way with broccoli, as described in *Julia Child & Company,* is less hearty. The French refinement is to sever stem from bud and to peel the stems severely down to the inner core of white. A quick blanch, a quick roll in browned butter and the broccoli's ready to go.

The Italian way produces a handsomer dish, however, when they keep the stalk and flower together by splitting the stalks lengthwise. The skin is then peeled from floweret to butt end, the stalks are blanched and then finished off in a quick sauté of oil, garlic, and parsley. Unlike the French, Italians often brown their garlic rather than wilt it in oil. For some, the browner the garlic the better because the more bitter. Marcella Hazan, in her *Classic Italian Cook Book,* suggests in her recipe for sautéed broccoli that the garlic be colored lightly, but many of us lovers of hopelessly unclassic American-Italian restaurants long for the bitter black flecks that do something to "winter cauliflower" that nothing else can do.

## Proportions

for 4 servings, 1 head broccoli (about 1½ pounds) to ¼ cup olive oil and 2 to 3 cloves garlic

| | |
|---|---|
| **1 head (1½ pounds) fresh broccoli** | **Salt and freshly ground black pepper to taste** |
| **2 to 3 cloves garlic, minced** | **2 tablespoons minced parsley** |
| **¼ cup olive oil** | |

1. Wash the broccoli and trim off the bottom end of the stalks. Peel the stalks from the flower to the end so that the stalks will cook as quickly as the buds. Split the stalks in halves or quarters, depending on thickness.

2. Bring a large pot of salted water to a boil. Add the broccoli and cook it, uncovered, for 3 to 5 minutes, or until the stalks are just tender but still crunchy. Drain immediately and set aside until ready to serve.

3. In a large frying pan, brown the garlic in the oil for a minute or two. Add the broccoli and salt and pepper, and stir-fry quickly to coat the stalks in oil and to reheat them if necessary. Sprinkle with parsley.

*Serve with a fresh Italian pasta or roasted chicken or beef.*

# GRATED ZUCCHINI SAUTÉ

When early cookbook writers refer to summer squash, they usually mean the greenish white rounds with scalloped edges that we call scallops or patty-pans and that they called *cymlings*. Since their word was based on Latin and Greek for "a swollen sprout," it's not surprising that their word disappeared as the study of Latin and Greek declined. Today, summer squash means usually either yellow straight or crook-necked squash or the striped-green squash we call zucchini. But curiously our cookbooks do not refer to zucchini until the 1940s. Fisher's 1949 *Alphabet for Gourmets* helps explain why when she calls zucchini "the nearest decent gastronomical counterpart to those overgrown pithy garden monsters called vegetable marrows in England."

What the French call *courgettes* and the Italians zucchini is really a dwarf species of the old monster marrows of England. In 1902, Mrs. Rorer described dwarf vegetable marrow as resembling "long narrow cucumbers," much grown in England "but little known in the United States." Eighty years later summer home gardeners could be said to know little else. During the Second World War, home gardeners discovered that the dwarf marrow, with its division of the sexes into male and female, bred like rabbits in their Victory Gardens. Ever since, the problem with zucchini has been one of overpopulation and underconsumption, so much so that one gardener I know throws away the squash and eats only the blossoms, batter-fried and sprinkled with salt.

One advantage of the breeding propensities of the zucchini is that we can afford to crop them young and small. About an inch in diameter is ideal and fortunately more markets now are making them available. As for cooking, Child has always advocated the zucchini sauté, grated plain or with any combination of onions, green and red peppers, garlic, and even fresh spinach leaves. The quickest stir-fry keeps the zucchini crisp, and with the advent of the processor for grating, the zucchini practically leaps from vine to skillet. A few batter-fried flowers on top for garnish will score points for the gardener as well as the cook. But a sprinkling of fresh garden herbs will serve almost as well.

## Proportions

for 4 servings, 4 to 6 small zucchini

| | |
|---|---|
| 4 to 6 small firm zucchini (about 1 pound) | 2 tablespoons minced fresh herbs, such as parsley, |
| ½ teaspoon salt | chervil, tarragon, or 12 |
| 2 tablespoons butter | zucchini blossoms, if |
| 2 tablespoons olive oil | possible |
| Freshly ground black pepper to taste | |

1. Wash the zucchini and trim the ends. Grate by hand or put through the shredding attachment of a processor. Toss the zucchini with the salt in a colander and let sit for 5 to 10 minutes. Put the shredded zucchini in a kitchen towel and twist the ends to squeeze out the liquid, or squeeze by handfuls in heavy-duty paper towels.

2. Heat the butter and oil in a heavy frying pan, add the zucchini, and stir rapidly over high heat for 1 to 3 minutes, just enough to take the raw edge off.

3. Serve them with a sprinkling of black pepper and minced herbs, or make ready a garnish of fried blossoms.

*Note:* To fry blossoms, gently wash and pat dry. Cut off the stems and dip the blossoms in a batter of ⅓ cup flour mixed until smooth with ½ cup water. Deep-fry quickly in enough hot vegetable oil to cover, brown on both sides, drain, and salt.

*With blossoms, the dish is special enough for a first course. Its crispness also makes it a good accessory for sauced meats.*

# *RATATOUILLE*

What is aubergine to France and England is eggplant to us. Tom Stobart, the author of *The Cook's Encyclopaedia*, notes that when he was a boy in India, the first aubergine he ever saw looked exactly like an egg in size, shape, and *color*. So at least the *white* eggplant justifies its name even when it has been largely supplanted by purploid eggs, footballs, and balloons. Miss Leslie advised that "the purple egg plants are better than the white ones" and suggested stewing them with bread crumbs, marjoram, butter, and cloves to be eaten at breakfast rather than dinner.

Since the eggplant came to Europe from India by way of the spice route, it established itself early and plentifully around the Mediterranean, where it was stewed with other plentiful Mediterranean plants, such as onions, zucchini, tomatoes, and peppers. Fisher first knew the mixture as a "Minorcan stew," which you begin by finding some fine fresh vegetables, a large earthen pot and time to contemplate their particular beauties —their shapes, colors, and smells.

Child insisted on the particularity of each kind of vegetable when she introduced us to a French version of *ratatouille* in *Mastering I*. Child cooks each vegetable layer separately, which most cooks don't bother with. Most follow Beard's and Claiborne's method of beginning with onions and garlic, then adding the solid vegetables and ending with the liquid-yielding tomatoes.

I've followed their simpler method below because the virtue of this vegetable stew is that you can vary the ingredients according to what's on hand, and you can vary the cooking time according to what's wanted in the way of texture. A fully integrated mixture takes no more than half an hour for a traditional *ratatouille* but, of course, you can do a crunchy vegetable sauté in half the time.

## Proportions

for 4 to 6 servings, 2 to 3 pounds vegetables

| | |
|---|---|
| 1 **large onion, sliced** | 8 **tomatoes, peeled, seeded,** |
| 3 **cloves garlic, minced** | **and chopped** |
| ⅓ **cup olive oil** | **Salt and freshly ground** |
| 1 **unpeeled eggplant, diced** | **black pepper to taste** |
| 2 **green bell peppers, sliced** | 2 **tablespoons minced parsley** |
| 4 **small zucchini, sliced** | |

1. Sauté the onions and garlic in the oil until wilted. Add the remaining vegetables except the tomatoes and parsley, stir well, and add more oil if necessary (depending on the size of the oil-absorbent eggplant). Cover tightly and simmer for 10 minutes.

2. Add tomatoes and salt and pepper, cover and simmer for 5 minutes longer. Remove the cover, turn up the heat to reduce the liquid, and stir the vegetables until they reach the desired doneness. Sprinkle with parsley before serving hot, cold, or at room temperature.

*You can make a full meal of this, with a soup before, or serve it as a first course or a salad.*

# CUCUMBERS WITH SNOW PEAS

"Cowcumbers" they were in *Martha Washington's Booke of Cookery* and were used mostly for pickling because their summer abundance made for a green in winter dearth. Fresh fried cucumbers, however, were in use from the time of Miss Leslie, who suggested dredging the slices in flour and frying them in butter. By the time of Mrs. Harland, fried cucumbers were *de rigueur*. "Many declare that cucumbers are never fit to eat unless fried," Mrs. Harland declared, "and they are assuredly far more wholesome than when served raw."

American markets have long distinguished between the fat, seedy, watery, and often waxed commercial kind grown year round and the small warty kind grown seasonally and labeled Kirby, or "pickling." The pickling kind are usually better for all purposes. A third kind favored by Europeans and Orientals, a long skinny, nearly seedless hothouse variety called sometimes "English" and sometimes "Chinese," has made a welcome inroad at last among our swollen green truncheons. For taste and texture there is no comparison, and only their high price prevents the European type from being better known here.

The French tend to bake or poach cucumbers to accompany meats as the Japanese steam them to accompany fish. France's newish cuisine has made fried cucumbers fashionable again by cutting them in pale green sticks or ovals as part of their color-coded vegetable array.

Bitterness varies according to breed and age. The only sure test, once again, is to taste. The quickest cure for bitterness is to blanch the cucumber slices for a minute or two, as Beard suggests. But the better method, if you have time, is the old-fashioned one followed by Child in which you salt the slices and let them sit for half an hour to purge them of both water and bitterness at once. Beard's suggestion, however, of sautéing cucumber sticks with snow peas (in *The New James Beard*) is such a good one, and so evocative of both Japanese and new French ways of calling attention to subtle gradations of color and texture, that I have followed it here. We've come a long way from cowcumbers.

## Proportions

for 4 servings, 1 long English or 3 short commercial cucumbers to 1 pound snow peas

| | |
|---|---|
| **1 long English or 3 short commercial cucumbers** | **Salt and freshly ground black pepper to taste** |
| **½ teaspoon salt** | **2 tablespoons chopped fresh mint** |
| **1 pound snow peas** | |
| **3 tablespoons butter** | |

1. The English greenhouse cucumber need not be peeled or seeded, but scooping out the core of tiny seeds will make for more uniform sticks. Cut the long cucumber in 3-inch lengths, split, seed, and cut into slivers ¼ inch thick. Regular cucumbers should be peeled, split, seeded, and cut similarly.

2. Toss the sticks with ½ teaspoon salt and let sit for 30 minutes in a colander. OR blanch quickly, about 2 minutes, in boiling water and drain thoroughly. Either way, pat dry with paper towels.

3. Wash, trim, and string the snow peas. Melt the butter in a wide frying pan like a wok. Add the cucumbers and peas and toss constantly over high heat until the peas turn a brighter green. Season to taste. Sprinkle with fresh mint before serving.

*The cucumbers and the crispness of the podded peas make this a good accompaniment for baked, grilled, or poached fish.*

# GRATED POTATO PANCAKE

Fried potatoes, whether sliced, diced, or chopped raw or boiled, are so much a part of our pioneer and hash-house tradition that they have become *déclassé* during our current Europeanization. But Beard speaks with loving memory of the short-order cooks of his childhood who diced potatoes directly into the hot fat by means of "a 2-pound baking powder can with holes punched in the bottom." They then tossed the dice in the pan until crusty on all sides. "Few potatoes," he says, "ever tasted or looked better to me."

Any potato lover knows that fried raw potatoes are superior in taste and texture to boiled potatoes, chopped or mashed, before hashed. But thrift often made such niceties irrelevant. Often, but not always. Raw peeled potatoes, cut in shavings, and fried in salt pork with tart apples and sliced onions appear in Mrs. Webster's *The Improved Housewife. The Buckeye Cookbook,* too, offers a recipe for Fried Raw Potatoes that is close to Beard's own Hash-Brown Potatoes in *American Cookery,* using the same combination of melted butter and beef drippings to pour over the crisping slices.

But the idea of grated raw potatoes, pressed into a hot frying pan to form a thin crusty pancake browned on both sides, seems to have come to us from German-Jewish traditions. The usual potato pancake in nineteenth-century American cookbooks was made of mashed potatoes, shaped into flat cakes, floured and fried. The German one was grated raw, spread thin in the bottom of a skillet and reversed to brown on the other side.

In *Julia Child & More Company,* Child comes up with a hybrid name, Giant Straw Potato Galette, for what is in effect a grated raw potato pancake. Because the processor makes grating a matter of minutes instead of hours, the recipe is quickly and easily done. This is one recipe in which the cut potatoes should not be soaked in cold water because their starch is needed to bind. Because grated raw potatoes can turn brown with oxidation almost within seconds, the fat must be on the fire before you start to grate. Child suggests clarified butter for the fat, as the watery milk of unclarified butter may cause the potatoes to stick. Another solution is to use beef dripping (from rendered beef suet) or leaf lard or even a little bacon fat instead of all butter. The taste is wonderful and since this is not a diet dish in any way, let taste be your guide.

## Proportions

for 4 servings, 4 Idaho baking potatoes, ⅓ cup of fat

**4 Idaho baking potatoes, peeled and grated**

**6 tablespoons butter, or butter mixed with beef or pork fat**

**Salt and freshly ground black pepper to taste**

1.   Drop the potatoes into cold water as you peel them. Melt the butter in a heavy cast-iron or other nonstick frying pan before you start to grate. Grate the potatoes by hand or by the shredding attachment of a processor. Quickly pat them dry with paper towels and press the potatoes into the hot fat until they mat together.

2.   Sprinkle with salt and pepper and, after 2 or 3 minutes, lower the heat to cook the upper layer. As soon as the bottom is brown enough to stick together, lift the edge of the cake with a spatula to make certain the bottom does not burn.

3.   To turn, slide a spatula under the pancake and slip it onto a large plate or baking sheet. Turn the frying pan upside down over the pancake and reverse it so that the browned side is up. Raise the heat and brown quickly to crisp the underside.

*Especially good with beef roasts or pot roasts or grilled birds, such as quail.*

# PARSNIP PURÉE

Considering their ancient and honorable lineage, parsnips, says James Beard, are one of the most neglected and maligned of vegetables. For Beard, they make a delectable purée, his favorite vegetable at a Thanksgiving feast. For the author of *Martha Washington's Booke of Cookery,* they were good to make a tart of, bedewed with rose water and wine and lemon and sugar and baked in a crust. Mrs. Harland boiled and fried and mashed and creamed and frittered them. Mrs. Rorer, always a bit fancier, made a timbale of them to serve with corned beef or salt fish.

Perhaps their very commonness brought them into disfavor and they became stigmatized as Depression food. Because of their natural sugar, however, they were once prized as a sweetmeat, preserved in honey, and were even used in England for wine-making. But now they are lucky to be chosen for a soup pot or at best for a mixed vegetable sauté. Claiborne was echoing earlier uses when he suggested candying them with brown sugar and orange juice. But if they have been given a new lease recently it is through the vogue for purées that came in with both the processor and the French *nouvelle* vogue.

Beard heads his parsnip crusade with a purée flavored with Madeira, a recipe so central to his strategy that he repeats it in *The New James Beard.* He also gives marketing tips: Avoid stringy roots in favor of fat-topped ones to minimize the waste of woody cores. I remember with revulsion the woody parsnips we were forced to clean from our plates during the Depression dinners of my childhood, so I can speak as a convert only lately enlightened by the possibilities of a creamy white parsnip purée as smooth as rum ice cream.

## Proportions

for 4 servings, 3 pounds parsnips to ¼ pound butter and ¼ cup Madeira

| | |
|---|---|
| 3 **pounds parsnips** | 1 **teaspoon sugar** |
| ¼ **pound (1 stick) butter, melted** | ½ **teaspoon salt** |
| | **Grated nutmeg or ground** |
| 4 **tablespoons heavy cream** | **mace** |
| 4 **tablespoons Madeira** | |

1.   Scrub the roots well and boil unpeeled in salted water to cover, anywhere from 20 to 45 minutes, depending on size. Drain, run under cold water and, when cool enough to handle, trim the ends and peel them. Discard any woody portions.

2.   Cut the parsnips in pieces and put in a food processor with the melted butter, cream, Madeira, sugar, and salt. When completely smooth, transfer to a baking dish and heat for 20 to 30 minutes in a 350-degree oven. Sprinkle with a dusting of nutmeg or mace before serving.

*Especially good with pork or duck, and also game birds, such as pheasant or guinea hen.*

# SOUR SWEET POTATO PURÉE

While the sweet potato and the yam are kissing cousins, the sweet potato and the white potato are related only by name and confusion, the confusion of Spanish and English adventurers confronted by savages and the weird roots they called *batatas.* Like the ginseng root today, "batata" roots of both kinds were once exotic and doubtless full of magic. The white was forbidden in some places for causing leprosy. The sweet was encouraged in some places for its capacity, said Gerard in his *Herbal,* to "comfort, nourish, and strengthen the body, vehemently procuring bodily lust." Conserved in sugar, the sweet potato was a handy after-dinner sweetmeat to satisfy one appetite and provoke another.

Americans tended to do as the Indians did and roasted their sweet potatoes in the ashes. By the time of Mrs. Harland's 1880 *Common Sense,* when the stove had replaced the fireplace, such methods were regarded as quaint but still somehow symbolic of the New World. Mrs. Harland reminds her readers that it was a roasted sweet potato with which General Francis Marion feasted a British officer. "The feast," she explains, "was cleansed from ashes by the negro orderly's shirt-sleeve, and served upon a natural trencher of pine-bark."

Mrs. Rorer outlined ways in which to boil them and bake them, mash them and stuff them and even broil them, but they took on the onus of a low-class food because they were common and, therefore, cheap. In the South that raised them they became the nourishment, both starch and sugar, of the poor. But among traditionalists they have lingered on as symbolic of New World feasting for the annual Thanksgiving table. The candied yam or sweet potato, whipped with egg and milk and put into a pie, was an alternative to pumpkin. The puréed sweet potato, sweetened further by brown sugar and whipped with butter and cream, was an alternative to the mashed white potato.

The problem with the traditional sweet potato casserole, however, is that it is just too damn sweet. For sugar addicts, that is its virtue, and some have been known to gild the lily by dotting the top with marshmallows. For most of us, however, something is needed to cut the sweetness. Claiborne, as a southerner, came up with tangerines in a recipe in his first book. Tangerine segments folded into the purée give a slight tang and a surprising contrast of texture. Yogurt, I've discovered, does the job more completely. So completely, in fact, that the first question a guest asks of the pale creamy lemony purée is, "What is it?" It's a question treasured by a cook, who can then reply, "An old aphrodisiac called sweet batata."

## Proportions

for 6 servings, 6 sweet potatoes (about 2 pounds) to 1 pint of combined yogurt and cream

|   |   |
|---|---|
| 6 sweet potatoes (the dry yellow kind, not the oranger yam) | ¼ teaspoon cinnamon |
|   | ¼ teaspoon nutmeg |
|   | Salt and white pepper to |
| ½ cup heavy cream | taste |
| 1½ cups plain yogurt | 4 tablespoons butter, melted |
| 2 to 3 tablespoons dark brown sugar |   |

1.   Wash the potatoes but do not peel them. Bake them in a 400-degree oven for 40 to 60 minutes, until soft, or boil them in enough water to cover until fork tender. When cool enough to handle, peel and chop.

2.   Put half the potatoes in a processor with half the cream, yogurt, sugar, and spices. (You can adjust sweet or sour by adding more or less yogurt and sugar.) Process until smooth. Repeat with the remaining ingredients.

3.   Whip the two batches together with a heavy wire whisk to make the purée light and pile it into a baking dish. Pour the melted butter over the top. Warm in a 300-degree oven to blend the flavors. Good reheated the same way. Keeps well for 2 or 3 weeks in refrigerator.

*Particularly good with roast turkey or hams.*

# GRAINS

*It will be seen by the charts [Food Materials Obtained for 25¢ or Less] that corn meal, whole-wheat flour, oatmeal, dried peas and beans are*
THE CHEAPEST FOODS.

—*Mrs. Mary Lincoln*
Boston School Kitchen Text-Book
*(1887)*

When beef sirloin was at the top of Mrs. Lincoln's charts at 25 cents a pound, Indian or cornmeal was at the bottom, at 3 cents a pound. Mrs. Lincoln characterized Indian corn as "a cheap, wholesome food, adapted to strong laboring people, and to those who are deficient in natural warmth." Herewith the first law of food snobbery: Whatever is cheapest is scorned. As soon as strong laboring people the world over change blue collars for white, or loincloths for serge suits, they change grains for meat. It is one of the first marks of a change in status.

Because cornmeal was the cheapest of "the cheapest foods" in Mrs. Lincoln's America, cornmeal was the first to go in America's post-Second World War affluence. Dishes requiring cornmeal became quaintly regional, like Philadelphia's Scrapple or Boston's Indian Pudding or Carolina's Corn Dodgers. After the war, dried corn, as distinct from fresh green corn on the cob, was principally used for toy food like popcorn or cornflakes. Gone were the mills for grinding the meal by stones and gone were the tubs of lye, made from wood ash and water, to soak and bleach the hulls from corn to make "hominy." Corn as a grain, the commonest and cheapest grain in a country which produces over half the world's crop, was the one grain that was definitely "out."

Other grains were "in," principally grains with exotic connections—such as wheat from the Middle East or rice from the Far East. By the dictionary, the word "corn" means "grain": that is, the seed or kernel of any cereal plant. In England, "corn" means the most common grain, which is wheat; in Scotland, oats; in America, maize. Because maize is the grain native to the Americas and cultivated by its inhabitants for at least 3,000 years, familiarity had to breed contempt.

After the war, health food stores began to burgeon with exotic grains that were supposedly good for you because they had not been milled to death. There was the cracked wheat called variously bulgar or bulghur, from the Middle East. There was the husked buckwheat called kasha, or buckwheat groats, from Russia. There was brown rice, the unpolished, unskinned seeds of the cereal grass that was a latecomer to America, not arriving until 1694. And there was the most prestigious—because the most expensive—wild rice, not a cereal at all but a marsh grass native to the ponds and lakes of Minnesota.

The biggest change, however, was in America's exchange of corn for rice. The exchange repeated an exchange that took place some five centuries earlier when the Spanish and Portuguese took corn from America to Europe and Asia and when the English, eventually, brought rice to the colonies and planted it in South Carolina. From then on, rice was considered to be a southern food, so that to cook it at all was to cook it, as Mrs. Webster cooked it in her *Improved Housewife*, in the "Southern Manner of Boiling Rice." Mrs. Lincoln gives another clue to its regional association when she says, "It is cheap, and is largely used by people in very hot climates." That in itself rules out any place north of Dixie, but she qualifies further: "It should always be used with milk, egg, or some fatty substance, and is a suitable summer diet." Rice, it seems, came to American cooking by way of the English rice pudding. Nineteenth-century American cookbooks are full of rice pudding recipes for dessert, but for a filling starch to accompany meats, the potato from the old cold sod of Ireland had it all over rice from Kandy and Cathay.

Today, Mrs. Lincoln would be astonished at the number and variety of rice recipes that pack the cookbooks of our current masters: rice Pilaf, Oriental, Persian, Risotto Milanese, Paella, Indonesian, Caribbean, Feijoda, rice from dozens of very hot climates. She would be surprised at the variety of rice kernels themselves: long-grain, short-grain, converted, instant, Arborio from Italy, Basmati from India. She would be more respectful of the fact that rice comes in 10,000 varieties and that rice has been cultivated for some 5,000 years in the Far East and for half that time in the Near East. And she might even agree that it is about time that rice caught up with the potato on American menus.

The alternative food to the seeds of grains or grasses is that large family known as legumes. The family of *leguminosae* is so very large that from its 12,000 species it furnishes the bulk of protein for the world's population of people and animals. Many members of the family are not edible, but when they are we call their edible pods "legumes." And we call the edible seeds within "pulses." Beans are the most common form of pulses, then peas and then lentils.

The most common native American bean is the small white bean called "pea bean" or "navy bean," and the slightly larger variety called the Great Northern bean. This is the bean that the Indians of the Northeast would dry and cook in a bean hole. They would bury a container of beans in a hole heated by stones or embers for a slow simmering with syrup from maple sap and with fat from a plump skinned bear. The bean pot came out of the ground and into the oven with Boston Baked Beans, but the tradition of sweet and fat for flavoring lingered on until Campbell replaced the pot with the can.

The biggest change in American bean use again came from the East, in the displacement of dried beans white, green, red, and black with the soybean, dried, pressed, curded, and sprouted. The triple wave of health food fans, vegetarians, and religious cultists has brought tofu down from the Zen mountain and into the marketplace of middle America, even into the heart of the corn belt itself. Where dried beans were once a cheap protein substitute for meat, now bean curd is demonstrating its versatility toward the same end as it is smoked, fried, and grilled. For the moment, the soybean is benefiting from a reverse snobbery where the cheapest is best, as long as it has the glamour of the unfamiliar. One of the latest crazes is tofu (bean curd) ice cream. But the progression from Western corn to Eastern soy has its own kind of logic. Now that corn dodgers are more remote to the current palate than soybean curd en brochette, who knows? Maybe the products of Indian meal will regain status as the handiwork of our own ancient native tribes.

# POLENTA WITH CHEESE AND CHILIES

While cornmeal mush is definitely "out," polenta is "in." Polenta, of course, is cornmeal mush, but its Italian name suggests the romance of earthy peasant villages rather than a Depression kitchen redolent of Ovaltine and Vick's Vapo-Rub. Fisher, in *How to Cook a Wolf*, tried to make a case for polenta by claiming the Italians use a coarser "grind" for their meal, but the meal is the same wherever stones are used for the milling. Health food stores today supply us with good stone-ground meal, white and yellow, with plenty of crunch and character, so that we don't have to use the machine-milled degerminated product that our forefathers welcomed as a refinement.

The difference between cornmeal mush and polenta, Beard claims, is in the making. The Italians add cornmeal slowly in a thin steady stream to a pot of boiling water, stirring constantly, so that the water absorbs the meal gradually. Actually this is also the method of such American stalwarts as Mrs. Sarah Rorer, who suggests allowing the meal "to run slowly through the fingers, while you stir with the other hand."

The point with cornmeal is to avoid lumps, so the basic method of Italian or American is the same: to dissolve the meal first over direct heat, then to cook the meal slowly over indirect heat—a double boiler or a corner of a wood-burning stove. Claiborne doesn't list cornmeal mush, but his recipe for Basic Polenta is the same as Beard's. After an initial softening, dissolve the meal in boiling water over direct heat in the top half of a double boiler; then put the top over boiling water to steam slowly.

Where polenta does differ from cornmeal mush is in its uses. Americans traditionally have eaten cornmeal mush like porridge for breakfast, hot, with a big pat of butter. Or, they have molded it, chilled it, sliced it, and fried it until crisp and brown, and doused it with maple syrup. The combination is like a quick Indian pudding or like a corn-flavored version of French toast or pancakes or waffles. It was my favorite childhood breakfast, as it was one of Beard's, and the old-fashioned tradition held until the war took GIs to Italy and polenta.

The advantage of mush or polenta is that you use the meal as a binder, like rice, for other ingredients, spicy things like sausages or creamy things like cheese. Beard in *The New James Beard* suggests Polenta with Fontina Cheese, with Spinach, with Salt Cod. Claiborne suggests Polenta with Gorgonzola or Bel Paese. But a suggestion of Fisher's is one I like best, perversely perhaps, because it returns polenta to American roots by combining it with an American cheese like Monterey goat cheese. The addition of a Mexican green chili, a mild one like Poblano used in Chili Rellenos, cuts the blandness of both meal and cheese, and reminds us that Italian polenta came originally from American Indian corn.

## Proportions

for 6 servings, 1½ cups cornmeal, 1 cup of cheese, 2 green chilies

4½ cups water
1½ cups yellow or white cornmeal, stone-ground if possible
1 teaspoon salt
1 cup diced Monterey Jack cheese

2 to 4 green canned Poblano chili peppers
4 tablespoons butter
4 tablespoons grated Parmesan cheese

1. Stir 1 cup of cold water into the cornmeal in the top half of a double boiler and mix until smooth. Bring the remaining water to boil in a separate pan and pour it into the cornmeal. Stirring constantly, cook directly over low heat until the mixture comes to a boil. Add the salt. Put the top over the lower part of the double boiler to steam, covered, for about 1 hour.

2. Stir in the diced cheese, diced peppers, and butter. Stir until the cheese and butter are melted. Pour into a buttered baking dish, smooth the top, and sprinkle with Parmesan cheese. If you are serving immediately, run the dish under the broiler to brown the cheese. You can also

keep the dish warm in a heated oven for as long as you want or you can reheat it when needed.

*A good dish for a simple luncheon but also a fine rich companion to grilled hot sausages, pork chops, roasts, or braised beef.*

# RICE: WHITE/BROWN/WILD

The simple old-fashioned way of boiling rice, in the Southern Manner, was outlined by Miss Eliza Leslie in what she called "a Carolina receipt." You were to pick the rice clean and wash it before boiling it vigorously in a large pot of water, which you then drained. "Afterwards," she said, "set the sauce-pan in the chimney-corner with the lid off, while you are dishing your dinner, to allow the rice to dry, and the grains to separate." We don't need to wash rice anymore because we don't buy it from barrels or sacks at the general store but in clean sealed packages. Otherwise, the general method is still valid: Follow a fast rolling boil with a quick dry. Beard suggests boiling rice for 15 minutes before draining, then drying it for 2 or 3 minutes, and finally fluffing it up with a fork. This is the simplest foolproof way of producing rice that is never gummy because the grains have been boiled in a quantity of water to remove their thin coating of starch.

The second way is to parboil and then steam. This is the way suggested by Fisher and Child. "There are two ways to boil rice correctly," Fisher wrote in 1942 and amended in 1951: "How arbitrary can you be? I should have said: 'I *think* there are . . !' " To parboil, you pour a cup of rice into a lot of boiling salted water "and let it race around until a grain of it smashes between the fingers." Child suggests the proportions of 2 cups rice and 2 tablespoons salt to 4 quarts boiling water and a cooking time of 8 to 9 minutes until the grains are not quite fully tender: "Bite into several grains to be sure." She then suggests draining in a colander and rinsing in hot water to remove any remaining starch. It's well to remember that the water in which rice was boiled was once used for making "a good starch for muslin." Child then finishes off the rice by setting the colander over a steam kettle, covering the rice with a damp towel to keep it from drying out, and letting it steam about 10 minutes just before serving. The advantage here is that you can parboil rice hours ahead and reheat by steaming at the last moment.

There is yet a third way to boil rice "correctly," and that is the way followed by most rice packagers in their directions printed on the box. Roughly the formula is twice as much water as rice, brought to a quick boil, stirred once and simmered, covered, over low heat for a specified time. There are problems with this method. The cooking time specified is usually too long and there is nothing to prevent the starch from gumming the grains together. It is the least foolproof of methods.

The most foolproof *and* the most flavorful involves yet a fourth way to boil rice "correctly," and that is the method called variously pilaf and pilau after its Middle Eastern origins. Actually it is a method of braising rice, rather than boiling it, because you first sauté the kernels in butter, which lightly browns the coating of rice flour and guarantees that each and every grain will be separate and equal. For this reason Claiborne and Franey call this method the way to produce A Perfect Batch of Rice. The only disadvantage to the method is that often you need plain white rice rather than golden flavored rice.

The main trouble with brown rice is that it's no substitute for white rice, but tastes and acts like a different sort of grain entirely. To health-fooders it's a far superior grain because it carries with it the coat it was born with, but to most of the world's rice-eaters (of whom there are more than any other kind and for whom rice is often the only food) the coat is an excrescence. What matters are the tiny nude pearls within, stripped of their wrappings like nymphets in a boudoir. So little does mere nutritional need govern our responses to food that white rice has stood for the conquest of nature by art for as long as men have harvested it. While white rice has a rich culinary tradition dating back to our most ancient civilizations, brown rice has none at all. Brown rice is a modern "invention."

The main limitation of brown rice is that it lacks the versatility of white and speaks in its own rough voice of husky grains like the groats of buckwheat or wheat. Brown rice is simple enough to cook, boiled or parboiled and steamed, just as you would cook white rice, only it takes twice as long. If you boil white rice in a kettle of water for 15 minutes, boil brown rice for 30. Like white, brown should not be cooked to a mush and, like white, brown benefits from a lavish dollop of butter.

Until recently, wild rice came close to being an authentic "natural" food because it actually grew wild in the shallows of the Great Lakes and because it was harvested by Indians in their time-honored way of shaking grain from stalk as they passed in their canoes. While the rice is now less wild than cultivated, it is still grown and harvested almost exclusively by the Indians of the Chippewa White Earth Reservation. Its expense is a result of its hand-picked tribal source.

According to the letter of an early trader, quoted by Waverley Root in *Food,* the Chippewas prepared wild rice the way the Algonquins prepared beans. "When it is Cleaned, fit four youse," the trader scrawled, "They Boile it as we Due Rise and Eat it with Bairs greas and Sugar." In these latter days of fancier restaurants and duller orthography, we omit sugar or other mapled sweetness and substitute butter for bear's grease. But it still needs to be washed and boiled, taking slightly longer to boil than white rice and slightly less than brown. Because its character is so distinct, it is excellent plain or mixed with white and brown rice. Beard suggests other mixing variants, like toasted walnuts or pine nuts, goose fat and mushrooms, or bacon and minced onions, when your larder runs short of bear's grease and sugar.

# BOILED WHITE RICE
## Proportions

for 4 to 6 servings, 1½ cups of rice to 4 quarts of water

| | |
|---|---|
| **4 quarts water** | **1½ cups long-grain Carolina** |
| **1 tablespoon salt** | **rice** |

Bring the water to a boil and add the salt. Pour the rice in gradually, so that the water continues to boil vigorously. Boil uncovered for about 15 minutes (bite into a kernel after 12 minutes to test). Drain in a colander and shake well. The rice should be fluffy but not splayed. Serve plain or with melted butter.

*You can use boiled rice interchangeably with steamed rice as a base for the full spectrum of food from soups to puddings.*

# STEAMED WHITE RICE
## Proportions

1½ cups of rice to 4 quarts of water

| | |
|---|---|
| **4 quarts water** | **1½ cups long-grain Carolina** |
| **1 tablespoon salt** | **rice** |

1. Bring the water to a boil and add the salt. Pour the rice in gradually, so that the water continues to boil vigorously. Boil, uncovered, for 7 or 8 minutes, or until the rice is not quite tender but still chewy. Drain in a colander and rinse under cold water to stop the cooking and remove any starch.

2. Fifteen minutes before serving, cover the colander with a lid or towel and set over a kettle of boiling water to steam for 10 to 15 minutes. Toss the rice with a fork to fluff it up.

# BOILED OR STEAMED BROWN RICE

## Proportions

for 4 to 6 servings, 2 cups of rice to 4 quarts of water

Use the same method as above, but cook twice as long: 30 minutes for boiled rice, 15 minutes for parboiling steamed rice. Where white rice will triple in quantity, brown rice will only double.

*Good with distinctive meats like beef heart or kidneys or with strong roast birds like duck.*

# WILD RICE

## Proportions

for 4 to 6 servings, 1½ cups of rice to 4½ cups of water

4½  cups water
1½  teaspoons salt
1½  cups wild rice

**Freshly ground black pepper to taste**

1.   Wash the rice in cold running water until the water runs clear. Bring 4½ cups of water to a boil and add the salt. Pour in the rice all at once and return rapidly to a boil.
2.   Stir the rice once with a fork, cover the pan, and reduce the heat to low. Cook, covered, for about 20 minutes, or until the grains puff and are tender but still slightly chewy. Season with freshly ground black pepper before serving.

*Classic with game birds like quail or Rock Cornish hens, but also good with domesticated turkey.*

# BRAISED WHITE RICE

This is the method favored by Claiborne and Franey to produce "A Perfect Batch of Rice," the method usually labeled Rice Pilaf or Pilau. The Claiborne-Franey formula does indeed produce a consistently good-textured, good-flavored rice that can be eaten on its own or as an accompaniment to flesh, fish, or fowl.

## Proportions

for 4 servings, 1 cup of rice to 1½ cups of liquid

| | | | |
|---|---|---|---|
| 2 | tablespoons butter | Pinch of cayenne pepper | |
| ¼ | cup minced onion | 1 bay leaf | |
| 1 | cup long-grain Carolina rice | ¼ teaspoon dried thyme | |
| | Salt and freshly ground black pepper to taste | 1½ cups chicken stock or broth | |

1.   Melt the butter in a saucepan and cook the onions briefly until they are soft. Add the rice and stir until the grains change color and become milky white (2 to 3 minutes). Add the salt, pepper, cayenne, bay leaf, and thyme.

2.   Bring the stock to a boil and pour it over the rice. Cover tightly and bake in a 400-degree oven for 17 minutes. Or, cook over low heat on top of the stove. Either way, don't uncover the pot for 17 minutes to keep in the steam. When uncovered, rice should be served immediately.

# ITALIAN *RISOTTO*

Since *riso* is the Italian word for rice, *risotto* refers to their typical way of sautéing in butter or olive oil and simmering in stock to make a European form of Braised Rice. But what makes *risottos* in Italy special is first the kind of rice they use and second the method by which they add liquid to it. Unlike our long-grain Carolina rice, the rice most favored by the Italians is the short-grain Arborio of *superfino* quality. It absorbs more liquid than other kinds and slowly swells to become plump and creamy. The creaminess is what distinguishes a well-made *risotto* and makes it a high-class dish worthy to be flavored by white truffles or fresh seafood or colored by saffron.

The Italian method is to add liquid gradually as the rice absorbs more and more until, finally, the plumped grains can hold no more. That is the moment the rice is done, usually about 25 to 30 minutes, resulting in a grain that is slightly *al dente* in the way that a well-cooked pasta is. The liquid should be of first quality, usually a chicken or fish stock, sometimes combined with white wine. Parmesan cheese is an unvarying requirement. Because the stock-swollen rice is rich in itself, it makes a good one-dish meal for lunch or supper, especially when it is made to contain nuggets of shrimp and scallops and clams, or strips of chicken breast or of smoked salmon or asparagus tips. If you add seafood, use fish stock instead of chicken.

*Risotto,* as Fisher advises, "can be made plain or fancy, and named for any town between Milano and Los Angeles, according to the wind and the weather and what is in the cupboard."

## Proportions

for 4 servings, 1½ cups of rice to 3½ to 4 cups of liquid

4 tablespoons butter
1 small onion, minced (¼ cup)
1½ cups Italian white rice, superfino Arborio if possible
Salt and freshly ground black pepper to taste

½ teaspoon saffron threads (optional)
¼ cup dry white wine
4 cups chicken stock or broth
½ cup grated Parmesan cheese

    1.  Melt the butter in a casserole and cook the onion until wilted. Add the rice and stir until the grains are coated and translucent. Add the salt, pepper, saffron, and white wine and stir until the wine is absorbed.

    2.  Bring the stock to a simmer and keep it at a simmer while adding 1 cup to the rice, stirring until the stock is absorbed. Repeat with a second cup, then add stock ½ cup at a time, stirring the rice gently over moderate heat, until the rice is plump, creamy, and tender (about 25 to 30 minutes). When done, gently stir in half the cheese with a fork and pass the rest in a dish.

*    This is a completely filling main dish that goes well with a vegetable or green salad and is best concluded with a bowl of ripe fruit.*

# PERSIAN RICE

    Persia, or, as it is now called, Iran, grows and cooks some of the best rice in the world. It is the rice from which India makes its *birianis* and the Middle East its *pilafs*. It is the rice we know as Basmati and that Persians know, in its highest grade, as *domsiah,* or royal rice. A royal way of preparing it is to soak, parboil, and then steam its long curved grains in butter in a lining of crusty potatoes. Often the rice is flavored with dill, but dill is not necessary to the sumptuousness of a rice that has slaked its thirst on butter.

## Proportions

for 6 to 8 servings, 2 cups of rice to ¾ cup of butter to ½ cup of fresh dill

| 2 cups rice, Basmati if possible | 1 to 2 Idaho potatoes |
| 4 tablespoons salt | ½ cup chopped fresh dill, or 2 |
| ¾ cup (1½ sticks or 12 | tablespoons dried |
| tablespoons) butter, melted | |

1. Put the rice in a strainer and wash in cold running water until the water is fairly clear. Soak the rice with salt in cold water to cover for 1 to 2 hours before cooking.

2. Drain the salted water into a large kettle, add 3 to 4 quarts more water, and bring to a boil. Add the rice gradually and boil vigorously for about 5 minutes, or until the rice is tender on the outside but chewy on the inside. Drain immediately and rinse with cold water to stop the cooking.

3. Melt the butter and pour a small amount of it into the bottom of a casserole to film it. Peel and slice the potatoes into ¼-inch-thick slices, enough to cover the bottom of the casserole in a single crowded layer.

4. Mix the dill gently into the rice with a fork and heap the rice in a cone-shaped mound on top of the potatoes. Pour the rest of the butter over the rice (the cone shape helps even distribution) and cook over medium heat until the rice starts to steam.

5. Cover with a small bath towel (or other absorbent kind of towel) before covering with a lid. Seal the lid by covering with a double layer of foil so that no steam escapes. Steam for about 45 minutes.

6. To serve, heap the rice on a platter and garnish with a layer of potato slices, which should be beautifully crusted from the butter. If they are not, raise the heat briefly to finish them. (You can make this dish without potatoes and then it is the rice that becomes crusty on the bottom, deliciously so, but the potatoes also release water for steam.)

*The quantity of butter makes this a rich rice dish that goes well with grilled meats, such as kebabs (page 254), and broiled fish or chicken.*

# KASHA WITH MUSHROOMS

When a nutty grain is wanted, I find the husked whole grains of buckwheat, made into the groats the Russians call *kasha,* far tastier than brown rice. Buckwheat is not a true cereal, but the seed of a starch plant that did not migrate from Russia to western Europe until the fifteenth century, when it became known as "Saracen corn." It has kept its Russian associations in this country because it was sold largely in Russian Jewish delicatessens or restaurants before health food stores introduced it to a larger grain-hungry populace.

Kasha is so strong in character that it can stand happily alone with hot butter or sour cream or, as Fisher says her daughter liked it, cold with brown sugar and sweet cream. Fisher also suggests substituting chicken fat or goose fat for butter or adding gamy flavors like the drippings from wild pheasants which, she admits, constitutes "a blatant example of rich-bitch deviation from a basically 'poor' recipe." Mushrooms don't suffer from the same class adhesions, even though few have plucked them for free in any thicket wilder than a crowded supermarket aisle. Mushrooms, nevertheless, taste of the woods and steppes in which we can imagine fields of Saracen grain.

## Proportions

for 4 servings, 1 cup of buckwheat groats to 2 cups of liquid to 1 egg

| | |
|---|---|
| 1 **cup buckwheat groats** | **Salt to taste** |
| 1 **egg, beaten** | ¼ **pound mushrooms** |
| 2 **cups boiling mixed or beef stock** | 6 **tablespoons butter** |

1. Heat the groats in a heavy frying pan or Dutch oven. Add the beaten egg and stir vigorously to coat each grain and toast it slightly. Add the boiling stock and salt, cover, and lower the heat. Simmer (or bake in a 350-degree oven) for 30 minutes.

2. Meanwhile, slice and sauté the mushrooms quickly in the butter to brown them. Add at the last moment to the cooked buckwheat, adding more butter if needed.

*This makes a healthy luncheon dish on its own but is also a good alternative to costly wild rice when a distinctive grain is needed.*

# BULGHUR

From the Middle East comes the cracked wheat sold in America as bulghur and in England as burghul. Since it is a whole wheat kernel that is cracked open by boiling rather than milling, anybody can make bulghur by boiling, drying, and then grinding the kernels in a coffee mill. But recently the boxed product has become more available through health-food and quality-food stores and through the increased popularity of Middle East specialities like *tabbouleh,* where bulghur is mixed cold with olive oil, lemon, onion, and parsley and served with pita bread. I like it best of any of the nutty crunchy berries, plain, with plenty of butter.

## Proportions

for 4 servings, 1 cup of cracked wheat to 2 cups of liquid

| 3 tablespoons butter | 2 cups boiling chicken stock or |
| 1 small onion, minced (2 | broth |
| tablespoons) | Salt and freshly ground black |
| 1 cup cracked wheat | pepper to taste |

1.  Melt the butter and cook the onion until soft. Add the wheat and stir to coat and slightly toast the grains. Add the boiling stock and seasonings and return to a boil.

2.  Cover tightly, lower the heat, and steam gently for about 15 minutes. Like rice, wheat should be tender but not mushy and the liquid should all be absorbed. Cracked wheat reheats well by sautéing or steaming.

*This is a grain that can be eaten as a cereal for breakfast, a protein for lunch, and a starch for dinner. Good as a bread, rice, or potato substitute.*

# AMERICAN PORK AND BEANS

There's no reason why Boston should get all the credit for a dish as widespread in this country and as venerable as baked beans, usually with pork and often without molasses. In her *Frugal Housewife*, Mrs. Lydia Child calls for a pound of pork to a quart of beans, but says not a word about molasses. She does, however, call for pepper: "A little pepper sprinkled among the beans, when they are placed in the bean-pot, will render them less unhealthy." The digestive effects of beans remained a problem and many suggested adding baking soda or saleratus to counter them. I have not found that pepper or anything else renders beans less "unhealthy," but pepper, and especially hot pepper, flavors them better to my taste than molasses.

Beard is of the anti-molasses school and cites recipes from mesdames Crowen, Rorer, and Harland in support of an unsweetened bean pot. To those for whom no bean pot is complete without molasses or maple or brown sugar, Child gives a good Boston recipe in *Child & Company,* which balances the sweet of molasses with the acid of tomato purée and the spice of Dijon mustard.

In the recipe below I have forgone any sweetener in favor of a southern trick of adding a little vinegar to cut the blandness of beans and enforcing it with hot pepper. Smoked ham hocks, if available, are another southern touch that makes the bean stock richer. The result is a bean dish that is closer to one of the great bean dishes of France, the *cassoulet* of Toulouse.

The small white beans we call pea beans or navy beans, or the larger white Great Northern beans, are traditional for the bean pot, but there's no reason to limit ourselves to one kind in America's abundance of dried beans. I used five kinds among those suggested below to see how they would mix and to lend variety to the main ingredient itself. I found that the split peas dissolved in the cooking and made a good thickening for the other beans that remained distinct and interestingly different.

## Proportions

for 10 to 12 servings, 2 pounds of beans to 4 cups of onions and 2 ham hocks

| | |
|---|---|
| 2 **pounds assorted dried beans or peas, such as pea or navy, Great Northern, lima, kidney, pinto, black beans, split green or black-eyed peas (1 cup equals ½ pound, so estimate accordingly)** | 2 **cloves garlic, minced** |
| | 2 **smoked ham hocks, or ½ pound salt pork with rind** |
| | 1 **tablespoon wine vinegar** |
| | 1 **small hot red pepper, minced** |
| | 1 **tablespoon salt or to taste** |
| | 2 **bay leaves** |
| 2 **large onions, diced (4 cups)** | 1 **teaspoon thyme** |

1. Wash the beans and pick over carefully to remove any small stones. Soak overnight in cold water to cover or use the quick-soak method: Bring the beans quickly to a boil, boil, uncovered, for 2 minutes, remove from the heat, cover, and let sit for 1 hour.

2. Add the remaining ingredients and enough water to cover. Bring to a boil, skim, and simmer, covered, for about 20 minutes, or until the beans are just tender but firm. Bake in a covered bean pot or casserole in a low oven (275 degrees) for 2 to 3 hours. Pea beans can cook 8 to 10 hours without pulping, but other varieties will soften and become too mushy with long cooking.

*Traditional with hearty American baked meats like ham but nowadays better used as a substitute for ham, particularly when accompanied by wilted collard or dandelion greens.*

# LENTILS WITH HERBS AND SPICES

The seeds known as lentils have traveled East and West from the Middle East in coats of brown or green, concealing interiors of yellow, salmon, red, and cream. The tiny green ones from the Auvergne in France seldom make it to America, but we grow our own rather large brown ones in Oregon and Washington and package them for supermarkets. We can buy the small red ones (originally from Egypt) in specialty stores and these are the ones most commonly available in England and the Continent, where lentils have long been an alternative to beans and rice.

Because lentils are high in protein and are cheap to grow and harvest, they are a staple in India where many people eat little else. In America, vegetarians have made lentils more popular here by making them aromatic with herbs and spices in the Eastern manner. In *The New New York Times Cookbook,* Claiborne includes one of the most traditional of India's many lentil dishes, this one with lemon. Use supermarket lentils if you must, but not the quick-cooking kind unless you have to; and if you can, get the small red Egyptian kind.

## Proportions

for 6 servings, 1 pound of lentils to 5 cups of liquid

1 pound lentils, Egyptian if possible
1 medium onion, finely chopped
4 tablespoons butter or peanut oil
1 cinnamon stick, broken in pieces
2 cloves garlic, minced
1 teaspoon minced fresh gingerroot
5 cups diluted chicken broth (half stock, half water), heated

1 bay leaf
1 teaspoon turmeric
1 teaspoon salt
⅛ teaspoon freshly ground black pepper
1 small hot chili pepper, or ¼ teaspoon cayenne pepper
1 whole lemon
¼ cup chopped fresh coriander or parsley for garnish

1.   Wash the lentils and pick them over carefully. Cook the onion in the oil or butter until it is wilted. Add the cinnamon, garlic, and ginger and stir for 2 or 3 minutes. Add the lentils and hot broth and bring to a simmer. Add the remaining ingredients with the exception of the lemon and coriander, cover, and simmer for 30 to 40 minutes.

2.   Slice the lemon, remove the seeds, and add the slices to the lentils. Cover and simmer for 5 to 10 minutes longer, or until the lentils are tender but not mushed. Serve with a sprinkling of fresh coriander. (You can vary the amount of hot pepper to taste.)

*A satisfying meal by itself, but the dish goes well with a traditional Eastern meal, such as lamb—roasted, stewed, or ground for kebabs.*

# BREADS

*In most households, I am very sorry to say, the hands are still used for the purpose of kneading. A kneading machine is much more hygienic. It is almost impossible to make the hands sterile, and at the same time safe for bread kneading. Materials for the thorough cleansing of the hands would be poisonous to the food.*

—Sarah Tyson Rorer
Mrs. Rorer's New Cook Book
*(1902)*

I n 1900, the American housewife, unlike her counterpart in France or England, did all her own baking at home, kneading the weekly supply of bread with her all too human hands. In 1900, the age-old process of kneading, proofing, and baking bread was fraught with hazard because of the recent discovery of an invisible and therefore infinitely dangerous poison—the germ. The whitest purest loaf was unhygienic. The wheat "germ" had fortunately been got rid of in the milling, along with the dyspeptic bran, but there was still the yeast. Yeast, as described by Mrs. Lincoln in her *Boston School Kitchen Text-Book,* is "a germ of the fungus tribe, of which mould, mildew, etc., are familiar forms."

All *too* familiar, the housewife might have said, tossing out the mildewed loaf, opening the bin of rancid weevil-infested flour, and adding a lump of pearl-ash to the bottle of corked yeast that had gone sour at the end of the week. If the dough she had set to rise overnight had also gone sour by the morning, she might sprinkle on more pearl-ash and knead it in with septic fingers. But why bother with the nasty fungus tribe at all? Why bother with the hops and malt and rye and potato and molasses and all the bottling when the ferment got lively, but not too lively to explode the bottle? The yeast that brewed bread brewed other poisons, like beer and wine. Why not forget yeast and use only the purifying pearl-ash to leaven dough? Pearl-ash could be got as easy as flour, first as saleratus, then baking soda, and by mid-nineteenth century —with a little added acid—as baking powder.

Bread-making was hard enough without the germs of yeast. First there was the problem of firing the bake oven with the "pine wood, fagots, brush, and such light stuff," that Mrs. Lydia Child advised for thrifty housewives. Then there was the problem of temperature. "A smart fire for an hour and a half is a general rule for common sized family-ovens," Lydia Child advised. To test the heat, the housewife should throw a little flour on the oven floor, once it was cleared of coals. If the flour burns black, "the heat is too furious." If brown, just right. Once the loaves were in, a housewife fearful of scorching them might "wet an old broom two or three times, and turn it round near the top of the oven till it dries."

And even if the housewife conquered the hazards of yeast and heat, what with the changes in the weather and the children and the cow down sick and Pa home drunk, the weekly bread might still turn out sour, heavy, ill-baked, unpalatable, unwholesome, and "not to be eaten." Even before the discovery of the germ made kneading and baking a danger to health, the home baker was warned by Miss Eliza Leslie: "These accidents so frequently happen when bread is made at home by careless, unpractised or incompetent persons, that families who live in cities or towns will generally risk less and save more, by obtaining their bread from a professional baker."

Considering the logic of her advice it's amazing how few housewives followed it. In 1900, 95 percent of the flour sold in America was bought by the American housewife still stubbornly baking at home. It took two world wars, a Depression, a sexual and an urban revolution to persuade the American housewife that time spent baking was time ill spent. It took almost a century to reverse the statistics, so that by 1970 only 15 percent of the flour sold in America was bought by a person baking at home. The professionals had won. But the professionals were not bakers. They were chemists or, as they prefer to be called, "food engineers." And in their laboratories they created a test-tube product as pure, white, and sanitized as the product it most resembles, the one housewives are warned please not to squeeze.

This was the century of the Great Bread Murder. And who killed the American Loaf? The purists, the professionals, the pressed-for-time. Of these three, the pressed-for-time mattered most. Time was the enemy to be conquered and destroyed. Instant baking began with the commercial ready-mix of baking soda and cream of tartar to make baking powder. Instead of the slow loaf, better the fast bread, pancake, and biscuit, biscuit so quick you could call a ready-mix Bisquick. If you were stuck with yeast, still you could buy it ready-made, since 1868, in a square of foil. Since yeast brewed faster with sugar, add sugar. Since two risings were faster than three, cut them to two. Since gas and electricity were faster than wood and coal, throw out the old oven. Come to think of it, why bake at all? Why sully the purity of hands cleansed by emollients guaranteed to be 99 and $\frac{9}{10}$ths percent pure and softened by lotions guaranteed to bleach their dishpan redness white as flour?

There was a fourth killer of the American loaf and that was poverty. When bread in the nineteenth century became the meat and potatoes of the poor, England, with its highly stratified class distinctions, led the way in discriminating rich from poor on the basis of color. White signified "upper" in bread as in class, race, and creed. To forsake the coarse, the black, the brown, the germ-laden, was to join the refined, and millions of the industrial poor died of malnutrition in that forlorn hope. White bread was here to stay. White bread was a wonder that might magically beget social rise.

That the WASP loaf is now déclassé among the privileged is an irony peculiar to social castes and the perversities of history. Today, home baking itself is the labor of the leisure, not the working, classes. The working-class man or woman does not have time for bread because what leisure he has he would rather spend in other time-consuming activities. Bread takes its own sweet time and that is one of its pleasures for people who have it. Bread-making may end as the dalliance of kings, even as it is now a hobby of the middle and upper classes, and of those too young or too old to be fully and gainfully employed. But meantime, we have discovered that in today's high-tech kitchens anybody can make bread that is neither sour, heavy, ill-baked, nor unpalatable. Nor need it be sweet, bleached, sterile, and dead, lined in rows in cellophane coffins and laid to rest in supermarket morgues.

Bread that is alive is full of germs, wheat germs and yeast germs and other strange ferments, that grow and decay as do the human hands that have warmed and massaged and pounded and shaped the dough that made the loaf. Those who want the living loaf have discovered both its cost in time and its rewards in pleasure, in being in touch literally with a changing *brew* from which bread takes its name. In the last decade there have been more books devoted to bread-making in all of its processes than to any other single food. In the last five years, there have been more kinds of flour available from hard and soft wheats, whole wheats, ryes and barleys and oats, and available from different kinds of mills, with germ, with bran, without bleach, without additives. In the last year an unbleached, hard-wheat high-gluten sack actually labeled "Bread Flour" sits on the supermarket shelf beside the sack of all-purpose flour. Is there hope that murder will out, at last, and that the smell of good bread baking will once again corrupt a deodorized land?

# THE ALL-WHITE AMERICAN LOAF

The traditional American loaf is essentially the English loaf, as it evolved through nineteenth-century industrialization. While the Continent retained its taste for dark and coarse loaves of rye, pumpernickel, and whole-grained wheat, England at the vanguard of progress and technology assumed the burden of an all-white loaf along with other white man's burdens. Refinement was the key, as far removed from *lumpen* peasantry as possible. In terms of bread, refinement meant a fine, light, tender crumb, relatively soft in texture, with only a thin wrapping of crust. The French call such a bread *pain de mie*, where the crumb (or *mie*) is the thing that counts and the crust can be cut off for canapés or sandwiches.

The great white bread hope began in the 1840s with the substitution of rollers for rotary grinders, in the milling of wheat, that got rid of bran and germ at once. Soon the refinement of porcelain rollers ground the wheat even whiter and finer. In quest of absolute whiteness, bleaching agents were used, either agene or chlorine gas, to oxidize the flour and "mature" it instantly.

Not only a white loaf but a quick loaf was wanted, quite understandably, by housewives as much as by professional bakers. Increasingly in the nineteenth century, housewives relied more heavily on professional baker's yeast, because it speeded up the time needed for fermenting. Homemade yeast was a finicky and chancy business because yeast too young was too weak and yeast too old was too sour. The stronger the yeast the faster the rising, but too much yeast produced a bitter taste.

Homemade yeast was made from hops, bran, potatoes, malt, or even pumpkin, with a little sugar or molasses, and jacked up with a teacupful of strong yeast from the brewer or the baker or from a previous home-made brew. Cookbooks throughout the century supplied recipes for yeast and for the two-step "sponge" method which helped ensure that the yeast was working. The housewife made up a sponge of water, yeast, and flour (and sometimes potatoes and sugar if the yeast was weak) in the proportion of one part "wetting" to two parts flour. She poured it in a large stone crock, covered it with a folded clean blanket, and let it work overnight. In the morning ("just at the peep of day," *The Buckeye Cookbook* advises), she beat the sponge into a larger quantity of flour, added salt which would have slowed fermentation if added earlier, and the dough was ready for kneading.

In 1902, *Mrs. Rorer's New Cookbook* followed the usual recipe for Home-made Yeast with a new recipe labeled Twentieth Century Bread, made of liquid, flour, salt, and a compressed yeast cake. The mixture should be light and spongy, Mrs. Rorer claimed, in a mere 3 hours in winter and 2½ in summer. The overnight sponge required by homemade yeast was done for. Mrs. Rorer did not add sugar in switching from homemade to compressed yeast, but others did. Everyone knew that sugar speeded up the fermenting process and they were accustomed to the necessity of some sweetening, usually sugar, in homemade yeast. When housewives forsook homemade for compressed yeast, they hung on to the sugar habit and sugar became a standard component of twentieth-century bread where salt alone had seasoned bread before.

Today's recipes for white bread center on the sugar controversy. Purists condemn its use and hearken back to the earlier "honest" loaf, innocent of capitalist exploitation by sugar-mongers out to make a buck by producing both an instant and a long-lasting commercial loaf. Sugar speeds yeast. Sugar preserves. Sugar sweetens. A sugar addict always wants more. Yet even a health addict, who condemns white refined sugar as he would arsenic, will often not merely condone but demand a sweet loaf—of honey, molasses, caster, Demerara or brown sugar—of anything but granulated white. A sweet tooth still demands sweet bread, and the twentieth-century American loaf has been, despite Mrs. Rorer's sugarless recipe, noticeably sweet.

The homemade white loaf now, however, is less sweet than twenty years ago. One can chart the wane of sugar in the sequence of recipes over the last two decades for Basic White Bread provided by the man whose name is so closely associated with bread-making that he makes it an anagram in *Beard on Bread*. In Beard's general cookbook of 1959 he calls for 2 tablespoons of sugar to 6 cups of flour. By 1973, in *Beard on Bread*, Beard has lowered the sugar ratio to 2 teaspoons of sugar to 4 cups of flour. In *The New James Beard* of 1982, while the proportion of sugar to flour is the same, his use of 1½ cups yogurt for liquid diminishes the sweetness.

All the same, Beard is a consistent user of sugar with yeast even in his "French-style" or "Cuban" bread because yeast, he believes, "must have something to feed on." The statement is misleading because yeast, whether in a compressed cake, granulated or freeze dried, does not need sugar. All it needs is warmth and wetness and flour. Sugar speeds the process of fermentation but, as Child says, "The villain in the bread basket is speed." Longer and slower fermentations improve both the taste and texture of bread. Worst of all, sugar, inevitably, tastes of sugar.

Whether a sugar taste is essential to a traditional American white loaf depends on which tradition you pick, the earlier one of Eliza Leslie or the later one of Fannie Farmer. Fisher picked the later one in her recipe for White Bread in *How to Cook a Wolf*, in which she calls for 2 tablespoons of sugar to 6 cups of flour. Claiborne calls for the same amount of sugar in the plain white dough he uses for Spiral Bread in his first cookbook, and even in his newest cookbook he gives a recipe for French bread with sugar "optional." It seems that the sugar habit of the American palate is far more ingrained than even the salt habit.

For those who don't like a sugar taste in bread, Elizabeth David in her extraordinary *English Bread and Yeast Cookery* (1977) traces the centuries-old tradition of sugarless bread. Her scholarship is so detailed about every aspect of bread-making that it may tell you everything you never wanted to know, but it will also tell you how historically conditioned our palates are. Even our taste for sugar.

Despite conditioning, my own taste is for bread without sugar, so I leave it out in the recipe below. I prefer the earlier tradition in which the only essentials are liquid, flour, yeast, and salt. But because I like the traditional loaf rich and tender, I use milk for richness and butter for tenderness. I like sour cream, yogurt, or buttermilk even more than plain milk or water because the sour gives a gutsier taste and the loaf lasts well.

The one constant in bread-making is time and it's time that determines the proportion of the other ingredients. As little as ¼ teaspoon of dry yeast can elevate 4 cups of flour given time enough in a warm place. How warm is warm? Seventy-five to 80 degrees is very warm. Seventy to 75 degrees is better, to give the flour time to develop a little character in the rising. Two risings are enough for the American loaf: The first rising takes about twice as long as the second. Once you've found your ideal warm spot, you can estimate time at least roughly. For me the best spot is an oven with a pan of hot water and the oven light on. You can slow everything down by putting the dough in the refrigerator overnight or longer. It's only rushing that dough does not like.

Dough does like to be slapped smartly about. Mrs. Harland in *Common Sense* is only one of many who disagreed with Mrs. Rorer on the superiority of the machine to human hands in kneading. "Spend at least twenty minutes—half an hour is better—in this kind of useful gymnastics," Mrs. Harland announces. "It is grand exercise for arms and chest." When correctly kneaded, she says, the dough "rebounds like india-rubber after a smart blow of the fist."

Generally I forgo this grand exercise and both mix and knead the dough in a heavy-duty electric mixer with a dough hook. Beard uses the electric mixer a great deal, he says, but prefers to do the final kneading by hand for the sheer pleasure of it. Beard's method of hand kneading is to push, fold, and turn. Push the dough away from you with the heel of your hand, fold it toward you, give it a quarter turn, and push again. The sticky mess will become satiny and elastic in about 10 minutes. The machine does the same job in 5 or 6. The reason dough becomes elastic is that kneading develops the gluten that will "glue" the particles of flour together, in a rubbery network, to trap the gas which is released when yeast turns starch and sugar to alcohol. With gluten, as with yeast, ripeness is all.

What to bake the risen loaf in depends on what you have. Fisher in *How to Cook a Wolf* gives an old-fashioned southern recipe for baking bread in "a greased lard bucket." Her friend Addie, on the other hand, used two-pound coffee tins to produce a long round loaf. ("Addie slashes her dough into pieces with a sharp knife and then slaps it into shape as if it were a Bad Boy," Fisher explains.) A French friend told her that he baked his loaves in clay flower pots, a method encouraged by Elizabeth David and the maker of a new clay or stoneware bread oven now on the market. The method of totally enclosing a loaf in iron or clay is the old one of baking in a Dutch oven, which produces a very crusty round loaf from the steam released by the dough as it bakes. Most people, however, use a standard metal bread pan to produce a rectangular loaf with a rounded top.

Once baked, homemade bread will keep better in a paper bag than a plastic one that shuts out all air. Since toast is one of the keenest pleasures afforded by a good loaf, if your bread begins to go dry and stale, simply slice it and freeze it. You can then toast the frozen slices one by one.

## Proportions

for 2 standard loaf pans (9 by 5 by 3 inches), 1 package dry yeast (¼ ounce) or 1 compressed yeast cake to 5 or 6 cups of flour to 2 cups of liquid

1 **package dry yeast**
½ **cup very warm water (110 to 115 degrees)**
1½ **cups milk (or 1 cup sour cream or yogurt and ½ cup water)**
5 **to 6 cups bleached or unbleached flour**

1 **tablespoon salt**
4 **tablespoons softened butter (optional)**
1 **egg white for glazing (optional)**

1.   Dissolve the yeast in the warm water in a large mixing bowl. The best method is to test the temperature by an instant thermometer. A temperature of 140 degrees will kill the yeast. At lower temperatures the yeast will work but more slowly. With pre-dated packages you don't really need to "proof" yeast (by waiting for bubbles to form to "prove" it's alive) but dissolving the yeast sets it in motion.

2.   Add the milk and other liquid, which should be at room temperature to keep the yeast going. Mix in 5 cups of the flour with the salt and butter, and keep adding flour until the dough is stiff. Either remove to a floured board for hand kneading or knead in the machine until the dough is supple and elastic.

3.   Place in a well-buttered bowl, turning the dough around to coat all sides with butter. Cover with a kitchen towel and place the dough in a warm, draft-free place to double in size. (It may take anywhere from 1 ½ to 2½ hours, depending on the warmth of the ingredients and of the place.)

4.   Punch the dough down, then slap it hard a couple of times to redistribute the gas bubbles. Knead it four or five times to encourage the yeast and gluten to work anew.

5.   Cut the dough in half. Fold the dough over on itself and round both ends toward the fold to make a nice rounded top. Place the dough fold side down into the buttered loaf pans. Cover the pans lightly with wax paper or a towel and let the dough rise again until it has doubled (about 45 minutes to an hour).

6. For a browner crust, brush the top of the loaves with a beaten egg white or simply with a little cold water. Bake in a 400-degree oven for 40 to 45 minutes, or until the bottom of the loaf sounds hollow when rapped with your knuckles. Cool on a rack. Don't wrap until thoroughly cool or the crust will soften.

*This is the traditional American loaf for sandwiches, toast, or dinner table.*

# THE FRANCO-ITALIAN LOAF

Some say that a genyouwine French loaf, one of those long crusty staves tucked under a blue-smocked arm of a Frenchman pedaling home on his bicycle for the two-hour lunch, does not exist outside France. Others say that today a good French loaf hardly exists *inside* France. French bread is rapidly going the way of commercial American and a local *boulanger* sweating over a wood-fired brick oven is as rare as a 5-franc meal. Today a Frenchman can pick up a loaf at the *supermarché*, even as you and I, for a quick snack before speeding back to work on his *motocyclette*.

The mystique of French bread, however, remains for generations of Americans and English who discovered the art and pleasure of eating in their first encounter with French bread. Instead of a soft maternal loaf of maximum crumb, here was a tough masculine rod that was all crust. If the Anglo-American loaf was baked by women, at home, to be served with milk or beer or tea, the French loaf was baked by men, in the bakery, to be served with a bottle of wine. The French loaf was professional. It commanded a different kind of respect.

Child told us just how professional the French loaf was in the twenty pages she devoted to it in volume II of *Mastering.* Her aim was to produce "as professional a system for the home baker as possible." The home baker was instructed to simulate professional equipment by acquiring a ¼-inch-thick piece of asbestos cement, a 3/16-inch-thick piece of plywood, a 9- by 12-inch roasting pan to hold water, and a sizzling hot brick or a solid 10-pound rock to throw in the pan for a great burst of steam. Still, however, your simulated loaf would not taste quite "French" because French bread flour is different. The gluten content is lower, the texture is coarser, and the flour is unbleached, since bleaching is, in fact, forbidden by French law for reasons of health. Given all this, was it worth the effort of the home baker to produce a fake French loaf, that was still fake whether you called it a *ficelle, baguette,* or *bâtard?*

Yes, if you wanted a vigorous, chewy, crusty loaf that might be Italian or Portuguese or Spanish or Cuban as well as French. America has had a long unbroken tradition of Italian and Portuguese bakers on both Coasts that even today run old-time family bakeries, turning out every dawn a batch of old-country bread. Such a loaf, divorced from the French mystique, is as easy to make as an American loaf once the principles are understood. Beard called his "French-style" loaf "Cuban bread" to avoid French expectations. The proportions of liquid, salt, and flour were the same as his Basic White, but he omitted butter and reduced sugar from 2 tablespoons to 1. In effect, there was little difference between his Cuban and white loaf except in shape.

The "French-style" of Child produced a Frenchier taste because she began with a stickier dough to allow for fuller fermentation, with the dough tripling in volume. The other essential she called for was steam. For those intimidated by the hot-brick method, she suggested spraying the loaves with a plant atomizer at regular intervals in the first part of the baking to achieve a really crisp brown crust. An additional device was a steady radiating surface, for which she suggested asbestos cement, but others suggested more readily available quarry tiles. Unglazed clay "baking" tiles are now sold in kitchen equipment stores, as more of us have learned how the tiles can give bread baked directly on them, as if on the floor of an old-fashioned bake oven, added volume and crustiness.

In the decade since volume II of *Mastering,* many have experimented commercially and at home with methods of baking a good "French-style" loaf. Claiborne provides two such experiments in *The New New York Times Cookbook* and Bernard Clayton Jr., a whole complete system in *The Breads of France* (1978). That an aura of professionalism still attends the French loaf is evident in the fact that it is the one area of baking that men go for without fear of emasculation. I have more than a few men friends who have specialized in producing the perfect "French-style" loaf who wouldn't dream of baking a cake.

But even women, busy with more mundane cooking, can do it. Anyone with a food processor can do it. Obviously a processor isn't necessary, but because the dough is a sticky one a processor or electric mixer with dough hook makes the kneading not only quicker but easier. Child's standard proportion of 3½ cups flour to about 1½ cups water is small enough for a processor to handle in one batch.

A French-style loaf requires three risings to create its characteristic ripe chewiness, with a fairly coarse texture full of holes. Child demands a minimum of 7 hours in order that the dough may *triple* in volume each time. I find that the three risings develop a sufficiently tasty dough even if the dough only doubles in volume. To simplify Child's rather complicated shaping, I use French-loaf baking pans that contain two 18-inch loaves to a sheet. But you can simulate the pans with a double layer of heavy aluminum foil on a baking sheet.

My "simulated baker's oven" is a compromise all the way. I line an oven rack with tiles and put the baking pans on the tiles. The pans eliminate the difficulty of getting loaves on and off the hot tiles without the aid of a baker's paddle. At the same time, the tiles do provide a constant radiating heat that helps brown the loaves evenly. In addition, I spray the top of the loaves with the kind of atomizer you use for spraying plants. This generates enough steam for a good crust without the hot brick business and its attendant hazards for the home baker trying to manage the thing with a pair of tongs or a faulty asbestos mitt.

Because the dough has no oil, the life span of a Franco-Italian loaf is brief. Born at dawn, it stales by night. If not used the same day, it should be frozen in airtight plastic or foil. When you are ready to use the loaf, Child suggests thawing a frozen loaf by unwrapping it on a baking sheet in a cold oven; turn the oven to 400 degrees and the bread will be thawed and crusty in 20 to 25 minutes. Or, you can thaw the unwrapped loaf at room temperature and crisp the crust with a last-minute bake at 400 degrees for about 5 minutes.

## Proportions

for 3 long loaves about 18 by 3 inches, 3½ cups (1 pound) of flour to 1½ cups of liquid

| | |
|---|---|
| 1 **package dry yeast** | 3½ **cups unbleached flour** |
| ¼ **cup very warm water (110 to 115 degrees)** | 2¼ **teaspoons salt** |
| | 1⅓ **cups water** |

1. Dissolve the yeast in warm water. Put the flour and salt in a processor bowl and process for a second or two to mix. Add the dissolved yeast and mix by processing for a few seconds. Add the room-temperature water slowly through the lid opening while the processor is running until the dough balls up on the blade. Let the dough rest for 4 or 5 minutes. The dough will be soft and sticky.

2. To knead, turn the processor quickly on and off four or five times. Or, scrape the dough onto a floured board and knead for 2 or 3 minutes by hand. Let it rest again for 4 or 5 minutes. Place the dough in a buttered bowl for the first rising. Cover the bowl with plastic wrap to generate a little steam inside and cover the plastic with a folded bath or kitchen towel to seal in the warmth. Place in a warm, draft-free spot for 1½ hours or more, until the dough doubles (or triples) in volume.

3. Punch the dough down with your fist, scrape it out onto a floured board, reshape into a round, and return it to the bowl for the second rising.

4. When the dough has doubled (or tripled again), punch it down

and turn it out on a floured board for shaping. Cut into three equal pieces with a sharp knife. Fold each piece in two and let rest for 4 to 5 minutes.

5. Flatten each piece into an 8-inch oval. Fold in half lengthwise and flatten again. Fold once more and flatten. Then indent the dough lengthwise with the side of your hand, fold it in two, and seal the edges. The aim is to coax the gluten into an unbroken skin like a balloon, that will stretch as you stretch the dough into a long sausage or fat rope. Lengthen the dough by rolling back and forth with your palms.

6. Place the ropes in lightly buttered pans or in foil that has been doubled and shaped in three parallel troughs with ridges between to keep the loaves separate. Place foil on a baking sheet for easy handling. Cover lightly with a towel and let rise again until double.

7. Place a layer of tiles (if you have them) on an oven rack and heat the oven to 425 degrees. Slash the top of each loaf with three diagonal lengthwise cuts by means of a razor, or cut with scissors. Put the pan or baking sheet directly on the tiles. After 3 minutes spray the loaves with the atomizer. Repeat twice more at 3-minute intervals. The bread will be done in 20 to 25 minutes. The loaf will sound hollow when rapped. Turn out onto a rack and cool.

*When serving, you can do as the French do: Put the loaf directly on the table and let each man tear off a hunk. But you can help your guests by slicing the loaf in 2-inch segments without cutting all the way through. This is the best loaf for soups, salads, and cheese because of its crustiness.*

# BRAIDED EGG BREAD

Every country that bakes yeast breads has discovered the lightness, richness, and delicacy added by eggs. For this reason, every European-ized country from Russia in the East to Ireland in the West has celebrated festive occasions by a special egg bread, specially shaped. The French egg bread, the *brioche,* is richest of all from its large proportion of butter. Made in a mixer or processor, *brioche* dough is not the messy, slippery affair of hand kneading it once was, where butter was smeared with the heel of the hand on a marble surface in a cool kitchen. But even so, one does not always want the buttery overload of *brioche.*

The Jewish egg bread, *challah,* because it is lighter in eggs and butter is easier on the cook, wallet, and waistline. But it still tastes and looks special in a traditional braided form of three, four, or six strands. Braiding is fun and looks more complicated than it is, which gives the baker easy points. Braids can be further shaped into circles to form Christmas wreaths, decorated with ribbons and holly leaves of dough. Braids can also be personalized with monograms of dough for gifts to family and friends. And because the eggs will swell on contact with oven heat, a light and lovely risen loaf is almost guaranteed.

Proportions of yeast to flour vary and so does the quantity of sugar. Most egg breads, including *brioche,* call for a small amount of sugar, which seems to go with eggs and butter and to signify, again, something special. One to 2 tablespoons of sugar to 5 cups flour is usual in recipes for *challah* and would change nothing in the recipe below except to give a sweeter taste to the dough. But I have cut the sugar to 1 teaspoon to appease my sweetless tooth. No sugar at all, I find, leaves the dough a little blah. Mix, braid, bake, and taste, and determine your own proportions.

## Proportions

for 1 large braided loaf (about 18 inches), 2 packages yeast to 5 cups of flour to 3 eggs to 4 tablespoons of butter

| | |
|---|---|
| 2 **packages dry yeast** | 2 **teaspoons salt** |
| 1 **cup very warm water (110 to 115 degrees)** | 3 **eggs, beaten** |
| 1 **teaspoon sugar** | 4 **tablespoons (½ stick) butter, softened** |
| 5 **to 6 cups bleached or unbleached flour** | |

### For the Glaze

| | |
|---|---|
| 1 **egg yolk** | ¼ **cup poppy seeds (optional)** |
| 2 **tablespoons milk** | |

1.   Dissolve the yeast in the water and add to 5 cups of flour mixed with the salt and sugar in a large mixing bowl. By hand, spoon, or electric mixer, stir in the beaten eggs and softened butter. Add more flour if needed to make the dough stiff. Knead by hand for about 10 minutes on a floured board or with the dough hook in the machine for about 6 minutes.

2.   Place the dough in a lightly buttered bowl and turn it to coat the surface with butter. Cover and let rise in a warm place until double (1 to 2 hours). Punch the dough down with your fist, reshape into a ball, and let rise again (about 45 minutes to an hour).

3.   Punch down again, and cut into three, four, or six portions, depending on the kind of braid you want. The three-strand braid is simplest. Roll the dough on a floured surface into ropes of equal length with the palms of your hands. Start the braid by overlapping the three

rope ends together. Take the middle strand each time and cross alternately right and left, as in the diagram below.

To make a four-strand braid, place the four rope ends together in the center of four compass points. Cross in sequence south to north, north to south, east to west, and west to east, repeating until the dough is used up. You will end with a high mound. Place the mound on a buttered baking sheet and push it over. It will fall into a thick braid. The diagram below is for a four-strand braid.

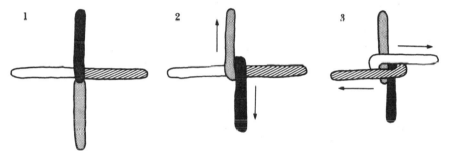

To make a six-strand braid, cut the dough into two pieces, one two thirds as large as the other. Cut each piece into three equal portions. and roll into six ropes of equal length, three thick and three thin. Make a three-strand braid of the thicker ropes. Paint with glaze. Make a braid of thinner ropes and place on top of the thicker braid.

  4.  Tuck the ends under the loaf and brush the top with the egg and milk glaze. Put in a warm place and let rise until double. Brush the loaf lightly again with the glaze and sprinkle with poppy seeds. Bake in a 375-degree oven for about 30 minutes, until the crust is brown and the loaf sounds hollow with a knuckle knock.

*An egg bread makes especially good toast, not only for breakfast but to serve with soups or pâtés.*

# SALLY LUNN BREAD

Although the Sally Lunn, "called after the inventress," Miss Leslie unhelpfully informs us, was often called a cake rather than a bread, it was in fact a type of Anglo-American *brioche*. It was made sometimes with yeast and sometimes with baking soda or powder but almost never with sugar until after the turn of the century. It was a quick bread because it was a batter bread that did not require kneading and that could be baked on the griddle in muffin or crumpet rings as well as in the oven in a square or round tin.

It was popular as long as the idea of English teatime was popular. It faded as the cocktail hour replaced the tea hour and as *croissants* and *brioches* replaced biscuits and tea breads. Now that the taste for *brioche* is fully developed, the Sally Lunn is worth reviving as a quick and easy butter and egg bread that is showy when baked in a tall tube pan and delicious when toasted the next day.

Beard gives two versions of such differing proportions that he proves his point about the multiplicity of Sally Lunns over the centuries. I prefer his version in *Beard on Bread* to the one in *American Cookery* because it is richer, although I have altered his proportions of sugar and salt to recover the salt taste of the earlier unsweetened Sally.

## Proportions

for 1 loaf pan, 4 cups of flour to 3 eggs to ¼ pound butter and 1 cup of liquid

| | |
|---|---|
| 1 **package dry yeast** | 1 **tablespoon salt** |
| ¼ **cup very warm water (110 to 115 degrees)** | 1 **tablespoon sugar** |
| | 3 **eggs** |
| ¾ **cup milk** | 4 **cups bleached or unbleached flour** |
| ¼ **pound (1 stick) butter** | |

1. Dissolve the yeast in the water in a mixing bowl or processor. Heat the milk with the butter, salt, and sugar to melt the butter. Cool to room temperature. Add the milk, eggs, and flour to the liquefied yeast and mix thoroughly.

2. Place the dough in a buttered bowl, cover, and let rise until doubled in bulk. Punch the dough down and beat with a large spoon or electric mixer for about 1 minute to redistribute the yeast bubbles.

3.  Scrape the dough into a well-buttered loaf pan or tube pan (or muffin tins), cover with wax paper, and let rise again until doubled. Bake at 375 degrees for 45 to 50 minutes for a loaf or tube pan (or at 400 degrees for 25 minutes for muffin tins). Turn out on a rack to cool.

*This bread has something of the coarse texture of an English muffin and tastes better hot than cold.*

# CRUNCHY HEALTH LOAF

During the Second World War when nutrition became a government concern, Cornell University applied the same kind of science that had produced a germ-free loaf to the cause of producing a germ-full one. The result was a sudden arraignment in the Great Bread Murder. Cornell called on unbleached flour, soy flour, and wheat germ, on honey instead of sugar, to testify on behalf of the defloured victim. Cornell Bread became a defender and champion for a new generation outraged at the injustice done the American loaf.

Health food stores burgeoned in the fifties and sixties, as Communist cells had in the thirties, to right the wrongs inflicted by the wicked. Where else could you buy unbleached flour, soy flour, and wheat germ, or the whole wheat flour called for in the Cornell Whole Wheat Loaf? Health-loaf recipes also burgeoned as earnest home or commune bakers passed the good word from friend to friend. As all kinds of flours and grains became available from their efforts, so did all kinds of breads—dense or light, smooth or crunchy, sweet or sour.

By the 1970s, the health movers and the hedonists joined hands and recipes in the cause of taste. Fisher had already praised the Cornell loaf in noting that researchers had discovered that animals fed solely on commercial bread "died young." Fisher suggested adding soy flour, skim milk powder, and wheat germ to breads, cakes, and cookies. Both Beard and Claiborne in their newest books have joined the cause by providing many more recipes for polygrained breads of high nutrition. Claiborne, in fact, cites a Nut and Seed Bread of varying flours and nutty crunches much like the recipe below that was called Mill Hollow Bread by the retired senior citizen who passed it on to me. He had gotten it, he said, from a baking grandchild with whom he exchanges recipes. The special virtue of such loaves for the baker is that the ingredients are almost infinitely variable in every specific, provided there is flour for gluten, liquid for moisture, yeast for leavening and—as here—seeds for crunch. The particular combination below produces a high-rising loaf of light texture, that is full of character, but not too sweet. Some sweetness helps counteract the non-gluten effect of whole wheat flour, but I have cut the original proportions of ⅔ cup honey by half.

## Proportions

for 2 standard bread-pan loaves, 7 to 8 cups of mixed flours to 2 yeast to 2½ cups of liquid

2 packages dry yeast
½ cup very warm water (110 to 115 degrees)
2 cups milk
3 tablespoons butter
1 tablespoon salt
⅓ cup honey
2 tablespoons molasses

4 cups white unbleached flour
3 cups whole wheat flour
½ cup rye flour
¼ cup bran flakes
¼ cup wheat germ
½ cup sunflower seeds
⅓ cup pumpkin seeds

1. Dissolve the yeast in water in a mixing bowl. Heat the milk with the butter, salt, honey, and molasses until the butter is melted. Cool to avoid killing the yeast when you add the liquid.

2. Save ½ cup of the whole wheat flour and add all the remaining flours and seeds to the yeast mixture. Stir in the milk and knead by hand or machine until the dough is elastic, adding the reserved ½ cup flour if needed to keep the dough from being too sticky.

3. Place the dough in a buttered bowl, cover with a towel, and put in a warm place until doubled.

4. Punch the dough down and knead it again a few times. Cut the dough in half. Put in buttered tins and let double again.

5. Bake at 350 degrees for about 40 to 45 minutes, or until the loaves sound hollow when rapped with your knuckles. Cool on a rack. Bread keeps well frozen and unfrozen.

# VEGETABLE BREAD

Potatoes used to be the only vegetables that found their way into bread, except for pumpkin. Both the starchy and the sweet vegetable were good feeders for homemade yeast. While potato breads are still baked and eaten wherever the tradition of solid peasant loaves has survived, pumpkin has been replaced by the more common carrot and even the zucchini. Health fooders are apt to stuff their loaves with these vitamin-rich veggies for the sake of health, ignoring the effects of the sickly sweet. Vegetable breads today, in fact, are often more like tea cakes of the kind that used to be made of nuts and oranges and bananas.

With the same vegetables, however, you can make a more consistently healthy loaf of distinctive taste and texture by omitting the sweet in favor of the sharp and pungent. One such loaf is a non-sweet zucchini bread, slightly soured by yogurt and sharpened by Parmesan cheese and grated onion. The grated raw zucchini disappears into the dough as liquid, except for intriguing flecks of green. Shaped into long French loaves, the interior grows light and moist while the outside becomes deliciously crusty. It's exactly the right kind of bread to experiment with, improvising with what's on hand or in the garden, like a little fresh chervil or basil, chopped with the zucchini.

## Proportions

for 3 French loaves of 18 inches, 4 cups of flour to 1 yeast to 1½ cups of grated zucchini to ½ cup of yogurt

| | |
|---|---|
| 1 **package dry yeast** | 2 **tablespoons grated onion** |
| ¼ **cup very warm water (110 to 115 degrees)** | 4 **tablespoons grated Parmesan cheese** |
| 4 **cups flour (3 unbleached white to 1 whole wheat is good)** | 1½ **cups grated zucchini** |
| | ½ **cup plain yogurt** |
| 1½ **teaspoons salt** | 2 **tablespoons butter, softened** |

1. Dissolve the yeast in warm water. Mix the flour with the remaining ingredients and pour in the yeast. Knead by hand or electric mixer or processor. (The dough will be very wet from the vegetables.)

2. Put in a buttered bowl, cover with a towel, and let rise until double in bulk. Punch down. Cut the dough into three equal portions to make long French loaves. Flour your hands to shape the dough because the dough will still be sticky. Butter French bread pans or aluminum foil shaped into troughs.

3. Bake in a 425-degree oven for 20 to 30 minutes. To get a good crust, spray the loaves with an atomizer of water three times during first 10 minutes. Cool on a rack. Bread keeps especially well because of its moistness.

# CINNAMON-PECAN COFFEE CAKE

America's love of sweetened breads for breakfast derives both from the teatime of the Anglos and the kaffeeklatsch of the Saxons. The English have their cakes and buns from Bath and Chelsea and Banbury, bearing their spiced and currant-laden pleasures with names like Ulverston Fair. The Germans and Swedes and Danes have their pastry rings and snails and claws, layered with jams and nuts, known everywhere but in Denmark as "the Danish."

A true Danish is halfway between a puff paste and a yeast roll and requires the turnings and foldings of puff paste for its flaky layers. (See

Bernard Clayton Jr.'s *The Complete Book of Pastry* [1981] for a complete rundown on the Danish.) What America calls "Danish" is usually a much simpler sweetened yeast dough shaped fancifully to contain nuggets of fruit and sweetmeats. Typical is the Snails House Cake contributed by Mrs. Dr. Westerborg Moeller (note the Germanic name) to *The Kansas Home Cook-Book* of 1886. A dough of flour, sugar, butter, eggs, and yeast is cut into strips, spread with raisins, currants, almonds, and citron, and rolled into many snails' houses.

Beard in *Beard on Bread* gives a good basic dough that he calls "my favorite of all the sweet breads." It is a rich soft dough that is easy to work and easy to keep without drying out because it contains sour cream. The addition of lemon juice gives the dough some spark and counters the sweet filling and glaze. You can shape the dough to your fancy, but Beard likes to roll the filling in the dough like a jelly roll and to coil it in a tube pan to rise.

## Proportions

for 1 ring loaf, 3 cups of flour, 2 yeast, 1 cup of liquid, ¾ cup of butter, 2 egg yolks, to about ¾ cup of filling

|  |  |
|---|---|
| **2 packages dry yeast** | **½ teaspoon vanilla extract** |
| **4 tablespoons sugar** | **½ teaspoon salt** |
| **½ cup very warm water (110 to 115 degrees)** | **2 egg yolks** |
| | **3 cups flour** |
| **½ cup sour cream** | **¾ cup (1½ sticks) butter, softened** |
| **2 tablespoons milk** | |
| **1 teaspoon lemon juice** | |

### For the Filling

|  |  |
|---|---|
| **2 tablespoons melted butter** | **¼ cup chopped pecans** |
| **¼ cup dark brown sugar** | **½ teaspoon cinnamon** |
| **¼ cup currants or raisins** | |

### For the Glaze

|  |  |
|---|---|
| **1 jar apricot preserves** | **1 tablespoon Grand Marnier** |

　　1.　Dissolve the yeast and 1 tablespoon of the sugar in the water in a large mixing bowl. Add the remaining sugar, cream, milk, lemon juice, vanilla, salt, and egg yolks and stir well.

　　2.　Cut the butter into 12 pieces and work into the flour as you would for a piecrust, either by hand, electric mixer, or in a processor. Combine the flour with the liquid mixture and knead for 5 to 6 minutes by hand on a floured board, or for 2 or 3 minutes with mixer dough hook, or 5 to 6 on-and-off pulses in a processor.

3. Put the dough in a buttered bowl, cover, and let rise in the refrigerator until doubled, about 4 hours. The dough needs to be cold to shape it around the filling.

4. Punch the dough down and roll it into a 10- by 14-inch rectangle. Brush with melted butter, sprinkle all over with sugar, cinnamon, currants, and nuts. Begin rolling the dough at the wider end, pressing the roll under as you go to make a tight roll.

5. Coil the roll into a well-buttered 9-inch tube pan, making sure the ends overlap. Cover and let rise until doubled. Bake in a 375-degree oven for about 45 to 60 minutes, or until the top sounds hollow when rapped.

6. Let cool for 10 to 15 minutes in the pan, then turn out on a rack to cool. Heat the apricot preserves to melt them. Stir in the liqueur and rub through a sieve over the top of the roll while the cake is still warm. The cake will slice better when cool, but it tastes best warm.

# BUCKWHEAT GRIDDLE CAKES

"The custom of making a breakfast of buckwheat cakes and syrup has been the cause of years of indigestion with many people," Mrs. Mary Lincoln opined and concluded, "Children should never eat them." Children and adults have continued the custom, in defiance of dietitians, doctors, and even good sense. Fisher recalled her grandmother's griddle cakes of homegrown buckwheat eaten with her grandfather's wild sage comb honey. "It was a heady meal," she remembered, "but if I ate it now I might sink like a stone . . ."

It was not good sense but the packaged pancake mix that took the fun and then the buckwheat out of breakfast griddle cakes. Jewish immigrants from Russia and Poland continued to make their blini of buckwheat flour to wrap around caviar and sour cream but not usually for breakfast. It was the health food store, ironically, that kept the breakfast buckwheat tradition alive.

That tradition was once as ritualistic as omelet-making. According to *The Buckeye Cookbook*, the devoted griddle-cake-maker bought only the purest buckwheat flour from grain "run through the smutter with a strong blast before grinding." She set her buckwheat sponge in a stone crock to ripen overnight and was careful not to stir the risen batter but to ladle it out cake by cake with a spoon set between times in a saucer. She then cooked her griddle cakes on an ungreased soapstone "never to be used for any other purpose."

Confronted with a hard-core buckwheat devotee, one can see the charm of an Aunt Jemima Pancake Mix made of baking powder, sugar, and very white flour. One can also see how the once-a-week pancake breakfast, even with a ready-mix, became a Sunday hobby for the leisured male. Daddy took over the pancake griddle as he took over the barbecue grill because he didn't have to do it every day.

A baking-powder griddle cake, however, wasn't a patch on the old fermented yeasty brew, just as bleached white flour wasn't a patch on buckwheat. Beard perpetuates the old tradition in *Beard on Bread* in a recipe for Yeast Buckwheat Cakes for new generations deprived by progress of earlier rituals. Like Sally Lunns, there are dozens of buckwheat cakes, but Beard's has the virtue of returning to the overnight rise.

## Proportions

for 10 to 15 medium pancakes, 2 cups of flour, 1 yeast, to 2 cups of liquid

| | |
|---|---|
| 1 **package dry yeast** | 1 **teaspoon salt** |
| 2 **cups warm water (about 100 degrees)** | ¼ **teaspoon baking soda** |
| 1 **cup buckwheat flour** | 2 **tablespoons molasses** |
| 1 **cup unbleached flour** | 1 **tablespoon melted butter** |

1.   Dissolve the yeast in the water in a large bowl. Add the flour and salt and stir well. Cover the batter and let rise in a warm place overnight. When ready to cook, stir in the soda, molasses, and butter, which will thin the batter out.

2.   Ladle the batter onto a sizzling greased griddle or heavy skillet. Brown a few minutes on each side and serve with melted butter and hot syrup or honey.

# RICH BAKING POWDER BISCUITS

From the beginning, quick breads suited the American perched in the wilderness, whether an Indian baking a flat corn cake or a colonist adding the aerated salt, *sal-aeratus* (better known as the sodium bicarbonate of baking soda), to make a baking powder biscuit. Such breads could be whipped up fresh before every meal in any pot that had a lid. A leavening agent that injected bubbles into meal or flour without the slow organic changes effected by the chemistry of yeast was a boon to the housewife who delved and spun as well as cooked and baked.

Toward the end of the nineteenth century, the Bread section of cookbooks was overtaken by quick breads of all kinds, including muffins, corncakes, griddle cakes, and waffles. But of all these, biscuits remained the most popular because they were the most versatile. They could be cut in squares for breakfast or enriched with buttermilk or cream and cut in rounds for fancier dinner. They could be sweetened with sugar for strawberry shortcake or loaded with cheese for a slice of ham. They could be made even quicker and easier by a prepackaged mix of everything but the liquid and sold for ten times the price of the ingredients under a catchy name and mass marketing. In the 1930s, Bisquick taught us to cover everything from soup to nutburgers with a thick layer of biscuit dough. In the forties, Pillsbury taught us how to peel open a cardboard "can" of Refrigerated Big Flaky Biscuits that needed nothing but an oven and a baking sheet. The next logical step was a biscuit that would cook on contact with air when opened on the plate. But by that time we'd been biscuited out and the good name of biscuits suffered a decline, along with the taste of the commercial product.

Considering the number of bad jokes about new bride biscuits, one might conclude that the success of the commercial product lay in the difficulties of achieving success at home. In 1871, Mrs. Harland complains of the frequency of "greenish-yellow streaks" in the dough and an odor "dissuasive to an educated appetite." "Few cooks make really good, quick biscuit," she concludes, "—why, I am unable to say, unless upon the principle of 'brains will tell.' "

Biscuits require few brains but they do require a quick light hand in the mixing because speed is everything with baking powder. Beard has done much to redeem biscuits by his recipe for the Cream Biscuits of his childhood, which calls for heavy cream instead of milk or buttermilk. The result is a wonderfully rich crumb, a bit like a risen piecrust, crisp on the outside and soft and tender in the middle. Patting the dough in shape, instead of rolling it, and cutting it in squares with a sharp knife, instead of in rounds with a cutter, make this quick bread ideal for a quick light hand.

## Proportions

for 16 small biscuits, 2 cups of flour to 1 cup of cream to 1 tablespoon baking powder

| | |
|---|---|
| 2 **cups flour** | 1 **cup heavy cream** |
| 1 **teaspoon salt** | 4 **to 6 tablespoons melted** |
| 1 **tablespoon baking powder** | **butter** |
| ¼ **teaspoon sugar** | |

1. Sift the dry ingredients together and quickly fold in the heavy cream with a rubber spatula, fingers, or fork. Turn onto a lightly floured board, knead no more than a minute, and pat into a square about ½ inch thick. With a sharp knife cut 4 strips one way and 4 strips the other to make square biscuits.

2. Pour half the melted butter into a 9- by 9-inch baking pan. Place the squares in the pan and pour remaining butter over them. Bake in a 425-degree oven for 12 to 15 minutes, or until the top is golden brown.

*Biscuits are ideal for a buffet table because they are not only tasty in themselves as a form of finger food but complement whatever they are served with, from salty hams to sweet conserves.*

# CORN BREAD WITH CORN

Corn bread has had as many names as ways of making. Mrs. Crowen in her *American Lady's Cookery Book* runs a nice gamut from Indian Corn Bread to Indian Meal Bread for Tea, Pone or Corn-Meal Breakfast Cake, Albany Breakfast Cakes, and Indian Meal Breakfast Cakes before she runs out of bread or cake tins and succumbs to flattened Indian Meal Griddle Cakes. The only essential elements in these varying breads are ground meal (pone, Indian, or corn), liquid, leavening, and a baking basin or tin.

The good thing about corn bread is that it is edible whether moist and dense, light and dry, salty or sweet. But to make really Delicious Corn Bread, Mrs. Crowen suggests in an appended recipe, you should add a portion of wheat flour to the freshly ground meal and a small amount of baking powder (cream of tartar and soda) to well-beaten eggs. Her "Delicious" is our more or less standard version of a corn bread that moves in the direction of a light and crumbly cake.

Beard cites as his favorite recipe for corn bread (in *Theory & Practice*) one which contains flour and cornmeal, baking powder and eggs, with an enrichment of cream and a lot of melted butter. Claiborne's favorite corn bread contains the additions of grated sharp cheese and canned cream-style corn. Even better, to my mind, is a corn bread that contains fresh corn kernels, if possible, or frozen kernels, if not.

To use both white meal and fresh white corn is to move in the direction of spoon bread, and a most delicious one. But here I've chosen yellow meal to provide a sturdier all-purpose corn bread as suitable for a turkey stuffing as for a breakfast, lunch, or dinner cake or bread. Corn provides its own sweetening, but those who like a sweet corn bread can add a little sugar, just as Mrs. Crowen, in some of her recipes, added molasses.

## Proportions

for a 9- by 9-inch pan, 1½ cups of cornmeal, ½ cup of flour, 1 cup of corn kernels to 3 eggs and 1 cup of milk

| | |
|---|---|
| 1½ cups cornmeal | 2 teaspoons salt |
| ½ cup flour | ½ teaspoon white pepper |
| 1 tablespoon baking powder | 1 teaspoon sugar (optional) |

| 1 cup corn kernels (scraped | 1 cup milk |
|---|---|
|    fresh or frozen) | 3 tablespoons melted butter |
| 3 eggs, beaten | |

1. Sift together the dry ingredients: meal, flour, baking powder, salt, pepper, and sugar. Add the corn kernels and the well-beaten eggs. Beat in the milk and melted butter and pour into a buttered 9- by 9-inch baking pan.

2. Bake in a 400-degree oven for about 20 to 25 minutes. Cut in squares and serve hot.

*We tend to associate corn bread with turkeys, chickens, and hams but it can go wherever yeast bread goes. An enriched version like this is half a meal in itself.*

# PASTES

*To make a light, crisp, and flaky crust, use a good, fine flour and none but
the best butter. Have everything, including yourself, cool.*

—Our Women's Exchange, *Xenia,
Ohio (1911)*

A good, fine flour, which we have neither to grow, mill, nor grind,
has now become so common that we forget how much depends
upon it. Without it, the whole world of Italian pastas, German
dumplings, and French pastries would disappear, not to mention staffs
of life like bread. When most foods were cooked at home, the men who
raised the wheat and the women who shaped and baked it understood the
capacities of flour to be both long and short. Moistened with egg, it could
stretch long and thin as a ribbon. Moistened with butter, it could flake
and rise like a feather. It could transform itself into noodle, dumpling,
and crust.

The last decade of kitchen hardware has renewed respect for materials
long forgotten as we cut butter into flour in the processor or cut floured
ribbons into noodles in the pasta machine. Machinery demands that we
understand the properties of the materials we use so that we can adapt
what we have to the machine at hand. And machinery has opened up a
world of uses that we might not have ventured upon had we not discovered how easy it was to make a basic paste and shape it ourselves.

We might have been stuck forever with packaged macaroni as our sole experience of the Italian staff of life. We might always have cooked our spaghetti soft and mushy had we not found on the tooth, *al dente,* the texture
of a fresh homemade noodle. We might have remained forever ignorant
of the myriad names and shapes of *fettucini* and *tagliatelli* and *tortellini.*

But there is a hazard with machinery. Many who are adept at turning
out Italian noodles in their pasta machine hesitate to make a piecrust
because there is no machine to roll it out and fit it in ring or pan. If the
frozen piecrusts at our supermarkets were made with "none but the best
butter," no home cook would need to know the art of pastry-making,
since crusts freeze perfectly once made. But beyond taste there is pleasure, again, in discovering the capacity of flour to puff like an atomic
mushroom when layered into puff paste or to wrap a fragrant fruit in an

edible case that remains crisp while the fruit becomes soft. There is pleasure in shaping dough, like modeling clay, into decorative lattices or leaves. There is pleasure in the pastry art.

To those who are afraid of working with pastry because they have never done it, Child quotes F.D.R.'s famous stricture against fear, "There is nothing to fear but fear itself." If the dough tears while rolling it out or if it won't stick together but crumbles at the edges, abandon the rolling pin. Put the dough directly in the pan and press it in with your fingers, working an edge around the top. If there are holes, patch them. If there are lumps, press them out. Since nothing will show but the border in a one-crust pie, the bottom can look a mess as long as it will hold together while it bakes.

If the pleasures of piecrust are large, the pleasures of puff paste are euphoric. If anybody can bake a cherry pie, as in the old song of Billy-boy, Billy-boy, anybody can make puff paste—with patience. Anybody who has watched through the glass door of an oven the actual rising of the paste as it vaunteth itself and puffeth up will know that patience, and the resulting spectacular pastry, is its own reward. For a knock-out finish at a dinner party, a little homemade puff paste beats all. It is then that the cook, warmed by the pleasure of his guests, best knows the virtue of having everything cool, including himself.

# HOMEMADE PASTA

Our recent revolution in buying and making fresh "homemade" pasta is due entirely to machines. While we admire the knowledge and skill of authentic Italian cooks like Marcella Hazan, who insist on the virtues of rolling out pasta by hand, few of us who have tried it have made it part of our daily routine. Most of us are not only content but eager to save labor and space by either a hand-cranked or an electric pasta machine. Beard claims, in fact, that the electric pasta machine revolutionized his life as a pasta addict by enabling him to have a mixed, kneaded, rolled, cut, and cooked pasta in thirty minutes. Moreover, the machine has the nursery pleasure of modeling in clay or making pies of mud, as you crank a lump of dough into endless ribbons that you can drape over chair backs, broom handles, and towel racks while you play "Italian kitchen."

By using another machine, a processor, to mix the dough, you may miss the mud-pie pleasure of stirring eggs into the flour by fork and finger, but you can make up that loss by kneading the dough by hand and shaping it for the rolling machine. With such happy tools, only the fear of fat need keep you from daily indulgence of your new pasta habit.

Pasta has come to mean, in American parlance, not the startling variety of simple flour and water pastes that the Italians cut like pencils or angel's hair or plastic tubing or wet mops, but the enriched egg noodle called *fettucini. Fettucini* is no peasant staple but an expensive first course or main dish, in a restaurant, sauced with the butter and cream of Northern Italy rather than the oil and tomato of the South.

In Italy the tenderest and thinnest of homemade egg noodles are made from a soft-wheat flour that is not widely available in this country. In this country Italian chefs like Hazan use semolina, the processed grain of a hard-wheat flour that the Italians call "durum." To duplicate a soft-wheat texture, Hazan reduces the usual proportion of ¾ cup flour for each egg to slightly more than ½ cup flour, but for the novice the standard proportion is easier to work with. To make the dough richer, you can add up to 3 egg yolks, but the more liquid the stickier the dough and the harder it is to roll out.

Anyone who wants to try kneading and cutting noodles by hand will find Hazan's directions quoted by Claiborne in *The New New York Times Cookbook.* He will also find a rule of thumb for deciding what sauce for which paste. The classic approach is to put chunky sauces on chunky containers like macaroni or shells and to put smooth sauces on smooth ribbons like *fettucini* and spaghetti, although there are always exceptions like linguine with clam sauce. Clinging sauces with cream, or "alla Panna" as the Italians say, go best with the delicate taste and texture of the egg noodle, as in Fettucini Alfredo.

There are so many cooking Alfredos in both Rome and New York, that the unwary may identify the sauce with a particular place. But the lovely blending of butter, cream, and cheese with fine noodles is at least as old as Catherine de' Medici who imported her cunning Italianate ways to France, along with several wheels of cheese from Parma, way back in the sixteenth century.

# PASTA DOUGH

## Proportions for Pasta Dough

for 2 large or 4 small servings, 1½ cups of flour to 2 eggs

| | |
|---|---|
| 1½ cups flour | 2 large eggs, at room |
| ½ teaspoon salt | temperature |
| 1 tablespoon olive oil | 1 tablespoon olive oil |

1. Put the flour in a processor with the salt and oil and process for 6 to 8 seconds. Add the eggs (if cold from the refrigerator warm in warm water for 5 minutes) and process until the dough forms a ball (10 to 15 seconds).

2. Put the dough on a lightly floured surface and knead with the heel of your hand for 2 or 3 minutes, or until the ball is smooth

and resilient. Divide in three pieces and cover with a damp towel.

3. Flatten one piece at a time into an oblong and put through the kneading rollers of a pasta machine set at the widest opening. Run the dough through five or six times, flouring and folding the dough in half each time, to knead thoroughly. Then run the dough through successively narrower openings until the dough is as thin as possible without its shredding or blistering.

4. Spread out the pieces to dry for 10 to 15 minutes (a folding wooden rack for drying clothes is ideal, but a chair back will do). Change the head of the machine to the cutting rollers and feed each piece through the machine. Flour the cut strips and dry them for 5 to 10 minutes longer.

5. Have ready 4 quarts of boiling water, to which you have added 1 to 2 tablespoons salt. Bring to a rolling boil, add the pasta, cover the pot, and return to a boil. Remove the cover and start testing by forking up a strand and tearing off a piece to bite. When the pasta has lost its flour taste but is still firm to the bite *(al dente)*, drain in a colander immediately and put into a warm serving dish with butter and cheese or sauce. Depending on its thickness, the pasta will be done in anywhere from 30 seconds to 3 minutes. Don't overcook or it will turn gummy.

# SAUCE ALFREDO OR ALLA PANNA

1 cup heavy cream
¼ pound (1 stick) butter
¾ cup freshly grated Parmesan cheese

Salt and freshly ground pepper to taste

Melt the butter with cream and put in a serving dish. Add the drained noodles, sprinkle with ½ cup of the cheese, season, and toss to coat the strands with liquid and cheese. Taste for seasoning and add more salt and pepper if necessary. Sprinkle the remaining ¼ cup of grated cheese over the top, or pass the cheese separately.

*Then there are pasta purists, like my son, who never puts anything but butter, salt, and pepper on his pasta, no matter what kind and no matter where. And who once outraged a waiter in Rome by sending back to the kitchen a pasta beautifully sauced in cheese and cream.*

# SPAGHETTI ALLA PRIMAVERA

To those of us raised on the sweet pink sauce of canned Franco-American spaghetti or the gummy orange sauce of American macaroni and cheese, a spicy sauce of tomatoes, garlic, onions, and ground meat was as daring as a trip to Sicily. Early culinary adventurers guarded with their lives the secret of their Italian spaghetti sauce, which usually turned out to be sugar in a sauce that simmered for a minimum of 4 hours to remove the taste of tin from the tomato paste. Those were the days when, for most of us, spaghetti came in boxes and sauces came in cans. So it was a revelation to learn from Fisher that spaghetti "should in the first place be good, and fresh, and made with honest semolina flour so that it is hard and horny when uncooked, and firm, clean, smooth when it comes from the pot."

Fisher's ideal spaghetti is now as commonplace as the canned tomato sauce is a rarity. Thank God. A quick glance at Beard's spaghetti sauces in his first cookbook shows a heavy reliance on the No. 2½ can of solid-packed tomatoes. Now that we have forgone the can for fresh vegetables of all kinds, spaghetti sauces are no longer limited to red or white but are often as multicolored as the vegetables of spring that give their name to Sauce Primavera. The sauce is typical of the current vogue for vegetables that must be as crunchy as the pasta is *al dente.* Also typical is the fact that cream rather than tomato is the binder.

While the vegetables can be as varied as the season provides, the one essential is to use plenty of them in proportion to the pasta and to cook them with as light a hand as possible. This is the kind of pasta dish that is as good cold as hot because it is really a hot salad to begin with. Ever since Claiborne confessed his addiction to cold spaghetti and supplied his sister's recipe for spaghetti in a mustard-flavored mayonnaise, spaghetti or *tortellini* salad has replaced the once-universal macaroni salad. It's a good way to use a Primavera pasta the second day. If the cream has solidified, the addition of a little oil and vinegar, as in a regular salad dressing, will dress it up as a cold salad.

## Proportions

for 4 to 8 servings, 1 pound spaghetti to 8 cups of chopped vegetables

| | |
|---|---|
| 1 **cup green beans, cut in 1-inch pieces** | 2 **cloves garlic, minced** |
| 1 **cup broccoli flowerets** | 1 **teaspoon dried basil, or 2 tablespoons fresh** |
| 1 **cup fresh peas or pea pods, such as snow peas or sugar-snap peas** | 4 **tablespoons minced parsley** |
| 1 **cup diced zucchini** | **Salt and freshly ground black pepper to taste** |
| ½ **cup olive oil** | 1 **pound spaghetti** |
| 2 **cups sliced mushrooms** | ½ **cup heavy cream** |
| 2 **cups cubed ripe tomatoes** | ¾ **cup grated Parmesan cheese** |
| 1 **small red or green hot chili, minced** | **Salt and freshly ground black pepper to taste** |

1. Parboil the green beans and broccoli, separately, 3 to 4 minutes in salted water. Parboil the fresh peas for 1 minute. Drain and run under cold water to retain color and crispness.

2. Stir-fry the zucchini for 1 or 2 minutes in 1 tablespoon olive oil. Stir-fry the mushrooms over high heat in 2 tablespoons olive oil for 1 or 2 minutes. In the remaining olive oil, heat the tomatoes with the minced chili, garlic, basil, and parsley for 3 or 4 minutes. Add the parboiled vegetables, salt, and pepper and taste for seasoning.

3. Cook the spaghetti in 4 quarts of boiling salted water until tender but firm to the bite (7 to 10 minutes with packaged spaghetti). Drain immediately and toss with the warmed cream, grated cheese, and additional salt and pepper.

4. Add the vegetable sauce and toss all together. Serve immediately with additional grated cheese.

*Pasta and salad have fortunately taken hold as a full meal for lunch or dinner. Because pasta is so filling, the best dessert is fruit or fruit ice.*

# GNOCCHI

The dough of flour and egg that makes noodles also makes cream puffs and dumplings. While the function of egg in a noodle paste is to bind the dough together to make the flattest, thinnest sheets possible, the function of egg in a *pâte à choux,* or cream puff paste (see DRINK FOOD), is to puff and swell the dough into the lightest and airiest of globes. When the French took over the Italian dumpling of semolina or potato called "gnocchi," they used a cream puff paste for a base because it was the surest way to bind and lighten at the same time. Child gives a number of recipes for this French version of gnocchi, including one in *Julia Child & More Company* that advises instant potatoes for mashed and a processor for the cream puff paste to make this traditional dumpling quick work.

Beard, on the other hand, in *The New James Beard,* begins the other way round with very mealy mashed potatoes to bind together flour, egg, butter, and cheese. I find that Beard's method makes for lighter dumplings of better taste, particularly if the flour is semolina or, as a substitute, farina breakfast cereal. Semolina gives the right texture, real potatoes give the right taste.

Traditionally, gnocchi are poached gently in salted water in the manner of *quenelles.* To do this, the mixture must be rolled by hand into golf balls and dropped into water kept just below the simmer. This makes for light dumplings but slow work. A faster method is to eliminate the poaching step and to shape the dough by cutting it with a biscuit cutter after it has chilled in the refrigerator. You then bake the rounds with *lots* of butter, as Beard says, and *lots* of cheese.

# Proportions

for 6 servings, 1½ pounds potatoes to 1 cup of flour, 2 eggs and 1 cup of cheese

1½ pounds Idaho or Maine
    baking potatoes
1½ cups milk, heated
 1 teaspoon salt
½ teaspoon pepper
¼ teaspoon nutmeg or mace
 1 cup semolina, or farina
    breakfast cereal

½ cup grated Swiss cheese
2 eggs, beaten
¼ pound (1 stick) butter
½ cup grated Parmesan
  cheese

1. Peel and quarter the potatoes and boil until tender. Drain and return to the pot, shaking over low heat to dry them out. Mash with a fork or put through a ricer. Gradually beat in the hot milk, salt, pepper, and nutmeg, and beat until the potatoes are smooth.

2. Put over low heat and gradually beat in the semolina, by hand or with an electric beater. Then add the grated Swiss. Remove the pan from the heat and beat in the eggs. Smooth the mixture into a flat buttered baking pan (15- by 10½- by 1-inch), cover with plastic wrap, and chill for 3 or 4 hours, or until ready to cut.

3. Cut the dough with a cookie or biscuit cutter into small rounds and place them, overlapping, in a buttered baking dish. Melt the butter and drizzle it over the top. Sprinkle heavily with grated Parmesan cheese and bake in a 375-degree oven for 25 to 30 minutes. The cheese should be crusted and brown and most of the butter should be absorbed.

*Can be served as a first course or a rich accompaniment to a simple meat or fowl.*

# AMERICAN SPOON BREAD

Urban Americans nowadays are more familiar with Italian ways of using cornmeal in dishes like polenta than with American ways of using cornmeal in dishes like spoon bread. But spoon bread is not a "bread" at all. It is a paste of egg and meal, rather than flour, in which the eggs are separated as they would be in a soufflé. There are as many variations as there are states in the Union for this indigenous method of transforming corn mush into something lighter than mush but more spoonable than corn bread proper, with its additional leavening of baking powder. Hot-tempered regionalists may quarrel over details but all agree that the one essential for an authentic spoon bread is a quality stone-ground meal, white or yellow.

The dish may be treated as an accompaniment for ham, game, chicken, or beef, like a Yorkshire pudding, or as a container for chopped ham, mushrooms, sausages, or cracklings. For the thrifty, Fisher suggests using the dish as a backbone for leftover gravy which you have enlivened with sautéed mushrooms, chopped olives, and sherry. Unlike corn bread or corn sticks, there is no sugar in spoon bread, which eliminates tea-room associations of gentility and returns us to the nitty-gritty of campfires and open hearths. You can push spoon bread, in fact, all the way back to the origin of its name and bake it in a cast-iron skillet with sizzling hot butter.

## Proportions

for 6 to 8 servings, 1 cup of cornmeal to 4 eggs to 2 cups of liquid

| | |
|---|---|
| 2 **cups buttermilk (or regular milk)** | 6 **tablespoons butter** |
| 1½ **teaspoons salt** | 4 **eggs, separated** |
| 1 **cup white or yellow cornmeal** | |

1. Bring the milk to the simmer (buttermilk will separate somewhat, but it doesn't matter). Add the salt and cornmeal and stir continuously for 5 minutes, or until thick.

2. Melt 4 tablespoons of butter in a 12-inch cast-iron (or enamel) frying pan and add to the cornmeal mixture.

3. Beat the egg whites until stiff but not dry. Beat the yolks with a little of the mush, stir in one quarter of the egg whites, and then fold in the rest.

4. Heat the remaining 2 tablespoons of butter in the frying pan until it sizzles. Spread the batter like a large flat pancake and bake in a 400-degree oven for about 20 minutes, or until the top has started to brown. The bottom will be nicely crusty from the hot frying pan.

*Spoon bread is also ideal for breakfast or brunch because of its soufflé qualities.*

# BUTTER CRUST

Some of us who had not learned to make apple pie or any other American pie at our grandmother's knee learned from Child how to roll out crusts for French tarts long before we tackled our double-crusted native fruit pie. One result was that standards of native crust improved, as we learned that the French partially bake their crusts before filling in order to keep them crisp and non-soggy.

From Child we also learned how to use an electric mixer instead of the wire pastry blender of our mothers or the fingertips of our grandmothers for the crucial step of rapidly blending butter into flour. We learned, too, how to vary the formula for short paste, or *pâte brisée,* according to use. We learned that *pâte brisée* could be *ordinaire, fine, à l'oeuf, sucrée, sucrée aux jaunes d'oeuf, sablée, à croustade,* and *à croustade à l'envers.* It could wrap up beef and turkeys and veal-and-pork pâtés. It could contain rich custards of bacon and leeks or cheese. It could display thin glazed slices of apple or strawberry or pears.

The French crust we learned from Child was made primarily from butter, mixed with shortening in varying quantities depending on the desired crispness or stiffness, mixed sometimes with sugar for dessert crusts and sometimes with egg yolks or whole eggs to make a free-standing crust that would hold its shape without a tin. We learned to use ice water instead of cold water. We learned to line a crust with foil and fill it with dried beans or rice to hold its shape during its first baking. The vogue of quiche and beef Wellington during the sixties was due entirely to the discovery that anybody, with a little care, could make an edible crust.

Then came the processor and the discovery that anybody could make the pastry for an edible crust in less than 10 seconds. The processor could be said to have taken some of the fun out of crust making by making it too simple, but there was still the rolling out to test one's powers and the intrepid could always plunge on to challenges like puff paste.

The principle of crust is to marry fat to flour with as little liquid as possible to make the pastry as "short" as possible and still hold together. Therefore a light quick hand is necessary in mixing and rolling so that the separate particles of flour and butter do not meld into a gummy paste that will turn tough instead of crisp, crumbly, or flaky.

The old-fashioned method was to literally cut the shortening or butter into the flour with a pair of knives or a wire pastry blender to avoid melting the fat with the heat of human fingers. The whirling blade of the processor accomplishes that feat in about 3 seconds, if you have cut the butter into ¼-inch pieces for quick assimilation. (Cut a stick of butter in fourths lengthwise, then in sixteen slices crosswise.) For this purpose, the colder the butter and shortening the better. Child suggests a mixture of butter and shortening, rather than straight butter as the French would do, because our flour is harder, more glutinous, and needs some shortening to tenderize it.

The recipe below, based largely on the proportions developed by Child, is for an all-purpose crust. To sweeten the crust for dessert, lessen the salt to a pinch and add 2 tablespoons of sugar to the flour. To stiffen the crust for wrapping meat, fish, or pâtés, anything *en croûte,* lessen the proportion of fat (to ½ stick butter and 3 tablespoons lard) and substitute egg yolks for part of the liquid (2 egg yolks plus ice water to make ⅓ cup).

Proportions are everything here, so measure flour with care by scooping it into a cup and leveling it off with a spatula. Prepare ice water by putting 2 or 3 cubes of ice into a 2-cup measure, filling with water until ready to use, and then measuring it into a smaller cup at the last moment.

## Proportions

for one 9-inch pie pan or tart shell, 1¾ cups of flour to nearly ¾ cup of fat to ¼ cup of water

| | |
|---|---|
| **1¾ cups flour** | **3 tablespoons shortening or** |
| **½ teaspoon salt** | **lard** |
| **¼ pound (1 stick) butter** | **4 to 5 tablespoons ice water** |

1.  Measure the flour and salt into a processor container fitted with a steel blade. Add the chilled butter, cut in ¼-inch pieces, and the chilled lard. Turn the machine on and off four or five times. Measure 4 tablespoons water. Turn the machine on and pour the water through the beaker. Turn the machine on and off four or five times until the dough just begins to stick together. Turn out on a piece of wax paper or plastic wrap and form into a ball. Flatten and wrap and chill in the refrigerator for at least 10 minutes.

2.  Roll the dough out on a lightly floured or cold surface by placing the pin in the middle of the dough and rolling away from you. Turn the dough a quarter turn each time and continue to roll away from the middle to the outer edge. This is the best way to roll dough evenly. Roll it ⅛ inch thick and about 2 inches larger than your tin. Roll the dough at the far side up over your pin and lay it into the pan. Fit it into the bottom and sides and trim off any excess with a scissors, knife, or by rolling the pin across the top.

3.  Chill for 30 minutes in the refrigerator to again relax the gluten. Fit a piece of foil over the dough and fill it with dried beans or rice so that the dough will hold its shape in the pan. Bake in a 425-degree oven for about 10 minutes. Remove the liner and beans, prick the dough all over with a fork so that it will not puff up. Return to the oven for 2 to 5 minutes longer to finish baking. If you are using a tart ring set on a baking sheet, let the baked shell cool on a wire rack.

*This is a classic crust for quiches, for pizza toppings (see page 89), for meat or chicken pies (see Chicken Pot Pie, page 233; Steak, Kidney, and Oyster Pie, page 268). With the addition of sugar it becomes a classic crust for fruit pies and tarts (see Apple-Pecan Pie, page 370; Pumpkin Chip Pie, page 372; and Lemon Meringue Pie, page 374).*

# LARD CRUST

American pie crust was often made with all lard; that is, rendered and purified pig's fat. For flavor and texture pure lard is far superior to the vegetable shortenings that have replaced it in daily home use since the introduction of Crisco and similar shortenings in the teens and twenties. But recently lard has been staging a comeback among pastry lovers undaunted by cholesterol scares. You can render your own lard by heating pork fat slowly in oven or double boiler, to prevent its coloring, then filtering it through cheesecloth and storing it in glass jars in the refrigerator. The best fat comes from around the kidneys.

An all-lard crust is much shorter and flakier than a butter crust, although Miss Eliza Leslie warns, "Lard for paste should never be used without an equal quantity of butter." Mrs. A. L. Webster in *The Improved Housewife* indicates why, when she says, "Pie-crust looks the handsomest made wholly of lard, but it does not taste so well as to have a proportion of butter." Like Miss Leslie, she gives a number of Common Pastes for Pies, including one all butter, one all lard, and one with a mixture of two teacups of lard to one of butter.

Anyone nostalgic for the taste of an old-fashioned American piecrust can get it by reversing the proportions of butter to lard in Child's formula to make ½ cup lard or shortening to 3 tablespoons butter. The lard needs to be chilled, as does the butter, before cutting into the flour.

# PUFF PASTE

Of all pastes, the multifoliate puff paste is both the king and queen of pastrydom. It is thought to have originated in the kitchens of the dukes of Tuscany in the fifteenth century and to have come to France by way of Marie de Medici, but however it began it remained a royal paste. Its French name, *pâte feuilletée*, suggests the tissue-thin leaves interlarded with cold butter that rise spectacularly when heat melts the butter and creates steam between the leaves. Hence the puff.

Because the dough freezes so well, it's a pity we can't buy frozen puff paste of the first quality at our local supermarket. Frozen paste, when available at specialty stores, is too often made entirely, or with a high proportion, of shortening or lard. This is one paste that should be made entirely of butter for both flavor and texture.

The principles are not difficult but the process is very time-consuming, so that it is best to make it in sizable quantities and to freeze whatever you do not immediately use. Child's instructions in volume II of *Mastering* were exceptionally clear in the illustrations, but to spell the process out in detail was also to deter the home cook from embarking. The only way to simplify puff paste is to do fewer than six turns, which produces nine layers of butter to make 10 leaves. You can, however, make Mock Puff Paste by spreading an ordinary piecrust dough with extra butter and then folding it several times as you would classic puff paste to produce multiple layers.

For *Mock Puff Paste,* roll butter-crust dough into a rectangle 20 by 8 inches, spread with 2 tablespoons softened but cold butter, and fold the dough in thirds, like an envelope. Rotate the dough from here ⬭ to here ⬚ , roll again into a 20-inch rectangle and spread with 2 more tablespoons butter. Fold again in thirds, wrap, and chill in the refrigerator for 30 minutes. Roll and fold twice more, without adding butter, to make a total of four turns. Chill until ready to use.

In *Classic Puff Paste,* the proportions of flour and butter are equal. American recipes call for a mixture of cake flour and all-purpose flour to weaken the high gluten content of our regular flour, which is good for bread but not good for pastry. The best method is to work a little butter into the flour and a little flour into the butter before rolling them out together.

## Proportions for Classic Puff Paste

for an 8-inch vol-au-vent, 8 to 10 small patty shells or a 16- to 18-inch rectangular shell: 1¼ pounds flour to 1¼ pounds butter

| | |
|---|---|
| 3¾ **cups all-purpose flour** | 1¼ **pounds unsalted butter** |
| ¾ **cup cake flour** | ½ **teaspoon lemon juice** |
| 1 **teaspoon salt** | 1 **cup ice water** |

1. Mix the flours and salt together and set aside ½ cup. Cut ¼ pound of the butter into small pieces and cut into the flour, as if making short paste. Add the ice water and lemon juice and knead quickly until the dough is no longer sticky. You can do this in an electric mixer or in two batches in a processor.

2. Flatten the remaining four sticks of butter with a rolling pin, cut into ½-inch slices, and toss them in ½ cup reserved flour. Chill for at least 15 minutes. Work the floured butter quickly with the fingers until smooth and shape into a 4- by 4- by 1½-inch square. Wrap in foil and chill again for at least 30 minutes.

3. Make a cross cut ½ inch deep in the ball of dough and push out each corner to make a four-leaf clover, leaving a thick mound in the center. Roll out each leaf to make the clover 1½ feet long in both directions.

4. Place the square of butter in the center of the mound. Bring each leaf up over the square and seal it well. Flour lightly, wrap, and chill for 30 minutes.

5. Roll gently and evenly into a 20- by 10-inch rectangle, being careful not to let the butter break through. If any does, flour it, brush off any excess, and continue to roll. Fold the dough back on itself about two thirds of the way up and then fold the remaining third back toward you to make an envelope. Indent one edge with a finger to mark the FIRST TURN. Wrap and chill for 30 minutes.

6. With the narrow end facing you, roll the dough again into a rectangle for the SECOND TURN, fold in thirds, indent it, and chill again. Repeat four more times to make a total of SIX TURNS, chilling the dough between each turn. Keep the board lightly floured to prevent the dough from sticking, but be sure to remove any excess flour from the dough or it will get rough and dry.

7. To make a round vol-au-vent, roll the dough ¼ inch thick, lay it on a dinner plate or cake pan for a model, and cut around it, running the knife straight down. Cut two circles. Cut a smaller circle from one to leave a rim an inch wide.

8. Brush the rim of the first circle with cold water. Place the cut-out rim on top. Scallop the edges every ¾ inch with the back of a knife. Cut a hairline around the inner circle with a knife point and score the top lightly with the knife to make a diamond design.

9. Glaze the top with beaten egg but be careful not to drip the glaze over the sides or the dough won't rise. Chill for 30 minutes, glaze again, and bake at 425 degrees for 20 minutes, then at 375 degrees for another 20.

10. Lift the center and remove the uncooked dough from the inside while it is still warm. You can store cooked vol-au-vent up to two days in the refrigerator and reheat when ready to use or freeze and store in a plastic bag.

*For dessert, fill with whipped cream flavored with liqueur, with a butter cream (see Praline Torte, page 382) or a chocolate mousse. For a main dish, fill with creamed sweetbreads and mushrooms (see page 270) or a seafood mixture like creamed crab (see page 88). Because of its high butter content, the paste should be at room temperature (or hotter) for the full taste and flake.*

# CHEESE

*Spiced*

Hungarian Cheese · 357

*Fried*

Deep-Fried Brie · 358

*Toasted*

Welsh Rabbit · 360
Italian Grilled Cheese Sandwich · 361

*Crumbled*

Gorgonzola, Walnut, and Pear Salad · 362

*Sugared*

Sugared Cheese Cream · 363

*Baked*

Marinated Baked Goat Cheese · 365

*"To Make an Excellent Winter Cheese"*—*To a cheese of 2 gallons of new milke, take 10 quarts of stroakings and 2 quarts of cream. put to it 4 spoonfuls of rennit, set it together as hot as you can from ye Cow . . .*

—Martha Washington's Booke of
Cookery *(1749)*

In 1983, it's hard to imagine a day when most American housewifes were cheese-makers, not to mention cow milkers, and when a daily concern was not how to get milk cold but how to get it as hot as you can from ye cow. It's almost as hard to imagine a day when milk was not pasteurized and cheese was not processed. In 1904, it would have been just as hard for a housewife to imagine a day when many cheese eaters and milk drinkers had never tasted new milk nor ever would.

In Chicago in 1904, when J. H. Kraft was a young man who began to peddle "canned cheese" wrapped in foil or jars to preserve it, he could hardly have imagined a day when 99 percent of American cheese would be canned and preserved, most of it in the name of Kraft. When, in 1914, Kraft finally found a way to blend a number of fresh cheeses and to cook them to abort their natural growth and decay, he could not have anticipated that Clifton Fadiman would condemn him for it, remarking that "processed cheese is the triumph of technology over conscience."

For the next fifty years the triumph of American technology over conscience produced cheese in two flavors, hard and soft. Cheese categories in the 1943 *Joy of Cooking* are thick yellow, sharp American, soft cream, soft blue, soft cottage, brick, and pimiento. In the edition twenty years later, a few imported cheeses have snuck in, Gruyère and Edam for hard, Gouda for semi-hard, and ricotta for soft. While American taste was changing, American milk laws were not. American milk laws forbade and still forbid the importing of any natural cheese—that is, cheese made of raw, unheated milk—that has not been aged for two months. Because milk laws in all but a few American states forbade and still forbid the *sale* of any natural cheese, imported or domestic, that has not been aged, American technology has triumphed over taste as well as conscience.

It is small wonder that in American menus the cheese rarely stands alone. In our cookbooks, cheese was a cake, a cracker, a biscuit, a sandwich, a soufflé, a rarebit, a fondu, a blintz, a cream, but seldom a separate course as in France or even England. The English often ended a meal with a rich Stilton or sharp Cheddar as a substitute for the savory, that final salt fillip that ended the food and opened the port. The French often ended with fruit and cheese because they complemented each other and because cheese offered an excuse for opening a really good bottle of even more complementary wine. In a proper French restaurant, the cheese tray dazzled eye and nose with its array of shapes, sizes, textures, and smells. In America, what was the point of a tray of uniformly pasteurized blends of green cheese, old cheese, emulsifiers and water, squeezed into different shapes like Play-doh and indistinguishable from toothpaste?

Still, after the war, aged European cheeses could again be imported and were. The chance to expand into the American market brought changes in European cheese-making, so that traditional natural cheeses like Brie and Camembert were increasingly pasteurized for export. In the fifties, pasteurized Brie was better than none until, of course, you got to Europe and tasted the real thing. Generations who had never tasted anything headier than Velveeta did get to Europe and sampled cheese as they sampled wine—fanatically. We learned names like Pont-l'Évêque and Reblochon as we learned regions like Mâcon and Rhone. We studied photographs in color, like the one in Claiborne's first cookbook, labeled "An assortment of international cheeses." We studied recipes in Child which seemed to specify exclusively Swiss or Parmesan, both imported. We learned from Beard how to find good cheeses even in America if you sent to California for Jack and Wisconsin for blue and Herkimer County, New York, for Cheddar.

With new demands new markets opened in the sixties and seventies and whole stores were devoted to cheese. Increasingly the cheese counter became the center of fine food stores and classy delicatessens. Americans who had for decades laughed at smelly ethnic cheeses like Liederkranz and Limburger, a pair of clowns in countless burlesque skits and funny papers, now sniffed along the cheese counters and paid handsomely for the privilege. As the European Common Market made available cheeses seldom smelled or heard of before, so it began to invent new ones under French-sounding names that would justify their ever increasing butter content and cost.

Today, imported processed cheeses have so proliferated that they too are often indistinguishable except as hard or soft. Whole countries as well as categories have become processed as we come upon Danish Gorgonzola and Finnish Swiss. The wheel has come full circle as young Americans are beginning to make "French" goat cheese like chèvre in the old "natural" ways as a home industry. As more local fresh cheeses are available, more young American cooks are devising ways to use them, as in a marinated and baked chèvre. Perhaps as more and more Americans encounter the full range of the world's cheeses, even our milk laws, as hardened as a forty-year-old Cheddar, will crumble and allow us to make an excellent winter cheese of new milk hot from ye cow.

# HUNGARIAN CHEESE

The idea of adding something to bland cheese—herbs, spices, condiments, vegetables, or meats—in order to jack up the flavor did not originate with the Pasteurized Process Blended Cheeses which are distinguishable from each other solely by the addition of ham flecks, stuffed olives, or pimientos. The Danish and Dutch were fond of flavoring their bland Edams or Samsoes with caraway. The English of Derbyshire ground up sage to turn their Cheddars green. But the Hungarians went all out in turning their briny sheep cheese called Liptauer into a powerful spread that could stand up to the vigor of their dark breads and the potency of their schnapps.

Schnapps or gin or dark beer, in fact, was one of the flavorings that helped to ripen an earthy Hungarian mixture of anchovies, mustard, caraway, paprika, and chives, smoothed out by cream cheese and butter. During the early days of the cocktail party, American cream cheese spreads were seldom spiked with anything stronger than curry powder or with anything smellier than blue cheese. This was a time when we rolled Cheddar cheese logs in walnuts and broiled crackers spread with American orange cheese and chutney. A Liptauer spread appeared as a subversive and exciting alternative to the bland leading the bland.

Claiborne's Liptauer recipe in his first *Times Cook Book* called for equal parts of cottage cheese and butter, but a mixture of cottage cheese and cream cheese was a more usual substitute for the soft Hungarian cheese from Liptow. Now that we are importing goat cheeses from everywhere, and even making our own, and now that the processor makes cheese blending easy, we can experiment with far more tasty cheese bases to make our own homemade Process Blended Cheeses.

Since the salty Greek cheese feta is widely available, I've suggested using a bit of that to give the goatish tang of Liptauer. But if you want to afford an American or French goat cheese for this spread, you can dismiss the other cheeses and use only the chèvre or substitute it for any one of the cheeses. The anchovies will in any case give saltiness and the butter creaminess. Hungarian paprika will lend its distinctive sweetness. And as for schnapps, gin, or dark beer, any of them will bring a whiff of the Carpathian mountains into our urban parlors when we serve up Hungarian cheese.

## Proportions

for 20 to 30 cocktail servings (or about 3 cups), 1 pound cheese, ¼ pound butter, 1 can of anchovies, ¼ cup of beer

| | |
|---|---|
| **1 pound cheese (such as ¼ pound feta plus ¾ pound cream cheese or cottage cheese. Or, ½ pound each of cream and cottage cheese. Or, ½ pound chèvre plus ½ pound cream or cottage cheese)** | **2 sardines (canned, or salted, skinned, and boned)** |
| **¼ pound unsalted butter** | **2 hard-boiled eggs, chopped** |
| **1 can anchovies with capers** | **1 teaspoon caraway seeds** |
| | **1 teaspoon Dijon mustard** |
| | **1½ tablespoons Hungarian paprika** |
| | **¼ cup beer, preferably dark, or gin or schnapps** |
| | **¼ cup chopped chives** |

1.   Bring the cheese and butter to room temperature and process or cream together by hand. Add the anchovies, including their oil, the sardines, and the eggs, and process into a smooth paste. Add the caraway, mustard, and paprika. Then add the beer gradually. The mixture will harden under refrigeration, so don't worry if it seems a bit soupy now.

2.   Pack into a bowl or wide-mouthed jar, cover, and refrigerate. Tastes best if left to ripen for about a week. Unmold and sprinkle with chives before serving, or beat in chives at last moment in processor if you want the spread creamily soft instead of firm like cold butter.

*Serve with thinly sliced rye or pumpernickel toast, with Euphrates crackers or toasted pita bread. Can be served as a first course in the way that you might serve Shrimp Butter (see page 91).*

# DEEP-FRIED BRIE

Where Beard had been born with a wheel of Brie in his mouth, supplied by early French émigrés to San Francisco, few of us before the war were so favored by birth or good fortune. Generally, Camembert was the only soft-ripening French cheese around and it could not ripen because it was sterilized at birth. So the Camembert choice was usually between a hard "green" round or a brown squishy one reeking of ammonia. Brie, on the other hand, when it first began to be imported in some quantity in the 1950s, revealed the quality Camembert was capable of but seldom showed this side the Atlantic. Brie came in spectacular milk-white wheels, downy as a baby's skin, seemingly firm but ready to run at the first opportunity. The trick was to get a cut piece of Brie home before it spread into a pool in hand or lap.

Thirty years later our cheese revolution is such that, today, Brie with a red, white, and blue Île de France label is a big wheel at the supermarket, but it doesn't run anymore. It stays as green as the day it was born. Meanwhile, a whole Milky Way of soft-ripening buttery creamy cheeses has replaced it at fancy cheese counters with ever fancier names and ever higher butterfat content. For a while, Brie-lovers ran to Crema Danica, Caprice des Dieux, Crème Royale, Boursault, Boursin, Une Gourmandise!!!, as cheeses from the Common Market took on the packaging and punctuation of Hollywood. But as new cheeses moved in and took over, a good Brie was hard to find. Brie is today where Camembert was fifty years ago, often a cheese in name only, with a texture and shelf life that would gladden the heart of any rubber manufacturer.

But one way to redeem the hardened supermarket Brie is to make it run artificially by deep-frying it. The result is showy and delicious, based on the principle of the Baked Alaska. You're not supposed to bake ice cream. You're not supposed to deep-fry cheese. If you coat it well with bread crumbs, however, and give it a quick hot bath, it will respond to your treatment by melting creamily inside as if touched by your kindness.

## Proportions

for 24 to 30 servings, 1 pound cheese, 2 cups of bread crumbs

| | |
|---|---|
| 1 **pound Brie (in circle or wedge)** | 1 **tablespoon water** |
| ½ **cup flour** | 2 **cups fresh bread crumbs** |
| 1 **egg** | **Vegetable oil for frying** |

1.   Cut the unpeeled Brie lengthwise and crosswise into squares and triangles to make large bite-sized pieces. Dip first into flour and then into egg, beaten with a tablespoon of water.

2.   Coat each piece well with bread crumbs and chill in the refrigerator until ready to use.

3.   Heat enough oil in a deep frying pan or deep-fat fryer to cover the pieces entirely (at least 2 inches). When the oil is hot but not smoking (360 degrees), add the Brie a few pieces at a time and stir constantly until golden brown. Drain each batch on paper towels. Don't worry if the cheese leaks a bit. Serve hot or warm. If necessary, you can reheat the pieces in a hot skillet or oven, but their shapes will be more wobbly.

*Serve as drink food or as a first course.*

# WELSH RABBIT

The English might have called this venerable dish of thickened cheese "Irish Rabbit" or "Scotch Rabbit" or even "Polish Rabbit," to suggest comic stupidity as well as poverty. But they didn't, and the Welsh must have complained toward the end of the last century at being singled out for ridicule. Cookbooks of the period begin to euphemize "Rabbit" to "Rarebit," as if in tribute to the taste and discrimination of the Welsh.

No Welshman, however, need have been ashamed of the dish itself as prepared by Eliza Leslie of "some fine mellow cheese," grated and put into a cheese-toaster with mustard, cayenne pepper, and a glass of fresh porter or red wine. She stirred the mixture over hot coals until melted, then browned it with "a salamander, or a red-hot shovel."

When a brick or wheel of fine mellow cheese was as necessary to a household as a loaf of bread, toasting or roasting cheese was as common as revivifying bread by the same means. Mrs. Crowen in her *American Lady's Cookery Book* suggests "roasting" grated cheese with egg yolks, bread crumbs, butter, and mustard to spread on bread heated in a Dutch oven. For her "Rabbit," she omits the thickening properties of yolk and crumb and thins the paste with milk, but the idea of a "roasted" cheese spread is the same.

About the time "Rarebit" takes hold as a name, the joke of a poor man's "rabbit" resurfaces in a dish of melted cheese and toast topped by a poached egg and labeled "Golden Buck." Claiborne, curiously, picks up the latter name (in *The New York Times Cook Book*) for a Welsh Rabbit enriched with a great many beaten eggs. The fact that he gives two recipes, one for a "Rabbit" and one for a "Buck," in his latest cookbook, may help rehabilitate this long-neglected supper dish that, made with milk, has soothed generations of weary children and, made with "ale, porter, beer, or Champagne" (as Mrs. Seely advises in her 1902 cookbook), has soothed generations of weekend weary adults. It may even, from time to time, have soothed hungry and none-too-bright Welshmen.

---

## Proportions

for 4 to 6 servings, 1 pound cheese, 6 tablespoons butter, 1 bottle (12 ounces) beer

1 **pound sharp Cheddar**
6 **tablespoons butter**
2 **teaspoons Dijon mustard**
4 **teaspoons Worcestershire sauce**
   **Tabasco sauce**

1 **12-ounce bottle dark beer (or stout or any good beer)**
4 **egg yolks**
   **Toasted English muffins or white or wheat bread**

1. Grate the cheese in a processor or by hand and put in the top of a double boiler with butter and seasonings.

2. Beat the egg yolks into the beer and add to the cheese while it is melting, stirring constantly to make the mixture smooth. Taste for seasoning and adjust to desired sharpness. Pour over toasted muffins or bread. Serve hot, but if there is any cheese left over, refrigerate and use as a cheese spread the next day. Keeps very well.

*Because this is a satisfying one-dish meal, which does indeed substitute for meat or fowl, serve with a simple green salad and ripe fruit.*

# ITALIAN GRILLED CHEESE SANDWICH

Every country that has cheese has some version of a toasted cheese sandwich, since melted cheese is a natural glue to stick slices of bread together. Americans have stuck bread together with melted Velveeta on thousands, probably millions, of luncheonette grills. The French have stuck bread together with melted Swiss, have tucked in a slice of ham, have browned it in a skillet with quantities of butter, and have called it Croque Monsieur. The Italians have stuck bread together with mozzarella, dipped it in egg, and deep-fried it to produce Mozzarella in Carozza.

Most Americans have encountered mozzarella first as the pale glucy sheet that sticks a tomato spread to a mattress of pizza dough. The rubber balls of processed whole or skim milk, wrapped tight in a plastic skin, that we find in our supermarket cheese counters bear little relation to the original peasant cheese of southern Italy made from the milk of oxen called "buffalo." No relation to the American bison. While fresh buffalo-milk mozzarella is just beginning to be imported now from Italy at fancy prices (*because* it is fresh, not cured and, therefore, subject to spoilage), freshly made cow's milk mozzarella is available at good Italian or specialty cheese stores and that is the mozzarella to use.

This bland dairy-fresh cheese has a natural affinity to the acid of tomatoes, complementing by contrast both taste and color. With their high visual sense, the Italians have exploited the contrast not only in their pizzas but in that simplest and best of salads composed of alternating slices of mozzarella and tomatoes, bathed in olive oil and scented with basil.

The contrast reappears in any grilled cheese and tomato sandwich, or should, if the cheese and tomato are not both composed of plastic. To anyone fond of making "grilled" cheese sandwiches at home by frying them on both sides in butter, which melts the cheese and butters and toasts the bread, mozzarella is a delicious alternative to Swiss or processed orange or yellow American. Child (in *Julia Child's Kitchen*) suggested the superiority of mozzarella to Swiss in making a Croque Monsieur. Similarly, I find that mozzarella transforms the old deli grilled cheese-and-tomato sandwich into a luncheon dish fit for my snootiest friends.

## Proportions

for 4 servings, ½ pound mozzarella, 2 tomatoes, 8 slices bread, 4 tablespoons butter

8 **slices good white bread**  
4 **tablespoons (½ stick) butter**  
½ **pound fresh mozzarella, sliced**

2 **fresh firm tomatoes, sliced**

1. Butter 8 slices of bread and put 4 of them butter side down in a large cast-iron frying pan. Cover each slice with a thin layer of cheese and 2 slices of tomatoes. Top each with a slice of buttered bread, butter side up.

2. Toast the bread in the pan over moderate heat, lifting the bottom slices with a spatula to see that the bread doesn't burn. When the bottom is golden brown, turn with the spatula to toast the other side (the butter keeps the bread from sticking). If this cheese doesn't melt properly (because the cheese is too cold and the pan is too hot), cover the pan with a lid to keep in the heat.

*Serve by cutting sandwiches in two on the diagonal. Garnish with a fresh radish or a leaf of basil.*

# GORGONZOLA, WALNUT, AND PEAR SALAD

Cheese has always belonged to the world of salads as it has always belonged to the world of breads. American and Swiss, cubed or shredded, have topped the standardized Chef's Salad, just as freshly grated Parmesan has rendered its tribute to Caesar's Salad. Roquefort or some lesser Blue has crumbled its way into dressings to coat each leafy green with salt and cream. Gorgonzola, that creamiest of Italian blues, has also had a happy association with fruit, especially pears ripened in the Italian sun.

Claiborne, in *The New New York Times Cookbook*, stuffs poached pears with softened Gorgonzola, sprinkles them with pistachios, and serves them warm for dessert. The same lovely combination of cheese, nuts, and fruit can make a salad to serve cold instead of a dessert.

# Proportions

for 4 servings, 1 head lettuce, ½ pound Gorgonzola, 1 cup of walnuts, 4 pears

| | |
|---|---|
| 1 head Boston lettuce, or similar soft green | 1 cup coarsely chopped walnuts |
| 4 ripe pears, peeled and sliced | 1 cup basic salad dressing, |
| ½ pound Gorgonzola, ripe and creamy | such as creamy yogurt or tofu (page 142) |

1.  Wash and dry the salad greens and arrange them flat on a serving plate. Peel the pears, halve them, and scoop out the cores with a spoon or melon-baller. Put the pears core side down in order to slice them. Slice each half quickly, slip a spatula underneath to retain the pear's shape, and place the halves in a circle on the greens, stem end toward the middle.

2.  Crumble the cheese over the pears or between them (as in spokes of a wheel). Sprinkle with the walnuts. Pour over the whole a creamy salad dressing or a fresh mayonnaise thinned with cream or a *crème fraîche* spiked with lemon or vinegar.

*Because of the nuts and cheese, this is a rich salad that would complement a bowl of soup to make a full meal.*

# SUGARED CHEESE CREAM

So accustomed are we to foil-wrapped packs of processed cream cheese designed for everlastingness that a recipe for "Milk Cheese" can startle us into recognition that the making of fresh cheese was once as important to daily life as the making of fresh butter. Cheese, as Vivienne Marquis and Patricia Haskell point out in *The Cheese Book* (1964), is simply preserved milk, so that cheese is to milk what wine is to grapes. "Fresh" cheese, then, like "new" wine, is the first stage of many in a process by which man utilizes the decay of nature to nourish his own brief span.

Nature thickens milk by separating it into curds and whey. Man helps nature along by heating the milk to hasten the "souring," by skimming the curd and draining it, by pressing the curd and sometimes salting it and sometimes adding cream to enrich it. He may ripen or cure the pressed curd to preserve milk over long periods of time or he may eat the curd fresh, salted, or sugared to heighten its flavor. If he begins with skimmed milk, he may call the resulting curd "Bonny-Clabber or Loppered Milk," as Marion Harland does in *Common Sense in the Household* (1893). If he begins with whole milk or thick sour milk which contains a goodly proportion of cream, he may call the result "Cheese-Cream" as Mrs. Crowen does in her *Lady's Cookery Book* (1866).

Under either name, the soft white curd was once a traditional American dessert as it has always been for the French, with their single, double, and triple creams indicating the degree of buttery richness. The French make dessert of a simple soured milk called Fromage Blanc, when they drain it in a heart-shaped wicker basket, cloak it in cream and sugar, and call it *Coeur à la Crème.* The Italians, for dessert, make a cheese of fresh cream and call it *mascarpone* to eat with sugar and fruit or frothed with brandy.

Fresh cheese, whether called farmer's or pot or cottage and whether made of milk or cream, sweet or sour, can be frothed and aerated in a processor or pressed and drained in a cheesecloth-lined sieve. It can be surrounded by fresh fruit like strawberries or raspberries or set in a pool of raspberry syrup or melted and sieved strawberry jam. Or it can simply be sugared and served with heavy cream or *crème fraîche* or sour cream. As Mrs. Harland said of Bonny-Clabber, "Few people know how delicious this healthful and cheap dessert can be made, if eaten before it becomes tart and tough, with a liberal allowance of cream and sugar."

## Proportions

for 4 to 6 servings, 1 pound fresh white cheese, 1 cup of heavy cream, ¼ cup of sugar

| | |
|---|---|
| 1 **pound fresh white cheese (such as farmer's, pot, cottage, goat, or cream cheese itself)** | 1 **cup heavy cream (or sour cream or *crème fraîche*)**<br>¼ **cup sugar, or to taste** |

1. Everything depends on the kind of curd you begin with and the effect you desire. To make the cheese light and airy, beat it with some of the cream in the processor or electric mixer. To make the cheese dense and compact, beat it with enough cream to smooth the curd, then press it into a sieve or mold lined with cheesecloth, and set over a bowl in the refrigerator overnight.

2. To unmold, invert the cheese onto a plate, sugar it well, and serve surrounded with fresh fruit. If desired, serve extra cream separately.

*Since creamed cheese is rich and filling, this is a good dessert to follow a light main dish, such as a roast chicken or broiled chop.*

# MARINATED BAKED GOAT CHEESE

California is one of the few states where raw milk, certified but not pasteurized, is allowed to be sold. Consequently, California makes some of America's best cheese from both cows and goats. Recently a goat cheese that equals French chèvre in quality, because it is made of the best goat milk by age-old French methods, is being made in Sonoma Valley, where quality wines have increased the demand for quality cheese. As a good wine needs no bush, a good cheese needs no marinade. But because the most common form of goat cheese is relatively mild, it is nicely complemented by herbs for flavor and oil for richness, so that it becomes a dish in itself, to be served at the beginning or end of a meal. I like to serve it with salad, so that the hot herbed oil becomes the salad dressing and a crusty loaf of French bread accompanies both salad and cheese at once.

## Proportions

for 6 servings, 1 long cylinder (in the shape called "montrachet") or 6 small rounds (called "crottin" or "cabecou") to ½ cup of oil

| | |
|---|---|
| 1 teaspoon thyme | 1 tablespoon freshly ground |
| 1 teaspoon rosemary | black pepper |
| 1 teaspoon coriander | 1 long or 6 small goat cheeses |
| ½ teaspoon savory | ½ cup olive oil |
| 2 bay leaves, crushed | |

1.  Mix the herbs and spices together, substituting others according to taste, press them into the cheese on all sides, and cover with oil in a dish or bowl. Cover the top with plastic wrap and let ripen in a cool place for a day before refrigerating. Will keep refrigerated more or less indefinitely.

2.  When ready to use, place in a baking dish with some of the oil and heat in a 400-degree oven for 5 minutes.

**Variation**

If you continue to heat the cheese another 10 or 15 minutes until it has melted, you end with a flavorsome and delicious cheese spread, whether served hot or cold. You can treat a whole-milk ricotta cheese the same way, either melting it for an herbed spread or shaping it into a cylinder or round.

# SWEETS

*To remove sugar from the kitchen were to deprive alimentation of many of its benefits and pleasures, as well as to rob woman of much of her allurement. She would become lean and scrawny, her rounded outlines would gradually disappear, the contours of her tailor-made gown would end by becoming rectilinear, and for her habiliment a straight-jacket would usurp the place of her proud corsage and bouffant petticoat.*

—George H. Ellwanger
The Pleasures of the Table
(1902)

Ellwanger was on to something when he saw sugar as the key to taste in fashion as well as food. His reasoning was impeccable and he can hardly be faulted for underestimating the fickleness of sexual fashion. Contemplating sugar-loaf contours fore and aft, he could hardly imagine that a woman might *want* to become rectilinear and straight-jacketed. The contemplative boulevardier was done in by underestimating the power of the new women dietitians. At the very time he was pleasuring himself at the table, Mrs. Sarah Tysen Rorer was lecturing the well-rounded women of Philadelphia from the stage. "Under protest I shall make for you some new desserts which I hope none of you will think of imitating," she told them. "Remember, desserts are both unhealthy and unnecessary as articles of food."

It would be good to know just what new desserts she then demonstrated that they were not to imitate. A chocolate mousse cake with sabayon sauce? A coconut cream pie? Whatever they were, she set the tone of the double-talk that plagues every woman trying to square her circles today to a rectilinear form and to every man trying to make time stand still. Through the preachments of women like Mrs. Rorer, sugar took the place of Satan in a Garden of Eden where the proffered apple was candied. Those unhealthy and unnecessary desserts became as thrilling as sin and as inevitable as guilt. No wonder today women have taken refuge in anorexia and bulimia while men jog themselves into cardiac arrest.

Never has chocolate, for instance, had such a very bad name and never has it been so egregiously consumed. And not just in little bonbons and foil-wrapped kisses but in solid one-pound bricks wrapped in gold. Chocoholics are confessing at the rate of the nuns of Loudon to demonic possession. Cookbooks, cooking classes, round-the-world tours devoted exclusively to chocolate do not begin to exhaust our chocomania. Chocomaniacs are rivaled only by ice-screamers. Secret screamers plug

SWEETS · 367

in the electric ice-cream maker while publicly nibbling lettuce and cottage cheese. Proclaimed dieters who condemn rolls and potatoes as fattening will down a quart of chocolate ice cream and still complain of withdrawal symptoms.

For many Americans the unnecessary dessert is not only the climax of the meal but a pleasurable pain as anticipated and delayed as sexual climax. Not so for the French. The traditional French menu was shaped around the climax of the entrée and everything after—vegetable, salad, cheese, fruit, and dessert—was lumped together as the *entremets,* meaning after the entrée. Even the word "dessert" is nugatory in French since it derives from "de-servir," meaning to clear the table. The dessert course was designed to clear the dining room like those vaudeville acts designed to clear the house for the next show.

To end a meal with fruit is decidedly French and not English. Ellwanger quotes the authority of a seventeenth-century Englishman to convey the harmful effects of fruit: "As for frute after fude, it's a downright abomination, and coagulates on the stomach like sour curds." When Americans thought to imitate the French, they did as Paul Pierce did in his *Dinners and Luncheons* of 1907. They skipped the fruit and concentrated on "small cold sweets, such as *éclairs,* fancy cakes called *petits-fours,* confectionery, candied fruits, nuts, individual moulded jellies, ices and creams, *glacés* and *café noir.*" Thank God for the *café noir.* When Americans thought to imitate the English, they went all out for puddings, creams, cakes, candies, possets, pastes, and pies.

Pies, above all. The American housewife not only baked her own bread, she baked her own pies. For her there was no ritual Sunday noon visit to the *patisserie* for éclairs or strawberry tarts any more than a daily visit to the *boulangerie* for bread. Her dessert thoughts were not classified as the French housewife's were into homemade sweets like simple fruit compotes and store-bought everything else. If an American housewife wanted fruit dressed up in a buttery crust, she had to do it herself. And she did. Her pies became a symbol of homespun Americana as sacred as the American Mom they resembled in shape.

When the Reverend Henry Ward Beecher extolled the American apple pie, he made a proper crust the aim of every righteous woman: "Aim at that glorious medium in which it is tender without being too fugaciously flaky," he warned his parishioners, "short without being too short; a mild, sapid, brittle thing, that lies upon the tongue, so as to let the apple strike through and touch the papillae with a more affluent flavour." That must have sent them reeling back to their rolling pins, with trembling papillae.

So important was the symbolic value of the American pie that George Rector, addressing himself in 1934 to What Men like and Why, asserted that pie belonged not to women but to men. He granted that women made pie, but women were always worrying too much about their rounded outlines to eat it. Pie was a man's dish because it was made for men and men ate it. It symbolized the manliness of the American male and "his inalienable right to holler for a piece of apple and a cuppa Java."

In 1934, many men and women were worrying less about their inalienable rights than they were about starving to death. Pies were practical. Apples, flour, and lard were relatively cheap, and filling, like potatoes. Anything could be baked in a crust, thickened with flour, and sweetened with molasses. But cakes were something else. Cakes were costly and they were difficult. Housewives had always been warned against them. Eliza Leslie took a particularly severe tone when it came to cakes. "Unless you are provided with proper and convenient utensils and materials," she warned, "the difficulty of preparing cakes will be great, and in most instances a failure."

No self-respecting homesteader would take that kind of challenge lying down. Homesteaders responded then as they responded later to Mrs. Rorer's "unhealthy and unnecessary" articles or as smokers respond today to warnings from the Surgeon General. Cakes became the thing to bake: rich, thick, sweet, light, filled, layered, rounded, and squared. The greater their difficulty the more fanciful they became. They bore names that spoke not only of public dignity, names like Lady Baltimore, Hartford Election, Boston Cream, Cincinnati, but also of hotly contested bake-offs, names like Tin-Wedding, Watermelon, Aunt Hettie's, Hard-Money, Angel's Food.

Cakes were the *non plus ultra* of the homemaker's art, and cookbooks like *The Buckeye* devoted long sections to Ornamental Icing and Artistic Piping, with Diagrams, as outlined by Professor C. H. King. A wedding cake was an excuse for ornament as elaborate as embroidery. And farmer's wives who had no time for petit point or watercolor could yet express the arts of gentilesse by painting mauve or indigo roses of sugar on a background of palest pink.

During the thirties, as people grew poorer, their cake fancies grew richer. The dessert section in cookbooks ballooned to fill a third or sometimes half the book. It took the war to end the homebaker's pride and her flights of fancy. Not just by a shortage of sugar and fats but by streamlined rectilinear packaging, first for K-rations, then for cake mixes. The heyday of the homemade monster cake, swollen with creams and frostings, was over. The old-fashioned bake sale that once furnished a king's ransom of cakes and calories was no longer respectable. In the new double-speak of diets the rectilinear chocolate bar was more alluring than the fluffy contours of a double-layer devil's-food cake with coconut-marshmallow frosting.

But the sweet famished tooth was not pulled. It just sunk itself into richer and more condensed pleasures imported from abroad. Instead of American pies, it ate French tarts. Instead of baked custards, soufflés.

Instead of cakes, tortes and *dacquoises*. And for the cook short of time, there was always chocolate to fall back on, the very best bittersweet from Switzerland or Belgium, quickly rolled into truffles or whipped into mousse. If female beauty was inconstant, the sweet tooth was not. The sweet tooth was one thing you could count on, to the bittersweet end.

# APPLE-PECAN PIE

George Rector, advocate of the he-man American pie, recalled the response of "the colored counter boy" at a railroad lunch room in the 1880s when asked what kind of pies he had. " 'Well, gemmen,' he said, 'we got three kinds: Theah's kivered, unkivered and crossbarred'—and then he looked at us sadlike—'but they's all apple und'neath.' " A century of railroad-lunch-room pie with crust of cardboard and appleloid glue has not yet killed off our fondness for the taste of apples in a hot short crust —kivered, unkivered, and crossbarred.

One reason is that our apples are good, even if less various than a century ago, and another is that we have learned to make all kinds of good crusts. We have learned to make crusts with different proportions of butter and lard and to shape them into one-crust, two-crust, lattice-work, free-form, upside-down crusts. From the Germans we have learned to layer apples in strudels and from the French to layer them in open-faced tarts or puff paste.

Many of us learned how to make an American apple pie by first learning from Child how to make a French fruit tart. Scorning a pie cut in the pan, we experimented with the French *flan* ring, which allowed the crust to stand on its own when the metal mold was removed after baking. The first virtue of the French open-faced tart is that the crust becomes a display case for fruit arranged decoratively to show off its beauty. The second is that the crust is baked before filling so that it does not sog from juices exuded by the fruit in cooking. But the sweet short paste or sugar crust typical of a French tart, spread with cooked apple slices and glazed with apricot preserves, results in what Americans might call an apple cookie.

Americans traditionally like flakier crusts (see page 348), "tender without being too fugaciously flaky," as Henry Ward Beecher said. But again it depends on what tradition you pick—Mom's, Grandma's, or Miss Eliza Leslie's. Miss Eliza Leslie's Best Plain Paste was a puff paste of many folds and turns. Her Common Pie Crust was a quicker puff paste of fewer turns. She went on to Sweet Paste and Fine Puff Paste and to Suet Paste, Dripping Paste, and Lard Paste. Lard paste, she 'lowed, should always have an equal quantity of butter and should be used "for common pies."

The lard/butter controversy has less to do with national distinctions between American and French than with style—plain or fancy. Child's paste for fruit tarts is fancy, using a high proportion of butter to flour, with sugar added and sometimes eggs as well. Beard's paste has evolved from plain to plainer. He recommended an all-butter crust in his first general cookbook, but also tolerated margarine, vegetable shortening, and lard. In *The New James Beard,* he has moved to an all-lard crust, recommending the finest leaf lard rendered from pork kidney fat. Claiborne, in *The New New York Times Cookbook,* keeps a foot in both worlds by offering two pastes: one all-shortening and the other all-butter.

All of them continue to turn out recipes for apple pie. Claiborne calls his pie Tarte aux Pommes, and follows the more or less classic recipe Child gave in volume I of *Mastering.* This involves flavoring the apples with lemon and Calvados, rather than cinnamon, cooking half of them into applesauce, and reserving the rest for a decorative top. Once baked, the top is glazed with sieved apricot preserves. Child in *Child & Company* now moves to an American-sounding Apple Turnover, but the crust is a *Pâte brisée fine, sucrée,* wrapped around plain apple slices with cinnamon and lemon optional. Beard comes out with a frankly American Apple Pie of two crusts, with apples flavored by lemon, vanilla, and nutmeg.

As a gesture toward the problem of a soggy bottom crust, Beard suggests spreading a layer of bread crumbs over the pastry before filling with apples. Others suggest a layer of finely ground nuts or a thin glaze of jam. In my experience, none of them is proof against the quantity of juice released by apples as they cook. I know of no better way to achieve a perfectly cooked apple and a completely crisp crust than to combine American and French methods, to cook the apples and pastry separately, and to combine them at the last moment. Sugar, cinnamon, and nutmeg, with a sprinkling of lemon, would convey the taste of old-fashioned American apples in pie or sauce. But I prefer, for variety, combining the tart and the sweet in one operation by using, as below, orange marmalade. Marmalade, or some other preserve like apricot or raspberry, has the added virtue of both thickening and glazing. And anyway, a preserve tastes good with apples, whether they are bland or tartly sour. Nuts I add because apples are soft, and a good crunch reinforces a crust that is crisp. The result is a pie halfway between the formally arranged Tarte aux Pommes and the homely kivered or unkivered American pie.

## Proportions

for 6 to 8 servings from one 9-inch pie shell, 8 apples, 1½ cups of orange marmalade, 1½ cups of nuts

Pastry for one 9-inch pie (see Butter or Lard Crust on pages 348 and 351)

8 apples, such as Granny Smith, Gravenstein, New Jersey red, or other tart kind

1½ cups orange marmalade

4 tablespoons (½ stick) butter

1½ cups whole or chopped pecan halves

1. Bake the pastry shell in a 9-inch pie tin or 10-inch flan ring. This can be done a day ahead, but the crust should be reheated before filling.

2. Peel and core the apples and cut into slices about ½ inch thick. Melt the marmalade with the butter in a large frying pan. Add the apples and shake over high heat until the apples begin to brown but are still firm. Drain in a large sieve or collander over a pan to save the juice.

3. Quickly boil the juice down, with additional marmalade and butter if needed, to make a rich thick glaze. Arrange the apples and nuts attractively in the piecrust and pour the glaze over. Serve immediately if possible, or at least warm rather than cold.

*I find that a bowl of heavy whipped cream, served alongside, never goes amiss because the dieters can feel virtuous in abstaining and the wicked can enjoy indulging.*

# PUMPKIN CHIP PIE

In the Anglo-American tradition, desserts belonged to the Sweetmeats department, which included candying and thus preserving all manner of fruits, flowers, and herbs. The *Booke of Sweetmeats* presented to Martha Washington in 1749 taught her how to make marmalets and pastes of violets and eglantine, quidonies (jellies) of raspberries and red roses, and sirrups of mayden hayre fern. Such confections and distillations were dispensed then, much as pills are today, for the sake of health. Sugar, if you can imagine, was thought to be good for you.

Preserving by syrups of sugar remained one of the most important branches of the cooking, if not the healing, art until our own time, when freezing made sugar less vital. But at a time when every housewife put up all her own jellies and jams, the line between sweets for breakfast and sweets for dinner was not distinct. Conserves were part of every meal.

Eliza Leslie, for example, has an interesting recipe for Pumpkin Chips, made with lemon and sugar and cut into thin strips "the thickness of a dollar" to eat as a candy, a relish, or as a dessert in puff paste shells. In the same book, she has a recipe for Pumpkin Pudding, which consists of the spiced egg and cream custard that we learned to bake in a crust and label Pumpkin Pie.

Because pumpkin pie has become associated with Thanksgiving feasting, most of us serve it at least once a year but often to grumbling family members who claim to hate the stuff. Too bland, too squashy, they say. To die-hard traditionalists, like myself, who love the stuff, the challenge is to find something that will give enough added zing to break through the cliché and disarm the grumblers.

Claiborne, in *The New New York Times Cookbook,* makes the radical suggestion of starting with fresh not canned pumpkin purée. The processor makes puréeing steamed chunks of pumpkin easy, but often even fresh young pumpkins have little taste. It depends on the kind. The orange-red pumpkins of the Caribbean are much more flavorful than the domestic pale yellow-orange kind. As for Claiborne's custard, it is similar to the egg-cream of his first cookbook, except for leaving out molasses and suggesting grated fresh gingerroot instead of powdered ginger. Beard uses essentially the same custard in his Pumpkin or Squash Pie recipe in *American Cookery.*

But even a heavy dose of ginger, cinnamon, cloves, and nutmeg, and a rich custard of brown sugar and heavy cream, does not silence my grumblers. Over the years I've taken advice from various hands and added a couple of tablespoons of Grand Marnier and grated orange rind, or chopped up crystallized ginger or black walnuts. Anything to cut the uniform dull squashiness. The most successful solution I've found, however, is to combine Eliza Leslie's Pumpkin Chips with Pumpkin Pudding. The result is a splendidly decorative open-faced pie halfway between a French tart and a classic American pie. The grumblers are too busy asking about the chips to remember to complain about the pudding.

## Proportions

for 6 to 8 servings from one 9-inch pie shell, 2 cups pumpkin to 3 eggs and 1 cup of heavy cream, plus 2 to 3 cups of pumpkin chips (1½ pounds pumpkin meat)

### For Pumpkin Chips

1½ lbs. pumpkin meat, cut in chips
2 cups sugar

1 cup fresh lemon juice
Rind of 3 lemons

1. Cut pumpkin in uniform chips 6 inches long by 1 inch wide, "the thickness of a dollar," meaning thin. Cover with sugar and lemon juice and let stand overnight in a cool place.

2. Boil gently in a pan until the chips become transparent but are still firm. Spread the chips to cool in a single layer so they won't go on cooking. Save the sugar syrup.

## For the Pumpkin Pudding

2 cups pumpkin purée, fresh
  or canned
3 eggs, beaten
½ cup dark brown sugar
½ cup sugar-lemon syrup from
  the chips
1 cup heavy cream

½ teaspoon each ginger and
  cinnamon
¼ teaspoon each nutmeg and
  salt
Pastry for a 9-inch pie shell
  (see Butter or Lard Crust,
  pages 348 and 351)

1. In a large bowl, combine all the ingredients except the pastry, and mix well. Taste for seasoning and add more spices if desired.

2. Pour the custard into the shell and bake at 425 degrees for 15 minutes, then lower the oven temperature to 350 degrees for 30 minutes, or until a testing knife inserted in the center comes out clean.

3. Arrange the chips on top of the pie in an attractive pattern. The pie will be easier to slice if you run the chips lengthwise from the center like spokes in a wheel. Best warm or at room temperature.

# LEMON MERINGUE PIE WITH ALMOND CRUST

Lemon creams and puddings were common sweets in England and France as far back as Queen Elizabeth. And both countries seemed to have a particular fondness for lemon tarts. Even when lemon cream was served in a jelly glass rather than a crust, as in Miss Eliza Leslie's recipe, still she suggested eating the cream accompanied by tarts. Mrs. Webster, in *The Improved Housewife,* indicates that "Lemon Pudding or Lemon Pie" was synonymous, baked in a pudding dish with a puff paste for a pudding or in a shallow pie plate for a pie. Either way the cream was rich with eggs, butter, sugar, lemon, and heavy cream. No nonsense about cornstarch or flour.

By the time of Mrs. Harland's *Common Sense* in 1871, lemon pies came in several versions, the richest calling for nutmeg and brandy and a meringue to spread over the top. But the idea of a tart still held. "They are very nice baked in pattypans," says Mrs. Harland. In *The Kansas Home Cook-Book* of around the same date, lemon pies and tarts are interchangeable, one of them bearing the whimsical name "$5 Pie," presumably from the cost of eggs, since the only other ingredients were lemon and sugar. The richest of the *Kansas* recipes is for a lemon cream with beaten whites folded in, to make a kind of soufflé. "Particularly nice," the contributor says, but warns, "we think too rich for a dyspeptic woman."

In the lean years of the twentieth century, the pie was thought too rich altogether. Starch was substituted for butter and eggs. In Rombauer's 1943 *Joy of Cooking,* only one of her three lemon meringue pie recipes lacks cornstarch or flour and for that one she apologizes: "A cousin was highly indignant when I failed to put this luxurious recipe in my first cookbook." This luxurious recipe called for ½ cup of butter to 4 eggs, which meant the sauce was thickened like a hollandaise. It was far easier and cheaper, however, to thicken the mixture with starch, as Beard does in *American Cookery,* at the ratio of 6 tablespoons to 3 egg yolks. When instant pudding mixes came along, consisting almost wholly of starch and sugar and a little artificial lemon flavoring, the pie seemed destined for well-deserved obloquy.

We who scorned the lemon meringue, however, were instantly ravished by the Tartes au Citron that Child introduced in *Mastering I.* One was a soufflé-type with egg whites folded into the egg and sugar base. Another was a lemon cream enriched by ground almonds which also helped to thicken it. In *Child's Kitchen,* Child added a third that was thickened with grated apple, an innovation she attributes to the French cook Mme. Saint-Ange, but which is frequent in nineteenth-century American recipes.

We rediscovered the true nature of the American lemon meringue pie by way of the fancy French tart. Recently we have come full circle in a recipe Claiborne attributes (in *The New New York Times Cookbook*) to the great master of French *patisserie,* Gaston Lenôtre. Lenôtre calls his creation Lemon Meringue Pie, and he thickens his eggs with cornstarch and milk. My first attempts to recapture the starchless lemon creams of the nineteenth-century American ladies seemed self-defeating with the quantities of butter required, so I have compromised and added cornstarch. The result is an intensely lemon curd that can be piled into Lenôtre's delicious almond crust and topped with his "French meringue" for this very un-French American pie.

---

## Proportions

for 6 to 8 servings from one 9-inch pie shell, 4 eggs, 2 lemons, 1½ cups of sugar, ¼ cup each of butter and cornstarch

### For the Almond Crust

¼ **cup pulverized almonds**
1 **cup flour**
¼ **teaspoon salt**
3 **tablespoons confectioners' sugar**

6 **tablespoons (¾ stick) butter, cold**
¼ **teaspoon vanilla extract**
1 **egg, beaten**

1.   Combine the almonds with the flour, salt, and sugar in a food processor. Cut the butter in half lengthwise, and in ½-inch slices crosswise. Turn the processor on and off to mix in the butter until the butter is about the size of a pea. Beat the vanilla into the egg and pour through the opening in the lid with the processor going until the ingredients just begin to crumble. Turn out onto plastic wrap, push into a ball, and refrigerate overnight if possible.

2.   This dough is too crumbly to roll easily. The best way is to press the dough rapidly with your fingers onto the bottom and sides of the pie pan, making a thick edge. Flute the edge with your fingers or press it down with a fork. Prick the shell all over with fork tines to keep the pastry from puffing. Line the shell with foil and fill the foil with beans to keep the shell from shrinking. Bake at 375 degrees for 6 to 7 minutes. Remove the beans and foil, prick the shell again with a fork, and continue baking until very lightly brown, about 10 to 12 minutes longer. Sugar crusts brown faster than other kinds, so watch the timing.

## For the Lemon Cream

4 tablespoons cornstarch or arrowroot
¾ cup water
¾ cup granulated sugar

4 egg yolks
½ cup lemon juice, plus rind of 1 lemon
4 tablespoons butter

## For the Meringue

3 egg whites (from above)
⅓ cup granulated sugar
⅓ cup confectioners' sugar

¼ teaspoon almond extract
Pinch of salt

1.   For the filling, dissolve the cornstarch in the water in the top half of a double boiler. Add the sugar and cook over direct heat until the mixture is very thick.

2.   Add half the mixture to the beaten egg yolks, stirring constantly, then return all to the double boiler. Beat well with a wire whisk or wooden spoon over simmering water while the mixture thickens.

3.   Remove from the heat to add the lemon juice, rind, and butter, a tablespoon at a time. Beat until smooth. The mixture will thin from the juice so it must be very thick to begin with; the mixture will thicken somewhat more as it cools, but it will be soft rather than a stiff paste. Refrigerate until needed.

4. For the meringue, beat the egg whites in a mixer or by hand until they stand in soft peaks. Beat in 1 tablespoon of sugar and continue beating until stiff. Then beat in the almond extract and salt. Mix the two sugars and sift over the whites while beating. Spoon over the filled pie shell and shape the meringue with a spatula. Put in the top third of a 500-degree oven for about 2 minutes to brown—but not burn—the top of the meringue. Serve as soon as possible so that meringue does not begin to "weep."

*Because this is a rich pie in each of its elements, save it for the climax of a preceding light meal.*

# WHISKEY-NUT CAKE

The pound cake was once the mainstay of the home baker because it was the easiest to make, it kept well, and it could be eaten at any time of day like a slice of bread. The pound cake takes its name from equal measures of its four ingredients: a pound each of butter, sugar, flour, and eggs. When the cup began to replace the scale as the most convenient kitchen measure, the cake was called the One, Two, Three, Four Cake from the increasing quantity of its four ingredients: 1 cup of butter to 2 cups of sugar to 3 cups of flour to 4 eggs (not cups but units on the last).

Like fruit cakes, pound cakes were often flavored with brandy or rum to ripen and preserve them. At the same time, the batter was a good one in which to preserve nutmeats, at a time when hickory and hazel and black walnuts fell in abundance. The result was that most delicious of all pound cakes, one flavored with liqueur and studded with nuts. It's a cake Beard put in his first general cookbook as Whiskey Cake, adding some unnecessary raisins to give it a holiday flair. In *The New New York Times Cookbook,* Claiborne gives a darker version with brown sugar and maple syrup to complement the bourbon and pecans.

Any kind of nuts can be used. I've used English walnuts often and would use black walnuts always if I could get them. If you're as fond of maple syrup as I am, use it. If not, simply substitute white or brown sugar, on the principle of ½ cup of butter to 1 cup of sugar to 1½ cups of flour to 2 eggs for a single loaf or Bundt pan. Beard's cake is lighter than a true pound cake because he uses a higher proportion of eggs to flour and separates the eggs to leaven the batter by beaten egg white. Claiborne's cake calls for a larger proportion of flour because of the liquid syrup.

## Proportions

for one 9-inch loaf, ¼ pound (½ cup) butter, ½ cup each of sugar and maple syrup, 2 cups of flour, 2 eggs, ½ cup of bourbon, 1½ cups of nuts

| | |
|---|---|
| ¼ pound (1 stick) butter, at room temperature | Pinch of salt |
| ½ cup dark brown sugar | ½ cup maple syrup |
| 2 eggs | ½ cup bourbon whiskey |
| 2 cups flour | 1½ cups chopped walnuts or pecans |
| 1 tablespoon baking powder | |

1. Beat the butter with an electric mixer or hand beater. Gradually add the sugar until creamy, then add the eggs one at a time.

2. Sift the flour with baking powder and salt. Add alternately to the butter mixture with the syrup and bourbon. Fold in the nuts. Spoon the batter into a buttered 9-inch loaf or Bundt pan.

3. Bake in a 350-degree oven for about 50 to 60 minutes. Cool in the pan for 10 minutes before trying to remove the cake from the pan. Cake freezes well or will keep indefinitely wrapped in foil and refrigerated. If it begins to dry out, splash some bourbon over the top.

*Makes a good accompaniment to a fruit ice or homemade vanilla ice cream or is good by itself for breakfast, lunch, and tea.*

# ORANGE-ALMOND SPONGE CAKE

A sponge cake is to American cakemaking what a génoise is to the French. The major ingredient in both is eggs, sweetened and thickened by sugar and held together by a little flour, to make a "sponge." The French add butter to the egg mixture to make a rich and fine textured cake. Americans add a little baking powder and no butter to make the cake even lighter and airier. With a génoise, you beat whole eggs with the sugar until your arm falls off, since the only leavening is air. With a sponge cake, you separate the eggs, folding the yolks and sugar into stiffly beaten egg whites as you would in a soufflé.

That both these egg cakes have the same Italian source is clear in Miss Eliza Leslie's directions for Sponge Cake. Her method is the whole-egg method of a génoise but without butter. The housewife is told to beat 12 eggs with sugar and lemon "for a long time" before folding in the flour quickly and pouring into little square tins or paper cases made of thick letter paper pasted or sewed at the corners. The cakes are generally called, she says, "Naples biscuits."

We can see the modern sponge cake evolving from the Genoa or Naples biscuit in Mrs. Webster's *Improved Housewife,* where she gives two recipes for sponge cake, one the whole-egg method as above; the other the separated-egg method, in which the egg white is the leavening without the aid of saleratus or baking powder. By the time of Mrs. Harland's

*Common Sense,* the egg white is being fortified by "1 scant teaspoonful of Cleveland's Baking Powder," but the idea of square tins or molds lingered on. Mrs. Harland specified a brick shape, which she had learned from a friend "celebrated among her acquaintances for her beautiful and delicious sponge-cake" and who claimed that the shape was necessary to the taste. It would seem that our round cupcakes were once square, even though they were called "Sponge Cups" instead of "Petits Fours."

Sponge cakes were generally flavored by lemon juice and rind before vanilla became a household staple. But eggs and citrus are natural complements, as is the delicate almond, so there is no shortage of lemon cakes and orange cakes and almond cakes.

Flavoring was no problem, but heating was. Miss Leslie warns the housewife to pile live coals on top of the Dutch oven in which her square tins were baking and then to diminish the fire to a moderate heat. The later *Buckeye Cookbook* warns the housewife how to work the damper to adjust the intensity and direction of the heat in the wood-burning oven. After advising that "there is no other cake so dependent upon care and good judgment in baking as sponge-cake," the anonymous editor abandons the task of judging oven temperatures by hand (if the hand can be held in the oven for 20 to 35 seconds, it's quick; 35 to 45 seconds, it's moderate; 45 to 60 seconds, it's slow). "All systematic housekeepers will hail the day," she concludes, "when some enterprising Yankee or Buckeye girl shall invent a stove or range with a thermometer attached to the oven, so that the heat may be regulated accurately and intelligently."

In *American Cookery,* Beard gives a simple quick-method sponge cake using a little orange juice and rind for flavoring. In *The New New York Times Cookbook,* Claiborne gives an elaborate Génoise with Oranges, elaborately named Rosace à l'Orange, from Gaston Lenôtre. Somewhere in between is the Orange and Almond Spongecake given by Child in *Mastering I,* which calls for the ingredients of a génoise with the method of a sponge, and with the texture of almonds to replace some of the flour. In the same volume, she provides another orange sponge with an orange-butter filling or buttercream icing. But in these simpler days of cakemaking, a cake that has all the flavor inside seems preferable to a cosmetic frosting.

---

## Proportions

for a 9-inch cake pan, 3 eggs, ¼ pound butter, ⅓ cup of orange juice, ¾ cup of pulverized almonds, ¾ cup of flour, ⅔ cup of sugar

| | |
|---|---|
| ¼ **pound (1 stick) butter** | ⅓ **cup orange juice** |
| 3 **eggs, separated** | ¼ **teaspoon almond extract** |
| ⅔ **cup granulated sugar** | ¾ **cup pulverized almonds** |
| **Rind of 1 orange** | ¾ **cup cake flour** |

1.  Melt the butter so that it will cool while you mix the batter. Beat the egg yolks with an electric mixer or beater. Gradually beat in the sugar and beat at high speed for 5 to 10 minutes, or until the mixture is thick and lemon-colored. Add the rind, juice, and extract. Beat in the almonds and quickly fold in the flour until just mixed.

2.  Beat the egg whites separately until stiff but not dry. Fold the melted butter (omit the residue at bottom) quickly into the batter. Stir in one quarter of the egg whites, then quickly fold in the rest.

3.  Bake in a buttered and floured cake pan in a 350-degree oven for about 30 to 35 minutes. A cake-tester needle or toothpick should come out clean if plunged into the center. Let stand for 10 minutes before reversing onto a cake rack. Turn so that puffed side is up. When ready to serve, sprinkle with confectioners' sugar.

*Can be served by itself but especially complements fresh fruit, like strawberries, sliced oranges, peaches, or nectarines.*

# PISTACHIO-NUT CHEESECAKE

It's hard to know whether the dessert we call "cheesecake" is really a pie or a free-standing pudding. The one thing it would seem not to be is a cake. But cheesecakes they have been since at least the second century A.D. when, as Fisher reminds us, Athenaeus of Rome described the cheesecake sent to Socrates by his lover Alcibiades. Socrates' wife took it in snuff and stamped on it. Athenaeus observed that she was not a true cheesecake lover, a sentiment with which any of the modern cheesecake faithful would agree.

To bake a cheese pudding or custard in a crust is a logical solution to the container problem and it was solved centuries ago. The "cheescakes" in *Martha Washington's Booke of Cookery* called for the usual "coffins of paste" to be filled with "stroakings of new milk" curdled by rennet and flavored with currants and spices and a little rosewater. The cheese, once it had wheyed, was to be thickened with eggs and cream, grated bread and "halfe a pound of fresh butter." In her edition of *The Booke,* Karen Hess gives instructions on how to make your own creamed cheese of curds and whey, which is good for the experimenter sick of the eternal sameness of factory cream cheese.

Cheesecake was not a standard recipe item in nineteenth-century American cookbooks, maybe because housewives were simply too busy wheying their new milk stroakings and churning fresh butter for the day to worry about custards and pies. Not until *The Settlement Cook Book* of 1915 do we find a plethora of "Cheese Pies or Kuchens." The custard was made of cheese, pressed dry, and put through a colander, to which various goodies were added besides butter, sugar, eggs, and cream. It might be baked in either pastry or the raised sweet dough called "Kuchen Dough," halfway between a cookie and a bread.

From such crossings of Middle-European traditions with English ones do we get today's strongly ethnic and urban product, whether it's called Lindy's Famous or Aunt Lulu's Infamous. Unfortunately, factory cheese-cake is as boring as the factory cheese of which it's made, but at the same time a light, moist, rich, and creamy pie, kuchen, or free-standing pud-ding is as worthy a lover's gift as any I know. And worth trampling a rival's into the dust.

All of our masters take a turn at it. Child suggests in *Child & More Company* a Cream Cheese and Lemon Custard baked in a tart. Beard and Claiborne in their newest books arrive at nearly identical recipes for a Hazelnut Cheesecake, which adds a welcome crunch to the softness of the cheese. Almonds and walnuts are also good, but I've chosen the path of pistachios as a reminder of the heritage of the cheesecake from those happy days in Ancient Greece when lovers strolled through the colon-nades and left their women back in the kitchen to bake or curdle the cheese.

## Proportions

for 8 servings from one 8- by 3-inch cake pan, 2 pounds cream cheese to 4 eggs to 1½ cups of chopped nuts

| | |
|---|---|
| 1½ cups roasted pistachios | 4 eggs |
| ⅓ cup cookie crumbs (macaroon, ginger, or graham cracker) | 1½ cups sugar |
| | ½ cup heavy cream |
| 2 pounds cream cheese | 1 teaspoon vanilla extract |

1. Shell the nuts and remove their skins. Chop in a processor or blender or by hand until finely chopped but not powdery.

2. Butter an 8- by 3-inch cake pan, and sprinkle the inside with cookie crumbs, preferably from ground macaroons. This is not a "crust" because you are going to unmold the cake and serve it upside down.

3. Mix the cream cheese, eggs, sugar, cream, and vanilla in an electric mixer (or with an electric hand beater) until perfectly smooth. Add the nuts and mix well. Pour into the prepared cake pan.

4. Put a roasting pan in a 325-degree oven, place the cake pan in the middle of it, and pour in half an inch of boiling water to surround the cake pan on all sides. Bake the cheesecake for about 2 hours. Turn the oven off and let the cake sit for another hour.

5. Remove the cake pan from the water and place it on a rack until cool. Put a plate over the cake and unmold. The texture will be very soft, but the cake should keep its shape. If you like, sprinkle the top with more

powdered macaroons or, if you prefer, reverse and serve browned side up.

# PRALINE TORTE

Child tells us that the French cake of layered nut-filled meringues called *dacquoise* is far easier to make than an American layer cake, which she demonstrates in eight easy pages. The meringue, except for macaroons, did not figure large in nineteenth-century American cooking partly for reasons of origin, I imagine, and partly for reasons of weather. High humidity kills a meringue as fast as a tumbler of water poured over a layer cake. So there are some summer days and some swampy places that render meringue making just not worth your while.

Then too, the English went in for cakes that were closer to puddings than to crisp cookies. It was the Germans and Austro-Hungarians who delighted in *torten,* those butterless cakes of eggs and nuts, made often with bread or cracker crumbs instead of flour. Not until the 1915 *Settlement Cook Book* do we find a full section of *torten,* made with everything from chestnuts, prunes and dates to chocolate and matzos. Tortes made of egg whites, without yolks, as in a meringue, were usually made with hazelnuts and called "Filbert" or with almonds and called "Macaroon."

When nuts had to be grated by hand, however easy the baking, the making of a torte was slow. One reason the *dacquoise* has become a standard feature of American Frenchified menus today is that nuts can be grated in a flash by the mechanical magic of blender or processor. I have a friend who still grates the pecans for his nut torte by hand because he swears the texture cannot be duplicated by crass machinery, but I attribute his stubbornness to male ego. If anybody can make a nut torte, as indeed anybody can on any but the swampiest day, the special virtues of the hand-grater seem diminished.

Nut tortes are easy to make today and the contrast of texture between the crunch of meringue and the creaminess of flavored butter makes them a sophisticated delight embodied in French names like "le Délice," "le Succès," "le Progrès." Almonds or hazelnuts, or preferably a combination of the two, are the traditional nuts to use because they are light. Meringue layers are shaped either by a pastry tube, if that is easiest for your particular hand, or with a spatula. The buttercreams that will glue the layers together are variously flavored of mocha, chocolate, and praline and scented with a dash of Cognac or rum.

In *The New New York Times Cookbook,* Claiborne gives a classic *dacquoise* of two flavored creams from the hand of Albert Kumin, now piping his meringues at the White House. His meringue is slightly less sweet than Child's formula: Child likes 1 cup of sugar to ¾ cup of egg whites; Kumin prefers a little over half a cup of sugar. Their buttercreams differ significantly in that Kumin's calls for egg whites only and Child's for egg yolks. The yolks are more practical for the home cook who has been separating out whites for a meringue and the yolks also make a richer creamier cream.

Instead of making circles, you can make a long cake of rectangles, as Child does in *Child & Company*. Here she layers a torte with liqueur-flavored buttercream and apricot purée. The settlers of *The Settlement Cook Book* used other fruits, like pears, blueberries, dates. Once you get the hang of meringue, it's a pleasure to make and assemble a variety of tortes. The assembled cake freezes well if wrapped airtight, but the meringue will soften somewhat in the thawing.

## Proportions

for 8 servings from three 8-inch meringues, ¾ cup of egg whites, ¾ cup of sugar, 1½ cups of nuts. For 5 to 6 cups of buttercream, ¾ pound sweet butter, 6 egg yolks, 1 cup of sugar, ¾ cup of milk.

### For the Meringues

| | |
|---|---|
| ¾ **cup egg whites (5 or 6 eggs)** | 1 **tablespoon vanilla extract** |
| ¼ **teaspoon cream of tartar** | ¼ **teaspoon almond extract** |
| **Pinch of salt** | ¾ **cup each toasted almonds** |
| ¾ **cup sugar** | **and hazelnuts** |

1. Prepare 2 baking sheets by buttering them and sprinkling them with flour. Coat evenly and shake off any excess flour. With a knife, outline three circles by drawing around the edge of an 8-inch cake pan inverted on the floured sheets.

2. Beat the whites with an electric mixer on slow speed until they are frothy. Add the cream of tartar and salt, increase speed until the whites form soft peaks. Gradually beat in half of the sugar together with the extracts and beat until the whites are stiff. Mix the nuts with the remaining sugar and fold quickly into the meringue mixture.

3. Spoon the meringue into a pastry bag fitted with a wide pastry tube and make a ring inside the perimeter of each circle. Continue spiraling to the center of each to make a meringue of even thickness. OR, spoon out meringue into the center of each and smooth toward the edges with a spatula. The point is to make a thin even layer.

4. Bake in a 250-degree oven for 40 to 50 minutes, or until very lightly browned and firm. Loosen the meringues from the sheet with a long spatula while they are still warm. Cool on a rack.

## For the Buttercream

6 egg yolks
1 cup sugar
¾ cup milk, heated

¾ pound (3 sticks) butter
1 teaspoon vanilla extract

To make the basic buttercream, beat the sugar gradually into the egg yolks in the top of a double boiler. Add the hot milk slowly and continue beating over simmering water until the sauce thickens. Pour into an electric mixer and beat until it begins to cool. Then beat in the butter gradually in ½-inch pieces until the mixture is thick and glossy. Add the extract and beat again. The mixture will look curdled until all the butter is in. If it does not smooth out by beating, add more tablespoons of butter until it does.

## For the Praline Flavoring

½ cup sugar
3 tablespoons water

1 cup blanched almonds, toasted

Dissolve the sugar in the water. Set over high heat, swirl but do not stir to dissolve any sugar on the sides of the pan. Cover the pan and boil for 2 or 3 minutes. Uncover and boil rapidly until the syrup turns caramel colored. Stir in the almonds and pour onto an oiled baking sheet. When cold, break in pieces and pulverize in a blender. Use ½ cup of the praline for one of the buttercreams and reserve the rest for garnish.

## For the Mocha Flavoring

1 tablespoon instant or freeze-dried coffee, dissolved in

1½ tablespoons of Cognac or rum

## For the Chocolate Icing

3 ounces bitter or bittersweet chocolate, melted

*To assemble the torte*
1. Divide the basic buttercream in three parts. Add ½ cup almond praline to one, the coffee and rum to another, and the melted chocolate

to the third. If the cream is not firm enough to spread and hold its shape, chill for a few minutes until the butter stiffens.

2. Spread the bottom meringue layer with the mocha cream. Spread another layer with the praline cream and place on top of the bottom layer. Place the smoothest meringue on top. Coat the top and sides with chocolate cream, smoothing the top as much as possible. Hold the cake on the palm of your hand and brush the sides all around with the remaining praline powder. If that's too tricky, sprinkle the praline powder over the top.

3. Chill for 1 to 2 hours or more to firm the buttercream and make the meringue easier to cut.

*While the buttercream is rich, the effect of the torte is one of airy lightness, so that you can get away with serving it after a meal that would preclude an obvious heavy like pumpkin pie.*

# BEST INDIAN PUDDING

When the Dutch oven was used to bake a cake or a pudding, the difference between the two was often slight. Lydia Child told the *Frugal Housewife* to use but a cup of milk for her Indian Cake, but a quart of milk for her Indian Pudding. If she was frugal, she might use skimmed milk. If she was splurging, she might add an egg and some "nice suet." If she was accustomed to boiling her puddings in the English way, she might boil her Indian with chopped suet and "thin slices of sweet apple." Probably no American dessert better embodies the juncture of two cultures than the English treacle and the Indian meal that, combined, became known as "Indian Pudding," not Cake.

Until recently the Indian Pudding has suffered neglect as an historical curiosity of New England, palatable only to eccentric old ladies and children. Those who ate S. S. Pierce's pudding in a can may have been reminded of the dank brown lump, as Fisher called it, that her very English Aunt Gwen served "with some pomp" as a Treacle Shape. But early recipes less frugal than Miss Child's suggest quite a sumptuous dish of butter and eggs, molasses and meal, liquefied by milk and scented by cinnamon, nutmeg, and grated lemon. Eliza Leslie, never one to cut corners, calls for 6 eggs and 2 cups of molasses to 1 quart of milk. And "to have an Indian pudding *very good*," she says, it should be mixed the night before and served up with wine sauce or more butter and molasses. Hardly an austere Pilgrim dish.

Now that American cooking is coming into its own, the poor unpitied Indian pudding is making a comeback. Beard included a butter and egg enriched pudding in his *American Cookery*. More surprisingly, Claiborne has included a suet and brown-sugar version in his *New New York Times Cookbook.* Child, in *Child & Company,* even returned to the recipe of "that primeval New England Puritan," Lydia Maria Child, adding a bit of grated apple to her Indian and glazing the top by floating milk over the half-baked pudding.

I have compromised the primeval Puritan by adding eggs and a little more butter and by substituting fresh grated ginger for ground. The proportions of milk to meal vary widely. One recipe will call for 1 quart of milk to 2 cups of meal and another will reverse it, calling for 2 quarts of milk to 1 cup of meal. I use a small amount of meal, ¼ cup, to a quart of milk, which makes the meal a thickener for a molasses custard, rather than a dense treacle shape. Needless to say, stone-ground meal will taste better and give a better texture than the standard supermarket brand. Julia Child suggests grinding your own corn, if you just happen to have a corn grinder handy, even though it's not the sort of equipment that would recommend itself to the frugal housewife.

## Proportions

for 6 to 8 servings, ¼ cup of cornmeal to 1 quart of milk to 1 cup of molasses, 2 eggs, and ¼ pound butter

| | |
|---|---|
| 1 **quart milk** | ¼ **teaspoon nutmeg** |
| ¼ **cup cornmeal, stone ground if possible** | 1 **teaspoon grated fresh ginger-root** |
| ¼ **pound (1 stick) butter** | 1 **tart apple, peeled, cored, and grated** |
| 1 **cup molasses** | 2 **eggs, beaten** |
| ¼ **teaspoon salt** | |
| ½ **teaspoon cinnamon** | |

1. Stir 3 cups of cold milk gradually into the cornmeal in a saucepan (hot milk will lump it). Set over moderate heat, add the butter, molasses, and spices, and stir frequently until the mixture comes to a boil. When the mixture is smooth, add the grated apple and boil slowly for 10 or 15 minutes, or until thick. Remove from the heat and stir in the beaten eggs.

2. Pour into a buttered 2-quart baking dish and bake in a 325-degree oven for 1 hour. Pour the remaining cup of milk over the top and bake for another hour or more, or until the top is nicely glazed. If not ready to serve, cover and keep warm in a 225-degree oven. Serve with butter and molasses sauce, whipped to a froth, or with heavy cream, whipped or plain.

*Because of the butter, the pudding is much better hot or warm than cold. It is also extremely filling and goes well with a soup and salad.*

# APPLE BREAD-AND-BUTTER PUDDING

In a land as abundantly provided with apples as America, we would expect to find apples turning up in dumplings and fritters and roly-poly puddings, in floats and snows and turnovers, in pones and pan dowdies and brown Bettys. And so they do. Under various names, they turn up most often with bread, either crumbed or buttered and sliced. Layered with crumbs and sugar or molasses, they are usually Scalloped Apples. Puréed and encased in bread slices, they are called Apple Charlotte. Sliced and spread over bread and topped with a rich egg custard, they may be called, as Claiborne does in *The New New York Times Cookbook*, Bread Pudding with Apples. There's no end to names or puddings.

Just to show that America has not cornered the market on apple puddings, Beard, in *The New James Beard*, provides a Polish dessert called *Sharlotka*, which is in effect a pumpernickel and apple charlotte pudding, moistened with red wine and lemon juice instead of cream and glazed with jelly. Fisher goes farther East with a recipe she learned, she says, "from a Russian woman when I lived in Vevey." This one is made of ladyfingers soaked in honey and kirsch to contain a kind of applesauce soufflé.

Then there is Child's Charlotte aux Pommes, an unnervingly rich concoction of apples puréed with rum and apricot jam to be poured into a bread-lined mold. But I have had such spectacular disasters unmolding this charlotte that I have returned to the sort of straight-up Bread-and-Butter Pudding suggested by Eliza Leslie (of which Claiborne's is a variant), fortified by Calvados or applejack if you can get it. Miss Leslie suggests a wineglass full of rose water for flavoring, but a little rum or brandy will do. Claiborne uses a shallow oval baking dish with one layer of bread on the bottom. I like Miss Leslie's alternate layers of bread and minced apples, which I have puréed here.

## Proportions

for 6 to 8 servings, 10 tart apples, 12 slices white bread, 1 cup of sugar, ¼ pound butter, 1 cup of apricot preserves, 4 eggs, 2 cups of milk, 1 cup of cream

| | |
|---|---|
| 10 tart apples, such as Pippins, Granny Smiths, etc. | 12 thick slices white bread |
| 1 cup sugar | ¼ pound (1 stick) butter |
| 1 cup apricot preserves | 4 eggs |
| 1 tablespoon vanilla extract | 2 cups milk |
| 2 tablespoons Calvados, rum, or brandy | 1 cup cream |

1.   Peel, core, and slice the apples. Heat in a covered pan over very low heat for about 15 minutes. Uncover, add ½ cup of sugar, the apricot preserves, vanilla, and Calvados, and mix well over high heat until the liquid has evaporated and the applesauce is fairly thick.

2.   Remove the crusts from the bread. Cut in strips about 2 inches wide. Divide the butter in 3 parts and the bread in 3 parts. Heat one third of the butter in a frying pan and sauté one third of the bread. Repeat until all the bread is browned on both sides.

3.   Put a layer of bread in the bottom of a 2-quart baking dish. Spread on half the applesauce. Put on another layer of bread, another of sauce, and top with a layer of bread.

4.   Beat the eggs with the remaining ½ cup sugar. Gradually beat in the hot milk and cream. Strain over the top layer of bread. Place in a larger baking pan and add boiling water to reach halfway up the dish. Bake in a 325-degree oven for about 40 minutes, or until the custard is just set and the top is nicely brown. Serve warm or cold.

# FLOATING ISLANDS

Until a few years ago, islands of white meringue floating in a sea of creamy custard were thought to be nursery food. Until, that is, the masters of French cuisine in their search for simplicity rediscovered the old-fashioned English sweet under its French label, *Oeufs à la Neige*. A dash of Cognac or rum, a dusting of praline, and nursery custard was transformed into the display piece it was originally. Eliza Leslie's Floating Island, for example, was a pile of sliced almond sponge cake, spread with raspberry jam, covered entirely with whipped cream and floated in sweetened cream, colored pink with currant jelly.

Mrs. Webster of *The Improved Housewife* reverses the color scheme by coloring her frothed egg whites pink with strawberry or raspberry marmalade and then floating her "Virginia" island in a sea of syllabub. And Mrs. Harland retains the tradition of a pink meringue by coloring it with currant "or other bright tart jelly" and decorating it with jelly cut in rings or stars.

Perhaps pink islands will return to fashion, along with syllabubs, but meanwhile the more classic white and yellow makes a pretty dish and a delicate understated dessert of what can only be called studied simplicity. Proportions and ingredients vary, as usual, among our current masters, but I've chosen roughly the proportions of Child in *Child & Company* and the poaching method of Claiborne in *The New New York Times Cookbook*. The meringue can be made in advance and the only question is whether to poach it or bake it. Child bakes the meringue (a big one of 12 egg whites) in a single casserole dish and cuts it in wedges to float. This makes for a solid stiff meringue but the shapes are not as island-like as when poached.

Claiborne follows the traditional French method of poaching meringues, piped from a pastry tube into 2-inch "beehives" or "rosettes," in simmering milk. You then drain the meringues with a slotted spoon, strain the milk, and use it for making the custard. If you like the meringues browned instead of snow-white, Beard suggests placing them in a pan of hot milk and running them under the broiler. Since I like them to look like floating icebergs, I forgo either browning or pastry-tube squeezing in favor of simple shaping with a large serving spoon. It's easier and gives them a good craggy look.

As for the custard, or Crème Anglais, Child likes to flavor it with dark rum or bourbon whiskey and to enrich it with softened butter. I prefer a lighter texture achieved by folding in heavy whipped cream.

## Proportions

for 6 servings, 10 egg whites, 8 egg yolks, 2½ cups of mixed milk and cream, 1½ cups of sugar

### For the Meringues

**10 egg whites, at room temperature**
**¼ teaspoon cream of tartar**
**Pinch of salt**

**1 cup superfine sugar**
**1½ teaspoons vanilla extract**
**2 cups milk**

### For the Custard

**8 egg yolks**
**½ cup sugar**
**Milk from the meringues**

**2 tablespoons vanilla extract**
**2 tablespoons dark rum**
**½ cup heavy cream, whipped**

1. Beat the egg whites with salt and cream of tartar in an electric mixer, beginning on slow speed and increasing to high. When the whites hold soft peaks, gradually beat in the sugar and vanilla. Continue beating until the whites are firm and glossy.

2. Heat the milk in a large frying pan. Scoop up meringue with a large serving spoon or ice-cream scoop and turn into the almost simmering milk. (The temperature should be less than 170 degrees.) Poach the meringues for about 1 to 2 minutes on each side, turning them over with a slotted spoon. When firm, remove and drain on paper towels.

3. Prepare the custard by beating the sugar gradually into the egg

yolks until they are thick and lemon-colored. Gradually add the strained hot milk and set over low heat for about 5 minutes, stirring constantly, until the custard begins to coat the spoon. Remove from the heat, stir in the vanilla and rum. Cover with plastic wrap and chill. When cold, fold in the whipped heavy cream.

4.   To serve, pour the custard into a serving bowl and float the meringue islands on top. Sprinkle them, if you like, with a little powdered praline (see Praline Torte, page 382) or macaroons or nutmeg.

*One of the reasons Floating Islands has been a French and English favorite is that, despite the eggs and cream, the effect is so light that you can follow even a heavy meal with this classic dessert.*

# SOUFFLÉ GRAND MARNIER

No one has done more than Child to deflate the mystique of the soufflé as a magical pouf attainable only by indentured servants of the Cordon Bleu. Her sweet soufflés in *Mastering I* floated a decade of soufflé making in domestic kitchens everywhere. We discovered that in the soufflé the only thing to fear was fear itself—and occasionally a faulty oven. Otherwise, Child's methodical analysis made the rising mushroom cloud of a soufflé as certain as the shape of an atomic explosion. Soufflés bloomed and trembled and sank on schedule to the wonder and applause of dinner guests who had not yet studied the works of Child.

The one incalculable in this otherwise perfect formula was timing the guests' rate of intake of earlier courses to avoid a half hour wait for dessert at the end. I miscalculated once and was forced to serve the dessert soufflé before the entrée. But ordinarily, if you have everything ready, you can whip and fold the egg whites quickly and pop the dish into the oven when the main course is cleared. Tell your guests a soufflé is coming and encourage them to dawdle over salad and/or cheese. Then you have primed them for the *coup de théâtre* of the soufflé's brief moment of glory.

Child's basic soufflé proportions in *Mastering I* were for a 6-cup charlotte mold, about two thirds as tall as round. Many people, however, use the shallower white porcelain soufflé dishes and with them you need to make a collar of wax paper or foil to give the soufflé sufficient height. I have given somewhat larger proportions for an 8-cup mold, which I find serves 4 to 6 people. A 10-cup mold will serve 6 to 8, but two smaller soufflés are easier to serve than one large one.

The richest and creamiest soufflés are made of a sweetened white sauce, thickened with egg yolk and leavened with egg white. You can flavor it with any liqueur, but Grand Marnier is classic for a reason: It has a silky nectar-like taste and texture lacking in some of the other liqueurs.

To intensify the flavor of orange, Child suggests the French device of rubbing a sugar cube over the skin of an orange, then mashing the cube as part of the sugar required. Since I seem never to find a sugar cube in my kitchen, I prefer simply to grate the orange rind, which gives a good fleck and tang.

There's no reason to serve an additional sauce with a soufflé, but a soufflé is unreasonable to begin with. So if you feel like having more and MORE, by all means soothe the unappeasable by a Grand Marnier sauce. One way to demand and get MORE is to wrap the soufflé inside a crêpe to produce the Crêpes Soufflé of many fancy French restaurants. Claiborne supplies a recipe in his *New New York Times Cookbook* for crêpes filled with praline soufflé, but you could also use the recipe below, which would stuff about eighteen small crêpes. Crêpes Soufflé has the advantage of being very easy to serve. To bake them, you simply put a dollop of soufflé in the center of each crêpe, fold each in two on a baking sheet, and bake at 400 degrees for about 10 minutes, or until the soufflé has puffed. Sprinkle with confectioners' sugar and serve with some Grand Marnier sauce on the side.

## Proportions

for 4 to 6 servings from an 8-cup mold, 6 egg yolks, 8 egg whites, 4 tablespoons flour, 3 tablespoons butter, 1 cup of milk, 6 tablespoons Grand Marnier; for the sauce, 4 egg yolks to ½ cup of sugar to 1¾ cups of milk

### For the Soufflé

4 tablespoons flour
1 cup milk
½ cup sugar
6 egg yolks
3 tablespoons butter, softened
1 tablespoon vanilla extract
Rind of 1 orange, grated

6 tablespoons Grand Marnier (⅓ cup)
8 egg whites
Pinch of salt
½ teaspoon cream of tartar
1 tablespoon sugar

1. Dissolve the flour in a little of the milk in a saucepan. Stir in the remaining milk and sugar. Heat, stirring vigorously, until the mixture thickens and boils. (The sauce should be very thick.) Remove from the heat, beat in the egg yolks gradually, then most of the butter, the vanilla, orange rind, and liqueur. Dot the remaining butter on top to prevent a skin from forming.

2. Beat the egg whites with salt and cream of tartar slowly until frothy, then rapidly until the soft peak stage. Sprinkle on the sugar and

beat until stiff but not dry. Stir a little of the egg whites into the yolk base, then quickly fold in the rest, keeping the whites as airy as possible.

3.  Turn into the prepared mold that has been buttered and coated with granulated sugar. (If needed, make about a 6-inch collar of wax paper or foil long enough to surround and overlap the baking dish. Butter and sprinkle with sugar the inside of the collar that will be exposed above the rim of the dish. Tie the collar to the dish with string just below the rim to hold it.) Put in a preheated 400-degree oven. Lower the oven temperature to 375 degrees and bake, without opening the oven door, for 30 minutes. Sprinkle the top with confectioners' sugar and bake for 10 or 15 minutes longer (total 40 to 45 minutes). Many prefer a wet center, so don't worry if the center is not as dry as the outside of the soufflé. Serve immediately. It will fall as you start to cut it. Cut it with a serrated knife and use a spoon to help get it out of the dish.

## For the Sauce

| | |
|---|---|
| 4  egg yolks | 1¾  cups milk, scalded |
| ½  cup sugar | 1  teaspoon vanilla extract |
| 1  teaspoon cornstarch | 1½  tablespoons Grand Marnier |

Beat the egg yolks with the sugar in an electric mixer until thick and lemon-colored. Gradually beat in the cornstarch and then the scalded milk. Put over low heat and stir constantly until the mixture thickens enough to coat a spoon. Remove and beat in the flavorings. Either serve the sauce separately or spoon some sauce at the side of each plate and put the soufflé serving next to it.

*Soufflés fool us into thinking we're eating nothing but foam, which makes it a near perfect dessert for any kind of sit-down meal that provides the right timing.*

# FRESH FRUIT ICES

Before the days of the processor and the electric ice-cream maker, sherbets outnumbered ices about 3 to 1. Sherbets used milk or beaten egg white to diminish the ice crystals formed by fruit purée, sugar, and water, frozen at ordinary home-freezer temperatures. Cookbooks instructed us to remove ices or sherbets from molds or trays while still slushy and to beat up the slush about every half hour to approximate the texture of a churn-frozen ice. This was a bother but not nearly as laborious as cranking by hand the old salt-filled ice cream freezer, even providing you had one on hand as a family relic.

The small electric churn-freezer was the first step in getting a creamy texture without a lot of hand beating or cranking. The processor was the second step, since the processor could not only purée fresh fruit rapidly, it could also purée frozen fruits and ices and sherbets that were crystalline instead of smooth and creamy. The processor has now revolutionized the world of fruit ices for the home cook because the combinations are endless and the pleasures are as instantaneous as Polaroid.

Fresh fruit has always been Beard's favorite dessert and because of that he has experimented widely with fresh fruit ices and fruit sherbets. In the past, he used the terms interchangeably, but in *The New James Beard*, he lists all of his frozen fruit, sugar, and water purées as "sherbets." One reason, I suppose, is that French new cuisine has popularized intense fruit ices and marketed them in America as "sorbets."

Beard makes fruit sherbet, ice, or sorbet making simple by explaining the basic principle of 3 cups of fruit purée to 1 cup of sugar syrup. The usual ratio for the syrup is 2 parts sugar to 1 part water. The less sugar in proportion to purée, the coarser the ice crystals. On the other hand, if there is too much sugar, the mixture won't freeze. You can keep the syrup ratio the same and still adjust tartness and sweetness by adding lemon juice, or other citric intensifiers, and liqueurs.

A quick list of Beard's fruit and liqueur combinations gives some idea of how rapidly you can empty both the fruit bin and the liquor cabinet. Orange juice with Grand Marnier, pineapple with kirsch or rum, strawberry with Grand Marnier, apples with Calvados, melons with port, cranberry with bourbon. For 1 quart of sherbet, the proportion generally is 2 cups of sugar to 1 cup of water for the syrup; you then use 1 cup of syrup with 3 cups of purée and 3 tablespoons of liqueur. If you have a churn-freezer, freeze until the mixture holds its shape but is still soft and spoonable. If you freeze in trays or a mold, you will need to beat the slush two or three times during the freezing. The processor will do this for you in a trice. The processor will also allow you to freeze the slush hard and soften it at the last minute for serving, by cutting it in chunks and purée-ing those as you would ice cubes.

Another processor dividend, publicized this time by Claiborne, is the miracle ice produced by a frozen banana. A peeled banana, frozen, then chunked and puréed in the processor produces an extraordinarily creamy texture that in itself makes a fine base for other fruits and flavors, obviating the need for sugar syrup as such, or milk or cream. Since the banana is bland, you can add lemon juice for tartness and a little honey or maple syrup for sweetness, or a spoonful of blackberry jam, or a little rum, or Kahlúa or crème de menthe. You can be elegant or outrageous. The one trick is to remember to freeze the peeled bananas in a bag with a little lemon juice so that the bananas don't discolor. Their creamy whiteness is part of the taste.

The following is a classic fruit ice, new way, that is good with a full range of red or blue or black fruits—strawberries, raspberries, blueberries, blackberries—colored and intensified by the liqueur called Cassis, made from currants. Cassis is very sweet, so you may want to increase the lemon and lime to counteract it. Everything depends, of course, on the exact sweetness of the fresh fruit at the moment it's used.

# STRAWBERRY-CASSIS ICE

## Proportions

for 4 to 6 servings, 2 pints fresh strawberries, 2 cups of sugar, 1 cup of water, ½ cup of lime or lemon juice, ½ cup of Cassis

| | |
|---|---|
| **2 pints (1 quart) strawberries** | **1 cup water** |
| **or other fresh berry** | **½ cup lime or lemon juice** |
| **2 cups sugar** | **½ cup Cassis** |

1. Hull the berries and purée in a processor or blender until smooth. Chill. Make a sugar syrup by boiling the sugar and water for 5 minutes to thicken it slightly. Chill, then add to the fruit purée. Add the juice and Cassis. Taste for sweet, sour, and intensity. Remember that freezing will lessen the flavor.

2. Pour into an electric churn-freezer or into trays for still-freezing. If the latter, beat in a processor or blender before it is fully frozen to smooth it out. Best if it is not frozen hard.

*Makes an excellent ice for ending a meal because of its balance of sweet and sour.*

# VANILLA-BEAN ICED CREAM

I scream, you scream, even George Washington screamed for ice cream. So entrenched is ice cream in the American psyche that at the very moment the official dietary goals proposed for the United States by McGovern's Senate Committee stipulated a sharp reduction of fat, cholesterol, and sugar consumption, Americans were gobbling up iced cream (milk and yogurt) at the rate of 23 quarts per person, or a total of 750 million gallons a year. That was in 1977. Since then, ice cream parlors, boutiques, holes-in-the-wall, street vendors on foot, carts, and automotive wagons have so proliferated that ice cream must be the single most screamed for sweet throughout the land.

Well, at least we come by it honestly. Honest George Washington bought his first "Cream machine for Making Ice" in 1784 in America's ice-cream-making capital, Philadelphia. During the summer of 1790 he spent $200 on the "iced creams" he served at his formal Thursday-night

White House dinners. White House ice cream was the epitome of swank for Thomas Jefferson as well, who entertained a "brilliant Assemblage—America's best," wrote one of his guests in 1801, at a perfectly appointed table of which the centerpiece was "a large, shining dome of pink Ice Cream."

Pink was probably from strawberries, since the first known reference to ice cream in America (according to Root and de Rochemont in *Eating in America*) was to a "Curious dessert" served by the Governor of Maryland and Compos'd of Ice Cream, Strawberries, and Milk. Strawberry ice cream was one of the popular flavors included by Eliza Leslie and Mrs. Webster, along with lemon, raspberry, almond, pine-apple, peach, and vanilla. Vanilla, of course, meant an honest New World vanilla bean, the extract not yet having been synthesized in chemical laboratories. Vanilla-flavored ice cream eventually outstripped strawberry, lemon, and peach in public favor, probably because it was not limited to seasonal fruits, but could be had year round. In America, vanilla now leads all other flavors by 2 to 1, even with simulated vanillin flavoring. Maybe vanilla ice cream is one of those placebo foods like Nabisco and Oreo cookies that remind us of happier ill-spent childhoods. Or maybe vanilla is welcome relief from the endless flavor proliferation of commercial ice-cream makers that have given us Banana Daiquiri, Chili Con Carne, and Pink Bubble Gum ice cream.

However it is, vanilla ice cream made with a vanilla bean is one of the most soothing of all sweets. The vanillin of a bean has other aromatics lacking in synthetic vanillin, so the long black withered pod is worth buying and keeping. Ordinarily the pod, or a piece of it, can be washed off and re-used after flavoring a custard or a syrup. But to intensify the flavor for ice cream, you open the pod and scrape into the cream the mass of tiny black seeds hidden therein.

Mrs. Webster explains that you can make "Ice Cream without Cream" by substituting for "a quart of rich cream boiled and set away till cold" a cooked custard of egg yolks, sugar, and milk. Her rich cream is really clotted or double cream, a splendidly thick cream that the English still make but we don't. Beard's Basic Vanilla Ice Cream, in *American Cookery*, comes closest to following the simple old-fashioned formula of freezing flavored and sugared rich cream, but even he calls for light cream. His French Vanilla, on the other hand, uses a custard base, plus a quart of heavy cream. Claiborne, in *The New New York Times Cookbook*, adopts the same custard method for his Vanilla Ice Cream but reverses the proportions of milk to cream to make a much lighter texture. For 6 egg yolks, Claiborne suggests 4 cups of milk and 1 cup of heavy cream, where Beard suggests 2 cups of milk and 4 cups of heavy cream. The point is that the custard will give you the creamy texture once achieved by the quality of the cream itself. You can vary its richness by adding more or less milk or cream. I have compromised by going half and half with milk and cream, which is still wonderfully rich without necessarily putting McGovern-diet followers into a state of permanent shock.

## Proportions

for 8 to 10 servings, 6 egg yolks, 2 cups of milk, 2 cups of heavy cream, 1 cup of sugar, 1 vanilla bean

6 **egg yolks**
1 **cup sugar**
2 **cups milk**
2 **cups heavy cream**

1 **vanilla bean (about 2 inches long)**
**Pinch of salt**

1.  Beat the egg yolks with the sugar in an electric mixer until thick and lemon-colored. Heat the milk with the cream, salt, and vanilla bean, split open with the seeds scraped into the liquid, along with the pod.

2.  Add the milk and cream gradually to the yolk mixture and beat in the top of a double boiler over simmering water until the custard thickens enough to coat a spoon. Chill in the refrigerator.

3.  When ready to freeze the mixture, remove the vanilla pod with a slotted spoon. Pour the mixture into a churn-freezer, if you have one, or into a metal mold for still-freezing. If the latter, stir well when the cream is half frozen. If the cream freezes harder than you'd like, cut it into chunks and put it into a processor just before serving. It will then have the texture of soft-frozen ice cream achieved by churn-freezing.

*Melted, the cream makes a fine custard sauce to serve with a fresh fruit salad or an apple and bread pudding.*

# CHOCOLATE MOUSSE CAKE

How to choose among chocolate confections? The American ideal of a chocolate dessert is a cross between a dense, creamy bittersweet mousse and a dense, creamy bittersweet cake. As a result, our famous restaurants have become famous for their dense, creamy bittersweet chocolate desserts named, variously, Chocolate Velvet at the Four Seasons, Coach House Chocolate Cake at the Coach House, Chocolate Mousse Cake at the late Café Chauveron—all in New York—and Chocolate Decadence at Narsai's on the West Coast.

Beard gives a French Chocolate and an Austrian Chocolate Cake recipe in *The New James Beard* and of one he says, "very rich and gooey"; of the other, "somewhere between a cake and a pudding, heavy and rich."

Claiborne, in *The New New York Times Cookbook,* gives the Café Chauveron recipe of chef Raymond Richez, appropriately named, who created the dish by accident when he put twice as much butter as usual in their regular mousse. The result, says Claiborne, is this "lasciviously rich, smooth, velvety confection served with an equally seductive rum-laden sabayon, otherwise known as zabaglione."

Child, in *Child & Company,* says that she was trying to reproduce a chocolate cake legendary in the thirties among New York connoisseurs for its "fat and unctuous texture." The result she named Le Gâteau Victoire au Chocolat, Mousseline, to celebrate "a very tender, moist, and delicate, and very chocolaty, dessert confection that is more like a cheese-cake or custard than a cake, yet it is a cake—almost." You see what I mean.

Child had given us a number of tender, moist, etc., etc., chocolaty confections over the years that would meet this description, but her latest one has the virtue of increased simplicity. A heretic might ask, "Why not just sink your teeth into the finest imported solid bar of chocolate that you can buy, or perhaps melt it and spoon it up?" But true believers know that chocolate must be mixed with something even smoother and more unctuous than itself, something like butter and cream and eggs—uncontaminated by flour, starch, baking powder, or other adulterants—to experience fully the pleasures of sin. If food in general has not replaced sex in the puritanical canon, chocolate in particular has. To read chocolate recipes in contemporary cookbooks is to encounter all the adjectives previously reserved for sexual encounters of the naughtiest kind.

For the hopelessly depraved, I have included a version of Child's Victoire, compounding her original sin by adding her recipe for chocolate-butter glaze from *From Julia Child's Kitchen.* I mean why not go whole hog, to slip into another fashionable and related metaphor? If you have hang-over rue the next day, you can always spruce up with Miss Piggy's special facial mousse, "a mixture of mocha, cooking chocolate, confectioners sugar, eggs, and cream (adjust the proportions to your own taste)."

## Proportions

for 8 to 10 servings from a 9-inch-square cake pan, 12 ounces semisweet chocolate, 4 ounces unsweetened chocolate, 6 eggs, 1 cup of heavy cream

| | |
|---|---|
| 1 tablespoon instant coffee (preferably Medaglio d'Oro) | 4 ounces unsweetened baking chocolate |
| ¼ cup hot water | 6 eggs |
| ¼ cup dark rum or Cognac | ½ cup sugar |
| 12 ounces semisweet chocolate bits or baking squares | 1 cup heavy cream |
| | 1 tablespoon vanilla extract |

1. Dissolve the coffee in the hot water and rum. Add the chocolate and heat slowly (over a Flame-tamer or over simmering water) in order to melt the chocolate without burning it.

2. Gradually beat the sugar into the eggs in the top of a double boiler over simmering water to increase their volume and thicken them to the consistency of lightly whipped cream.

3. Beat the heavy cream with the vanilla until it is thick and doubled in volume. Beat the melted chocolate and fold it into the egg mixture. When half incorporated, add the heavy cream and continue mixing as lightly as possible.

4. Turn into a cake pan prepared by lining the buttered pan with buttered and floured wax paper (or the cake will be impossible to unmold). Set in a pan of hot water in a 350-degree oven for 1 hour. Turn the oven off, leave the oven door ajar, and let cake sit for 30 minutes while it falls. Remove from the oven and let sit another 30 minutes before unmolding it. Sprinkle with confectioners' sugar, or a frosting of whipped cream or the chocolate glaze below.

# CHOCOLATE-BUTTER GLAZE

## Proportions

5 ounces chocolate to 2 ounces butter (½ stick)

1 teaspoon instant coffee
2 tablespoons hot water
3 ounces semisweet chocolate bits or squares

2 ounces unsweetened chocolate
2 ounces (½ stick) butter, softened

Dissolve the coffee in the hot water and add the chocolate. Melt in the top of a double boiler over simmering water. Gradually beat in the butter off the heat, and cool until it is right for pouring over the cake. If it becomes too thick, beat it over hot water until the butter melts again.

# CHOCOLATE TRUFFLES

Just to indicate how generally shiftless and irrational the human feeder is, it is a known fact that the better the meal and the greater the number of delicious and irresistible courses consumed, the greedier the feeder gets. Offer a plate of chocolate truffles with your demitasse espresso and hear the groans. Turn away for an instant and the plate is empty. Maybe it can only be explained chemically. Not simple greed but this craving for chocolate, which a prominent psychiatric institute explains as a craving for absent love. Chocolate, it appears, contains a substance called phenylethylamine, which is released by the primitive part of the brain of a human in love and craved by a human spurned. Perhaps a lover's gift of chocolates has a crude scientific—that is, biochemical—basis. If the affair goes well, the chocolate sustains the high. If badly, chocolate is there to compensate.

The fact that a chocolate truffle wrapped in its gold or silver foil costs about a dollar apiece in our fine food or chocolate boutiques is maybe the best explanation of the truffle's popularity. Given the truffle's high status, homemade truffles are one of the best gifts you can give—to a lover or guests. That they are one of the easiest of all candies to make in no way diminishes their value, or yours, as a gift-giver.

Child supplied us with a recipe for them as far back as *Mastering II*. The sly and crafty among us instantly seized on their possibilities for lovers, guests, charities, Christmas presents, and Parents Day competitions. They reappear in *Julia Child & Company,* heavily laden with bourbon or rum this time, and pulverized gingersnaps.

I say yes to the bourbon or rum and no to the gingersnaps. Just a plain ordinary rich dense intense bittersweet bourbon-laden chocolate truffle is good enough for me.

## Proportions

for 18 small nuggets, 8 ounces chocolate, ¼ pound butter, ¼ cup of bourbon or rum, ½ cup of cocoa

**6 ounces semisweet chocolate**
**2 ounces unsweetened chocolate**
**2 tablespoons strong coffee (instant plus water)**

**¼ cup bourbon or rum**
**¼ pound (1 stick) butter**
**½ cup unsweetened powdered cocoa**

1. Melt the chocolate slowly with the coffee and rum in the top of a double boiler over simmering water. Beat in the butter in small pieces with an electric mixer. Chill until the chocolate is firm enough to handle easily.

2. Scoop up hunks of the chocolate with a soup spoon and roll in the powdered cocoa. Can be frozen or simply refrigerated until needed. If the truffles look moist, roll in more cocoa.

*Put them on a silver platter, as if they were worth their weight in gold, and pass with espresso or other strong after-dinner coffee in demitasse cups.*

# SELECTED BIBLIOGRAPHY

I've chosen the most important or most characteristic works of our four masters to provide a sampling rather than a complete list. Many of these books are now in paperback, but I've indicated here first publication.

## M. F. K. FISHER

*The Art of Eating* (World: 1954)
> Collects five gastronomical works in a volume unique in the literature of cooking. A melange of autobiography, philosophy, recipes, and storytelling, the volume confronts the American experience in terms of food.
>> *Serve It Forth* (Harper: 1937);
>> *Consider the Oyster* (Duell, Sloan and Pearce: 1941);
>> *How to Cook a Wolf* (Duell, Sloan and Pearce: 1942);
>> *The Gastronomical Me* (Duell, Sloan and Pearce: 1943);
>> *An Alphabet for Gourmets* (Viking: 1949).

*A Cordiall Water* (Little, Brown: 1961)
> Reprinted by North Point Press in 1981, this is a brief booklet about the art, magic, and science of "The Recipe" in relation to healing.

*Map of Another Town* (Little, Brown: 1964)
> The experience of an American woman and her two daughters in Aix-en-Provence as they learn the French art of daily living.

*With Bold Knife & Fork* (Putnam: 1969)
> Gastronomical essays, with recipes, largely collected from *The New Yorker.*

*A Considerable Town* (Knopf: 1978)
> Reminiscences about Marseilles, its people, its personality, its fairs, and feasts.

*The Physiology of Taste* by Jean Anthelme Brillat-Savarin (Knopf: 1971)
> Translated and annotated by Fisher to make this classic work accessible to the American reader.

# JAMES BEARD

*James Beard's New Fish Cookery* (Little, Brown: 1976)
> A pioneering work when it first came out in 1954, it is still the most comprehensive collection of American fish recipes.

*The James Beard Cookbook* (Dell: 1958)
> Many times reprinted from its original paperback edition, this is a simple all-purpose cookbook of general American cooking.

*James Beard's Treasury of Outdoor Cooking* (Golden Press: 1962)
> The most complete of Beard's two earlier works on outdoor cooking, the book is useful for its variety of marinades as well as methods of barbecuing, grilling, spit-roasting, and pit-roasting.

*Delights and Prejudices* (Atheneum: 1964)
> Beard's autobiography, studded with recipes from his mother and her Chinese chefs. A delightful food memoir of growing up in the Northwest.

*James Beard's American Cookery* (Little, Brown: 1972)
> A massive collection of American recipes new and old, with emphasis on important women's cookbooks of the nineteenth century.

*Beard on Bread* (Knopf: 1973)
> A simple and still the best primer on basic bread-making.

*Theory & Practice of Good Cooking* (Knopf: 1977)
> An attempt to outline the basic principles of cooking; more useful for reference than for a beginner's practical guide.

*The New James Beard* (Knopf: 1981)
> Designed as a recipe book to be used with *Theory & Practice,* the volume is full of new ideas as well as old Beard favorites. Includes a useful concordance of American foods.

# CRAIG CLAIBORNE

*The New York Times Cook Book* (Harper & Row: 1961)
> A comprehensive selection of some 1,500 recipes that appeared in *The New York Times* between 1950 and 1960. International and eclec-

tic, recipes range in difficulty from basics like scrambled eggs to exotics like Venezuelan "hallacas" (stuffed tamales wrapped in banana leaves). Some useful photographs.

*The New York Times International Cook Book* (Harper & Row: 1971)
    A brief collection of national dishes arranged by country, to serve as a general introduction to the variety of the world's cuisines.

*The New New York Times Cookbook* (with Pierre Franey) (Times Books: 1979)
    The best recipes from *The New York Times* during the 1970s, many contributed by amateur and professional chefs at home and abroad. A celebration of the Franey-Claiborne kitchen team.

*Craig Claiborne's Gourmet Diet* (with Pierre Franey) (Times Books: 1980)
    Life without salt, or how to go on a salt-free diet with maximum pleasure and minimum pain.

*A Feast Made for Laughter* (Doubleday: 1982)
    "A Memoir with Recipes," the book includes Claiborne's recommended cookbook library and his hundred favorite recipes.

## JULIA CHILD

*Mastering the Art of French Cooking,* Volume I (with Simone Beck and Louisette Bertholle) (Knopf: 1961)
    The classic work in English on the terminology and techniques of French cooking in all its aspects. Detailed Master Recipes and variants.

*Mastering the Art of French Cooking,* Volume II (with Simone Beck) (Knopf: 1970)
    An encyclopedic extension of volume I, more useful for studying food than for cooking it.

*From Julia Child's Kitchen* (Knopf: 1975)
    A compilation of her first color television shows elaborated into a practical one-volume condensation of *Mastering.* Includes a useful culinary gazetteer, meat charts and comparative cuts, comparative weights and measures, and instructive photographs.

*Julia Child & Company* (Knopf: 1978)
*Julia Child & More Company* (Knopf: 1980)
    These two books in paperback, based on the later television series, are menu cookbooks that are simpler and more generally American than any of Child's earlier works. Include color photographs of what completed dishes should look like.


*Note:* The following are but a few among many important American cookbooks, arranged chronologically in order of the first known edition.

Where possible, I've indicated publisher and date of facsimile reprint. For the twentieth century, I've selected from works cited a mere handful important to my purpose. For good critical bibliographies, see John L. and Karen Hess, *The Taste of America* and Karen Hess' edition of *Martha Washington's Booke of Cookery*. For a description of some of the best current cookbooks designed for the American cook, see Claiborne's "Recommended Cookbook Library" in *A Feast for Laughter*.

## EIGHTEENTH CENTURY

*Martha Washington's Booke of Cookery,* Karen Hess, editor
A 1749 manuscript, transcribed and annotated by the editor and printed by Columbia University Press, 1981. Detailed scholarly history of colonial cooking by means of two English recipe collections, *A Booke of Cookery* and *A Booke of Sweetmeats.*
*American Cookery* by Amelia Simmons (Hartford: 1796)
Facsimile reprint by Oxford University Press, 1958. Thought to be the first cookbook by an American cook, in this case also "an American orphan."

## NINETEENTH CENTURY

*The Virginia Housewife: or Methodical Cook* by Mary Randolph (Washington, D.C.: 1824)
Facsimile reprint of the 1860 edition published by Crown, 1970. One of the earliest and best of the native American cookbooks.
*The American Frugal Housewife* by Lydia Maria Child (Boston: 1832)
Facsimile reprint by the Ohio State University, 1971. A favorite with Julia Child (no relation), who admires her "primeval New England Puritan quality."
*Directions for Cookery* by Eliza Leslie (Philadelphia: 1837)
Facsimile reprint by Arno, 1973. Miss Leslie, rare as a spinster among her cookbook writing peers, is favored by James Beard for the clarity of her directions and the forthrightness of her views.
*The Improved Housewife* by A. L. Webster (Hartford: 1844)
Facsimile reprint by Arno, 1973. Mrs. Webster was unusual for her knowledge of French as well as of English cooking.
*The American System of Cookery* by T. J. Crowen (New York: 1847)
Mrs. Crowen was an early systematizer of the kind Mrs. Beeton was in England.
*Hand-Book of Practical Cookery* by Pierre Blot (New York: 1867)
Facsimile reprint of the 1869 edition by Arno, 1973. One of the first French chefs in America to write a cookbook for Americans.

*Mrs. Porter's New Southern Cookery Book* by M. F. Porter (Philadelphia: 1871)
Facsimile reprint by Arno, 1973. Good regional recipes.
*Mrs. Parloa's Appledorf Cookbook* by Maria Parloa (Boston: 1877)
A popular cookbook writer in the 1880s.
*Buckeye Cookery* (Minneapolis: 1877)
Facsimile reprint of the 1883 edition, retitled *The Buckeye Cookbook* by Dover, 1975. A revelation of midwestern cookery, contributed by many hands.
*Common Sense in the Household* by Marion Harland (New York: 1871)
A "best-selling manual" of Anglo-Saxon categorical imperatives for women like M. F. K. Fisher's Grandmother Holbrook.
*Mrs. Lincoln's Boston Cook Book* by Mary J. Lincoln (Boston: 1883)
The original founder of the Boston Cooking School, later known through the works of Fannie Farmer.
*Delicate Feasting* by Theodore Child (New York: 1890)
A slim fastidious volume on the proprieties of ingestion, much enjoyed by James Beard.
*The Boston Cooking-School Cook Book* by Fannie Merritt Farmer (Boston: 1896)
Facsimile reprint by Crown, 1973. Latest revised edition by Knopf, 1979, under Marion Cunningham and Jeri Laber. Now a middle-of-the-road encyclopedic reference work, Mrs. Farmer's original text explained the chemistry of food in the new domestic science.

## TWENTIETH CENTURY

*Mrs. Rorer's New Cook Book* by Sarah Tyson Rorer (Philadelphia: 1902)
Head of the Philadelphia Cooking School that rivaled Boston's, Mrs. Rorer was a prolific writer, lecturer, and media celebrity in the new field of dietetics.
*The Settlement Cook Book* by Mrs. Simon Kander (Settlement Cook Book Co.: 1901)
One of the first cookbooks to bring Middle European cooking to Middle America.
*Joy of Cooking* by Irma S. Rombauer (Indianapolis: 1931)
Many later editions with her daughter, Marion R. Becker. An indispensable reference work that Claiborne has called "the finest of all-inclusive, comprehensive basic American cookbooks."
*Mrs. Rasmussen's Book of One-Arm Cookery* by Mary Laswell (Houghton Mifflin: 1946)
A pioneering work on food to cook while drinking beer. George Price illustrations.

*Dine at Home with Rector* by George Rector (Dutton: 1937)
> Son of the famed restaurateur, Rector takes a macho line halfway between Robert Benchley and Calvin Trillin.

*The Gold Cook Book* by Louis P. De Gouy (Chilton: 1947)
> The sophisticated cook's alternative, during the forties, to Fannie Farmer. An influential French chef who became thoroughly acclimated to American ways.

*The West Coast Cook Book* by Helen Evans Brown (Boston: 1952)
> Good regional recipes from a colleague of James Beard.

*Bouquet de France* by Samuel Chamberlain (Gourmet: 1952)
> One of the first postwar travel books to make food an imperative of the European experience. Recipes subsumed in art and architecture.

*The American Heritage Cookbook,* Helen McCully, Eleanor Noderer, and Helen D. Bullock, editors (American Heritage: 1964)
> A compilation of recipes from early cookbooks, adapted for modern kitchens, but full of historical detail.

*American Food: The Gastronomic Story* by Evan Jones (Dutton: 1975)
> A combination of history and recipes updated for current tastes and kitchens.

*Eating in America* by Waverley Root and Richard de Rochemont (Morrow: 1976)
> A social and economic history, lacking structure but full of interesting detail, covering the full span from the colonies to the present.

*The Taste of America* by John L. and Karen Hess (Grossman: 1977)
> A cantankerous view of the current food establishment, but knowledgeable in its prejudices.

*The New York Times 60-Minute Gourmet* by Pierre Franey (Times Books: 1979)
> An influential collection of recipes from Franey's column, focusing on the quick and easy in a simplified format.

# GENERAL INDEX

Acton, Eliza, 55, 61
*Aïoli,* 136, 139
Airline travel, 4
Alcibiades, 380
Alcoholic beverages, 76–78
*Ali-oli,* 139
Allen, Ida Bailey, 12, 76
*Alphabet for Gourmets, An* (Fisher), 258, 291
American cookery
 airline travel and, 4
 alcoholic beverages and, 76–78
 anticategorical habits and, 5
 appetizers, history of, 78–79
 author's development as cook, 11–18
 Beard, James (biography), 31–37
 beer and, 77, 80
 birds, 213–37
 blenders and, 135–36
 braising, 262–63
 breads, 316–39
 butchers, 239
 cakes, 377–82
 California wines, 79–80
 cereals. *See* Grains
 cheese, 354–65
 Child, Julia (biography), 47–53
 Chinese cooking, 57
 chocolate, 396–97, 398–99
 Claiborne, Craig (biography), 39–45
 Coca-Cola, 76
 cocktail party stand-bys, 78
 codification and, 5–6
 colonial life and, 54–55
 cookbooks, history of, 54–59
 crusts, 207, 349–50

desserts, 366–99
dips, 78
drink and drink food, 75–96
drinking habits and, 76–78
early history of, 54–55
eating on the move, 8
eggs, 174–76
as expression of culture, 6
in the fifties, 57
fish and shellfish, 185–212
Fisher, M. F. K. (biography), 23–28
food processors, 72, 108
French cuisine and, 5–6, 56
"frontiers" in, 7
garlic, 127, 136, 235
German-Jewish tradition in, 56
grains, 300–15
gravy, 123
green salads, 151–53
hamburgers, 257–59
health-food movement in, 58–59
herbs, 135–36
ice cream, 394–96
Indian cuisine, 57–58
inferiority feelings about, 4–5
international cuisine, 57–58
Italian cuisine, 57
ketchup, 123, 143–44, 248
kitchens, 7
Lucas, Dione, 57
masters of, 8–10, 23–53
meats, 238–73
melting-pot character of, 6
Mexican cuisine, 58
milk, 76

American cookery (cont.)
Moroccan cuisine, 58, 231
natural-foods movement, 58–59
nineteenth-century cookery, 55–56
pasta, 340–53
pies, 368, 370–77
poaching, 176, 177, 192–93, 230
poultry, 213–37
"professionalism of amateurs," 8
processors, 72, 108
purées, 108, 137, 297–99
raw vegetables, 81
recipes, discussion of, 60–66. *See also*
Recipe Index
revolution in, 3–10
Roasting Charts, 219, 244
salad bars, 151
salad dressings, 125, 141–42
salads, 147–73
salt and sweet tastes in, 6
sauces, 122–46
sautéeing, 257–58
in the seventies, 57–58
shellfish. *See* Fish and shellfish
sherbets, 392–93
in the sixties, 57
"sludge," 240
soufflés, 176–77, 182–84, 390–92
soups, 97–103
stir-frying, 224
stocks, 97–104
sugar, fixation on, 6–7
sweets, 366–99
systematizing household economy and,
55–56
tortes, 382
travel opportunities and, 3–4
turkey, 217–20
twentieth-century history, 56–59
vegetables, 81, 274–99
white bread, 319–24
wines and, 77–80
World War II and, 3–4, 14–15, 58
*American Cookery* (Beard), 6, 35, 83, 100, 120,
148, 155, 159, 167, 268, 269, 295,
330, 373, 375, 379, 385, 395
*American Cookery* (Simmons), 5, 55, 61
*American Frugal Housewife of 1832, The*
(Child), 55, 61, 67, 239, 262, 313,
385
*American Lady's Cookery Book* (Crowen), 55,
338, 360, 364
*American Women's Home, The* (Stowe), 12
*Among Friends* (Fisher), 25
"Anatomy of a Recipe, The" (Fisher), 60
*Apicius Redivivus* (Kitchener), 61
Appetizers. *See* Drink and Drink food
Apples, 387
Arliss, George, 143
*Art of Cookery* (Glasse), 55
*Art of Eating, The* (Fisher), 17

*Art of Good Cooking, The* (Peck), 57
Artichokes, 153, 278
cooking, 278
Asparagus, 279–80
cooking, 280
Asparagus Polonaise, 277
Aspic, 170
Aubergine, 293
Auden, W. H., 23
Aunt Gwen's Cold Shape, 241
Avocado, 81
Aykroyd, Dan, 47

Baba Ghanouj, 83
*Bagna cauda*, 279
Banana, frozen, 393
Barbecue sauces, 143–44, 248
Barthes, Roland, 67
Beans, 161–64, 302–03
navy, 302–03
pea, 302–03
soybeans, 303
Beard, James, 6, 8–9, biography of, 31–37;
39, 51, 64–65, 69; on drink and drink
food, 78, 79, 81, 83, 86, 92; on soups,
98, 99, 100, 102, 104, 105, 107, 108,
110, 112, 113, 116, 118, 120; on
sauces, 126, 131, 136, 138, 140, 141,
144, 145; on salads, 148, 152, 155,
157, 159, 162, 163, 164–65, 166,
167, 168, 172; on eggs, 175–76, 180,
183; on fish, 187, 189, 192, 195, 197,
201, 204, 207; on birds, 215–16, 221,
230, 231–32, 233, 235, 237; on
meats, 240–41, 242, 244, 245, 246,
249, 251, 253–54, 255, 258, 260,
261, 264, 265, 268, 269, 271, 272; on
vegetables, 277, 280, 282, 284, 287,
293, 294, 295, 297; on grains, 303,
304, 313; on breads, 321–22, 325,
330, 331, 334, 336, 337, 338; on
pasta, 343, 346; on sweets, 371, 373,
375, 377, 379, 385, 387, 389, 393,
395, 396
*Beard on Bread* (Beard), 321, 330, 334, 336
Béchamel, Marquis de, 124
Béchamel sauce, 124, 128
Beck, Simone, 16, 48, 58
Becker, Marion, 56
Beebe, Lucius, 23, 39, 56
Beecher, Catherine, 275
Beecher, Henry Ward, 368, 370
Beer, 77, 80
Beeton, Isabella, 55, 61, 149–50
Bemelmans, Ludwig, 39
Bertholle, Louisette, 16, 48, 58
*Beurre blanc*, 126
*Beurre manié*, 128
Billi Bi, 113
Billings, Josh, 10

Child (cont.)
84, 86, 87, 89, 93, 94; on soups, 98,
99, 100, 101, 104, 105, 107, 108,
110, 113, 114; on sauces, 123, 124,
127–28, 131, 134, 138, 140, 141; on
salads, 152, 153, 160, 161, 164, 170;
on eggs, 176, 177, 179, 180, 182–83;
on fish, 187, 190, 199–200, 204, 207,
208–10; on birds, 216, 221, 225, 226,
228, 230; on meats, 243, 244, 246,
247, 251, 253–54, 256, 258, 260,
261, 264, 268, 270–71; on vegetables, 277, 280, 284, 285, 286, 287,
289, 292, 293, 296; on breads, 321,
324, 325–26; on pasta, 342, 346, 349,
351; on cheese, 360–61; on sweets,
370, 371, 375, 379, 381, 382–83,
385–86, 387, 388, 390, 397, 399
Child, Lydia Marie, 55, 61, 67, 239, 241,
262, 313, 317, 385–86
Child, Paul, 47, 48, 49–50, 51, 52–53
Child, Theodore, 56, 99, 123, 128, 148, 151
Chinese cabbage, 155
Chinese cuisine, 57
Chocolate, 396–97, 398–99
truffles, 398–99
Chowder, 116
Cima alla genovese, 265
Claiborne, Craig, 4, 6, 8–9, 36, biography
of, 39–45; 51, 57, 64, 65, 69; on drink
and drink food, 77, 78, 79, 81, 83, 84,
86, 90, 94; on soups, 98, 105, 107,
110, 111, 114, 118, 120; on sauces,
140, 143, 144; on salads, 149, 151,
154, 157, 158, 164–65, 166, 167; on
eggs, 176, 177, 183; on fish, 190,
192, 195, 197, 202, 205–06, 207,
210; on birds, 215, 218, 223, 231–32,
233; on meats, 241, 242, 243, 244,
245, 246, 249, 251, 254, 255, 256,
258, 260, 264, 269; on vegetables,
277, 282, 284, 285, 289, 293, 297,
298; on grains, 303–04, 315; on
breads, 321, 325, 331, 338; on pasta,
343, 345; on cheese, 357, 360, 362;
on sweets, 371, 373, 375, 377, 379,
382, 387, 388–89, 391, 392, 395,
397
Clams, 117–18
Clancy, John, 9, 57
Classic Italian Cookbook, The (Hazan), 57, 290
Classic Puff Paste, 352
Clayton, Bernard, Jr., 325, 334
Coach House Restaurant, 107
Coca-Cola, 76, 78
Cocktail-party dip, 78
Coeur à la Crème, 364
Cold Cream of Sorrel Soup, 110
Coleslaw, 155–56
"Collops," 260

Common Sense in the Household (Harland), 175,
248, 283, 298, 322, 363, 374, 379
Complete Book of Pastry, The (Clayton), 334
Consider the Oyster (Fisher), 198
Cook, Anne, 123
Cook It Outdoors (Beard), 34, 253
Cook's Encyclopedia, The (Stobart), 293
Cookbooks, history of, 54–59
Cooked Dressing, 141
Cooper, James Fenimore, 7
Coq au Vin, 228
Coquilles St. Jacques à la Nage, 197
Cordiall Water, A (Fisher), 28
Cordon Bleu Cookbook (Lucas), 57
Corn, 281–82, 338
boiled, 282
bread, 338
cooking, 282
"shaved," 282
varieties of, 281–82
Corn bread, 338
Corned beef, 267–68
Cornell Bread, 331
"Corning," defined, 267
Cornish Hens, 236
Cornmeal, 301
mush, 303–04
Coulibiac of salmon, 207
Courgettes, 291
Cous-cous and Other Good Food from Morocco
(Wolfert), 58
Cracked wheat, 312
Cracklings, 221
"Craig Claiborne Journal, The" (newslet-
ter), 43
Cream Biscuits, 337
Cream of Watercress, 110
Crêpes Soufflé, 391
Crowen, Mrs. Thomas J., 35, 55, 338, 360,
364
Crudités, 81
Crusts, 207, 349–50
for desserts, 349–50
for fish, 207
Cucumbers
bitterness in, 294
varieties of, 294
Cuisines of Mexico, The (Kennedy), 58
Cunningham, Marion, 118
Cymlings, 291

Dacquoise, 382
Daikon, 202
Danish pastry, 333–34
Dannenbaum, Julie, 32
Dashi, 202
David, Elizabeth, 58, 62, 321, 322
David Eyre's Pancake, 245
Davis, Adelle, 58, 244

Timbale d'Asperges, 277
Tortes, 382–83
Tomata Catchup, 144
Tomato aspic, 170
*Tramp Abroad, A* (Twain), 2, 60
Travel opportunities, 3–4
Trichinosis, 246
Tripe, 272
Tripes à la Mode de Caen, 272
Tripes Lyonnaise, 272
*Tripier* pot, 272
Triplet, Clay, 32
Troisgros, Jean, 43, 58, 166
Troisgros, Pierre, 58
Trollope, Mrs. Frances, 3, 4, 12, 54
Tschirky, Oscar, 56, 156
Tsuji, Shizuo, 58, 202
Tull, Jethro, 12
Turkey, 217–20
 basting, 218
 high-temperature cooking, 218
 stuffing, 218, 220
Turner, Catledge, 42
Twain, Mark, 2, 25, 60
*Tzaziki,* 154

Vanilla, 395
Vanilla Ice Cream, 395 96
Veal Birds, 264
Veal scallops, 259–60
Veal Orloff, 264
Veau Prince Orloff, 134
Vegetables, 274–99
 breads, 332–33
 French tradition and, 276–77
 health, association with, 275
 purées, 297–99
 raw, 81
 *See also* specific vegetables
*Vegetarian Epicure, The,* 58, 277
Verdon, René, 43
Vergé, Roger, 58
Vergnes, Jean, 43
Vesiga, 207
Vichyssoise, 111–12
Victory Gardens, 14

*Victory Vitamin Cook Book,* 240
Vinaigrette, 125, 141
*Virginia Housewife, The* (Randolph), 35, 55,
 120
Vitamins, 276
Vitello Tomato, 264

*Walden Pond* (Thoreau), 29
Waldorf Astoria, 56
Waldorf salad, 156
Waring blenders, 15
Washington, George, 394
Washington, Martha, 54, 372
Waters, Alice, 58–59
Webster, Mrs. A. L., 55, 149, 295, 302, 351,
 374, 378, 388, 395
Wechsberg, Joseph, 39, 56
Welsh Rabbit, 360
*West Coast Cookbook, The* (Brown), 57, 82,
 159, 167
*When You Entertain* (Allen), 76
White, Alma, 12
White, Ellen A., 276
White bread, 319–24
White Pekin duck, 221
Whitman, Walt, 31
Whole Salmon Baked in Foil, 193
Wild rice, 302
Wines, 77–78, 79–80
 California, 79–80
 rules for, 79
*With Bold Knife and Fork* (Fisher), 23, 148,
 215
Wolfe, Tom, 10
Wolfert, Paula, 58, 231
World War II, 3–4, 14–15, 58

Yeast, 317–18, 320
Yeast Buckwheat Cakes, 336
Yorkshire Pudding, 245–46

Zucchini, 291–92, 332–33
 bread, 332–33

# RECIPE INDEX

All-white American loaf, 323
Almond crust, 375–76
American black bean soup, 107–08
American pork and beans, 313–14
American spoon bread, 347–48
Appetizers. *See* Drink and drink food
Apple bread-and-butter pudding, 387–88
Apple-pecan pie, 370–72
Artichokes *bagna cauda*, 278–79
Asparagus maltaise, 279–81
Aspic, raw vegetable, 170–71
Avocado dressing, 143

*Bagna cauda* sauce, 279
Baked cod in garlic mayonnaise, 204–05
Baked eggs with smoked salmon, 179
Baked shad with roe and sorrel, 205–07
Balsamic cream sauce, 130
Barbecue sauce, hot, 143–45
Basic salad dressing, 141–42
Bean(s)
  pork and, 313–14
  salad, 163–64
Beef rib roast: High/medium/low, 242–45
Best Indian pudding, 385–86
Birds, 213–37
  baked, 233–35
  chicken. *See* Chicken
  corn bread and sausage stuffing, 220
  duck with cracklings, 221–22
  fried, 222–24
  gin-marinated Rock Cornish Hens, 236
  grilled, 236–37

  quail, mustard-grilled, 237
  roast chicken, 215–17
  roast duck with cracklings, 221–22
  Rock Cornish Hens, gin-marinated, 236–37
  sautéed, 224–27
  stewed, 228
  stuffing, corn bread and sausage, 220
  turkey, quick-roast, 217–20
Biscuits, 336–38
Black bean soup, 107–08
Bluefish, grilled, 196–97
Boiled lobster, 190–92
Boiled white rice, 307
Borsch, Slavic, 105–07
Braided egg bread, 327–29
Braised white rice, 308–09
Breads, 316–39
  all-white American loaf, 323
  biscuits, 336–38
  braided egg, 327–29
  buckwheat griddle cakes, 335–36
  coffee cake, cinnamon-pecan, 333–35
  corn bread with corn, 338
  crunchy health loaf, 331–32
  egg, braided, 327–29
  Franco-Italian loaf, 324–26
  griddle cakes, buckwheat, 335–36
  quick, 336–39
  Sally Lunn, 330
  sweet, 333–35
  vegetable, 332–33
  white bread, 323
  wholegrain, 330–32
Brie, deep-fried, 358–59

Egg bread, braided, 327–29
Egg(s), 174–84
  baked, with smoked salmon, 179
  Benedictine, 177–78
  bread, braided, 327–29
  cheese soufflé, 182–84
  French omelet, 180–81
  *frittata*, 181–82
  omelet, foolproof French, 180
  poached, 177–78
  scrambled, 180–81
  whipped, 182
Eggplant
  caviar with Melba toast, 83–84
  *ratatouille*, 293–94

Fish and shellfish, 185–212
  baked, 204–12
  bluefish, grilled, 196–97
  boiled lobster, 190–92
  broiled swordfish steaks, 195–96
  cod in garlic mayonnaise, baked,
    204–05
  deep-fried smelts, 201–02
  flounder, sautéed, 199–200
  lobster, boiled, 190–92
  mackerel, marinated, 188–90
  oyster loaf, 198–99
  poached striped bass with fennel,
    192–94
  raw, 188
  salmon in a crust, 207–09
  scallops
    sautéed, 197–98
    -shrimp mousseline, 209–12
  shad with roe and sorrel, 205–07
  shrimp
    and scallops mousseline, 209–12
    tempura, 202–03
  smelts, deep-fried, 201–02
  stock, 103–04
  striped bass with fennel, poached,
    192–94
  swordfish steaks, broiled, 195–96
  tips on buying and cooking, 188
Fish stock, 103–04
Floating islands, 388–90
Flounder, sautéed, 199–200
*Fois gras*, peasant, 92–94
Foolproof cheese soufflé, 182–84
Foolproof French omelet, 180–81
Foolproof hollandaise, 138–39
Foolproof mayonnaise, 139–41
Forty-garlic chicken, 235–36
Franco-Italian loaf, 324–26
Franco-yankee pot roast, 262–64
Fresh fruit ices, 392–94
Fresh peach sauce, 137–38
French omelet, 180–81
French onion soup, 104–05

*Frittata*, 181–82
Fruit ices, 392–94

Garlic
  mayonnaise, 204–05
  -parsley butter sauce, 127
  purée, 136–37
Gazpacho, 120–21
Gin-marinated Rock Cornish Hens, 236–
  37
Gnocchi, 346–47
Goat cheese, marinated baked, 365
Gorgonzola, walnut and pear salad, 362–63
Grains, 300–15
  brown rice, 308
  bulghur, 312
  kasha with mushrooms, 311–12
  lentils with herbs and spices, 314–15
  Persian rice, 310–11
  polenta with cheese and chilies, 303–04
  pork and beans, 313–14
  white rice, 307–09
  wild rice, 308
Grated potato pancake, 295–96
Grated zucchini sauté, 291–92
Greek salad, 158
Green avocado dressing, 143
Green beans with walnuts, 283–84
Green garden salad, 151–53
Green herb sauce, 135–36
Green peas, French style, 285–86
Green sorrel soup, 110–11
Griddle cakes, buckwheat, 335–36
Grilled bluefish, 196–97
Grilled cheese sandwich, 361–62
Guacamole with corn crisps, 81–83

Ham with cider, 266–67
Hamburger four different ways, 257–59
Health loaf (bread), 331–32
Herb sauce, green, 135–36
Hollandaise sauce, 138–39
Home-corned beef, 267–68
Homemade pasta, 342–44
Hot barbecue sauce, 143–45
Hot Vichyssoise, 111–12
Hungarian cheese, 357–58

Iced cream, vanilla-bean, 394–96
Ices, fresh fruit, 392–94
Indian pudding, 385–86
Italian *frittata*, 181–82
Italian grilled cheese sandwich, 361–62
Italian *risotto*, 309–10

Jerusalem artichoke and spinach salad,
  153–54